THE MOST FEARFUL ORDEAL

THE MOST FEARFUL ORDEAL

Original Coverage of the Civil War by Writers and Reporters of The New York Times

INTRODUCTION AND NOTES
BY JAMES M. MCPHERSON

St. Martin's Press
New York

 For information, address St. Martin's Press, 175 Fifth Avenue, New York, N.Y. 10010.

www.stmartins.com

Library of Congress Cataloging-in-Publication Data

The most fearful ordeal : original coverage of the Civil War by writers and reporters of The New York times / the staff of The New York times ; introduction and notes by James M. McPherson.—1st ed.

p. cm.

ISBN 0-312-33123-1

EAN 978-0312-33123-8

1. United States—History—Civil War, 1861–1865—Sources. 2. United States—History—Civil War, 1861–1865—Personal narratives. I. McPherson, James M. II. New York times

E464.M8 2004

973.7—dc22

2003070872

First Edition: June 2004

10 9 8 7 6 5 4 3 2 1

CONTENTS

INTRODUCTION

Amid the Killing, 'Only Bread and The Newspaper' Really Mattered

By James M. McPherson

THE CENTRALITY OF THE CIVIL WAR TO THE AMERICAN experience is indisputable. At least 620,000 soldiers lost their lives from 1861 to 1865, constituting 2 percent of the American population. If the same percentage of Americans were to die in a war fought today, the number of American dead would be five and one-half million.

Were the results achieved by the Civil War worth this huge cost in lives? Any answer to this question must be subjective. But without doubt or cavil, the war did resolve two festering issues that had plagued the United States since its founding: whether this fragile experiment of a democratic republic could survive in a world where most republics through the ages had been swept into the dustbin of history; and whether the house divided would continue to endure half slave and half free.

Many Americans had doubted whether the republic would survive, and many Europeans regularly predicted its demise. Some Americans believed in the right of secession and periodically threatened to invoke it; 11 states did invoke it in 1860–1861. As Abraham Lincoln said in his address at Gettysburg in 1863, the conflict was a test whether a nation "conceived in Liberty, and dedicated to the proposition that all men are created equal" could "long endure" or would "perish from the earth." It did endure, and in such a way as to give promise of long life. Since 1865 no state or region has seriously threatened secession, not even during the South's "massive resistance" to desegregation from 1954 to 1964.

The war also gave America "a new birth of freedom," as Lincoln put it at Gettysburg. Before 1865 the United States, which boasted itself "a land of liberty," was the largest slaveholding country in the world. "The monstrous injustice of slavery," Lincoln had said in 1854, "deprives our republican example of its just influence in the world—enables the enemies of free institutions, with plausibility, to taunt us as hypocrites." With the abolition of slavery by Northern victory, that particular monstrous injustice and hypocrisy came to an end. At the cost of those 620,000 lives (37,000 of them black Union soldiers), more than four million slaves and their descendants achieved freedom and—on paper at least—equal rights as American citizens.

Those who experienced the Civil War were well aware that they were living through the most important events in the nation's history to date. "These are fearfully critical, anxious days," wrote the prominent New York lawyer George Templeton Strong in May 1864, in which "the destinies of the continent for centuries will be decided." Looking back a few years after the war, Mark Twain described the conflict as having "uprooted institutions that were centuries old, changed the politics of a people, transformed the social life of half the country, and wrought so profoundly upon the entire national character that the influence cannot be measured short of two or three generations."

The intensity of war experiences seemed to alter the very consciousness of time and space for its participants. For both soldiers and civilians, time seemed either to stand still or to rush forward at lightning speed as they fought great battles or gathered anxiously outside the telegraph offices of newspapers waiting for news from the front. "The excitement of the war, and interest in its incidents, have absorbed everything else," wrote Virginia's fire-eating secessionist Edmund Ruffin in August 1861. "We think and talk of nothing else." Three days later and five hundred miles to the north, Ruffin's words were echoed by the Yankee philosopher Ralph Waldo Emerson: "The war . . . has assumed such huge proportions that it threatens to engulf us all—no preoccupation can exclude it, & no hermitage hide us." Another Northern civilian wrote that the conflict had "crowded into a few years the emotions of a lifetime." And from as far away as London, where he served as secretary to his father in the American legation, young Henry Adams wondered "whether any of us will ever be able to live contented in times of peace and laziness. Our generation has been stirred up from its lowest layers and there is that in its history which will stamp every member of it until we are all in our graves. We cannot be commonplace. . . . One does every day and without a second thought, what at another time would be the event of a year, perhaps of a life."

The South's strategy in this war was to defend the 750,000 square miles of territory that constituted the 11 states of the Confederate States of America in 1861. The North, by contrast, had to formulate an offensive strategy to invade and conquer this territory and overthrow its government to bring these states back into the Union. The campaigns and battles described in the news stories from *The New York Times* in this anthology grew out of these competing strategies.

The first Northern effort in the summer of 1861 was the "On to Richmond" campaign to capture the Confederate capital, which came to grief along the banks of Bull Run, 25 miles southwest of Washington, on July 21. The next large-scale attempt occurred in the spring of 1862, culminating in the Seven Days' battles (June 25-July 1) in which the Confederate Army of Northern Virginia drove the Union Army of the Potomac back on its heels near Richmond.

Another part of Union strategy was a naval blockade of Confederate ports. The supreme Southern effort to break this blockade was the attack by the famous ironclad C.S.S. *Virginia* (popularly called the *Merrimac*) on Union warships, which was successfully countered by the U.S.S. *Monitor* on March 9, 1862, in history's first battle between ironclad ships. Meanwhile, the Northern strategy of gaining control of navigable rivers in the Southern interior achieved great success at Fort Donelson, Shiloh (Pittsburg Landing), and Vicksburg—all subjects of *Times* articles herein.

Robert E. Lee's victories in the Seven Days' battles persuaded him to launch spoiling offensives that led to a major Confederate triumph at Second Bull Run (Manassas) in late August 1862 and then to a Confederate defeat at Antietam in Maryland. Following two more Union failures in renewed On to Richmond campaigns, at Fredericksburg in December 1862 and nearby Chancellorsville in May 1863, Lee tried again, this time invading Pennsylvania and suffering his greatest defeat at Gettysburg in the first three days of July 1863. All of these big battles are described vividly in this anthology.

The tide set inexorably toward Union victory in 1864, as Ulysses S. Grant became the General in Chief and defined Union strategy as the destruction of Confederate armies as well as conquest of Southern territory. At great cost in battles like the Wilderness, Spotsylvania, Cold Harbor, and the 10-month siege of Petersburg, coupled with Sherman's capture of Atlanta, Grant finally brought Lee to bay at Appomattox on April 9, 1865. Readers of this anthology can relive these harrowing but eventually triumphant months, followed by the terrible tragedy of Lincoln's assassination, through the *Times* articles included here.

In times of crisis or war, Americans today tune into television or radio, or increasingly to the Internet. None of these media, of course, existed during the Civil War. Americans then got their news from newspapers. Most people experienced the battles and other crucial war events vicariously through their daily papers. "We must have something to eat, and the papers to read," declared Oliver Wendell Holmes in August 1861 as his son and namesake prepared to depart for Virginia as an officer in the 20th Massachusetts Volunteer Infantry. "Everything else we can do without. . . . Only bread and the newspaper we must have."

Americans were well served by newspapers in the late 1860's. The 3,300 newspapers in the United States were twice the number in Britain and one-third of all newspapers in the entire world. Circulation per capita was far greater than in any other country. Most of these papers were small-town weeklies. But even small cities had at least one daily newspaper, and most had two or more. New York City had 11 dailies—not including those in Brooklyn, then a separate city. Most dailies subscribed to the Associated Press, formed in 1848 to provide its members with dispatches via the newly invented telegraph. By 1861 the whole country (including California) was connected by copper wires that could transmit news in minutes across thousands of miles. During the Civil War, New Yorkers could read of events that happened a day or two earlier in Virginia or Mississippi.

That is, they could read such telegraphed news if Union Secretary of War Edwin M. Stanton allowed the messages to go through. In January 1862 Congress authorized the War Department to control the telegraph lines during the emergency. The ostensible purpose was to give priority to military communications, but Stanton also used the power to censor telegraphic dispatches by newspaper reporters. By 1862 a hundred or more such reporters were in the field with various Union armies scattered across a front of more than a thousand miles. The largest number were with the Army of the Potomac in Virginia, where most of the war's major battles would be fought. On several occasions these enterprising journalists, when denied the use of the telegraph to send in their reports, traveled 24 hours or more by horseback, rail and/or boat to New York or another Northern city, going without sleep and writing their stories by candlelight to score a "beat" (scoop) over rival newspapers by getting their story of the battle into print first.

One such famous beat was accomplished by *The New York Times* reporter William Swinton, whose seven-column story of the first three days of the battle of Chancellorsville (May 1–3, 1863) was published in *The Times* on May 5 and is reprinted in this anthology. Swinton was one of the top Civil War reporters. He proved to be a little too enterprising, however; during the battle of the Wilderness (May 5–6, 1865), a staff officer caught him hiding behind a tree to eavesdrop on a conversation between Gens. Ulysses S. Grant and George G. Meade, and expelled Swinton from the army. *The Times* therefore had no correspondents' reports during the bitter, relentless fighting at Spotsylvania, North Anna and Cold Harbor in May and June. Not until the armies reached Petersburg in mid-June did Swinton contrive to get close enough to the action to begin filing stories again.

The big three of Northern newspapers during the Civil War were all in New York: *The Times, The Tribune* and *The Herald.* Edited by Horace Greeley, *The Tribune* represented the radical antislavery wing of the Republican party. *The Herald,* owned and edited by the enfant terrible of American journalism, James Gordon Bennett, took the opposite political tack. *The Times* spoke for the moderate Republican position. Founded by Henry J. Raymond in 1851 and edited by him until his premature death from a stroke in 1869 at the age of 49, *The Times* was the foremost journalistic representative of Abraham Lincoln's brand of Republicanism. One of the founders of the Republican party in New York, Raymond turned *The Times* into an outstanding supporter of the Union in the secession crisis of 1861 and of emancipation as a Northern war aim in 1862–63. In 1864, while remaining in charge of *The Times,* Raymond also became chairman of the Republican National Committee, wrote a campaign biography of Lincoln and was elected to Congress.

In the early months of the war, Raymond had gone into the field himself and reported the first battle of Bull Run for his newspaper. Readers of the issue of July 24, 1861, included in this anthology, will notice the initials "R." and "H. J. R." after two dispatches in that issue. Thereafter *The Times,* like other major newspapers, sent "Special Correspondents" into the field to report military affairs. Army commanders were often wary of these reporters, fearing that their dispatches might provide information to the enemy, who frequently smuggled Northern newspapers into their camps. Nevertheless, the more enterprising of the correspondents managed to turn up at battles during or soon after the fighting and to file their stories—by telegraph, if possible, by courier or personal delivery if necessary. In addition to Swinton, *The Times* employed some of the best war correspondents—Samuel Wilkeson (for a time), George H. S. Salter ("Jasper"), L. L. Crounse, and William Conant Church ("Pierrepont").

Articles by all of these reporters, and others, are included in this anthology. *The Times* and other newspapers did not then follow a consistent policy on bylines. Some stories by "Our Own Correspondent" are unattributed; others carry a byline (always at the end of the article) with a pen name, or initials, or the last name only. Some carried the full name, as in the case of William Swinton, to distinguish him from his older brother John, who was on *The Times*'s editorial staff back in New York.

First-hand accounts by *Times* reporters are not the only form of war news included here. The initial reports of any important event—especially battles—came in the form of official telegrams from generals or from the War Department, printed verbatim in the newspapers. Associated Press dispatches and reprinted excerpts or summaries from other newspapers (a common practice at the time) were additional important sources of war news. *The Times* did not have its own full-time correspondents with Union forces in the Western theater, so the stories of the captures of Fort Donelson, Vicksburg and Atlanta, plus the battle of Shiloh found in this anthology, came from this composite of sources. Transcribing these historical documents created unique challenges. Due to the wear and tear of age, some words proved unintelligible despite best efforts and they are marked as such. Fortunately, these instances are relatively few.

News stories are the first draft of history. Like all first drafts, they are subject to correction and revision as fuller information and longer perspectives become available. Thus many of the initial reports of battles included here contain errors and exaggerations that subsequent accounts corrected. All of the first reports of Civil War battles by newspapers in both North and South tended to exaggerate—or even fabricate—the success and to minimize the casualties of one's own side while inflating enemy casualties. The initial report in *The Times* (Aug. 31, 1862) of the second battle of Bull Run headlined the story "Highly Important: Defeat of the Rebels on the Old Bull Run Battle-Ground." *The Times* and all other Northern newspapers based such over-optimistic reports on Gen. John Pope's telegrams to the War Department. Only in subsequent days did it become clear that Second Bull Run was a humiliating Union defeat. Likewise the first reports of the battle of Fredericksburg (Dec. 14, 1862) emphasized a limited Union success on one sector of the battlefield in what turned out to be another disastrous Northern defeat.

If this first draft of history is wrong in some respects, why make these *Times* stories available to modern readers? Precisely because these dispatches shaped the first impressions of Northern readers and thereby swayed public opinion and morale. These were the stories that caused "the excitement of the war" to "absorb everything else," in the words of the Virginia secessionist Edmund Ruffin—the news that made the morning paper more important to that generation than anything else except bread itself. These reprinted stories from *The Times* will give modern readers a "You Are There" feeling that will make it possible to empathize with people of the 1860's and to appreciate what they went through. From John Brown's raid on Harpers Ferry in 1859 through Lincoln's assassination and the trial of the conspirators in 1865, you will be there as you read these dispatches and stories. You will learn of Lincoln's election as president, of his Emancipation Proclamation and Gettysburg Address, of the terrible battles, and of the equally terrible draft riots in New York City in July 1863 when *Times* employees stationed three newly invented Gatling guns on the roof to scare off rioters bent on burning down the building.

Also included are obituaries of the war's leading protagonists, which demonstrate how important the memories of this war were to the generation that lived through it. The obituary of General Grant in the July 24, 1885, issue of *The Times*—among the fullest and longest newspaper obituary ever published—offers a fitting climax to this most vivid anthology of first-hand Civil War experiences.

JAMES M. MCPHERSON is a professor of history at Princeton University. He is the author of many books on the Civil War era, including Battle Cry of Freedom, *which won the Pulitzer Prize in 1989. His most recent book, published last year, is* Crossroads of Freedom: Antietam.

PART ONE

1859—1861

The New-York Times.

VOL. IX.—NO. 2520. NEW-YORK, TUESDAY, OCTOBER 18, 1859.

John Brown was an abolitionist who believed that peaceful efforts to end slavery would never succeed. His favorite Biblical quotation was "Without shedding of blood there is no remission of sin" (Hebrews 9:22). America's greatest sin, he believed, was slavery, and he intended to do something about it no matter what the cost in blood. On October 16, 1859, he led eighteen white and black followers in an attack on the federal arsenal at Harpers Ferry, Virginia. With the weapons he captured there he hoped to arm the slaves he expected to flock to his banner, and then to move south with this "army" along the Appalachian chain to spread slave insurrections through the South. But thirty-six hours after it began, this war to liberate the slaves was over. A force of U.S. Marines led by Colonel Robert E. Lee and Lieutenant J. E. B. Stuart captured or killed Brown and most of his men. The following story in *The Times* reflected the first facts and rumors coming out of Harpers Ferry.

October 18, 1859.

SERVILE INSURRECTION.

The Federal Arsenal at Harper's Ferry in Possession of the Insurgents.

GENERAL STAMPEDE OF SLAVES.

United States Troops on their March to the Scene.

Dispatches from our Special Correspondent.

Washington, Monday, Oct. 17.

The report that negroes have taken possession of Harper's Ferry, and now hold the Government Armory, has created great excitement here. It is said that troops from Fort McHenry, Baltimore, will be dispatched forthwith to the scene of disorder.

Dispatches to the President and Secretary of War confirm the report from Harper's Ferry. The President has telegraphed to Postmasters at Frederick and Baltimore for particulars. The train was fired into on the Bridge, and one man was killed. The insurgents have possession of the Bridge. A special train at Baltimore has been ordered to carry on troops, Frederick Volunteers have offered services.

Washington, Monday, Oct. 17.

The latest account says the insurgents are Government employes, headed by one Anderson, lately arrived there. It is believed to be an Abolition movement to protect runaways. A large number of negroes stampeded last evening from several localities. It is supposed that they are making for Harper's Ferry.

Relay House Baltimore and Ohio Railroad, Monday, Oct. 17.

Gov. Floyd announced in the Cabinet meeting this morning that two months ago he received an anonymous letter stating that an Abolitionist movement was on foot, which would exhibit itself first at Harper's Ferry, about the middle of October, but he treated it with levity, and had not thought of it since. This seems to give the key to the insurrection.

A train has just arrived here with three companies, but without ammunition.

The eighty-five marines in company are fully equipped and supplied, and may divide. The marines were ready at Washington depot in one hour and twenty minutes from the first notice of the order.

BALTIMORE AND OHIO RAILROAD PLANE NUMBER 4—9 P.M.

Our train of seventeen cars, with two hundred and ten Baltimore troops, eighty from Marines, and one hundred and twenty from Frederick, is just going on. Besides the above, there are one hundred and eighty Artillerymen from Fort Monroe. *These constitute the whole force*. Major REYNOLDS has command, until Major LEE, who is behind on a special train, with ammunition, comes up.

The insurgents have pillaged the pay-office. GOV. WISE has ordered out the Jefferson Regiment, and a horseman has been dispatched by the Baltimore and Ohio Railroad, with the Governor's orders This messenger will endeavor to pass through the country, and deliver his message by three o'clock to-day. It is yet doubtful whether the troops will make an attack to-night or wait for daylight.

MONOCACY BRIDGE, MONDAY, OCT. 17.

A train has just returned from Harper's Ferry having been refused permission to pass. The insurgents are increasing. The baggage-master of the train was permitted to pass into town, when he was marched into the Armory, where he found about six hundred runaway negroes. Mr. WASHINGTON, of Jefferson, also came down with his wife and servant. The latter was taken prisoner, and Mr. WASHINGTON and his wife were tied in their carriage. The place appeared to be deserted by the inhabitants. A few only remained. The baggage-master was permitted to return.

The same party reports about two hundred white men engaged in the insurrection. Everything had been plundered, and all appeared determined to fight. Mr. DIFFEY, master of trains, has telegraphed from Martinsburg, *via* Wheeling, that a body of armed men have taken possession of the Armory at Harper's Ferry and have planted guns in one bridge. The telegraph wires are cut and there is no communication East. A body of armed men are getting ready to leave here at once to clear the bridge, that our trains can pass.

There is great excitement all through the neighborhood. It is now evident that the insurgents have fortified themselves and will make a desperate resistance. The Directors and families of the Pennsylvania Central Railroad are on an excursion, and have also been stopped at Harper's Ferry.

The following are the first dispatches received from the scene of disturbance, that were communicated to the Government:

"The express train east has been detained at Harper's Ferry in consequence of the railroad bridge and Armory being in the possession of an armed organized band of Abolitionists. They are 100, and perhaps more, in number. I took my baggage master and proceeded through the bridge, when I was stopped by three men having arms, who ordered me to halt or be shot down. I retired from the bridge and made my escape. *I have been frequently shot at,* and so have many others. All the watchmen of the bridge and Armory are under arrest. Moreover, every bridge around is guarded. HAYWOOD, the colored man, has been shot through the left side, greatly endangering his life. Inform the United States officials at once. There are some eight or ten men in the neighborhood of the Ferry in the greatest anxiety to know the issue of this dreadful affair. The captain of the band told me to notify you that no other trains should pass the bridge. Had you not better notify the Secretary of War of the circumstance?"

Our train is ordered to let Major LEE overtake us. The Frederick companies went at 3 o'clock, P.M., but have not since been heard from. We take on at this place two additional pieces of artillery, and an additional supply of ammunition from Frederick.

HARPER'S FERRY, MONDAY, OCT. 17.

Train arrived and halted below town, where runners communicated the state of affairs. Jefferson County Regiment had entered town, from Virginia side, and Frederick troops crossed the bridge; there had been a deal of firing. Some nine persons killed.

Mr. BECKHAM, Agent of the Railroad Company, was shot through, and his murderer fell almost at the same instant, pinned by a rifle ball from a friend of Mr. BECKHAM.

The troops have landed, and are in the town. The insurgents are willing to surrender, but on terms of safe conduct out of difficulty, otherwise they threaten to sacrifice the lives of LEWIS WASHINGTON and Col. DANGERFIELD, who they now hold as prisoners. Capt. AARON STEPHENS, of Norwich, Conn., is now dying of wounds, and makes the following statement:

"The plan has been concocting for a year or more. The parties rendezvoused at a farm a few miles from here, rented for the purpose by Capt. BROWN, of Kansas notoriety, under the name of Smith. Among the insurgents are KAGG, of Ohio; TODD, of Maine; WM. SEAMAN and MR. BROWN, of Ohio."

From the Associated Press.

BALTIMORE, MONDAY, OCT. 17.

A dispatch just received here from Frederick, and dated this morning, states that an insurrection has broken out at Harper's Ferry, where an armed band of Abolitionists have full possession of the Government Arsenal. The express train going east was twice fired into, and one of the railroad hands and a negro was killed, while they were endeavoring to get the train through the town. The insurrectionists stopped and arrested two men, who had come to town with a load of wheat, and seizing their wagon, loaded it with rifles, and sent them into Maryland. The insurrectionists number about two hundred and fifty whites, and are aided by a gang of negroes. At last accounts fighting was going on.

The above is given just as it was received here. It seems very improbable, and should be received with great caution, until confirmed by further advices.

Baltimore, Monday, Oct. 17.

A later dispatch received at the Railroad Office, says the affair has been greatly exaggerated. The reports had their foundation in a difficulty at the Armory, with which negroes had nothing to do.

Baltimore, Monday, Oct. 17—P.M.

It is apprehended that the affair at Harper's Ferry is more serious than our citizens seem willing to believe. The wires from Harper's Ferry are cut, and consequently we have no telegraphic communication beyond Monocacy Station. The Southern train, which was due here at an early hour this morning, has not yet arrived. It is rumored there is a stampede of negroes from this State. There are many other wild rumors, but nothing authentic yet.

The Secretary of War has telegraphed to Fort Monroe for three companies of artillery, who are expected to be in Baltimore to-morrow morning. A company of marines will leave the Washington Navy-yard at 3:20 o'clock to-day for Harper's Ferry

Baltimore, Monday, Oct. 17—12 P.M.

Another account received by train says the bridge across the Potomac was filled with insurgents, all armed. Every light in the town was extinguished, and the hotels, closed in all the streets, were in possession of the mob, and every road and lane leading thereto barricaded and guarded. Men were seen in every quarter, with muskets and bayonets, who arrested the citizens, and pressed them into the service, including many negroes. This done, the United States arsenal and government pay-house, in which was said to be a large amount of money, and all the other public works were seized by the mob. Some were of the opinion that the object was entirely plunder, and to rob the government of the funds deposited on Saturday at the pay-house. During the night the mob made a demand on the Wager Hotel for provisions, and a body of armed men enforced the claim. The citizens were in a terrible state of alarm, the insurgents having *threatened to burn the town.*

The following has just been received from Monocacy, this side of Harper's Ferry: "The mall agent on the Western-bound train has returned to Monocacy, and reports that the train was unable to get through. The town is in possession of the negroes, who arrest every one they can catch, and imprison. The train due here at 3 P.M., could not get through, and the agent came down on an empty engine."

Baltimore, Monday, Oct. 17—2½ P.M.

The Western train on the Baltimore and Ohio Railroad has just arrived here. Its officers confirm the statements first received touching the disturbance at Harper's Ferry. Their statement is to the effect that the bridge-keeper at Harper's Ferry, perceiving that his lights had been extinguished, went to ascertain the cause, when he was pursued and fired upon by a gang of blacks and whites. Subsequently the train came along, when a colored man, who acted as assistant to the baggage-master, was shot, receiving a mortal wound, and the conductor, Mr. PHELPS, was threatened with violence if he attempted to proceed with the train. Feeling uncertain as to the condition of affairs, the conductor waited until after daylight before he ventured to proceed, having delayed the train six hours. Mr. PHELPS says the insurrectionists number two hundred blacks and whites, and that they have full possession of the United States armory. The party is commanded or led by a man named ANDERSON, who had lately arrived at Harper's Ferry. Mr. PHELPS also confirms the statement in a previous dispatch, that the insurrectionists had seized a wagon, and loading it with muskets had dispatched it into Maryland. The military of Frederick had been ordered out.

Dispatches have been received from President BUCHANAN, ordering out the United States troops at this point, and a special train is now getting ready to convey them to the scene of disturbance. He has also accepted the volunteered services of Capt. SENICK's Company of Frederick, and has likewise ordered the Government troops from Old Point Comfort to proceed immediately to Harper's Ferry. This intelligence is authentic.

BALTIMORE, MONDAY, OCT, 17—3½ P.M.

The mail train going West got as far as Sandy when Mr. HOOD, the baggage master, and another party, started on foot to the bridge. They went through the bridge, and were taken and imprisoned, but subsequently went before the captain of the insurrectionists, who refused to let anything pass. All of the eastward bound trains laying west of Harper's Ferry have been taken; persons from this side the river, tying them together, and taking off the slaves. The mail train bound West has returned to Monocacy. There are from five hundred to seven hundred whites and blacks concerned in the insurrection.

The United States marines at Washington are under order for Harper's Ferry. There is great excitement in Baltimore, and the military are moving. Several companies are in readiness to take the train, which will leave soon.

BALTIMORE, MONDAY, OCT. 17—4 P.M.

An account from Frederick says a letter has been received there from a merchant at Harper's Ferry, sent by a boy who had to cross the mountain and swim the river, which says that all the principal citizens are imprisoned, and many have been killed; also, that the railroad agent had been shot twice, and that the watchman at the depot had been shot dead.

BALTIMORE, MONDAY, OCT. 17—5 P.M.

A train filled with military, including the Law Greys, City Guards, Shields' Guards, and other companies, left here at 4 o'clock for Harper's Ferry. Representatives of the press accompanied the military.

Baltimore, Monday, Oct. 17—7 P.M.

A dispatch from Martinsburgh, west of Harper's Ferry, received *via* Wheeling and Pittsburgh, confirms the report of the insurrectionists having possession of the arsenal at Harper's Ferry, and says they have planted cannon at the bridge. All the trains have been stopped. A body of armed men was getting ready to proceed thither to clear the road. There was great excitement at Martinsburgh, Va.

Richmond, Monday, Oct. 17.

It is reported and believed that the Governor of Virginia has ordered volunteer troops to Harper's Ferry.

Washington, Monday, Oct. 17—4 P.M.

On the receipt of the intelligence from Harper's Ferry, orders were issued for three companies of artillery at Old Point and the corps of marines at Washington Barracks to proceed thither without delay. The marines, ninety-three in number, left in the 3:15 P.M. train, with two twelve-pound howitzers and a full supply of ammunition. It is reported that they are under orders to force the bridge to-night at all hazards. Col. Faulkner accompanies them.

It is reported, on good authority, that some weeks ago Secretary Floyd received anonymous epistles stating that about the 15th of October the Abolitionists and negroes, and other disaffected persons, would make an attempt to seize the arsenal and hold the place, but the statement was so indefinite and improbable as to cause no fears of such an outbreak.

Washington, Monday, Oct. 17—9 P.M.

In view of the possibility of the disturbances at Harper's Ferry extending to this vicinity, the Mayors of Washington and Alexandria have taken precautionary steps for its suppression. The President, through the Mayor of Washington, ordered a strong detachment of volunteer Militia to be posted at the National and Company armories, which was promptly done. Two hundred stand of muskets and a supply of ammunition will also be placed in the City Hall, for emergency. It is suggested by well-informed persons that the cause of the insurrection is the reported fact that not long since the contractor for the construction of a Government dam, at the Ferry, absconded, largely indebted to several hundred employees, who have taken this step to indemnify themselves, by the seizure of the Government Funds, which it was supposed were transported thither on Saturday. A gentleman just in from Harper's Ferry, thinks the blacks participated in the outbreak *only on compulsion.*

RICHMOND, MONDAY, OCT. 17—9 P.M.

There is great excitement here. Company F, with full ranks, has just left the Armory, expecting to take a special train to-night. There is a new company, with a similar uniform to the Greys.

The Greys leave for Harper's Ferry early in the morning. The Governor left to-night for Washington.

BALTIMORE, MONDAY, OCT. 17—9 P.M.

The *American*'s special reporter telegraphs from Plane No. 4, 45 miles from Baltimore, and 31 from Harper's Ferry, at 8 o'clock, that the train consists of seventeen cars, with four hundred troops, under Maj. REYNOLDS, with a roadmaster and laborers to repair the track, and telegraphers to mend the lines. Three companies from Frederick were in an advance train. Col. HARRIS, of the United States Marines, commanding the expedition, follows in a special train. They will not reach Harper's Ferry before 10 o'clock.

MONACOCY BRIDGE, MONDAY, OCT. 17—10 P.M.

The train arrived here at 9 o'clock. LUTHER SIMPSON, baggage master of the mail train, gives the following particulars: I walked up the bridge; was stopped, but was afterwards permitted to go up and see the captain of the insurrectionists; I was taken to the armory, and saw the captain, whose name is BILL SMITH; I was kept prisoner for more than an hour, and saw from five hundred to six hundred negroes, all having arms; there were two or three hundred white men with them; all of the houses were closed. I went into a tavern kept by Mr. CHAMBERS; thirty of the inhabitants were collected there with arms. They said most of the inhabitants had left, but they declined, preferring to protect themselves; it was reported that five or six persons had been shot.

Mr. SIMPSON was escorted back over the bridge by six negroes.

The train with the Frederick military is laying at Point of Rocks. A train with the directors of the Pennsylvania Railroad on board, is on the other side of Harper's Ferry. It was believed that the insurrectionists would leave as soon as it became dark. Orders have been received here that the train shall stop at Sandy Hook until Col. LEE, who is following in a special train, arrives. There are any amount of rumors, but nothing is certain.

MONOCACY, TUESDAY, OCT. 18—1 P.M.

The special train, with Col. LEE's command, passed this station at 11:30 P.M. It is supposed that there is difficulty in adjusting the breaks in the road this side of Harper's Ferry, as nothing has since been heard of the expedition.

The state of Virginia tried John Brown and his followers for murder, treason, and insurrection. Brown and six others were convicted and sentenced to hang. Brown's calm demeanor during the trial and his disapproval of any effort to rescue him by force won the grudging admiration of even his captors. As he walked to the gallows in Charlestown, Virginia on December 2, he handed one of his jailors a note: "I John Brown am now quite *certain* that the crimes of this *guilty land* will never be purged *away* but with Blood." Brown had become a martyr to many in the North; at the hour of his execution, church bells tolled in many Northern villages, cannons fired solemn salutes, and prayer meetings adopted memorial resolutions. This outpouring of sympathy shocked Southerners and drove many of them toward disunion.

December 3, 1859.

EXECUTION OF JOHN BROWN.

His Interview with his Wife.

SCENES AT THE SCAFFOLD.

Profound Feelings Throughout the Northern States.

Special Dispatch to the New-York Times.

CHARLESTOWN, VA., FRIDAY, DEC. 2,
HALF-PAST 3 O'CLOCK, P.M.

BROWN was executed to-day at a little after 11 o'clock. There was no attempt at rescue, nor any indications of any disposition to interfere with the course of justice in any way. Indeed, there was very little excitement of any kind.

I visited the field in which the gallows had been erected at an early hour this morning. The day was very fine and the air warm. All strangers were excluded from the town. Indeed, no railroad trains were allowed to enter during the entire day.

The gallows was erected at 7½ o'clock, and all preparations for the execution immediately completed. The reporters who had secured the privilege of being present were allowed to enter soon after.

On being summoned, BROWN appeared perfectly calm and collected. He took formal leave of each of his fellow-prisoners and gave each one a quarter of a dollar as a token of remembrance. He remarked to COOK that he did not tell the truth when he said that he had been induced by him to take up arms and enter upon this project. COOK replied that he did—that BROWN did invite him to the course he had pursued. BROWN replied, "I *did not.*"

As he left the jail Cook bowed to acquaintances outside.

He rode to the scaffold in an open wagon, seated upon his coffin.

At the gallows Brown was still perfectly cool. He made no remarks. As soon as he had mounted the scaffold the cap was put down and drawn over his face.

He was not standing on the drop. The Sheriff told him to get upon it.

Brown said, "I cannot see—place me on it, and don't keep me waiting."

He stood upon the drop nine minutes and a half when it fell. He suffered but little.

After three minutes, there were no convulsions, or indications of life. At the end of twenty minutes his body was examined, and he was reported dead.

[FROM THE REPORTER OF THE ASSOCIATED PRESS.]

Harper's Ferry, Friday Dec. 2.

John Brown was hung at Charlestown at 11½ o'clock to-day.

The military assembled at 9 o'clock, and were posted on the field leading to the place of execution, and also at various points as laid down in the general orders.

Everything was conducted under the strictest military discipline, as if the town were in a state of siege.

Mounted scouts were stationed in the woods to the left of the scaffold, and picket guards were stationed out towards the Shenandoah mountains in the rear.

The military on the field formed two hollow squares. Within the inner one was the scaffold, and between the inner lines and outer lines, the citizens were admitted, no one being allowed outside the lines, except the mounted guards.

At eleven o'clock the prisoner was brought out of the jail, accompanied by Sheriff Campbell and assistants, and Capt. Avis, the jailer.

A small wagon, containing a white pine coffin, was driven up, on which he took his seat.

Six companies of infantry and riflemen, and one company of horsemen, and the general and a staff numbering twenty-five officers, headed the procession and moved towards the place of execution.

Brown was accompanied by no ministers, he desiring no religious services either in the jail or on the scaffold.

He looked calmly on the people, was fully self-possessed, and mounted the scaffold with a firm step.

His arms were pinioned by the Sheriff.

Brown then bid farewell to Capt. Avis and Sheriff Campbell, and at half-past eleven the trap of the scaffold was pulled away, and, with a few slight struggles, John Brown yielded up his spirit.

The body was placed in a coffin, and is now on its way to Harper's Ferry, to be delivered to his wife, under a strong military escort.

CHARLESTOWN, VA., THURSDAY, DEC. 1.

The day has passed quietly.

Mrs. BROWN was escorted over from the Ferry at 3 o'clock, when the entire military were brought out to make a demonstration. She was received with full military honors, but her companions were not allowed to accompany her from the Ferry. After remaining four hours with her husband, she was escorted back to the Ferry at 9 o'clock, there to await the reception of her husband's body.

THE INTERVIEW BETWEEN BROWN AND HIS WIFE— INCIDENTS OF THE EXECUTION.

CHARLESTOWN, FRIDAY DEC. 2.

The interview between BROWN and his wife lasted from 4 o'clock in the afternoon until 8 o'clock in the evening, when Gen. TALIAFERRO informed them that the period allowed had elapsed, and that she must prepare for departure to the Ferry. A carriage was again brought to the door, the military took possession of the square, and with an escort of twenty men, the *cortège* moved off, Capt. MOORE, of the Montgomery Guard, accompanying her. The interview was, I learn, not a very affecting one—rather of a practical character, with regard to the future of herself and children, and the arrangement and settlement of business affairs. They seemed considerably affected when they first met, and Mrs. BROWN was for a few moments quite overcome, but BROWN was as firm as a rock, and she soon recovered her composure. There was an impression that the prisoner might possibly be furnished with a weapon or with strychnine, by his wife, and before the interview her person was searched by the wife of the jailor, and a strict watch kept over them during the time they were together. At the time of separation they both seemed to be fully self-possessed, and the parting, especially on his part, exhibited a composure either feigned or real, that was truly amazing. I learn from Capt. MOORE that she rather repelled all attempt on his part to express sympathy with her under her affliction.

She resented the idea that Capt. BROWN had done anything to deserve death or to attaint his name with dishonor, and declared that the ignominious character of the punishment that was about to be inflicted upon him was as cruel as it was unjust. She regarded him as a martyr in a righteous cause, and was proud to be the wife of such a man. The gallows, she said, had no terrors for her or for him. She stated that she had not seen him since last June, about six months ago, and that they had been separated, with the exception of a few days, for nearly two years. They had, however, corresponded, and she had always felt a deep interest in the cause in which he was engaged.

The character of this interview may be judged to some extent from this conversation with Capt. MOORE, which took place previous to it.

I learn from Capt. AVIS, the jailor, that the interview between the prisoner and wife was characteristic of the man, and the directions given for the management and distribution of his property embraced all the minor details of his last will and testament.

Gen. TALIAFERRO was also present, and Capt. BROWN urged that his wife be allowed to remain with him all night. To this the General refused to assent, allowing them but four hours.

On first meeting they kissed and affectionately embraced, and Mrs. BROWN shed a few tears, but immediately checked her feelings. They stood embraced, and she sobbing for nearly five minutes, and he was apparently unable to speak. The prisoner only gave way for a moment, and was soon calm and collected, and remained firm throughout the interview. At the close they shook hands, but did not embrace, and as they parted, he said, "God bless you and the children." Mrs. BROWN replied, "God have mercy on you," and continued calm until she left the room, when she remained in tears a few moments and then prepared to depart. The interview took place in the parlor of Capt. AVIS, and the prisoner was free from manacles of any kind.

We sat side by side on a sofa, and, after discussing family matters, proceeded to business. He stated that he desired his property to pass entirely into her possession, and appeared to place full confidence in her ability to manage it properly for the benefit of his younger children. He requested her to remain at North Elba, N.Y., on her farm, where she now resides, and which belongs to her. He desired that his younger children should be educated; and if she could not obtain facilities for their education at home, to have them sent to a boarding-school. He then gave direction, and dictated to Sheriff CAMPBELL a will, which directed that all his property should go to his wife, with the exception of a few presents and bequests which he made. To one of his sons he gave a double spy-glass, and to another a watch; while a third was directed to take a tomb or monument that marks the grave of his father at North Elba, and have his name, age, and the manner of his death, together with the cause for which he had suffered, engraved upon it. He directs that it shall remain at North Elba as long as his family resides there. To each of his children he bequeathed the sum of fifty dollars, and to each of his daughters a Bible, to cost five dollars—to be purchased out of money coming to him from his father's estate. Also, he directs that a Bible, to cost three dollars, shall be presented to each of his grand-children, and that $50 each be paid to three individuals whom he named, if they can be found, and, if not, to their legal representatives. During the course of conversation Mrs. BROWN asked him if he had heard that GERRIT SMITH had become insane, and had been sent to the Asylum at Utica. He replied that he had read of it in the papers, and was sorry to hear it, but immediately changed the subject.

The subject of the death of his two sons was spoken of, and Mrs. Brown remarked that she had made some effort while at Harper's Ferry, for the recovery of their bodies, to which object she said Col. BARBOUR had kindly consented to give his assistance. Capt. Brown remarked that he would also like the remains of the two

THOMPSON's removed, if they could be found, but suggested that it would be best to take his body, with the bodies of his four sons, and get a pile of pine logs, and burn them all together; that it would be much better, and less expensive, to thus gather up all their ashes together, and take them to their final resting place. Sheriff CAMPBELL told him that this would not be permitted within the State, and Mrs. BROWN objected to the proposition altogether.

The prisoner said that he contemplated his death with composure and calmness. It would undoubtedly be pleasant to live longer, but as it was the will of God he should close his career, he was content. It was doubtless best that he should be thus legally murdered for the good of the cause, and he was prepared to submit to his fate without a murmur. Mrs. BROWN becoming depressed at these remarks, he bid her cheer up, telling her that his spirit would soon be with her again, and that they would be re-united in heaven.

With regard to his execution, he said, that he desired no religious ceremonies either in the jail or on the scaffold from ministers who consent or approve of the enslavement of their fellow-creatures; that he would prefer rather to be accompanied to the scaffold by a dozen slave children and a good old slave mother, with their appeal to God for blessings on his soul than all the eloquence of the whole clergy of the Commonwealth combined.

PUBLIC EXPRESSIONS OF SYMPATHY.

PRAYER MEETINGS IN NEW-YORK.
PRAYER MEETING IN DR. CHEEVER'S CHURCH.

The small lecture-room of Dr. CHEEVER's Church was filled yesterday morning, it being announced that a prayer meeting for JOHN BROWN would be held. Among those present were ERNESTINE L. ROSE, C. L. BRACE, LEWIS TAPPAN, OLIVER JOHNSON, and Count DE GUROWSKI. The exercises lasted from 10½ A.M. to 12½ P.M., consisting of addresses, singing, and prayer.

Dr. CHEEVER read a passage of Scripture relating to Stephen's martyrdom, drawing a parallel between JOHN BROWN and the Apostle. He considered JOHN BROWN as God's first martyr in this land for the Anti-Slavery cause.

Mr. TAPPAN made a prayer, speaking of BROWN as a Christian martyr in the hands of an infuriated mob, and praying that posterity would rise up and call him blessed.

A Baptist clergyman offered a prayer, asking the spirit of God to imbue his servant JOHN BROWN, and that God's presence would be felt by the sufferer when surrounded by those who gnash their teeth and thirst for the blood of his kind and benevolent heart.

Rev. Mr. FRENCH renewed the parallel between JOHN BROWN and Stephen and prayed that his martyrdom should work greater good for the slave than had ever been worked before.

Dr. CHEEVER read the hymn containing the following:

> "Through grace I am determined
> To conquer, though I die."

At the reading of this portion the audience responded by fervent cries of "Amen."

At the suggestion of Mr. BERRY, the audience, at twenty minutes past 11, under the supposition that JOHN BROWN was then suffering his severest trial, devoted five minutes to silent prayer. [It appears that exactly at 11½ o'clock the fatal noose was tightened.] During the five minutes the silence was only broken by sobs and partly-audible prayers.

Dr. CHEEVER, near the close of the meeting, made an address, urging his hearers to "remember them that are in bonds as bound with them." Let them trust in the power of God to lead them on to victory.

A gentleman in the audience wanted to call attention to the trial of the first slave case thirty-five hundred years ago, when God was the plaintiff—when God had said, "Let my people go." He had determined that they should go. He did not believe that a slave could be got to heaven. They had got to rid the slave out of the hands of his master.

Another gentleman thought it perhaps better that JOHN BROWN had not carried out his scheme, because otherwise this meeting would not have assembled, and they would not have caught his spirit, as they would most assuredly under the present circumstances. JOHN BROWN had consecrated himself to the great and good cause.

Another gentleman said they depended too much on God's carrying on his work, without remembering that they were all instruments. They were awaiting God to show His power. Had it not been so with the reference to the rescue of their brother, JOHN BROWN? They should act as well as pray.

Dr. CHEEVER spoke of the day as a sacred and holy day, and as a fit season for prayer. He hoped there would be a large attendance at the evening meeting.

The church was a little more than half filled in the evening. A number of those present were evidently there only from motives of curiosity. After the preliminary exercises, Rev. C. J. WARREN delivered an address, in which he stated that the subject of their prayers was beyond the reach of prayer or pain. But his bereaved wife and family needed their prayers, his comrades, still bound in chains, should have their sympathy and prayer. Let the angel of the Lord light up their cells. [Amen.]

Dr. CHEEVER read a number of extracts from the Scriptures, with the design of showing God's comfort to the martyrs, and his ultimate purpose to overcome Slavery. He supposed that there was hardly a man in the nation who did not believe that JOHN BROWN was now in Heaven. His bitterest enemies ought to allow that God had taken him to Himself. He read several extracts from BROWN's letters to show his character. One letter, stating that he (Brown) considered himself worth much more for hanging than for any other purpose, was indorsed by a deep-toned "Amen" from a gentleman in the audience. He spoke of the circumstance of Brown's declining the services of the Southern minister, on the ground that their views on the subject of Slavery were incompatible with their joint profession of any religion. Dr. Cheever thought this was glorious. [Applause in various parts of the church.]

A Lady Voice—So do I. [Continued applause, by standing and clapping of hands.]

The Christian Church ought to take this to heart, and only needed the union of the religious world to remove this curse from our land in ten years.

Mr. Oliver Johnson said he felt exultant in the present crisis. John Brown's movement was God's own earthquake, shaking American Slavery to the centre. He read several verses eulogizing John Brown, and the principle for which he claims to have suffered, which were applauded by both clapping of hands and stamping of feet.

A shrill female voice at this point said: "I believe a great deal in bone and muscle." The lady told the fable of Hercules and the wagoner, in which the latter was advised
16 to put his shoulder to the wheel and then call upon the gods to help him. She wanted to see the ministers, women, and old men do the praying, but the young men ought to fight. She wouldn't have been afraid to head an army herself to help rescue John Brown. He should never have been hung. [Prolonged applause, as before.]

Dr. Cheever thought these manifestations were inappropriate to the deep solemnity that pervaded the meeting of the morning, and should characterize this. He believed the gigantic sin of Slavery was to be overcome by the power of the word of God leading the movement.

Mr. Fairbanks prayed, saying: It was sad that there were laws in the Nineteenth Century to put the Christian to death for obeying the laws of God. It was sad that the Government was on the side of the oppressor and the unjust laws, and pledged to extend their power. He prayed that God would make John Brown's death to call the attention of every slave-holder to the sin of Slavery, until they should break every yoke, and let the oppressed go free.

Dr. Ritter said he did not come here to exonerate John Brown and his associates, although he thought they were conscientiously wrong. He thought it a proper occasion to pray for John Brown, but he hoped they would say nothing that would lead it to be supposed that they did not know and believe that Brown and his associates were in error. They could praise Brown's heroism and honest aversion to Slavery, and pray for him consistently. He thought that the whole occurrence would tend to the overthrow of Slavery.

Mr. Fairbanks contrasted the scene of the reception of Lafayette, at the Bunker-Hill Monument, with the hanging of John Brown at Charlestown. The only difference he saw was that Lafayette fought for white men, while Brown only fought for the black. Lafayette succeeded and was honored, JOHN BROWN failed and was hung. He did not want to die a better death than while fighting for humanity. [Loud applause.]

Dr. CHEEVER suggested the immediate time was the best for making the collection for BROWN's family. While the plates were being passed, he took occasion to cite a passage from JOHN MILTON to sustain JOHN BROWN, ending with the following: "They dispute as to precedents, forms and circumstances, when the Commonwealth well-nigh perishes for want of deeds in substance done with just and faithful expedition." "JOHN BROWN's action," said Dr. CHEEVER, "stands unshakeable in righteousness and truth." [Prolonged plaudits.]

Rev. Mr. SLOAN said he had not believed that JOHN BROWN would be executed until he read it in the papers this evening. If proper demonstrations had been made, JOHN BROWN would be now alive. [Applause.] Gov. WISE had proposed if a Republican President was elected in 1860 to resist his inauguration. Now JOHN BROWN had only preceded Gov. WISE. Virginia's chivalry was nothing but a laughing-stock. Virginia could be whipped easily. [Applause.] Virginia was like a poor-house in the town in which it was established. It was a burden to the North. But the North would not let them go away. He never was an Abolitionist until this afternoon [applause;] but, now, he had determined to be a rabid Abolitionist, and do all he could to humiliate the South. That insolent, oppressive, pauper people must be humbled.

Mr. FAIRBANKS suggested that the brother was rather out of order. The meeting was called for prayer.

Mr. SLOAN said he had no disposition to pray over the matter at all. [Applause.] He was glad to be surrounded by praying men, but, he confessed he hadn't the spirit of prayer to-night. [Laughter and applause.]

Dr. CHEEVER said they had met for the purpose of prayer, and he hoped the brother would give way.

Mr. SLOAN said he had been so wrought up that he must give utterance to his feelings. Henceforth he was bound to act his best for Abolitionism. [Great applause.]

A Gentleman near the door said he had more confidence in 35,000 clergymen than in all the bayonets in the world. The people needed a religion like that of JOHN BROWN, that would treat Slavery as a crime. Let the Church get right.

Rev. Mr. MATTISON (Methodist) said he was here as a Methodist preacher, in harmony with the spirit of this meeting. He wished he could say he was a representative of the Methodist ministers. There was one other Methodist—brother FRENCH. He hoped they would keep their ministerial garments "uncottonized" until they got to heaven. Another crisis was approaching. The representatives of the Methodist Church were to meet in Buffalo within ninety days, and the question was to be discussed whether a slave-holder could be allowed in the communion of the Methodist Church. They had ministers who owned from one to twenty slaves. He was glad that JOHN BROWN had served the son of old Bishop WAUGH as he did. If that minister came to New-York he couldn't occupy his pulpit. The day had been a sad one to him.

After a prayer by Mr. MATTISON, and a few words from Rev. J. C. WARREN, the meeting separated.

MEETING AT THE SHILOH CHURCH.

A large assemblage, nearly all colored persons, filled the Shiloh (colored) Presbyterian church, yesterday forenoon. After singing, Rev. CHARLES B. RAE offered a prayer asking that God would rouse the consciences of men to see the wrongs done by the banditti of slaveholders as they never had been seen before, and that God would be with the wife and children of Mr. BROWN, and with all his friends and acquaintances in this day of trial.

After reading of the Scriptures by Rev. A. G. BEAMAN, Rev. H. H. GARNETT made an address. He said that the 2d of December would hereafter be called "Martyr's Day." Tyrants and despots would everywhere upbraid us for inflicting so ghastly a wound on the fair brow of Liberty, in a land nick-named the "Model Republic." After saying that JOHN BROWN was actuated by a desire to carry out the golden rule, Mr. GARNETT concluded as follows: "The withered hand of an old man, whose hairs are white with the frosts of nearly seventy Winters, has given the death-blow to American Slavery. His heroic deeds will be inscribed on marble, and his grave will be visited by troops of pilgrims. Virginia will be famed in history for having been the home of WASHINGTON, and the theatre of JOHN BROWN'S cowardly execution. Farewell, brave old man! God be with thee. Step forth from the scaffold which cannot dishonor thy name, or tarnish thy glory, into the chariot of fire that awaits thee. Go up to meet the army of departed heroes that have gone before thee to the kingdom of heaven. Go, and with joy receive thy martyr's crown, which the Lord has prepared for thee. Succeeding ages will cherish thy memory, and do justice to thy deeds of renown; and thy amazing courage will be the fruitful theme of orators, and the glowing songs of poets. Hero-martyr, farewell!

Rev. J. B. DUNN followed. He thought the occasion analogous to that scene, 1,800 years ago, when Christ ascended Calvary. Sisters and mothers were there to sympathize, as they are now present to console with JOHN BROWN. [Yes.] The prayer of all Christians should be, "Father, forgive them, for they know not what they do."

Rev. H. JOHNSON, who is quite an old man, then made some remarks and was succeeded by Rev. Mr. BAHN and Mr. GOODELL. Before the latter gentleman spoke a collection was taken up for the family of JOHN BROWN. It was stated that a movement was on foot to establish a permanent "Liberty Fund." The meeting was continued until 1 o'clock, one hour beyond the time fixed for adjournment.

Rev. SAMPSON WHITE deemed the occasion a very solemn one, when he thought of their friend who was in a short time to enter the eternal world. He believed that whatever might be done for liberty, God would approve of it. If it could not be achieved without shedding of blood, then it was their duty to do so. [Yes, yes.]

Rev. R.C. HENDERSON, of the Demarara Mission, made a few remarks upon the example of England in emancipating her slaves in the West Indies.

MEETING AT PHILADELPHIA.

A meeting assembled at National Hall yesterday morning, to offer prayers for JOHN BROWN. The following letters were read by Rev. Mr. FURNESS:

Charlestown, Jefferson Co., Va., Nov. 8, 1859.
Dear Wife and Children, every one:

I will begin by saying that I have in some degree recovered from my wounds, but that I am quite weak in my back and sore about my left kidney. My appetite has been quite good for most of the time since I was hurt. I am supplied with almost everything I could desire to make me comfortable, and the little that I do lack, (some few articles of clothing, which I lost,) I may perhaps soon get again. I am, besides, quite cheerful, having (as I trust) the peace of God which "passeth all understanding" to "rule in my heart," and the testimony (in some degree) of a good conscience that I have not lived altogether in vain. I can trust God with both the time and the manner of my death, believing as I now do, that for me at this time to seal my testimony (for God and Humanity) with my blood, will do vastly more toward advancing the cause I have earnestly endeavored to promote, than all I have done in my life before. I beg of you all meekly and quietly to submit to this; not feeling yourselves in the least *degraded* on that account. Remember, dear wife and children, all, that Jesus of Nazareth suffered a most excruciating death on the cross as a felon—under the most aggravating circumstances. Think, also, of the prophets, and apostles and Christians of former days, who went through greater tribulations than you or I; and (try) to be reconciled. May God Almighty comfort all your hearts, and soon wipe all tears from your eyes. To Him be endless praise. Think, too, of the crushed millions who "have no comforter." *I charge you all never* (in your trials) to forget the griefs "of the poor that cry, and of those that have none to help them." I wrote most earnestly to my dear and afflicted wife not to come on for the *present at any rate*. I will now give her my reasons for doing so. First, it would use up all of the scanty means she has, or is at all likely to have to make herself and children comfortable hereafter. For let me tell you that the sympathy that is now aroused in your behalf may not always follow you. There is but little more of the romantic about helping poor widows and their children than there is about trying to relieve poor *"niggers."* Again, the little comfort it might afford us to meet again would be clearly brought by the pains of a final separation. We *must part,* and I feel assured for us to meet under such dreadful circumstances would only add to our distress. If she comes on here, she must be only a gazing-stock throughout the whole journey, to be remarked upon in every *look, word* and *action,* and by all sorts of *creatures,* and by all sorts of papers throughout the whole country. Again, it is my most decided judgment that in quietly and submissively staying at home, vastly more of generous sympathy will *reach* her, without such dreadful sacrifice of feeling as she must put up with if she comes on. The visits of one or two female friends that have come on here have produced great excitement, which is very annoying, and they cannot possibly do me any good. *Oh, Mary, do not come,* but patiently wait for the meeting (of those who love God and their fellow-men) where no separation must follow. "They shall go no more out forever." I greatly long to hear, from some one of you, and to learn anything that in any way affects your welfare. I sent you $10 the other day—did you get it? I have also endeavored to stir up Christian friends to visit and write to you in your deep affliction. I have no doubt that some of them at least will heed the call. Write to me, care of Capt. JOHN AVIS, Charleston, Jefferson County, Va.

"Finally, my beloved, be of good comfort." May all your names be "written on the Lamb's book of life"—may you all have the purifying and sustaining influence of the Christian religion—is the earnest prayer of your affectionate husband and father,

JOHN BROWN.

P.S.—I cannot remember a night so dark as to have hindered the coming day; nor a storm so furious or dreadful as to prevent the return of warm sunshine and a cloudless sky. But, beloved ones, *do remember* that this is not your rest; that in this world you have no abiding place or continuing city. To God and His indefinite mercy I always commend you. J. B.

NOV. 9.

Dr. FURNESS, in introducing the following, remarked that he would read the last letter received from BROWN by Mrs. BROWN.

Extract from the last letter received by Mrs. BROWN, before she started to go to Charlestown, Jefferson County, Va., Nov. 20, 1859, in which, after referring to his wife's being under Mrs. MOTT's roof, he proceeds to say:

***I remember the old lady well; but presume she has no recollection of me. I once set myself to oppose a *mob* at Boston, where she was. After I interfered, the police immediately took up the matter, and soon put a stop to mob-proceedings. The meeting was, I think, in *Marlboro-street* Church, or *Hotel, perhaps.* I am glad to have you make the acquaintance of such old "Pioneers" in the cause. I have just received from Mr. JOHN JAY, of New-York, a draft for $50 (fifty dollars,) for the benefit of my family, and will enclose *it* made payable to your order. I have also $15 (fifteen dollars) to send to our *crippled and destitute* unmarried son; when I can, I intend to send you, by express, two or three little articles to carry home. Should you happen to meet with Mr. JAY, say to him that I fully appreciate his great kindness both to *me and my family.* God bless *all* such friends. It is out of my power to reply to *all* the kind and encouraging letters *I get; I wish* I could do so. I have been so much relieved from my lameness for the last three or four days as to be able to sit up and to read and write pretty much all day, as well as part of the night; and I do assure you *and all other friends,* that I am quite busy, and *none the less happy* on that account. The time passes *quite pleasantly;* and the near approach of my great change is not the occasion of any particular dread.

I trust that *God* who has sustained me *so long* will not *forsake* me when I most feel my need of *Fatherly aid and support.* Should He hide His face, my spirit will drop and die; *but not otherwise, be assured.* My only anxiety is to be properly assured of my *fitness* for the company of those who are "washed from *all filthiness;" and for the presence of Him who is Infinitely pure.* I certainly *think* I do have *some "hunger and thirst* after righteousness." If it be only *genuine,* I make *no doubt I "shall* be filled." Please let all our friends read my letters when you can; and ask them to accept of it as *in part for them.* I am inclined to think you will not be likely to succeed well about getting away the bodies of your family; but should that *be so, do not let that grieve you.* It can make but little difference *what is done with them.*

You can well remember the changes you have passed through. Life is made up of a series of changes, and let us try to meet them in the best manner possible. You will not wish to make yourself and children any more burdensome to friends than you are really compelled to do—*I would not.*

I will close this by saying that if you *now feel* that you are *equal* to the undertaking, do *exactly as you feel disposed to do* about coming to see me before I suffer. *I am entirely willing.*

YOUR AFFECTIONATE HUSBAND,

(Signed) JOHN BROWN

Remarks were subsequently made by Dr. TURNER, Mr. THEORDORE TILTON, of the *New-York Independent*, Mrs. MARY GREW, Mrs. LUCRETIA MOTT, and others.

DEMONSTRATION IN MASSACHUSETTS.
ACTION OF THE LEGISLATURE.

BOSTON, FRIDAY, DEC. 2.

At the meeting of the Senate to-day, after prayer by the Chaplain, Mr. LUCE, of the Nantucket district, moved that the Senate adjourn on account of the execution of

John Brown. Mr. Rich, of Suffolk, opposed the motion, and the yeas and nays stood 8 for adjournment and 11 against.

In the House, Mr. Ray, of Nantucket, moved an adjournment, offering at the same time a resolution of sympathy for Brown. A spicy debate followed, when the motion to adjourn was defeated, yeas 6, nays 141.

THE FEELING IN BOSTON.

Boston, Friday, Dec. 2.

John Brown's execution to-day attracted considerable crowds about the newspaper offices as the evening editions were issued, and several individuals promenaded the streets with crape attached to their persons. Religious services were held in several of the colored churches the most part of the day. Otherwise there were no manifestations unusual to everyday life in this city.

Rev. Mr. Grimes, colored, held late prayer-meetings at his church last night, for John Brown, and is continuing them to-day.

The bells in Plymouth and New-Bedford were tolled at noon.

MEETING IN TREMONT TEMPLE.

Boston, Friday, Dec. 2.

Tremont Temple was crowded, this evening, to commemorate the death of John Brown.

All the colored population of Boston and its vicinity were present, together with many ladies, a large number of whom attended out of mere curiosity. On the platform were seated many of the most prominent Abolitionists of New-England, and erected upon which was the standard of Virginia, with its coat-of-arms draped in black. In front the rostrum was decorated with a large black cross, underneath which was a photograph likeness of John Brown, which was draped in mourning.

Mr. Sewall made the opening speech, stating the object of the meeting was one of sympathy, and to commemorate the death of John Brown, who he designated as a "martyr to freedom." He concluded by characterizing Gov. Wise as the modern Pontius Pilate.

Wm. Lloyd Garrison then read the various letters and documents which have emanated from John Brown. They have heretofore been published.

J. S. Marten, a negro of Philadelphia, followed. He lauded the acts of John Brown, at the same time slightly rapping the Republican Party for its lukewarmness in not doing likewise. A remark made by him that Virginia in her act today was the most guilty of all the guilty mothers of the American Government, was received by mingled hisses and applause.

J. Q. A. GRIFFIN, of Malden, a member of the House, next addressed the meeting. He claimed that the heinous offences of Pontius Pilate, in crucifying our Savior, whitened into virtue when compared with those of Gov. WISE, of Virginia, in his course towards JOHN BROWN. He also stated that it was the opinion of no less a Democrat than Hon. CALEB CUSHING, as a lawyer, that the proceedings of the Governor and Court of Virginia, in trying and condemning JOHN BROWN, were without the sanction of the Constitution and laws of the United States.

A letter was received from Rev. H. M. DEXTER, of the Pine-street Church, regretting his inability to be present, and stating that, while he did not justify the act of John Brown, he thought it would yet be glorified by its future good results to the cause of freedom.

Rev. Mr. PIERPONT made a few remarks in accordance with the tone of the previous speaker.

He was followed by Hon. R. H. DAVIS, of Fall River, a member of the Massachusetts Senate, who indorsed the action of JOHN BROWN, on the ground that its ultimate result would be good.

WM. LLOYD GARRISON then made a characteristic speech, glorifying BROWN and his associates, and thanked God that the time had been brought about by the act of today's martyr, when the sympathies of men of rank were identified with his, which would thus enable him to leave the arena after battling for thirty years for American freedom.

A collection was taken up, announced for the benefit of the family of JOHN BROWN. The meeting then dispersed at an early hour.

The election of 1860 was the most fateful in American history. For the first time a party and a candidate that were pledged to restrict any further expansion of slavery won the presidency. For the first time a president was elected by carrying every free state and no slave states. Having controlled the federal government most of the time before 1860 through their domination of the Democratic party, southern Democrats saw the handwriting on the wall. Charles Francis Adams, son and grandson of presidents and a founder of the Republican party, declared that with Lincoln's election "the great revolution has actually taken place. The country has once and for all thrown off the domination of the Slaveholders." The slaveholders thought so too; that is why they launched their counterrevolution of secession.

November 7, 1860.

THE PRESIDENTIAL ELECTION.

Astounding Triumph of Republicanism.

THE NORTH RISING IN INDIGNATION AT THE MENACES OF THE SOUTH.

Abraham Lincoln Probably Elected President by a Majority of the Entire Popular Vote.

Forty Thousand Majority for the Republican Ticket in New-York.

One Hundred Thousand Majority in Pennsylvania.

Seventy Thousand Majority in Massachusetts.

Corresponding Gains in the Western and North-Western States.

Preponderance of John Bell and Conservatism at the South.

Results of the Contest upon Congressional and Local Tickets.

RE-ELECTION OF GOV. MORGAN.

The canvass for the Presidency of the United States terminated last evening, in all the States of the Union, under the revised regulation of Congress, passed in

1845, and the result, by the vote of New-York, is placed beyond question at once. It elects ABRAHAM LINCOLN of Illinois, President, and HANNIBAL HAMLIN of Maine, Vice-President of the United States, for four years, from the 4th March next, directly by the People: These Republican Candidates having a clear majority of the 303 Electoral votes of the 33 States, over all three of the opposing tickets. They receive, including Mr. Lincoln's own State, from which the returns have not yet come, in the

New-England States	41
New-York	35
Pennsylvania	27
New-Jersey	7
And the Northwest	61
Total Electoral for Lincoln	171

Being 19 over the required majority, without wasting the returns from the two Pacific States of Oregon and California.

The election, so far as the City and State of New-York are concerned, will probably stand, hereafter as one of the most remarkable in the political contests of the country; marked, as it is, by far the heaviest popular vote ever cast in the City, and by the sweeping, and almost uniform, Republican majorities in the country.

The State of Pennsylvania, which virtually decided her preference in October, has again thrown an overwhelming majority for the Republican candidates. And New-Jersey, after a sharp contest has, as usual in nearly all the Presidential elections, taken her place on the same side. The New-England majorities run up by tens of thousands.

The Congressional elections which took place yesterday in this State have probably confirmed the probability of an Anti-Republican preponderance in the next House of Representatives, by displacing several of the present Republican members.

The new House of Assembly for New-York will, as usual, be largely Republican.

Of the reelection of Gov. Morgan there is little or no question. By the scattering vote thrown for Mr. Brady in this City, the plurality of Mr. Kelly over Gov. Morgan is partially reduced, while the heavy Republican majority in the country insures Gov. Morgan's success.

The rival Presidential candidates against Mr. Lincoln have probably divided the Southern vote as follows:

For Mr. Bell.

Virginia	15	Tennessee	12
Kentucky	12		

For Mr. Breckinridge

South Carolina 8	Florida 3
North Carolina 10	Mississippi 7
Georgia 10	Texas 4
Alabama 9	Arkansas 4

Doubtful.

Missouri 9	Delaware 3
Louisiana 6	Maryland 8

ELECTION DAY IN THE CITY.

ALL QUIET AND ORDERLY AT THE POLLS.

Progress of the Voting in the Several Wards.

THE CITY AFTER NIGHTFALL.

HOW THE NEWS WAS RECEIVED.

Unbounded Enthusiasm at the Republican and Bell-Everett Head-Quarters.

THE TIMES OFFICE BESIEGED.

Midnight Display of Wide-Awakes.

BONFIRES AND ILLUMINATIONS.

The clouds lowered gloomily over the City yesterday morning, when the polls were opened, and very shortly afterward rain began to drizzle, with every prospect of a wet day. Was it an omen, and if so, an ill omen to the Lincoln or Fusion ticket. It did not, at any rate, keep one or the other party from the polls, for never in the history of any political contest in this country, has more enthusiasm been exhibited, and the result has proved that though the "clouds" may have "lowered," the hopes of the Republican Party were not "in the deep bosom of the ocean buried." But of that anon and elsewhere.

People generally were awake—wide awake, in fact—very early yesterday, for they knew they had a duty to perform which could not occur but once in four years, and in the actual shape it assumed, perhaps not more than once in a lifetime. And whether they were Republicans or Fusionists, they went to work with a will. The clouds were dispelled; the sun shone forth as a beneficent sun should shine on such an occasion, and a general good time was the result. In short, although the stake to be played, according to the alarmists, was the continuation or severance of the Union, there was no disturbance, no discordance, no manner of ill-feeling, beyond the impatience produced by extreme difficulty in getting in "my vote, Sir, my prerogative as an independent citizen, Sir, which I would not barter for my life, Sir."

The vote polled in each Ward, and each District of each Ward, is said to have been the heaviest ever known in this City. At nearly every polling-place—and there were close upon three hundred in all the Wards—voters took their places *en queue,* and moved on very slowly to their duty as freemen. And wherever we had opportunities of observing them, they did it like men who were fully sensible of the responsibility, whether it came of conscience sake, or was derived from a recollection or a hope of "gilded gain."

Considerable delay was caused at many polls by an indiscriminate challenging process, which occupied so much time that in nearly every Ward at sunset, when the polls closed, some hundreds of votes had not been able to "save the country," and having given the day to that nobly patriotic purpose, they felt very naturally, slightly irascible thereat.

The proceedings at the several Wards are slightly sketched below. The harmony of the whole proceedings renders the detail of them slightly monotonous—a defect, if it is one, which should be placed to the credit of the excellent Police arrangements, for which Superintendent KENNEDY and his aids and abettors are responsible.

HOW THE NEWS WAS RECEIVED.

TAMMANY DISCONSOLATE.

Marshal Rynders, in an Irreverent Manner, Concedes the Victory to Lincoln.

The crowd which gathered about Tammany last evening, dispersed and reassembled several times before the old wigwam showed any signs of life. Not only was there no "Rynders pocket-piece," to scare the echoes in the Park, but there was no tar-barrel, there were no rockets or Roman candles. Not to speak of a full Band of music, there was not even a single drum or fife. Tammany was dismal. Tammany was abysmal. Tammany, in fact, was nowhere, till about eight o'clock, when the gas in the large room was partially lighted, and a tolerable crowd, in some twenty minutes, found admission. And then, where was the pride of Tammany? Three or four hundred men, and an equal number of boys, constituted the audience who were to listen to, approve and applaud the speakers. Councilman MCCONNELL, in the absence of Marshal RYNDERS, took the chair. He said that the object of the meeting was to receive

This rare photograph by Alexander Hesler of Abraham Lincoln was taken in June 1860 soon after his nomination to the presidency. (*Library of Congress*)

the returns of the election for the different Wards of the City, which he trusted would result in a great victory for the Union ticket. The Eleventh Ward, he knew, was 2,305 majority for that ticket.

A VOICE—Give us a song.

McCONNELL—I cannot sing, but I feel thunderingly anxious to give you a great majority.

A VOICE—What about the Seventh Ward?

McCONNELL— In The Seventh Ward there are 7,000 majority for the Union ticket.

The speaker continued to enlighten the audience concerning the majorities in favor of the Union ticket in the Sixth, Ninth and Eighteenth Wards, when just at this point Marshal RYNDERS made his appearance. Of course he was cheered very loudly. Of course he was called to speak immediately, and of course, with his accustomed modesty, he declined. But having declined, he was prevailed upon to reconsider the matter, and did it very effectively by mounting the platform, and yielding the election to LINCOLN. . . .

RYNDERS—A fellow once said to me that birds were of such a gender, I forget what gender, and perhaps he didn't know himself what gender, and so I say that the State is of a doubtful gender. But the City of New-York stands for Union, let other places have done what they have. Every man who lives in this City, who has voted our ticket, has a right to say to the world that we are a conservative City, [Don't knock that man's hat over his eyes, don't,] and if the people in the country will trample upon us, for the love of the Negro, let them bear the ignominy of it, and if the Union is dissolved, we can proudly say, "Never shake your gory fingers at us; we have stood by the rights of the white people of this country, and if we are beaten, we are beaten honorably."

The Marshal left the platform amid loud applause. Calls were made for the Chairman, but he had disappeared and there being no other speaker present, the audience lugubriously dissolved itself, the Marshal announcing it as his opinion that LINCOLN would be the next President.

AT THE REPUBLICAN HEAD-QUARTERS.

General Rejoicing.

The Republican rejoicings filled the City last night. They celebrated their triumph in the streets; they gathered in shouting crowds around the newspaper-offices; they inundated the Station-houses, and threw up their hats as the returns were announced; they assembled at the Head-quarters, No. 618 Broadway, in such numbers, that once wedged in one could not turn around to come out again. There Mr. DANIEL D. CONOVER took the Chair, and, with Gen. J. H. HOBART WARD and Mr. CHARLES SPENCER, received the returns, and from time to time computed the probable result. Mr. CONOVER read the figures, and every time he read the people cheered or jeered, according to the complexion of the news. The enthusiasm, which was wild, as soon as it was known how much below the estimate of the Fusionists was the result in the First Ward, increased steadily as the night wore on, and was incontinent at last. Never were there gathered together so many persons in so excellent a humor. While they were waiting for news from some Ward not yet heard from, all were talking and laughing at once; some were giving lusty cheers for LINCOLN and the whole Republican ticket; some were cracking jokes at the expense of the Opposition; those without were endeavoring to elbow their way in, and some within, half suffocated, were trying to force their way out. It was just such a hubbub of hilarity, in short, as you would expect to hear in the Republican Head-quarters on the night of the Republican victory. One, more enthusiastic, was incessantly proposing three cheers for somebody. He proposed three cheers for Gen. WARD; they were given with gusto. He proposed three more for Mr. CONOVER, and three more for Mr. SPENCER; they were given. Then he proposed "Three cheers for me." They were not given. Then, by way of variety, he proposed three cheers for Mr. CONOVER again. Here that gentleman interposed and requested that less noise should be made, and that men would stand still; he did not know how long the floor of the room would support such a mass of enthusiastic people. A man mounted a chair at the remote end of the room and shouted out the name of a friend, whom he said he wanted to go to a fire that was raging not far off. "There's a fire every where," said Mr. SPENCER, and that brought down the house—almost the floor—again. Loud as the din was during these interludes, as soon as the Chairman announced more returns, quiet was immediately restored—to be lost again amid a storm of cheers as soon as they were read. Thus, till a late hour, they kept it up at No. 618 Broadway.

At the Head-quarters of the various Republican Clubs, too, there were immense throngs. The City of Wide-Awakes were at their rendezvous in force, and at Stuyvesant Institute the jam was irrepressible. The interior of the building was choked with people, the entrance was blocked up, and the sidewalk in front was black with Republicans. With the thunders of the thousands there assembled, the vicinity like the rest of the City, was kept thoroughly and wide awake.

AT THE NEWSPAPER OFFICES.

If any one doubted last evening that the telegraph wires were big with the fate of this glorious Union, a walk in the vicinity of the different newspaper offices would have speedily convinced him to the contrary. Such crowds as were gathered around the doors of the TIMES, *Tribune* and *Herald* are only to be seen on these quadrennial occasions of the country's salvation or destruction. Even our mundane neighbor suffered from a temporary deluge of humanity, and crowds rushed to read the latest entries in the *Day Book.* The publication offices were soon filled; "happy thou," thought the crowd outside, who have gained admittance to the inner mysteries. It is very probable that the minnows in the North River envy those which are snugly boxed up and labeled sardines. Anxious to see as well as to hear the outside crowd flattened their noses painfully against the panes—one would have imagined that they thought to smell out the returns. They climbed on each other's shoulders and stood on each other's heads in a vain attempt to peer in at the second story windows. Curiosity, apprehension, exultation—these and all other emotions, were as plainly stamped on each individual countenance as the Eagle on a quarter or the Georgius Rex on an old-fashioned penny-piece. These emotions found expression whenever returns came in from a Ward or a County. There were cheers and groans and huzzas and hisses. And until the night had grown old and morning was born, the clamorous crowd demanded more news and later intelligence. They demanded to know the fate of the Union before daybreak, and many of them learnt it before they went home. But it is questionable whether the majority of them would find out during the coming Presidential term whether the country were saved or lost, if it were not for the information supplied by their party newspaper.

IMPROPTU WIDE-AWAKE PARADE.

They are Attacked by Armed Men.

A short time before 12 o'clock midnight, an impromptu gathering of the City Wide-Awakes took place, and preparations were made immediately for a demonstration. A banner bearing a full-length portrait of "Old ABE," with a broom in both hands, in the act of sweeping out the White House, and surmounted by the inscription, "Clear the track!" was carried in front of the procession. Forming in platoons of six abreast, they marched down Broadway, through the Park, and, halting in front of the TIMES office, gave rousing cheers for the success of the Republican ticket. The procession then marched down Park-row, headed by the banner, and marching to the tap of a drum. When they had reached a position opposite the Astor House, several rowdies broke into the procession and tore down the banner, while one of the party, at the same instant, struck one of the Wide-Awakes a heavy blow upon the mouth. This was the signal for a general fight; clubs and stones were freely used by all parties, and one of the rowdies, finding himself overpowered, drew a knife and made a rush at those nearest him, swearing that he would murder every Wide-Awake that he could get a hold of. Another drew a revolver and threatened to blow the first man's brains out who approached him. These actions and threats kept the Wide-Awakes at some distance, when one of the party shouted, "What, shall three or four loafers frighten us?" and instantly a rush was made, and before either party could use their weapons they were disarmed and badly beaten. Another of the assailants drew a heavy club, while the two parties were fighting at the corner of Broadway and Vesey-street, and struck one of the Wide-Awakes a severe blow upon the head, felling him to the ground. Hardly had he committed the assault, however, than he was seized by a number of the Wide-Awakes and most unmercifully pummeled. Finally he broke from them and entered an Eighth-avenue car, which had just started, and escaped. A number of the Wide-Awakes now went up Broadway, preceded by the banners, and the rest dispersed.

As the telegraph flashed news of Lincoln's election across the South, one state legislature after another called for the election of delegates to a convention to consider secession. South Carolina's convention met first and on December 20 passed a resolution of secession by a vote of 169-0. Mississippi, Florida, Alabama, Georgia, Louisiana, and Texas followed suit during the next six weeks. In February 1861, delegates from these states met in Montgomery to create a constitution and government for the Confederate States of America.

December 21, 1860.

THE DISUNION CRISIS.

The Formal Secession of South Carolina.

Unanimous Adoption of the Ordinance Declaring the Union Dissolved.

Interesting Discussions in the Convention.

HIGHLY IMPORTANT FROM THE FEDERAL CAPITAL.

Reception of the News of the Action of South Carolina.

The Commander of Fort Moultrie Instructed to Surrender.

The U.S. Arms in Charleston Arsenal Delivered to the City Authorities.

CONGRESSIONAL PROCEEDINGS.

Passage of the Pacific Railroad Bill in the House.

SPEECH OF SENATOR PUGH, OF OHIO.

Important from the Home of Mr. Lincoln.

SOUTH CAROLINA STATE CONVENTION.

WEDNESDAY'S PROCEEDINGS.

The full report of Wednesday's proceedings having been received too late for the insertion in our entire edition of yesterday, we reproduce in the following portion:

J. P. REED introduced a resolution, first ordering the President to appoint a Cashier and Deputy-Cashier; second, ordering the Clerk to superintend the printing of the Convention; third, that reporters for public journals shall be allowed access to the hall for the purpose of reporting; fourth, that the regular hour for meeting shall be 10 o'clock, subject to a special order; fifth, that an alphabetical list of their members, with their Post-office address, be provided; sixth, that a journal be published and laid on the tables of the members before the time of meeting.

Mr. KEITT moved to amend by substituting 11 o'clock. Accepted.

Mr. MIDDLETON moved to strike out the last resolution. Objection was made.

Mr. SUNON desired to know how far the resolution extended respecting the admission of reporters.

Mr. ENGLIS moved that the reporters of the State only be admitted.

Mr. QUATTLEBAUM moved that each resolution be voted on separately. Carried.

The reporters' resolution is still up.

Mr. CHEVIS said that a Convention of the people, or a deliberative body in discussion should sit with closed door. To sit with open doors was essential to the satisfaction of the public mind. Visitors, whether by States or foreign countries, look at us otherwise than unfavorably. Let us sit at all times with open doors, till some question should be discussed among ourselves. We must satisfy the public mind. We had better get a more suitable hall, so that we can more readily sit with closed doors. He moved to lay it on the table.

Mr. MEANS seconds the motion.

Mr. MAGRATH believed the people of Charleston didn't wish to intrude, although they had a curiosity. He didn't believe there were ten men in Charleston who would not sacrifice their curiosity and strangle their desire to see and hear their deliberations.

Mr. RICHARDS said this is the best place in the city, and there should be no discrimination between a friend or foe, as to his knowing what is transpiring inside.

Mr. MIDDLETON—We should then obviate the difficulty of settling with closed doors and employ an artisan to erect a barrier, spectators then can be admitted without interference.

A motion was then made to refer the whole matter to the Charleston delegation, and the substitute for sitting with closed doors was withdrawn.

Mr. REED moved to lay the whole subject on the table.

Mr. BONNEAU withdrew his resolution.

Mr. DARGEN—What is before the meeting. Here is a resolution authorizing the President to issue tickets for admission to the reporters at his discretion; which was adopted.

The printing of an alphabetical list was taken up.

Mr. PRIESTLY moved to insert the occupation of the members.

Objection was made, and the motion was withdrawn.

The sixth resolution was lost.

A resolution was offered to adopt the rules of other Conventions for the government of the present body.

Mr. QUATTLEBAUM moved to lay it on the table.

Mr. REED—the Conventions of 1833 and 1852 had published rules. These would be convenient to members now.

Mr. MEMMINGER—Such rules embarrass the proceedings. The President refers to the rules for governing the House of Representatives, or parliamentary rules.

Mr. QUATTLEBAUM withdrew his motion, and the resolution was adopted.

Mr. WARDLAW said we had better leave the question of admitting the reporters to be decided between the editors and the President.

Mr. MEMMINGER—Does the resolution apply to the reporters of the Southern States alone?

Mr. SIMONS—Let the question be left alone to the reporters themselves.

Mr. CHEVIS called for the adoption of his amendment.

Mr. CURTISS—We should do everything in order, and know what we are doing.

Mr. MEMMINGER moved that a bar be erected, and access granted to the Convention through the Sergeant-at-Arms only.

Mr. BONNEAU offered the following:

Resolved. That the Mayor of Charleston be requested to have a proper policeman stationed at the door of the Convention to see that members only gained access to it.

Mr. REED thought that it would be better to appoint the Charleston delegation to make all the necessary arrangements.

Mr. BONNEAU thought it would be best to pass his resolution. It might be necessary for us to sit here with closed doors for two days or more.

Mr. CHESNUT thought it impracticable to sit with closed doors.

It was here moved that the communications from the Georgia Legislature be taken up and referred to the Committee to prepare an address to the people of the Southern States.

Mr. MIDDLETON—This is not a communication from the Georgia Legislature, it is merely from sundry persons calling themselves members of the Legislature of Georgia. May we not incur risk for proceeding in this way. This will afford an opportunity for communications from New-York and Pennsylvania, and we will then be bound to refer to the same Committee all similar papers. Let us lay this resolution on the table, and let it be understood that this body will not consider unofficial documents.

Mr. CALHOUN moved that the communication be refused.

Mr. QUATTLEBAUM moved to lay the matter on the table.

Mr. WARDLAW—This is the only paper from a respectable body of persons, who are citizens of Georgia, and who hold important positions. Shall we repulse them by saying they shall not hear anything from us?

Mr. MIDDLETON said, where is the evidence of its authenticity? The signatures are all in the same handwriting. We must preserve our self-respect.

Mr. WADLAW—The telegraph from Gov. Moore is similar.

Mr. SIMONS hoped official communications only would be received.

Mr. DARGEN—The document is couched in respectful terms. There is no reason why we should not consider it. Georgia is the Empire State of the South.

Mr. ENGLIS—We must draw a line somewhere.

Mr. QUATTLEBAUM reported that the Printing Committee had performed their labors. They had awarded the contract to Messrs. EVANS & COGGSWELL.

The appointment of four Special Committees was then made.

Mr. HUTSON said the business of the Convention will be greater and wider than that of any other ever held in South Carolina.

Mr. SMITH proposed that the Committee on Commerce also be the Committee of Postal Arrangements.

Mr. MAZYCK—Small Committees work with greater certainty.

The Committee on Commerce and Postal Arrangements was increased to 13.

The Convention adopted a resolution that a Committee in relation to the slave-holding States of North American be appointed.

The third resolution of the Committee on Commercial Intercourse and Portal Arrangements was taken up.

Mr. MCCURDY—We only propose to make a change for the people while in a transition state. We must take special care of the postal arrangements. Our Legislature now has no power, we are the power. Let us pass it subject to their revision and alteration. You are not to break in upon arrangements which are necessary to the convenience of our citizens and those of other States. I think the Convention are bound to make arrangements with the Post-Office Department. The mails can be carried as usual, and we will pay the contractors.

SPEECH OF CHANCELLOR DUNKIN.

Chancellor DUNKIN said: Mr. President, I do not know that a particular amendment is of very much consequence. I supposed this Committee would have authority to take into consideration what has been termed postal arrangements, and I think so now.

A VOICE—That's so.

Mr. DUNKIN—Its very difficult to define and distinguish, but when you come to consider what we have to do, it will be no great stretch to say that a Committee on Commercial Relations might take into consideration our portal arrangements as part of its commercial relations; and I do supposed, when my friend submitted his resolution for appointing the Committee, that it would have that authority; and with due deference to the gentleman, whom I greatly respect, I would that there might be a question upon this. I do not believe the Convention entertains a doubt about the Committee. They may, if they think proper, take into consideration postal arrangements. The President has done me honor by placing me on the Committee to prepare an ordinance of the withdrawal of this State from what has been called the Federal Union. I do not think I act in violation of confidence as a member of that Committee to act upon the matter; they are united. [Smothered applause.] If any delay takes place it will be simply for the purpose of preparing an ordinance in a manner consistent with its effect and the dignity of the State. Sir, I am sure that the ordinance will not be submitted to-morrow. We have been working this morning, and again will work this evening. We don't intend to be hasty. We purpose to lose no time. We are anxiously engaged in it, and I say, without violation of confidence, we are engaged only upon the matter of form. Upon that we shan't be long in agreeing. Mr. President, I will, in the remarks I intend offering—I will assume that this State will be out of the Union in a very few days, if not in many hours. Then, Mr. President, we have

something to look to. For many purposes the Union has worked well. The machinery is convenient and advantageous—in small matters very convenient. Sir, having a determination to go out of the Union, we should endeavor to do it with as little harm to the ordinary transactions of the community as is practicable and consistent with the position we have assumed, a character which we purpose to maintain. Sir, the machinery has worn well, and you can't stop it suddenly unless you get some break in it in some way. Now, Sir, I can't illustrate what I desire to say in a better manner than by referring to the first matter to be considered—the commercial relations, or marine relations, if you so please to call the ports, harbors and Custom-houses. This is a great purpose, and I cannot illustrate, nor elaborate, but suggest in reference to Custom-houses, and I would refer to the conduct of the gentleman who now occupies the Collectorship of the port and who has illustrated to me his idea. Sir, all I know I have seen in the public papers. I know nothing more. I saw the Collector a few times directly after the announcement of the election of LINCOLN. The feelings of the gentleman would have promptly caused him to instantly throw up his commission. He didn't desire for one moment to remain an officer of the National Government when he perceived what would happen. But, Sir, what would have happened if immediate acceptance had taken place in the reception at Washington of his commission? Sir, it is well known to every man in the community that if Mr. BUCHANAN received it and appointed another to fill the thrown-up commission for that purpose. I need not say that no Southern man would have accepted it; no man of South Carolina would have been allowed to do it. [Applause.] Sir, Mr. COLCOCK saw that he is a practical man. If he had sent in his commission, and it had been accepted, as I presume it would, I ask any man who knows anything of the commercial relations of Charleston, what would have been the consequence? All the power of the British Navy would not have as effectually stopped the port of Charleston. It is well known that if a vessel passes the bar of Charleston without the regular papers, signed by the Collector of that port, that vessel is liable to be taken up in twenty minutes as a vagrant or pirate. No vessel would venture that peril. The Collector knew this. He didn't do it. He gave notice he would hold his commission subject to the direction of the Convention of the people of South Carolina, when here assembled. He knew that a sudden stoppage would have been accompanied by the most mischievous consequences. He is prepared now, and he holds his commission under the direction and at the will of the Convention, or of this body, to which he expects to owe allegiance, and to whom he expects to owe allegiance alone. Let us pass to postal arrangements. Mr. President, MIRABEAU, many years ago, said that the fiercest insurrections were those which arose from the stomach. People without bread won't have reason; their patriotism is dead. Sir, next to bread, in our artificial state of society, is light. I don't mean the glorious light of the heavens—I mean the information and intelligence. Next to bread, people must have information. They must have light. If, Sir, you suddenly withdraw this light for eight and forty hours, or cause an interruption in postal arrangements, you stop the means of communications. Sir, the perilous consequences which would result from it will be easily appreciated by every thinking man in every corner of the State. Sir, it should not be done suddenly. We should have a little time to effect common arrangements. Now, in regard to postal arrangements, it is to be done by a Congress. Don't let me be misunderstood. I assume that to-morrow we take the attitude of a sovereign State; I will assume that the national men at the head of the Federal Government when the matter is presented to them, will see that the rights we assume—our rights—must be recognized. Without that they will be prepared soon to hear we are out of the Union. By slowly acting they will then be prepared to treat with us in confidence upon postal arrangements, upon any other matter. Let me say, Mr. President, I don't use argument from their feelings, but their interests, as important to them as to us, and a certain time should be given. As in the instance of a co-partnership proposed to be drawn up, it is reasonable that ordinary time be given to effect our purposes. You can't act until you are out of the Union.

The object should be to make arrangements, and that very shortly, so as to keep up commerce. If we please, the postal arrangement, which I consider a part of the great commercial relations of the country, can we keep them up until we hear the government is prepared to say yea or nay? Mr. President, I have said I got my information about the Collector from the newspapers, as to the Postmasters of the States, I think I might say the same thing. From a number I know I could say they are ready; they are only desirous of knowing from the Convention what is proper for the welfare and the advancement of this great cause. Mr. President, what I have said as to the Collector of Charleston, I could only specify from what I read in the papers. For the Postmaster of Charleston, I have a right to speak a little more authentically. I say, Sir, that at this very moment, he is prepared to put his commission in the hands of the Governor of the State to be forwarded to the Department whenever, in the opinion of the Governor, through this Convention, it shall be deemed expedient for the welfare of South Carolina, to which alone, after its withdrawal, he will look. I do injustice, however. I come short. He has lived to the time appointed for man, and rather beyond it, and I say, in all the difficulties and troubles he may have encountered in that long period of time, that they have been as nothing to the relief which he is afforded. He has intimated that he is ready to put his commission this night in the hands of the Governor of this State. Now, Sir, we know what the Collector will do, we know what the Postmasters throughout the State are prepared to do. Now, Sir, I have a resolution which I intend to offer to this Committee, not entirely for them, but to find out what temporary or permanent arrangements it is expedient to adopt, in reference to the withdrawal of this State from the Union, for commercial and postal arrangements. Sir, I supposed that the Committee would only report until it had conferred with the Governor. So that better not to disturb the ordinary relations, and not until it had heard what was proposed to be done on the subject. Some gentlemen suggest an allowance for conference of ten days, some suggest one month, some suggest a longer time, say two months, or after the assembling of the two Conventions of our sister States which meet on the 7th of January. It was suggested that a temporary arrangement could go into operation on the 20th of January, so that time would be given for the General Government to know our views and make ready to answer yea or nay, whether they are disposed to treat, but in the meantime the ordinary occupations of our citizens are to go on. One matter more as to the revenues. The Postmaster of Charleston, most likely would keep an account up till the transaction was settled, Jan. 17. My friend from St. Michael's proposed one item. It was proposed that the money received by the Postmaster, or any of them, should be considered in account and settled with the General Government on the day of the ratification of the ordinance. At the sitting of this Convention a month hence, all these matters will be arranged as between two parties. In the meantime, the accounts should go on so that no sudden disruption should take should take place. Sir, I merely suggest this, as it has been spoken of by others. Secretary Cobb said that the revenue of South Carolina from the Custom-house didn't near pay the expense of customs. For the last quarter, I understood from the best authority, that the Post-offices of South Carolina cost the Government $240,000, and the receipts have been less than $50,000. Therefore, Mr. President, there is no great apprehension in that way. But accounts should be kept. In the meantime the usual business transactions should be allowed to proceed until it was ascertained what were the views regarded by the Administration, which I have no doubt are entirely friendly to us and will do everything that can be done in order to prevent any inconvenience. Mr. President, I have only a word more. I will then take my seat. We are at the inauguration of a great cause. All of us look with an undivided eye to the consequences of that move. One of the most prominent and most favorable is the unanimity which prevails in this State of South Carolina, and unanimity not only unexpected, Sir, but unprecedented. I might go farther and say as to the sympathy found in other States; it is to a certain degree unexpected. It has surpassed, I take to say, every expectation. The great object should be to preserve unanimity and form, and not chill this sympathy of our Southern sisters. Now, Mr. President I have said stop for a day, shut up for a day, the port of Charleston, and the ships now loading with the products of our country would rot before they would go to sea. If an ordinance was passed, they will have no papers; they are stopped. Pass your ordinance, and what is the consequence? Why, Sir, we are stopped a single day. If we were stopped two days, all the eloquence of Mr. STEPHENS would be but a penny-whistle compared with the astounding causes among ourselves. The stoppage of postal arrangements is an argument that will make a man silent. This will be but the beginning. The port of Charleston shut, the post arrangements stopped, the people united, their ships rotting at the wharves, and the whole of our ordinary transactions will stop. Is there any argument that can obviate it? Look at the States. One State hesitates, some are more than ready. Georgia, whose cooperation we desire more than any other, is a State having exactly the same position with us, and lies side by side by us. Mr. President, I have a resolution which I intend soon to ask to offer to an appropriate committee. I propose to refer to that committee to inquire whether it is in contemplation, on withdrawal of the State from the Union, either to make permanent or temporary arrangements in reference to the officers of the Post-office or our Custom-house, and that they should report thereon. This is what I propose. I think it may be done without offering a resolution, unless great objection is made.

Mr. GREGG—We can dissolve the union with the United States, and make arrangements for a continuance of the mail service.

Mr. ADAMS—This debate is out of order.

Mr. GREGG—The Minister to the United States will have the matter in charge.

The amendment of adding "Postal Arrangements" for the consideration of the Committee on Commerce, was adopted.

The fourth resolution was then adopted.

The special order, the second resolution, relating to the secession portion of the message of the President of the United States, was taken up.

SPEECH OF JUDGE MAGRATH.

If we were now in a condition of profound peace, and about inaugurating this act of secession of South Carolina from the brotherhood of States is a condition of good will and good wishes, that resolution would be immediately proper and necessary; but when we are about to consummate this great act, without the good will and without the good wishes of many of the States of the Confederacy, it is most important that the State of Southern Carolina should know if their rights claimed in behalf of these

States were to be exercised. It would be well to define its rights to be exercised within the limits of her own State. The President of the United States affirms his rights, his Constitutional duty and high obligation to protect what he calls the property of the United States within the limits of South Carolina, and enforce, after the secession of South Carolina, the laws of the United States within its limits; and it is true, Sir, that he says he has no Constitutional power to coerce the State of South Carolina if she shall secede, while at the same time he denies her the exercise of her legitimate right of secession which she claims, and I apprehend there will be, Mr. President, an attempt to coerce the State of South Carolina in the form of protecting the property of the United States within the limits of South Carolina. I am disposed, at the very threshold, to consider the accuracy of this logic, and weigh well the conclusion which the President of the United States has arrived at in his consideration of this matter. There never has been a day, no, nor an hour, when anybody could claim the property within the limits of the State of South Carolina—whether the claims were made by an individual, or corporation, or community, or nation. Is it not as sacred under the constitution as the laws of South Carolina, and as when that right is claimed by one of our own citizens? And if there be, as is asserted, property of the United States within the limits of South Carolina—the property, after the succession of the State, according to opinion, consistent with the dignity and honor of the State—can, I say, after the act of secession, receive only that protection which it has received—I mean that protection which has been derived from the laws of South Carolina. Mr. President, look at it: there is property which, while we are in this Union, belongs to the Union of the States, as an independent State. Has it been protected by the arms of the United States? When was it, Sir, that the United States considered it necessary, within the limit of South Carolina, to consider this property needful of that material protection which it seems disposed to assert for it? Because the act of secession makes the people of South Carolina occupy by the people of the United States the position of robbers, so potentially is it asserted that the rights of the United States are only to be maintained in our limits by material force? No. No, no. It cannot be so, that the United States can, consistently with the honor and dignity of South Carolina, own within the limits of South Carolina. The President of the United States says that this property has been bought by the Union of the States; that the United States has paid for it, and therefore claim the right to hold it. It must be remembered that when South Carolina secedes from this Union her sovereign rights arise, and are to be considered in connection with this assertion of the right of property. In this Convention, in the face of the whole world, it is for her to decide to raise the barrier of justice, and let every one see whether we owe the United States. If there be a dollar claimed which is not justly due the United States, let South Carolina be desolated before that dollar is paid. [Smothered applause.] There is one condition of public affairs to which I wish for a moment to advert in consequence of the remarks which fell from the gentleman on the resolution just disposed of. It is this: When the State of South Carolina and this Convention have passed this ordinance of secession; when in full consideration of these responsibilities which are about to issue, shall it be the determination of South Carolina to uphold the position of an independent State, it becomes us, as men who represent the public sentiment of South Carolina, to look boldly in the eye of the responsibilities of the position. I shall vote against any action if there is to be a joint ownership, co-partnership or agency of any kind between the United States and South Carolina. Unless they stand to each other in this relation of equal independence, (sovereign,) mutually recognizing one in another. If I have to make an act of secession, if I have to qualify this ordinance after it is passed, all of it shall be for the dignity of Carolina. One word more. There is one position to which we may be brought, and it is the position—which, so far as one man is concerned, I shall avoid above all others—it is the position of having the State of South Carolina to seem to the world to be allowed to exercise its right of secession by the permission of the United States. Other States are preparing to secede. There are States going into Conventions. Provisions might be made to arrest their progress. I don't want South Carolina to secede because Mr. BUCHANAN or any other man, besides the people of South Carolina, desire not to see it. Come what may, whatever consequences it may involve, I think it best becomes the people to meet these consequences in the largest assertion. It may be Mr. BUCHANAN is the friend of South Carolina. I don't say he is. I disclaim that he is. I admit no other conclusion, from the events transpiring before me, except that in the issue now before the country, the President of the United States will consummate this declaration which will inevitably arouse war with the incoming President. Mr. MAGRATH then asked pardon of the Convention for inflicting a speech.

Mr. MILES—I have not the least idea that the President of the United States will send reinforcements here. In a conversation, and subsequently in written communication, I know this to have been said to him. "If you send a solitary soldier to those forts, the instant the intelligence reaches our people—and we will take care it does reach us in good season—the forts will be taken, because they are necessary to our self-preservation." Mr. MILES spoke about the repairs to Fort Sumter, and mentioned the cause of the resignation of Secretary CASS. Capt. ANDERSON is needful of troops. He (MILES) felt the necessity of being watchful, lest a few Carolinians should surprise the fort in a night. Let us wait awhile, as all the repairs will be to our advantage.

The blank in the resolution appointing the Committee was, on motion of Mr. BARLEE, filled with thirteen.

Mr. SHINGLER moved to insert the debt of the United States in the resolution. The resolution seemed to be one-sided.

Mr. BARLEE moved to lay the motion on the table. Carried.

The resolution was then adopted.

Mr. MEMMINGER introduced a resolution for the appointment of a Committee of seven members to draft a summary statement of the causes justifying South Carolina to withdraw from the Union.

The resolution was adopted.

Mr. DUNKIN offered a resolution that a Committee be appointed to inquire and report what measures, temporary and permanent, can be adopted in reference to customhouses and postal arrangements in consequence of the withdrawal of South Carolina from the Union.

Mr. HAYNES introduced the following resolution:

Whereas. The causes which have produced a separation of South Carolina from the Federal Union, have emanated from the States north of Mason and Dixon's line, which use hireling labor only; and whereas, it has not been against the Constitution of the United States that South Carolina has opposed her sovereignty, but usurpation by the Government in violation of this instrument.

Resolved. That a communication be sent to each of the Slave holding States, bearing a copy of the ordinance of secession, and proffer each State, or any one or more of them, the existing constitution of the United States as the basis of a Provisional Government, to be adopted on the part of South Carolina an another State or States, which, after seceding from the present Federal Union, shall be willing to unite with South Carolina in the formation of a new Confederacy; and we do hereby ratify and confirm from the date thereof any action taken by such Commissioner or Commissioners, and with the consent of the Governor of South Carolina, in the formation of such provisional Union. And we do further earnestly recommend that in ____ days after two or more States, in addition to South Carolina, shall have acceded to the said provisional Union, an election shall be held for Senators and members of the House of Representatives of the new Congress, and a President and Vice-President of the new Confederacy.

Resolved. That three Commissioners be appointed to carry an authenticated copy of the ordinance of Secession to Washington, to be laid before the President of the United States, with the request that the same shall be communicated to the Congress now in session, and said Commissioners are hereby authorized and empowered to treat for the delivery of the forts, magazines and light-houses, and also for the other real estate, with the appurtenances thereto, within the geographical limits of South Carolina, and that the authority to treat upon these subjects be extended to ____ day of February, in the year of our Lord 1861; provided, in the meantime, the said forts, magazines and other places are allowed to remain in the condition in which they may be at the adoption of this ordinance; and they shall be further empowered to treat upon the subject of the public debt, and for a proper division of all other property within the above, now held by the Government of the United States, as the agent of the States now embraced in the said Confederacy, until such time as a new Confederacy of States shall be formed, of which South Carolina shall be one.

This elicited a debate, in which Messrs. RHETT, REITT and MIDDLETON participated.

The first one referred to a Committee on Foreign Relations, and was ordered to be printed.

Mr. MEMMINGER introduced the following:

Resolved. That a commission, consisting of three, be elected by ballot of the Convention, to proceed to Washington to negotiate with the United States, and act through their General Government, as to the proper arrangements and measures to be made or adopted in the existing relations of the parties, and for the continuance of peace and amity between them.

Resolved. That five persons be elected by this Convention, who shall be authorized to meet such deputies as may be appointed by any other slaveholding State for the purpose of organizing or forming a Southern Confederacy, with power to discuss and settle upon a Constitution or plan of union, to be reported to said States for their ratification, amendment or rejection; and that the said deputies shall invite a meeting at Columbia, or such other place as may be agreed upon among the deputies of the several States, and shall report to the Convention such Constitution, or articles, as may be agreed on by the said deputies.

The first was referred to the Committee on Foreign Relations, and the second to the Committee on the Slaveholding States of North America:

Mr. MAZYCK introduced the following:

Resolved. That a Committee to consist of ____ members be appointed, whose duty it shall be to inquire and report to this Convention how much of the legislation of Congress would be *ipso facto* abrogated, so far as this State is concerned, by the secession of this State from the National Union, and how much of it might remain of force, notwithstanding the act of secession.

This was made the special order for to-morrow.

Mr. ORR moved to adjourn, and at 3:10 the Convention adjourned.

THURSDAY'S PROCEEDINGS.

CHARLESTON, THURSDAY, DEC. 20.

Prayer was offered, the roll called and the journal read.

A resolution was offered to invite the Mayor of Charleston to a seat on the floor of the Convention. It was amended by inserting the Governor of the State, the President of the Senate and Speaker of the House, and passed.

The chair announced the appointment of the Committee to draft a summary of the cause of the Secession of South Carolina; also of four standing Committees.

Mr. RHETT's resolutions to appoint a Committee of Thirteen for the purpose of providing for the assemblage of a Convention of the seceding States, and to form a Constitution, was adopted.

Mr. INGLIS made a report from the Committee to prepare and draft an ordinance proper to be adopted by the Convention.

An Ordinance to Dissolve the Union between the State of South Carolina and other States united with her under the compact entitled the Constitution of the United States of America:

We, the people of the State of South Carolina, in Convention assembled, do declare and ordain, and it is hereby declared and ordained, that the ordinance adopted by us in Convention, on the 22d day of May, in the year of our Lord 1788, whereby the Constitution of the United States of American was ratified, and also all Acts and ports of Acts of the General Assembly of this State ratifying the amendments of the said Constitution are hereby repealed, and that the union now subsisting between South Carolina and other States under the name of the United States of America is hereby dissolved.

The ordinance was taken up and passed by an unanimous vote of 109 members at 1¼ o'clock.

As soon as its passage was known without the doors of the Convention, it rapidly spread on the street, a crowd collected, and there was immense cheering.

Mr. MILES moved that the Clerk telegraph to the members at Washington. Carried unanimously.

Mr. DESAUSSURE moved that the ordinance be engrossed on parchment, under the direction of the Attorney-General, and signed by the President and members, this evening, at Institute Hall, and that it be placed in the archives of the State.

Six and a half o'clock was agreed upon as the hour to proceed to Institute Hall, for the purpose of signing it.

The following is a summary of the debate on the passage of the ordinance:

Mr. MAGRATH—I think the special matter of the ordinance should be immediately considered. To my understanding there is no Collector of the Port nor Postmaster now within the limits of South Carolina. What you have done to-day has extinguished the authority of every man in South Carolina deriving authority from the General Government. I am in favor of this body making such provisional arrangements as may be necessary in the interval which may exist between this moment and the time when the Legislature may act. I am not, however, to be implicated as sanctioning the idea that there is no lawful authority within the limits of the State except the General Government.

Mr. GREGG—After South Carolina abrogated the Constitution of the United States, are its laws still in force? I think not. All the laws of Congress fall instantly to the ground on the act of Secession.

Mr. CHEVIS—As an immense chasm will be made in the law, and as it is necessary to avoid inconvenience to the people, we must make some temporary arrangements to carry on the Government.

Mr. GREGG—There is no law on the subject of the collection of the duties in South Carolina now. We have now accomplished the work after forty years.

Mr. HAYNE—The Congress of the United States is no longer our Government. It will be for our Legislature to say what laws of the United States shall be continued and what not. The simple act of secession does not abrogate all the laws. We have a great many laws on our statute books which were passed by the Governor and the Privy Council.

Mr. GREGG—The Congressional laws for the collection of revenue are for the support of the Federal Government at Washington, and all our Post-office laws fall on our dissolution with that Government.

Many soldiers in the Civil War were still boys. (*Library of Congress*)

Mr. MILES—We have to deal with facts and stern realities. We must prevent confusion, anarchy, and the derangement of our Government affairs. Things must for the present remain in *status quo,* or confusion will arise.

Mr. HAYNE—Sudden action is injurious.

Mr. CHESNUT—Two questions are involved—power and duty. We must preserve our people, not only from inconveniences, but chaotic condition. We must revivify such laws as will best preserve us from calamities. As to duty, will you turn the ship of State adrift, what will become of the officers?

Mr. MAZYCK—There is no duty for the Collector of the Port to do. The Post-office has been swept off. My opinion is that the present system of postal arrangements is a nuisance. The public can be better served by private parties between cities like Philadelphia and New-York, one cent instead of three, and between less important ten or more cents.

Mr. CALHOUN—We have pulled a temple down that has been built three-quarters of a century. We must clear the rubbish away to reconstruct another. We are now houseless and homeless, and we must secure ourselves against storms.

Mr. DUNKIN—If that ordinance be passed things will go on in the Custom-house and Post-office exactly as now, until other arrangements can be made by this Convention. There is nothing in the Ordinance to affect the dignity, honor and welfare of the State of South Carolina. We must keep the wheels of the Government going. The Constitution of the United States is not entirely abrogated by the Ordinance. What is legal tender in the payment of debts? Is it not gold and silver of the United States? In the case of clearing and entry of vessels, we are very liable to have the same confiscated.

Mr. Carroll—The present venue would be continued till an act of the Legislature authorized otherwise.

Mr. Brown—There is no longer communication with the Government from which we are just separated.

Mr. Dunkin—The spirit of the ordinance must be temporarily sustained till we treat with the General Government.

Mr. Gregg—The President of the United States has thrown down the gauntlet in his Message. He has said that it was his duty to collect the revenue and that he would do it. On one side the Federal Government claims the right and declares its intention to execute the power of collecting revenue in our ports; on the other side, we have declared that we are free. I desire no compromise. Is it necessary to maintain the fifteen to thirty per cent duties imposed by the Congress of the United States? Should these duties continue to be levied our people will suffer a great calamity. For carrying the mails let the present contracts be assumed by South Carolina instead of the United States.

Mr. Rhett—This great revolution must go on with as little danger as possible to the country. By making the Federal agents ours, the machinery will move on. The Federal laws of taxation must not exist over us. I trust that the present system of taxation has fallen forever.

Mr. Barnwell—We have seceded from the United States and established our independence. We can't allow the United States to exercise authority over us any more. Let postal convenience be sacrificed if necessary. There never was anything purchased worth having, unless it cost a sacrifice.

Mr. Mazyck said, in regard to the mail, restrictions must be removed. Let us appoint our own officers. Let the Collector of the Port battle with the difficulties as they come.

At 3:40 P.M. the Convention took a recess to meet at Institute Hall at 6½ o'clock, for the purpose of signing the ordinance.

As the Convention were leaving St. Andrew's Hall, the chimes of St. Michael's Episcopal Church pealed forth "Old Lang Syne" and other tunes.

DISPATCH FROM COLUMBIA.

Columbia, S.C., Wednesday, Dec. 19.

The Methodist Conference of this State have passed resolutions in favor of secession.

Hon. Lawrence M. Keitt has resigned his seat in the House of Representatives of the United States.

Ex-Governor McDonald, of Georgia, died at his residence at Marietta, on Wednesday night.

There were eleven new cases of small-pox here on Tuesday,

OUR WASHINGTON DISPATCHES.

Washington, Thursday, Dec. 20.

Orders have been issued to Major Anderson to *surrender Fort Moultrie if attacked.*

I am reliably informed that Major Anderson telegraphs here that *he had surrendered a large number of arms which had been removed from the arsenal to Fort Moultrie, to the authorities of Charleston,* on a demand being made for them. This was done *in obedience, as he says, to the spirit of orders he had received from Washington.*

An official dispatch, giving information of the passage of the ordinance of secession, was received this afternoon by President Buchanan. A number of Southern men were with him at the time, and I learn that he exhibited much agitation on hearing the news.

The news of the passage of the ordinance produced intense excitement in Congress to-day. The South Carolina members were congratulated by the Southern men. Gen. McQueen, who has been for years a consistent advocate of secession, was surrounded. They dine this evening with Trescott, and retire from Congress on Monday.

When the news reached the House of Representatives Garnet, of Virginia, was speaking in opposition to the Pacific Railroad bill, and availed himself of the opportunity to make the first allusion to it. One State, he said, had just left the Confederacy, and crowding events were hastening the departure of his own; and he notified gentlemen that Virginia would never consent to pay one cent of the three hundred millions of public debt proposed to be created by the bill. Little else is talked of in political circles to-night.

The Committee of Thirty again discussed, to-day, a proposition for dividing the Federal Territory between the sections. Hon. C. Francis Adams made an eloquent speech in opposition. It is believed the proposition will pass the Committee in a shape acceptable to the Conservative States. Dunn of Indiana, and Nelson of Tennessee, made strong Union speeches. A vote will be taken, to-morrow, on Rust's proposition.

The Senate Territorial Committee had under consideration, to-day, Thaddeus Hyatt's petition in behalf of Kansas, and indefinitely postponed it without action. All Territorial questions were postponed until after the House shall have acted.

Hon. D. Taggert announces that Gov. Curtin and Senator Cameron have pledged themselves to secure him the Philadelphia Collectorship or the Superintendent of the Mint.

Arrangements are being made, it is said, to secure the election of Hon. JAMES K. MOORHEAD, of Pittsburgh, to the United States Senate.

The Pacific Railroad bill, which passed the House to-day, is one of the most important measures that ever came before Congress. Nearly all the Republicans and conservative Southern men voted for it. It was regarded as not only a great financial enterprise, but the argument was used that it was a peace measure, which will bind the Pacific and Atlantic States together firmly, and give Oregon and California to freedom in the future. Several California and Oregon men have been pressing it to the utmost: here—among them Senator BAKER; Dr. RABE, Secretary of the California Pacific Railroad Convention; Judge STOUT, of Oregon; Mr. FAREWELL, of the *Alta California*, and Mr. SIMONTON, Editor of the *Bulletin*, of San Francisco. Great credit is due to Mr. CURTIS, the Chairman, and the other members of the House Committee. There is general rejoicing tonight among the Pacific Coast men. The main features of the bill are already well known.

PUGH's speech in the Senate to-day, in reply to WADE, was able in some respects, but lacked substantiation in facts. In point of clearness and boldness it does not compare with WADE's. The Republicans claim that it misrepresents Northern men. The galleries were densely crowded with spectators and the scene was exciting.

The House came near adjourning to-night till Monday, but the Republicans opposed and beat it.

When the dispatch came and it was announced that South Carolina had passed the ordinance of secession, and it was privately reported that South Carolina members remaining had prepared a farewell address, to be delivered to-morrow morning for the purpose of going out in a body and creating an impression. The Republicans immediately renewed the proposition to adjourn, and carried it, and the South Carolina members must wait till Monday to make their demonstration.

The case of Judge WATROUS, reported in the House to-day, comes up the first of next week. The House will report an impeachment to the Senate, beyond a doubt.

The *Illinois State Journal* of the 17th inst. reached here to-night, containing an article written by the editor of the *Journal*, a nephew of the President elect, evidently written under Mr. LINCOLN's own eye, saying:

"We feel indignant sometimes when we hear timid Republicans counseling an abandonment in part of Republican ground. We are asking for nothing that is not clearly right. We have done nothing wrong. We have nothing to apologize for—nothing to take back, as a party. We have fought a hard battle. We have come out of it victorious; and shall we now call back the routed, flying enemy, and basely surrender all we have gained? Never! Let us stand firm as the Eternal Hills upon the Republican Platform, and turn this Government back into the channel in which the framers of the Constitution originally placed it. Some there are, who are counseling Mr. LINCOLN to take into his

Cabinet two or three gentlemen who do not agree with him politically. They do not know the man. ABRAHAM LINCOLN never betrayed a friend—never violated a promise, and will he do it now? He will carry out the policy of the Republican Party and the two millions who elected him."

This article has created quite a sensation among the Republicans, especially among those who regard it as an expression of Mr. LINCOLN's sentiments.

Only three Republicans in the Committee of Thirty are doubtful; CORWIN, of Ohio; DUNN, of Indiana; and STRATTON, of New-Jersey. The rest are firm.

Mr. HAMLIN goes home to-morrow, and will not return until he comes to assume his seat as Vice-President. His successor will be elected in January, and he will not resign until after that.

WASHBURN, of Maine, Governor elect, has gone.

Notwithstanding the injunction of secrecy on the New-York caucus last night, the whole thing was divulged to the Associated Press by a member of the House, who says the injunction was removed after certain members left.

An informal meeting of the Pennsylvania Delegation took place this evening at the Avenue House. Several members have left for home, and consequently the caucus was not full. A discussion occurred regarding the position of the Republican Party regarding compromises with the South, and it was agreed that no compromises admitting the Constitution to extend Slavery to Territories, or looking to its protection there would be acceptable to the Republicans under any circumstances. The expression of opinion was very decided and firm.

O.P.Q.

DISPATCH TO THE ASSOCIATED PRESS

WASHINGTON, THURSDAY, DEC. 20.

A report that South Carolina had passed an ordinance of secession, was brought to the House at 4 o'clock this afternoon. It produced intense excitement among the members, and for a long time confused the proceedings . . .

Mr. CLARK said the rumors abroad did more to increase the excitement than anything else. He thought the resolutions were the best way to find out the truth of the whole matter. He had no desire to do anything to increase the excitement. He was for peace.

Mr. LANE, of Oregon, (Dem.,) objected to taking up the resolutions.

Mr. HUNTER wanted to postpone until he could see if the Committee of Thirteen did anything to allay the excitement.

Mr. MASON, of Virginia, (Dem.,) said he supposed the object of the mover was, after he got the information by another resolution to require troops to be sent to those forts in a few days. Events will be presented for the consideration of Congress when the question comes practically up. He never doubted the perfect right of a State to determine for herself whether she would longer continue in the Union.

Mr. CLARK, said the Senator from Virginia misunderstood his object. He wanted to gain information. He had seen different accounts in the papers. The President could give the truth. He had no object to move further resolutions.

Mr. DAVIS, of Mississippi, (Dem.,) contended that the inquiries were improper to make of the President. They might only embarrass. The President could not send troops now without bringing about the very collision dreaded. Of the idea to withdraw the troops, the President was a better judge than the Senate. He trusted there would be no collision. If there were any danger there were troops there.

Mr. TRUMBULL said he did not know of anybody who had an idea that the General Government intended to declare war against a State or coerce a State. The Government has power to coerce or punish individuals.

Mr. MASON said action to force one State against another was war.

Mr. TRUMBULL asked, what was rebellion?

Mr. MASON said it was resistance by a portion of the citizens to the laws emanat-
50 ing from a common Government—the citizens being an integral part of one common Government. The States are as sovereign to-day as when they formed the Constitution of the United States, and being so, a State has power to absolve its citizens from the obligations of the Federal compact which the State entered into before. When the States thus absolve its citizens they become as completely foreign as citizens of France.

Mr. TRUMBULL denied that a State was as sovereign as when she entered the compact.

The Deficiency bill from the House was referred to the Committee on Finance on motion of Mr. HUNTER.

Mr. SLIDELL, of Louisiana, (Dem.,) said he had received a note from the agent of the Associated Press about what he said yesterday. He did not believe the reporter in the galleries ever sent the dispatch, but he had received no assurance that the man who did should be punished. He therefore moved the expulsion of the reporter from the gallery.

The special order, being Mr. JOHNSON's resolution, was taken up.

Mr. PUGH, of Ohio, (Dem.,) said over thirty millions of people in this country, and all the nations of the world, are looking to us to restore the country to something like peace. His colleague (Mr. WADE) spoke of peace. When he left home he left in anarchy and confusion. He adverted to his colleague's speech, denouncing it as inflammable. His colleague put his party on the defensive, and said they never had the power of the Government. That fact was enough to make it necessary to put the party on trial. He (PUGH,) did not know as to the complaints made against the Federal Government, but he charged that the Republican Party of the Northern States had not conducted themselves as to inspire alarm in the Southern States. If that party did not intend to infringe upon any of the rights of the Southern States, what objection could there be to their making proper explanation? His colleague (WADE) had said that the only difficulty was, that the minds of the people of the South were poisoned against the people of the North. The fact that men who appeal for another section are blamed by the Republican Party of the North, is sufficient evidence of the sectionalism and hostility of the party to which his colleague (WADE) belonged. The difficulty is that the South has read and heard too much of that party. Do you deny that they are in favor of excluding a certain portion of the people of the Southern States from the Territories? Do you deny that they intend to surround the people of the Slave States with a cordon of Free States so as to compel them to emancipate their slaves? Did not his colleague (WADE) boast that they would conquer Mexico and make it the best government in the world—better than this? Do you deny that they are opposed to the execution of the law for the recapture of fugitive slaves? Do you deny that they are in favor of extending the right of suffrage to blacks and mulattoes, and was this ever done except in the States under the control of the Republican Party? In the State he represented in part, (Ohio,) in defiance of the Constitution, this has so far been done as to control the State election! He (PUGH) did not regard the Personal Liberty bills as of any practical value; their only object could be to insult the people of the Southern States. Mr. PUGH here returned to the decision of Gov. DENNISON, and said that he thought it was entirely wrong. Now when the Senator from Kentucky (CRITTENDEN) comes forward with a plan for a fair line of partition between the Northern and the Southern States, not one voice was heard in favor of it from the Republican side. Why could not gentlemen come forward and meet as if they were of one great family? Is the Institution of Slavery so very hateful to them that they will never permit it to go to any place where they can prevent it? If this is so how can they ever hope for peace? Cannot they permit Slavery to exist in the arsenals and navy yards of the Slave States? If their hatred of Slavery is so great, will they not feel it their duty when they have power to amend the Constitution so as to abolish the institution? There can be no objection to the proposition of the Senator from Kentucky, (CRITTENDEN,) unless there is a determination to carry on intestine strife? His colleague (WADE) had said that Mr. LINCOLN's character was such as to prevent any fear from his conduct, but he (LINCOLN) was the most obscure man that had ever been elected to the Presidency. His colleague might have studied the record and character of Mr. LINCOLN, but he (PUGH) did not believe that nine hundred and ninety-nine voters in a thousand knew anything about him.

Mr. WADE, of Ohio, (Rep.,) asked if he (PUGH) had studied Mr. BUCHANAN's character before he voted for him? [Laughter.]

Mr. PUGH said that he had, and voted for him knowingly. Mr. PUGH then read from Mr. LINCOLN's speech, where he says, "a divided house cannot stand; that it must fall or cease to be divided or that it must become all one thing or all the other." This crisis, he said, had now arrived, and by the election of the very man who had uttered these sentiments. He thought that the Southern States should have some guarantee that the administration of such a man would not be hostile to them. Heretofore the question of Slavery in an election had never been carried so far as to cause such a division as existed in this house. His colleague had said that the South did not make any specific charges. There was great fear and apprehension felt, and justly felt, of the character of the coming Administration. He did not design to offend the Senators of that party, but to show the vast responsibility resting on them. They have the power, while all the opposing parties are shattered. They were coming into power with every assurance of a continuance on condition of their good behavior. But if they intended to live on the agitation of the Slavery question, the party is at an end. The next dispatch may inform us that one of the States has placed herself out of the Confederacy, so far as is in her power. Six other States have called delegates to consider the propriety of following. It is eminently the duty of the party coming into power to do something to avert the consequences. But his colleague says the day of compromises is past. If so, the day of the Union is past. For the Union was founded on compromise. One of the noblest letters of Washington was the one on this very subject of compromise. Mr. Pugh read a letter written by Washington in 1789. Gentlemen on both sides, who avow that the day of compromise is past, avow unconstitutional sentiments. His colleague complains of the weakness of past compromises. Then let us put this where it cannot be broken, into the Constitution of the United States. No one intends to alter the Constitution, but only so to amend it as to carry into effect the true spirit of the Constitution. He hoped, so far as the Territorial question was concerned, all parties would unite on the basis of the resolutions of his friend from Kentucky (Mr. Crittenden.) He hoped the Senator from Kentucky would so arrange his amendment as to take the subject entirely away from Congress—thus the question which has distracted us so long can be put at rest forever. But his colleague thinks it dishonorable for Mr. Lincoln to make terms before his inauguration. He thought not in view of the long recess. Jefferson never thought himself dishonored because his election disclosed a defect in the Constitution. We may expect to hear tomorrow of the separation of one State, and we are told that others will follow. We can either make a fair division with the States that go out, or make such an adjustment of the difficulty as to hold many States; and in a little while bring back those who have gone out, or we may make war. War makes itself, and it makes no difference whether we send an army to disperse the Convention of South Carolina, or whether we attempt to collect the revenue. He did not care whether they called it coercion or enforcing the law. They and he knew it meant civil war, and he called on those who lived in distant States to help to avert a calamity which would fall chiefly on the border States. Some Senator had said we should not discuss the abstract right of secession. We should not put forth the hand to lift the veil which hides the Atlas of State Sovereignty, which supported the Government on its shoulders.

But if we listen, he seems to move uneasily, and when he speaks his voice will be that of the earthquake and the avalanche. Let us not go into those questions. It is a question of empire and not a question of customary legislation. He read from the letters of JAMES MACKINTOSH, to show the duties of politicians, and from ALEXANDER HAMILTON to show that coercion of a State is of no avail. He also read from JOHN QUINCY ADAMS' fourth annual message, to show that no conflict of the State and Federal Government was ever contemplated in the Constitution, and that the States never delegated the right to pronounce an act of Congress unconstitutional. He read from JACKSON'S message that the Union could not be perpetuated by force of the General Government, but by the fraternal feeling of the States, and that each State has the unquestionable right to regulate its own concerns, and that all acts calculated to disturb the peace are in direct opposition to the spirit of the Constitution. He also read from the debate in the Senate on the 11th June, 1858, between Messrs. WADE and TOOMBS, on the sovereignty of the States, when Mr. WADE said he was as good a nullifier as the Senator from Georgia. He then referred to what his colleague said about making war. Shall we make war upon the people of a State or try to conciliate them and lay deeper the foundations of our Government. He (WADE) would commend the counsels of JOHN QUINCY ADAMS. Mr. PUGH here read from a message of Mr. ADAMS to show that he deprecated force in such a case. The idea that the Constitution compels the President to rush forward into war is utterly amazing. It is a question for Congress. Yet we are told we are to be pushed headlong into war with our fellow-citizens. It is monstrous! We could learn from history that when a man desires to commit an atrocity, he tries to convince himself that he is in the service of God. What no man would do individually, force us into a war with a sister State, is now fashionable! We are told that we must try and convince our conscience that such is our duty! We must try and force back a State which we can win back by kindness and conciliation! In this connection the Senator from New Hampshire (CLARK) could not see the impropriety of asking the President to give as all the orders he had given to the troops at Charleston, and how many he had sent there. If the people desire to take the forts, that is just what they want, and it is far better to take the troops and shoot them. He then read the first Article of the tenth section of the Constitution, and said, South Carolina has already violated some of these provisions, and if it is a duty to compel obedience by the sword, then it is the duty now of the President to go to war. But do we ever carry out these provisions by force? Who would collect the revenue? Is that the maintenance of the Union? He was for peace and conciliation, and therefore would stand by the side of his friend from Kentucky (Mr. CRITTENDEN,) and hold open the door as long as possible. He would not debate the right of secession. He thought this the path of duty and wisdom—not the wisdom of demagogues and tyrants, but the wisdom of patriots. He was against the idea, under whatever name, of proclaiming civil war. When the Prince of Wales was here, he might have remembered that if his grandfather had listened to the counsels of EDMUND BURKE, this country might now be a province of England. Mr. Pugh here read from a speech of Edmund Burke's to show that he was against using force to compel the colonies to submit. He Pugh was opposed to the idea of plunging the whole country into civil war. War was horrible even when waged in the holiest and best of causes—but war waged by one part of the American people against the other is too horrible to be described. Yet we are told that we have not the power to put off this catastrophe. He (Pugh) believed that if the programme put forth by his colleague (Wade) was carried out, we should be driven to the verge of ruin. As he (Pugh) said years ago, separate confederacies have no charms for him. If discord, coercion and civil war are to be the consequence, he had no desire to see the day when the country, carved in capitals and graven on the columns of this glorious palace, should see blazed forth, as by some horrible enchantment, the gory eyes of the demon of discord—when, instead of gorgeous inscriptions of "Union," displayed on every side, above, below, beneath, and around, we should see only the fingers of a man's hand, writing over against the candlestick, on the plaster of the wall, such dreadful words as pronounced the doom of Babylon: "The days of thy kingdom are finished, for thou art weighed in the balance and found wanting. Thy Kingdom is divided and given to the Medes and Persians." It may be that, for a season, the continual sunshine and refreshing shower will remain, and that art, science and the comforts of civilization will continue to bless our people as now, but over all, the destroying angel, that has turned so many realms of happiness into desolation, will slowly and silently, but inevitably, extend his pinions until the fair palaces of this country become like the faded cities of the Imperial Republics of the Old World.

As they left the Union the seceding states seized federal property within their borders: post offices, customs houses, mints, arsenals, and forts. The only such property still in federal possession by February 1861 were two remote forts on the Florida keys, Fort Pickens on Santa Rosa Island off Pensacola, and Fort Sumter (often misspelled Sumpter at the time) right in the middle of Charleston Bay. Fort Sumter became by far the most visible and volatile symbol of the crisis. The Confederate government demanded its evacuation by the eighty-odd American soldiers whose presence in the fort maintained the principle of U.S. sovereignty and defied the principle of Confederate sovereignty. Neither President Abraham Lincoln of the U.S.A. nor President Jefferson Davis of the C.S.A. was willing to back down. When Lincoln announced his intention to resupply the garrison, Davis ordered the Confederate guns to open fire on a fort flying the American flag. At 4:30 a.m. on April 12, 1861, they did so. Thus began a four-year war that would result in the deaths of 625,000 Union and Confederate soldiers.

April 15, 1861.

FORT SUMTER FALLEN.

PARTICULARS OF THE BOMBARDMENT.

The Fort on Fire and the Garrison Exhausted.

NO ATTEMPT AT REINFORCEMENT.

The Cessation of Firing and the Capitulation.

NO LIVES LOST ON EITHER SIDE.

Major Anderson and his Men Coming to New-York.

How the News was Received in Washington.

Call for Seventy-Five Thousand Militia.

AN EXTRA SESSION OF CONGRESS.

War Feeling Throughout the Northern and Western States.

FORT PICKENS REINFORCED.

CHARLESTON, SATURDAY, APRIL 13—EVENING.

Major ANDERSON has surrendered, after hard fighting, commencing at 4½ o'clock yesterday morning, and continuing until five minutes to 1 to-day.

The American flag has given place to the Palmetto of South Carolina.

You have received my previous dispatches concerning the fire and the shooting away of the flagstaff. The latter event is due to Fort Moultrie, as well as the burning of the fort, which resulted from one of the hot shots fired in the morning.

During the conflagration, Gen.BEAUREGARD sent a boat to Major ANDERSON, with offers of assistance, the bearers being Colonels W. P. MILES, and ROGER PRYOR, of Virginia, and LEE. But before it reached him, a flag of truce had been raised. Another boat then put off, containing Ex-Gov. MANNING, Major D. R. JONES and Col. CHARLES ALLSTON, to arrange the terms of surrender, which were the same as those offered on the 11th inst. These were official. They stated that all proper facilities would be afforded for the removal of Major ANDERSON and his command, together with the company arms and property, and all private property, to any post in the United States he might elect. The terms were not, therefore, unconditional.

Major ANDERSON stated that he surrendered his sword to Gen. BEAUREGARD as the representative of the Confederate Government. Gen. BEAUREGARD said he would not receive it from so brave a man. He says Major ANDERSON made a staunch fight, and elevated himself in the estimation of every true Carolinian.

During the fire, when Major ANDERSON'S flagstaff was shot away, a boat put off from Morris Island, carrying another American flag for him to fight under—a noteworthy instance of the honor and chivalry of South Carolina Seceders, and their admiration for a brave man.

The scene in the city after the raising of the flag of truce and the surrender is indescribable; the people were perfectly wild. Men on horseback rode through the streets proclaiming the news, amid the greatest enthusiasm.

On the arrival of the officers from the fort they were marched through the streets, followed by an immense crowd, hurrahing, shouting, and yelling with excitement.

Several fire companies were immediately sent down to Fort Sumter to put out the fire, and any amount of assistance was offered.

A regiment of eight hundred men has just arrived from the interior, and has been ordered to Morris Island, in view of an attack from the fleet which may be expected tonight.

Six vessels were reported off the bar, but the utmost indignation is expressed against them for not coming to the assistance of Major ANDERSON when he made signals of distress.

The soldiers on Morris Island jumped on the guns every shot they received from Fort Sumter while thus disabled, and gave three cheers for Major ANDERSON and groans for the fleet.

Col. Lucas, of the Governor's Staff, has just returned from Fort Sumter, and says Major Anderson told him he had pleasanter recollections of Fort Moultrie than Fort Sumter. Only five men were wounded, one seriously.

The flames have destroyed everything. Both officers and soldiers were obliged to lay on their faces in the casemates, to prevent suffocation.

The explosions heard in the city were from small piles of shell, which ignited from the heat.

The effect of the shot upon the fort was tremendous. The walls were battered in hundreds of places, but no breach was made.

Major Anderson expresses himself much pleased that no lives had been sacrificed, and says that to Providence alone is to be attributed the bloodless victory. He compliments the firing of the Carolinians, and the large number of exploded shells lying around attests their effectiveness.

The number of soldiers in the fort was about seventy, besides twenty-five workmen, who assisted at the guns. His stock of provisions was almost exhausted, however. He would have been starved out in two more days.

The entrance to the fort is mined, and the officers were told to be careful, even after the surrender, on account of the heat, lest it should explode.

A boat from the squadron, with a flag of truce, has arrived at Morris Island, bearing a request to be allowed to come and take Major Anderson and his forces. An answer will be given to-morrow at 9 o'clock.

The public feeling against the fleet is very strong, it being regarded as cowardly to make not even an attempt to aid a fellow officer.

Had the surrender not taken place Fort Sumter would have been stormed to-night. The men are crazy for a fight.

The bells have been chiming all day, gun firing, ladies waving handkerchiefs, people cheering, and citizens making themselves generally demonstrative. It is regarded as the greatest day in the history of South Carolina.

FORT SUMTER EVACUATED

Charleston, *via* Augusta, Saturday, April 13.

FORT SUMTER HAS SURRENDERED.

The Confederate flag floats over its walls.

None of the garrison or Confederate troops are hurt.

Another correspondent says:

The bombarding has closed.

Major ANDERSON has drawn down the stripes and stars, and displays a white flag, which has been answered from the city, and a boat is on the way to Sumter.

CHARLESTON, SATURDAY, APRIL 13—P.M.

The Federal flag was again hoisted over Fort Sumter, when PORCHER MILES, with a flag of truce, went to the Fort.

In a few minutes the Federal flag was again hauled down by Major ANDERSON, and a white one unfurled.

CHARLESTON, SATURDAY, APRIL 13.

Gen. BEAUREGARD, with two Aids, have left for Fort Sumter.

Three fire companies from Charleston are now on their way to Sumter to quell the fire before it reaches the magazine.

Fort Sumter has unconditionally surrendered.

Ex-Senator CHESNUT, Ex-Governor MANNING and W. P. MILES have just landed and marched to Gov. PICKENS' residence, followed by a dense crowd wild with joy.

It is reported that the Federal flag was shot away by the Palmetto Guards at Morris Island.

In all two thousand shots have been fired. No Carolinians killed.

Major ANDERSON and his men, under guard, were conveyed to Morris Island.

The bells are ringing out a merry peal, and our people are engaged in every demonstration of joy.

It is estimated that there are nine thousand men under arms on the islands and in the neighborhood.

THE LATEST DISPATCHES.

CHARLESTON, SATURDAY, APRIL 13.

I have seen W. PORCHER MILES, who has just returned from a visit to Fort Sumter. He assured me that no one was killed at Fort Sumter. This is reliable, and puts at rest all previous reports about Sumter.

Maj. ANDERSON has reached the city, and is guest of Gen. BEAUREGARD.

Our people sympathize with Maj. ANDERSON, but abhor those who were in the steamers off our bar and in sight of our people, and did not even attempt to reinforce him.

The Fairfield regiment, one thousand strong, has just passed the *Courier* office, on their way to Morris Island.

There are now ten thousand men under arms in the harbor and on the coast.

Judge MAGRATH, who has just returned, reports that the wood-work and officers' quarters at Fort Sumter were all burnt.

None of the officers were wounded.

The Fort will be taken possession of to-night by the Confederate troops.

A boat from one of the vessels outside the harbor communicated with Gen. SIMONS, in command of the forces on Morris Island, and made a request that one of the steamers be allowed to enter the port for the purpose of taking away Major ANDERSON and his command. An arrangement was agreed upon by the parties to stay all proceedings until 9 o'clock tomorrow.

CHARLESTON, SATURDAY, APRIL 13.

Hostilities have for the present ceased, and the victory belongs to South Carolina. With the display of the flag of truce on the ramparts of Sumter at 1½ o'clock, the firing ceased, and an unconditional surrender was made.

The Carolinians had no idea that the fight was at an end so soon.

After the flag-staff of ANDERSON was shot away, Col. WIGFALL, Aid to Gen. BEAUREGARD, at his Commander's request, went to Sumter with a white flag, to offer assistance in extinguishing the flames. He approached the burning fortress from Morris Island, and while the firing was raging on all sides, effected a landing at Sumter. He approached a port-hole, and was met by Maj. ANDERSON. The Commandant of Fort Sumter said he had just displayed a white flag, but the firing from the Carolina batteries was kept up nevertheless.

Col. WIGFALL replied that Major ANDERSON must haul down the American flag; that no parley would be granted; surrender or fight was the word. Major ANDERSON then hauled down his flag, and displayed only that of truce.

All firing instantly ceased, and two other of Gen. BEAUREGARD'S staff—Ex-Senator CHESTNUT and Ex-Governor MANNING—came over in a boat and stipulated with the Major that his surrender should be unconditional for the present, subject to the terms of Gen. BEAUREGARD.

Major ANDERSON was allowed to remain with his men in actual possession of the fort, while Messrs. CHESTNUT and MANNING came over to the city, accompanied with a member of the Palmetto Guards, bearing the colors of his Company. These were met at the pier by hundreds of citizens, and as they marched up the street to the General's quarters, the crowd was swelled to thousands. Shouts rent the air and the wildest joy was manifested on account of the welcome tidings.

After the surrender, a boat with an officer and ten men was sent from one of the four ships in the offing to Gen. SIMONS, commanding on Morris Island, with a request that a merchant ship or one of the vessels of the United States be allowed to enter and take off the commander and garrison of Fort Sumter.

Gen. SIMONS replied that if no hostilities were attempted during the night, and no effort was made to reinforce or retake Fort Sumter, he would give an answer at 9 o'clock on Sunday morning.

The officer signified that he was satisfied with this, and returned. This correspon-

Southern volunteers after the firing on Sumter, April, 1861.
(Library of Congress)

dent accompanied the officers of Gen. BEAUREGARD'S staff on a visit to Fort Sumter. None but the officers were allowed to land, however. They went down in a steamer and carried three fire engines for the purpose of putting out the flames. The fire, however, had been previously extinguished by the exertions of Major ANDERSON and his men.

The visitors reported that Major ANDERSON surrendered because his quarters and barracks were destroyed and he had no hope of reinforcements. The fleet lay idly by during the thirty hours of the bombardment, and either could not or would not help him; besides, his men were prostrate from over-exertion.

There were but five of them hurt, four badly and one, it is thought, mortally, but the rest were worn out.

The explosions that were heard and seen from the city in the morning, were caused by the bursting of loaded shells. These were ignited by the fire, and could not be removed quick enough. The fire in the barracks was caused by the quantities of hot shot poured in from Fort Moultrie. Within Fort Sumter everything but the casemates is in utter ruin. The whole thing looks like a blackened mass of ruins. Many of the guns are dismounted. The side opposite the iron battery of Cumming's Point is the hardest dealt with. The rifled cannon from this place made a great havoc with Fort

Sumter. The wall looks like a honey-comb. Near the top is a breach as big as a cart. The side opposite Fort Moultrie is honey-combed extensively, as is that opposite the floating battery.

Fort Moultrie is badly damaged. The officers quarters and barracks are torn to pieces. The frame houses on the islands are riddled with shot in many instances, and whole sides of houses are torn out.

The fire in Fort Sumter was put out, and recaught three times during the day.

Dr. CRAWFORD, Major ANDERSON's surgeon, is slightly wounded in the face. None of the Carolinians are injured.

Major ANDERSON and all his officers and men are yet in Fort Sumter. I approached near enough to the wall to see him bid adieu. In addition to this, conversations were had, which have been repeated to me.

A boat was sent from the Fort to-night to officially notify the fleet at the bar that Major Anderson had surrendered. It is not known when the Carolinians will occupy Fort Sumter, or what is to be done with the vanquished.

Everyone is satisfied with the victory, and happy that no blood was shed.

In the city, after the surrender, bells were rung and cannon fired.

CHARLESTON, SUNDAY, APRIL 14.

Negotiations were completed last night. Major ANDERSON, with his command, will evacuate Fort Sumter this morning, and will embark on board of the war vessels off our bar.

When Fort Sumter was in flames, and ANDERSON could only fire his guns at long intervals, the men at our batteries cheered at every fire which the gallant Major made in his last struggles, but looked defiance at the vessels of war, whose men, like cowards, stood outside without firing a gun or attempting to divert the fire of a single battery from Sumter.

FIVE OF ANDERSON'S MEN ARE SLIGHTLY WOUNDED.

CHARLESTON, SUNDAY, APRIL 14.

The steamer *Isabel* is now steaming up, and will take Gen. BEAUREGARD to Sumter, which will be turned over by Major ANDERSON to the Confederate States. ANDERSON and his commend, it is reported, will proceed to New-York in the *Isabel.*

CHARLESTON, SUNDAY, APRIL 14.

Maj. ANDERSON and his men leave to-night in the steamer *Isabel* at 11 o'clock for New-York.

The fleet is still outside.

It was a thrilling scene when Maj. ANDERSON and his men took their formal leave of Fort Sumter.

THE TIMES CORRESPONDENT IMPRISONED.

WILMINGTON, N.C., SUNDAY, APRIL 14.

I saw the first gun fired at Fort Sumter at 4 o'clock, A.M., April 12. I witnessed the battle for six hours. At noon I was arrested by order of Gen. BEAUREGARD as a Federal spy, and was imprisoned for twenty-four hours, and then sent out of the city by Gov. PICKENS, destitute of funds. In Wilmington I was aided by Mr. PRICE, of the *Daily Journal,* and will be with you in thirty-six hours.

There are conflicting reports as to the number killed. It is generally believed that nobody is hurt.

JASPER

PROCLAMATION BY THE PRESIDENT.

SEVENTY-FIVE THOUSAND VOLUNTEERS AND AN EXTRA SESSION OF CONGRESS.

BY THE PRESIDENT OF THE UNITED STATES.
A PROCLAMATION.

Whereas; The laws of the United States have been for some time past, and now are opposed, and the execution thereof obstructed in the States of South Carolina, Georgia, Alabama, Florida, Mississippi, Louisiana and Texas, by combinations too powerful to be suppressed by the ordinary course of Judicial proceedings, or by the powers vested in the Marshals by law—now, therefore, I, ABRAHAM LINCOLN, President of the United States, in virtue of the power in me vested by the Constitution and the laws, have thought fit to call forth, and hereby do call forth, the militia of the several States of the Union to the aggregate number of seventy-five thousand, in order to suppress said combinations, and to cause the laws to be duly executed.

The details for this object will be immediately communicated to the State authorities through the War Department. I appeal to all loyal citizens to favor, facilitate and aid this effort to maintain the honor, the integrity and the existence of our national Union and the perpetuity of popular government, and to redress wrongs already long enough endured.

I deem it proper to say that this first service assigned to the forces hereby called forth will probably be to repossess the forts, places and property which have been seized from the Union, and in every event the utmost care will be observed, consistently with the objects aforesaid, to avoid any devastation, any destruction of, or interference with property, or any disturbance of peaceful citizens in any part of the country, and I hereby command the persons composing the combinations aforesaid to disperse and retire peaceably to their respective abodes, within twenty days from this date.

Deeming that the present condition of public affairs presents an extraordinary occasion, I do hereby, in virtue of the power in me vested by the Constitution, convene both Houses of Congress. The Senators and Representatives are therefore summoned to assemble at their respective Chambers, at 12 o'clock noon, on Thursday, the fourth day of July next, then and there to consider and determine such measures as in their wisdom the public safety and interest may seem to demand.

In witness whereof, I have hereunto set my hand, and caused the seal of the United States to be affixed.

Done at the City of Washington, this fifteenth day of April, in the year of our Lord one thousand eight hundred and sixty-one, and of the Independence of the United States, the eighty-fifth.

By the President, ABRAHAM LINCOLN.

William H. Seward, Secretary of State.

AID FOR THE GOVERNMENT.

Advices from Albany state that Gov. Morgan will to-morrow issue a call for twenty-five thousand men, for the assistance of the Federal Government.

A private letter from Gov. Curtin, of Pennsylvania, to a prominent citizen of New York, states that he can have one hundred thousand Pennsylvanians in Washington within forty-eight hours, if required.

THE AVAILABLE MILITIA.

Should the Government require it, a military gentleman states that the following number of men can be forthcoming at short notice, and probably in about the following contingents:

Maine 5,000
New Hampshire 5,000
Vermont 5,000
Massachusetts 15,000
Rhode Island 2,500

Michigan 10,000
Illinois 15,000
Wisconsin 5,000
Iowa 5,000
Minnesota 5,000

Connecticut	5,000	Kansas	2,500
New-York	25,000	Indiana	5,000
New Jersey	2,000		
Pennsylvania	30,000	Total	154,500
Ohio	12,500		

The estimate would give to an army of three divisions: 62,500 for the Eastern, 54,500 for the Central, and 37,500 for the Western Division. This would do to make a beginning.

THE NEWS IN WASHINGTON.

WASHINGTON, SUNDAY, APRIL 14.

THE EXCITEMENT AT THE CAPITAL.

The excitement here throughout the day has been intense. People gather in groups on the streets and in the hotels, discussing affairs at Charleston and the probabilities of the future.

There is great diversity of opinion relative to the reliability of the news that Major ANDERSON has surrendered. The dispatches to the Associated Press are evidently full of blunders, which cast suspicion on the whole.

DISPATCHES TO THE PRESIDENT.

The President, nevertheless, has intelligence which satisfied him that the news is too true. Private dispatched from Charleston, signed by trusty men, also confirm it; but as the telegraph is known to have been constantly tampered with by the secession authorities, it is feared that even private dispatches may have been mutilated for the purpose of cutting the Government off from all possible means of correct information.

THE CREDIBILITY OF THE TELEGRAMS.

The statement that the fleet had asked a cessation of hostilities until morning especially puzzles everybody, for if the Fort had surrendered the fleet could only have asked a cessation for its own sake, and we have thus far no information that it had been engaged. The vessels had only to steam out of range.

Still the opinion of men in high military authority here is that the news of the surrender is too true. They say no battery for the defense of the harbor could long withstand a skillful bombardment by heavy metal, where the garrison assailed is too weak to reply effectively and distract or annoy the assailants.

Besides, it is well-known here, and I have it from an authentic official source. Major ANDERSON's provisions were all exhausted yesterday, leaving him without an ounce to refresh his men after tl hard day's work. There is apparently good reason here to believe the report that Major ANDERSON has embarked seaward.

Still many wagers are taken here to-day that the whole story of the surrender is false. The Union men absolutely refuse credence.

STREET FIGHTS IN WASHINGTON.

To-day's excitement has betrayed many secessionists who hold public office, and who could not conceal their joy at the reduction at Fort Sumter. Several fights occurred, and decided knock-downs. Gen. NYE, among others, has knocked down a couple of secessionists within the last day or two. The fact is, Northern men have got tired of having treason crammed offensively down their throats, and are learning to resent it by force, the only argument the chivalry seem to appreciate.

JOHN M. BOTTS ON SECESSION.

Hon. JOHN M. BOTTS, who is here, is violent in his denunciations of secession. He has been all day the stoutest disbeliever in the story of Major ANDERSON's surrender. He insists that the whole story is manufactured for the purpose of precipitating Virginia into the secession movement. He predicts that it will utterly fail.

THE COURSE OF VIRGINIA.

Everybody here sees that now war has commenced, the question which the Virginia Convention has to decide is simply whether Virginia will declare war against the United States or stand by the Government; whether she will invite the battle upon her soil, to her utter ruin, or aid in bringing the fratricidal strife to a speedy termination by sustaining the Government and Union.

THE NORTH A UNIT.

The news from the North of the unanimity of public sentiment in favor of the Government and the strongest policy for the suppression of rebellion gladdens every heart. It is fully believed that all partisan considerations henceforth will be suspended, and that every effort will be directed to saving the country.

THE PRESIDENT'S PROCLAMATION.

You have the President's proclamation, making a requisition for seventy-five thousand volunteers, called from all the adhering States except California and Oregon. That news will thrill like an electric shock throughout the land, and establish the fact that we have a Government at last.

UNANIMITY OF THE CABINET.

The Cabinet is a unit on these measures, and no man among them was more decided and active in their support than Mr. SEWARD, who urged conciliation and forbearance until the Disunionists were put clearly and thoroughly in the wrong.

THE QUOTA OF TROOPS FROM EACH STATE.

The War Department is engaged to-night in calculating the number of troops which each State is entitled to furnish. New York will be entitled probably to ten regiments. Pennsylvania and Massachusetts to a few less. The estimates are based upon the Federal representation of the States.

This proclamation is the fruit of a prolonged Cabinet meeting held last night.

THE BLOCKADE OF SOUTHERN PORTS.

No policy relative to closing the ports of the Seceding States is yet understood to be settled upon in detail. It is probable, however, that arrangements will be speedily made to cut off all communication with them by sea. There need be no doubt about the power of the Government to do this under its authority to prevent smuggling.

But, independent of that, the occasion justifies the Executive in assuming responsibility. He may well emulate Gen. JACKSON, who, when BOB LETCHER asked him under what law he could bring the Nullifier leaders of South Carolina to Washington for trial and execution, replied that if the Attorney-General could not find a law for it, he would get another Attorney-General who could. Self-preservation is the Government's first duty, and its masters, the people, will justify it in every wise measure addressed to that end.

ACTIVITY OF GEN. SCOTT.

Gen. Scott has been at work all day, with all the energy of the soldier in the prime of life, making calculations for the disposition of the forces to be raised.

PROBABLE ATTEMPT TO SEIZE WASHINGTON.

The Administration has satisfactory information that the Confederate States have proposed, immediately after reducing Fort Sumter, to march on Washington with their army of twenty thousand men, for which they will have nothing else to do. Until recently, JEFFERSON DAVIS was disposed to postpone that step until the secession of Virginia and Maryland was effected, but as he despairs of that now, he believes that at the approach of his army those States will immediately unite their forces with his. Men who know those States well say he is in error.

PREPARATIONS FOR ITS DEFENCE.

There is one regiment of volunteers now in Baltimore ready to obey the call of the Government immediately, and they will be mustered into service. Virginia also is ready to furnish her quota. The Government designs to bring a force of volunteers to this city not only strong enough to defend it against all comers, but to render an attack on it improbable. Several additional companies of regulars are also ordered here. It is not improbable that this point will be made a grand rendezvous from which troops can readily be sent wherever required.

THE SINEWS OF WAR.

Congress is called in extra session on the 4th of July—a glorious day for a glorious work! This is essential in order to get the money that will be needed to enable the Government to sustain itself, and to pay as it goes. War is a costly experiment, as the Disunionists will find. It is no longer child's play, and will impoverish them utterly in a few months, if they persist in it, for they must themselves be the aggressors, and transport their troops and supplies long distances. The hopelessness of their unrighteous struggle must speedily force itself upon their minds when they learn how vigorous is the Government in its present hands, and how unanimous the people are in sustaining it.

MARTIAL LAW AT THE CAPITAL.

The President had not at nine o'clock to-night determined upon putting Washington under martial law. But there is little doubt that it will be done within a day or two. If so, it is hoped that possession will be taken of the telegraph office to prevent its employment by Disunionists for treasonable purposes.

The rumor that it has been decided to cut off all the mails from the seceded States is premature, to say the least. The Government does not recognize secession, and does not wish to punish the true men of the South together with the traitors. Wherever the mails are interfered with, they will be cut off, but probably not elsewhere. At least no determination otherwise has yet been arrived at by the President, notwithstanding his reference to the subject in the following letter to the Committee of the Virginia Convention, delivered by the President yesterday:

To Hon. Messrs. Preston, Stuart, and Randolph:

GENTLEMEN: As a Committee of the Virginia Convention, now in session, you present me a preamble and resolution in these words:

Whereas, In the opinion of this Convention, the uncertainty which prevails in the public mind as to the policy which the Federal Executive intends to pursue towards the seceded States is extremely injurious to the industrial and commercial interests of the country, tends to keep up an excitement which is unfavorable to the adjustment of the pending difficulties and threatens a disturbance of the public peace; therefore,

Resolved, That a committee of three delegates be appointed to wait on the President of the United States, present to him this preamble, and respectfully ask him to communicate to this Convention the policy which the Federal Executive intends to pursue in regard to the Confederate States.

In answer, I have to say that having, at the beginning of my official term, expressed my intended policy as plainly as I was able, it is with deep regret and mortification I now learn there is great and injurious uncertainty in the public mind as to what that policy is, and what course I intend to pursue. Not having as yet seen occasion to change, it is now my purpose to pursue the course marked out in the inaugural address. I commend a careful consideration of the whole document as the best expression I can give to my purposes. As I then and therein said, I now repeat, "The power confided in me will be used to hold, occupy and possess property and places belonging to the Government, and to collect the duties and imports; but beyond what is necessary for these objects, there will be no invasion, no using of force against or among the people anywhere." By the words "property and places belonging to the Government," I chiefly allude to the military posts and property which were in possession of the Government when it came into my hands. But if, as now appears to be true, in pursuit of a purpose to drive the United States authority from those places, an unprovoked assault has been made upon Fort Sumter, I shall hold myself at liberty to repossess it, if I can, like places which had been seized before the Government was devolved upon me; and in any event I shall, to the best of my ability, repel force by force. In case it proves true that Fort Sumter has been assaulted, as is reported, I shall, perhaps, cause the United States mails to be withdrawn from all the States which claim to have seceded, believing that the commencement of actual war against the Government justifies and possibly demands it. I scarcely need to say that I consider the military posts and property situated within the States which claim to have seceded, as yet belonging to the Government of the United States as much as they did before the supposed secession. Whatever else I may do for the purpose, I shall not attempt to collect the duties and imposts by any armed invasion of any part of the country; not meaning by this, however, that I may not land a force deemed necessary to relieve a fort upon the border of the country. From the fact that I have quoted a part of the Inaugural Address, it must not be inferred that I repudiate any other part, the whole of which I reaffirm, except so far as what I now say of the mails may be regarded as modification.

Postmaster-General BLAIR sent special agent BRYANT to Pensacola last week to reestablish the Post-office there. BRYANT stopped at Montgomery on his way, where Confederate States Postmaster REGAN forbade him to fulfill his mission, but failed to give any reason therefor.

RECRUITS FOR THE SECESSION ARMY.

Recruiting for the regular army of the Southern Confederacy has been going on sometime at Baltimore. The men are sent South *via* Norfolk as rapidly as they are obtained. Recruiting was also going on for the same service in this city yesterday. No objection is made to it, as it is deemed desirable to be rid of such men. A reliable Union man as Collector at Baltimore now, would do much good in watching these enlistments and detecting anticipated efforts to obtain a navy for the Confederated States at that port.

FORT PICKENS.

The Government has no advices from Fort Pickens, but you may rely upon it that relief has been sent to it. Dispatches hence to Pensacola have positively announced the fact to Gen. BRAGG, and it is very probable that fighting has begun there also by this time. No apprehension is entertained on its behalf, as it has abundant men and supplies, and, if needed, additional forces can be sent it from Fort Taylor and Tortugas.

While the Executive does not indicate his purpose in that respect, it is generally understood to-night that the contest will be waged at Charleston vigorously for the vindication of the flag at that point and the recovery of the public property there.

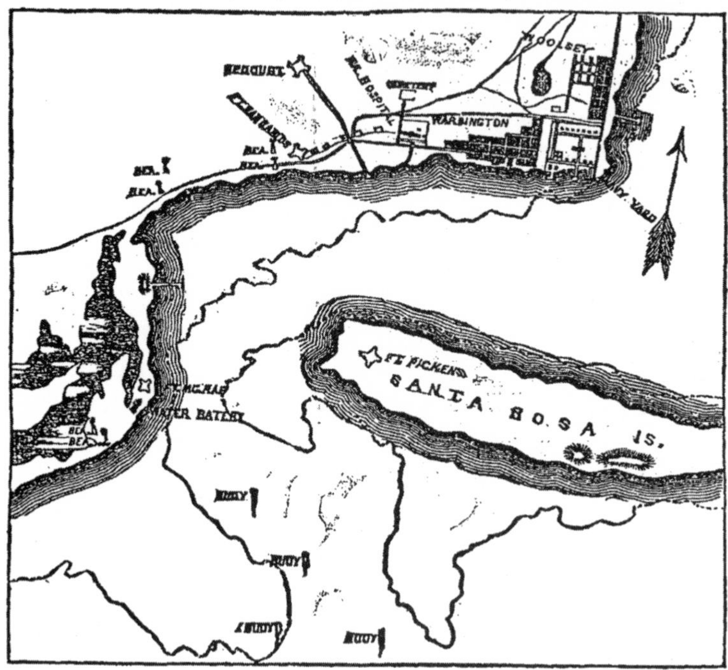

FORT PICKENS AND THE HARBOR OF PENSACOLA.

MISCELLANEOUS MILITARY MATTERS.

Five additional companies of the District militia were mustered into service today, making 2,500 men here now under arms.

The National Rifles, a Disunion corps, held a meeting last night to rejoice over the reduction of Fort Sumter and reorganize their corps. Martial law would suppress this nest of traitors.

One POWELL, a clerk in the Sixth Auditor's office, and an officer in the District militia, who last week took the oath to support the Government, stated publicly on the street to-day, that if Maryland should secede he would go with her. He will probably lose both his office and commission to-morrow. No mercy henceforth will be shown to Disunionists in the public employ.

Twenty men from the Second Cavalry were stationed all last night as a guard at the White House. Mounted troops are stationed to-night outside the city, with rations for their horses. They are guarding every approach to the city. They are stationed four at each point, and relieved every four hours. Signals have been arranged for more speedy communication. One hundred and fifty men are stationed in the Post-office Department; three hundred at the Treasury; two hundred at the Capitol, and two hundred near the White House. Gov. CURTIN, of Pennsylvania, who is in town, received dispatches to-day, assuring him that Pennsylvania volunteers to any number are ready to take this field, and urging the President to call on Pennsylvania first.

A number of citizens propose to organize, to-morrow, a corps as an independent patrol guard for the protection of the city.

The two companies of the Second Cavalry which arrived yesterday will be fully mounted during the present week with horses procured in this neighborhood.

THE OFFICE-SEEKERS.

Appointments to civil office are necessarily suspended, and numerous applicants have wisely left town. The military spirit, too, has caused a sudden cessation of the rush for civil positions, while the applications for military commissions are very numerous.

FROM ANOTHER CORRESPONDENT.

WASHINGTON, SUNDAY, APRIL 14.

THE RECEPTION OF THE NEWS.

The excitement consequent upon the news of the bombardment and surrender of Fort Sumter is most intense. For a long time the accounts of the surrender were utterly discredited, even the Secessionists refusing to believe the statements transmitted by their friends. When, this morning, there was no room to doubt the story, the people warmly discussed the probable effects upon the country. The Avenue was crowded from the Treasury to the telegraph offices, and the one subject was the universal theme. It seemed difficult to comprehend the possibility that after twenty hours a fort pronounced impregnable had surrendered to its assailants without having inflicted the slightest injury upon the masses engaged in the assault.

Among the Northern men there was a general determination that Major ANDERSON had at least proved untrue to the trusts reposed in him by the Government, and unworthy of the praise bestowed upon him when he evacuated Fort Moultrie and retired to Fort Sumter. Indeed, at this time, the first suspicion of his unfaithfulness has settled into a conviction so strong that nothing but an official report and justification to the Government will remove it.

I think the facts, when known, will, however, show that Major ANDERSON deserves the commendation of the country, for a most brave and vigorous defence of his command, and that he did not surrender until it became an inevitable necessity. He will probably show by his official communication to the Government, that his men had not tasted bread for the five hours previous to the surrender; that they were utterly exhausted with the labor of firing the heavy gun; that a shell from the Cummings Point Battery fell among the shells of the Fort, causing an explosion and setting fire to the wood-work of the Fort, and that the smoke of the burning structures was so dense as to render it impossible to continue the combat, and that his force was unable to put out the flames, or even to save their own private property.

It was under these circumstances that he was at last compelled to hoist a flag of truce, and eventually to stipulate for a surrender. He is now at sea with his command, and will probably soon be landed at New-York.

WASHINGTON, SUNDAY, APRIL 14.

Efforts are still making to concentrate a formidable military force in and around Washington to be prepared for all emergencies.

Information continues to be received from private sources of secret plots in various localities in Maryland and Virginia, having in view the seizure of the public property and even persons, the highest officers of the Government.

Though these accounts are not generally credited, they are believed in official quarters, and hence the precautionary movement. At all events they are considered necessary, no one knowing what turn events may take during the prevalent excitement. Roads and avenues leading to Washington are closely watched. Arrangements have been made to promptly concentrate the military forces at any threatened point.

There is the greatest anxiety everywhere to hear further news from the South. Groups discuss the war news, and its future effects on the country.

Information from what are deemed reliable sources was received last night to the effect that the Secessionists of Delaware, whose head-quarters are reported to be in Virginia, were about to make a sudden attack upon Fort Delaware, opposite Delaware City, for which they were preparing last month. Immediate steps were taken by the Secretary of War to prevent the consummation of the plot.

Five officers of the Navy yesterday tendered to the Navy Department their resignations, which were refused. Their names will probably be stricken from the list as dismissed, as in the recent cases of several officers of the Army under similar circumstances.

The Virginia Commissioners returned to Richmond to-day. They were cautious in expression their opinions relative to the President's reply.

The National Volunteers last night passed a resolution severely denouncing the military operations of the Government, and expressing sympathy with the Secessionists. It is said these volunteers are several hundred strong.

The military guard at the general Public Departments was largely increased last night.

An additional number of Federal troops arrived to-day by special train.

The President, in the exercise of his discretion to designate a newspaper here in

Confederate volunteers 1861. *(Library of Congress)*

which the Executive advertisements shall be published, in addition to the two papers publishing them by virtue of their circulation, has designated the *National Republican.*

Official advices from Montgomery indicate that the Confederate Congress will, on reassembling, at once declare war against the United States. It is believed that in the act of declaration a distinction will be made between alien friends and alien enemies, the former including the Border States, and such citizens of the North as oppose a coercive Administration. All obligations to this class are as much to be respected as though in time of peace.

Senator DOUGLAS called on the President to-night. He had an interesting conversation on the present condition of the country. The substance of it was, on the part of Mr. DOUGLAS, that, while he was unalterably opposed to the Administration on all its political issues, he was prepared to sustain the President in the exercise of all his constitutional functions to preserve the Union, maintain the Government, and defend the Federal Capital. A firm policy and prompt action were necessary. The Capital of our country was in danger and must be protected at all hazards, at any expense of men and money.

He spoke of the present and future without reference to the past.

Mr. LINCOLN was very much gratified with the interview.

Three Cavalry Companies from Texas and SHERMAN's Light Battery of Artillery are expected here to-morrow.

Additional volunteer companies will be mustered in to-morrow.

THE NEWS IN THE NORTH

HOW IT WAS RECEIVED IN NEW-YORK.

No event in which has occurred within the recollection of the present generation, it is safe to assume, ever occasioned so profound and wide-spread excitement as that which has pervaded all classes since the attack upon Fort Sumter was announced. Beginning with Saturday morning, when the first general details of the alleged engagement were published, up to a very late hour of the night, and throughout the day and evening of yesterday, *the war* was the absorbing topic among all classes of citizens. The newspaper offices, particularly in Printing House-square, were besieged from an early hour in the morning on Saturday for copies of the papers containing the latest news from Charleston. A mass meeting of respectable size congregated at each corner where bulletins were posted, and where they continued to devour each item of intelligence as it was received and posted up. The regular editions being exhausted the presses were kept incessantly at work supplying fresh editions of Extras as each succeeding dispatch was received by telegraph—the demand almost outrunning the supply.

Strange to say, the more "news" the public receives the more incredulous they become, owing to the contradictory, absurd and evidently *one-sided* character of many of the dispatches which come over the wires. That the rebels, ten thousand strong, had opened their half dozen batteries upon the single beleaguered fortress and its seventy bravo defenders, was fully credited, and that Major ANDERSON was replying with his guns to the attack, but that the fleet lay quietly at anchor outside, taking no part in the action; that a granite bomb proof structure should be on fire, and the flames "bursting out through all the port-holes;" that a raft should have been constructed and launched, to enable the men to procure *water* to put out the fire, thus subjecting the poor fellows to "terrible slaughter," when there are full water tanks *in* the fort, and ample pumps to flood the place; that Major ANDERSON had displayed his flag at half-mast, as a "signal of distress;" that he was *gradually* blowing up the fort, with the supposed intention of escaping seaward—these and like announcements created a general belief that the dispatches were bogus, or at least the mere result of random conjecture, entitling them to no confidence.

No language, however, can depict the doubts to which all these stories gave rise in the public mind, and there were as many conflicting theories as there were different persons in explaining these incongruities. Assuming that the general tenor of the dispatches was true, the sad and final announcement that Major ANDERSON has surrendered not was unexpected, considering that no succor had reached him from the fleet outside. But then, "no one was hurt." Here again was strong cause for doubting the whole pretended report. That a fierce engagement between large forces, with the most destructive guns, could have been carried on for two days without killing a single person on either side, and that Major ANDERSON was the guest of Gen. BEAUREGARD, were regarded as the climax of absurdity.

Finally, at a late hour on Saturday, private dispatches of the most authentic character were received from Charleston, stating that as late as 4 o'clock on Friday "all was quiet" in Charleston, and that up to 4 P.M. Friday, "not a gun had been fired;" whereas, according to previous accounts, the firing commenced at 4 o'clock, A.M., on that day. It was, of course, impossible to explain these evident contradictions upon any other theory except that the rebels were using the telegraph, like everything else, for their own infamous purposes, and falsifying every statement for effect.

Thus, all day Sunday, anxious crowds continued to surround the newspaper bulletins, in expectation that these harassing doubts would be dispelled by some more *consistent* statements from the seat of war.

OPINIONS OF THE PEOPLE.

Twenty-four hours have charged the entire feeling in the City of New-York touching the secession matter. Judging from the plainest and most outspoken expressions from men of, nominally, all parties, there is but one sentiment in this City touching the duty of the citizen at this hour to sustain the Government. The most belligerent in tone, and resolute in the expression of their determination to stand by the Government now, at whatever cost, are *Democrats*. On every corner, yesterday, in every car, on board every ferry-boat, in every hotel, in the vestibule of every church, could be heard the remark: "I am a Democrat, dyed in the wool; I voted against LINCOLN, but I will stand by the Government of my country when assailed as it now is by traitors."

While the churches were more numerously attended than usual, to hear what leading clergymen would say on the all-pervading subject, every street had its corner gathering, where the same topics were discussed, but very few persons ventured to utter a word in defence of the secession conspirators, and if any one did so, he soon learned by an outburst of indignant rebuke that New-York is fast becoming too hot to hold outspoken traitors against the Government. The duty of hanging any Southerner who, in New-York, should care to justify the cowardly and treasonable conduct of the Carolinians, was openly advocated. On all hands persons were heard to declare their readiness to take up arms in defence of the Government, and to put down, once and forever, the conspirators against peace and order.

MAJOR ANDERSON ON HIS WAY TO NEW YORK.

The following note was received last evening in reply to a note of inquiry:

BREVORT HOUSE, Sunday Evening, April 14, 1861.

To the Editor of the New-York Times:

In answer to your note, I would say that Mrs. ANDERSON has not received any announcement from her husband of any kind since Tuesday last.

But in answer to numerous inquiries, she has sent to the office a note, which I will copy for your in formation.

"Mrs. ANDERSON received a dispatch from her brother at Charleston yesterday, saying that the fort had been surrendered, and that Major A. was uninjured. A letter from the Associated Press states that a dispatch has just been received stating that he will sail soon for New-York.

SUNDAY, 5 o'clock."

This is the exact copy of her note, and is all the information we have.

YOURS TRULY,
GEO. W. HUNT, FOR MR. CLARK.

THE NEWS IN ARMY AND NAVY CIRCLES.

All Saturday naval and military officers were in the dullest mood imaginable. They all know that, firing once commenced, it was not in the power of man to prevent surrender of Fort Sumter, under the circumstances. Moreover, they knew, what had been decided by the Cabinet as long since as the 2d of April, that all hope of reinforcing Major ANDERSON, by force, had been given up; and that it was only the method suggested by a distinguished engineer—that of strategically putting in men and provisions, without going to war—which was intended to be carried out, and which could succeed. But when news of the first hostile shot having been fired reached the City, the result was, in their minds, a foregone conclusion. At the commandant's office in the Navy-yard, everybody was as nervously excited as though the premises were besieged. When a messenger came from the town, he was frequently so impressed by the embarrassing anxiety of the authorities before him, that he stood speechless for moments in their presence.

At the head-quarters of the army in Eleventh-street similar excitement prevailed. Officers who happened to be in town on business or pleasure thronged Col. SCOTT's rooms and discussed the progress of events in the most doleful spirit. The premature disclosure of the Government's plans is chiefly blamed for the surrender of Sumter. Below this feeling is a deep and marked sense of humiliation and self-depreciation. No novice in military matters can understand the disgrace which persons in the service experience when the flag of which they are the chief protectors is dishonored and humbled. Our reporter saw two officers shed tears profusely yesterday afternoon, when speaking of the "scandalous nature of the attack" on Major ANDERSON.

PATRIOTIC MASS-MEETING.

The following is a call for a mass-meeting to be held in this City as soon as arrangements can be completed. We are informed that prominent men of all parties sign it freely, and that it will probably be the largest meeting ever held in New-York.

THE CALL.

FELLOW-CITIZENS: The darkest period in our nation's history has arrived. We are passing through the most fearful ordeal to which our experiment of popular institutions has ever been subjected. Our patriot sires struggled through a long and bloody conflict to secure to their children the blessings we have enjoyed, and labored to frame a government that would protect the rights and reflect the wishes of the people.

To guard against usurpations and foster healthy progress, they provided for frequent elections and a legal method of amending the Constitution, there-by *rendering resistance* to the laws, or revolution against the Government, not only unnecessary, but morally and legally criminal. Notwithstanding this wise and equitable method of correcting mistakes in policy, improving the laws, or altering the compact by peaceful means, misguided men have fomented passion and prejudice to such a degree that it has ripened into treason and rebellion, so that our once prosperous nation trembles to its very center.

The delusive dream and empty hope that the war-clouds that skirted the Southern horizon might pass away, has failed, and the dreaded catastrophe of an armed conflict is upon us.

The time has come when political differences should give way to a patriotism which knows no party but our country, recognizes no revolution but through the ballotbox, and acknowledges no man as brother who refuses allegiance to the Government.

All good citizens who price *liberty with order*, over USURPATION and ANARCHY, are invited to assemble in mass Convention to give expression to the views of the City of New-York on the present emergency. The time for assembling will soon be published.

IMPORTANT FROM VIRGINIA.

PROCEEDINGS OF THE STATE CONVENTION.

RICHMOND, VA., SATURDAY, APRIL 13.

The Virginia State Convention reassembled to-day . . . The debate then turned exclusively upon the surrender of Fort Sumter.

Messrs. CARLILE and BARLY deprecated the action of South Carolina in firing, and expressed devotion to the Stars and Stripes.

Leading Secessionists replied, and applauded the gallantry of South Carolina, and maintained that, whatever the Convention might do, the people would now carry the State out of the Union.

The Committee here rose, when a communication was received from Gov. LETCHER, inclosing a dispatch from Gov. PICKENS, dated Charleston, to-day.

The dispatch gives an account of Friday's bombardment of Fort Sumter, and says that not a man on our batteries is hurt. It adds:

> "Fort Sumter was furious in its fire on us. Our iron battery did great damage to the foot on its southern wall. Our shells fell freely into the fort, and the effect is supposed to be serious, as they are not firing from the fort this morning. Our battery dismounted three of the largest of the columbiads of the enemy. We will take the fort, and can sink the fleet, if they attempt to force their way up the channel. If they attempt to land elsewhere, we can whip them. We have now nearly seven thousand of the best troops in the world, and a reserve of ten thousand on the railroads. War is commenced, and we triumph or we perish. Please let me know what Virginia will do."

To this Gov. LETCHER stated, that he replied that the Convention would determine.

Mr. WYSON offered a resolution in view of the late information, recommending the people of Virginia at once unite in defense of their institutions and make common cause with the Confederate States.

Without taking action on the resolution the Convention adjourned.

It was openly stated in debate that the Southern army would march through Virginia to the North, and that thousands would join them.

Mr. EARLY said it would be invasion and should be repelled.

After the fall of Fort Sumter, President Lincoln called out the militia to suppress the insurrection and four more slave states seceded to join the Confederacy: Virginia, Arkansas, Tennessee, and North Carolina. Both antagonists began to recruit and train large armies, but for three months little fighting took place except in western Virginia, which had opposed the state's secession from the Union and proceeded to secede from the state, eventually to form the new state of West Virginia. Union troops from Ohio and Indiana helped the West Virginians expel small Confederate armies from the region. Meanwhile a Union army marched out from Washington in mid-July to battle the Confederate force defending the railroad junction at Manassas as the first step in a campaign to capture Richmond, which the Confederacy had made its capital. The two armies clashed on July 21 along a sluggish stream named Bull Run just north of Manassas. After Union gains in the early fighting, a Confederate counterattack in mid-afternoon drove the Federals from the field to win a decisive victory—whose decisiveness is minimized by these dispatches in *The Times*.

July 24, 1861.

THE GREAT REBELLION.

The Victory of Sunday, and How it was Lost.

Exaggerations of the First Reports Corrected.

THE NATIONAL ARMY NOT ROUTED.

A Body of Troops Still at Centreville.

Our Loss in Killed and Wounded not Over Six Hundred.

The Rebel Loss Estimated at Three Thousand.

THEIR TROOPS IN NO CONDITION TO PURSUE.

Shocking Barbarities Perpetrated by the Rebels.

They Make Targets of the Wounded Soldiers, Mutilate them with Knives, and Fire at the Hospital.

Brilliant and Dashing Bravery of the Fire Zouaves.

They Annihilate the Black Horse Cavalry.

Lists of Our Killed and Wounded.

SPECIAL DISPATCHES FROM WASHINGTON.

WASHINGTON, TUESDAY, JULY 23.

The feeling is much better here to-day. The enormous exaggerations of the runaway soldiers have ceased to have the effect which attended them yesterday. Our loss in killed and wounded will not much exceed six hundred, though the missing may be three times that number.

It is understood that the Government has already taken the necessary steps to bring one hundred thousand men into the field here, and this renews the confidence and determination of the people.

Col. RAMSAY's regiment has been accepted, and ordered to report at Washington within twenty days, and muster in by hundreds.

The losses of the New-York and other regiments have been greatly overstated. The Seventy-first has not lost over thirty in killed and wounded. The Fire Zouaves suffered more severely, as did also the Sixty-ninth. Capt. T. F. MEAGHER had a horse shot under him, but is untouched. All our losses were in advancing—none in falling back. There was no panic in front. This was confined mainly to the wagon drivers, straggling soldiers and fugitive officers, at the rear of the columns.

Our greatest deficiency was in cool and competent officers. The men fought nobly, and were ready for anything which experienced commanders would order them to do.

Gen. MCDOWELL behaved admirably. He was active, cool, and attended to everything in person, so far as possible; but he had not a sufficient staff, and was not properly supported by his subordinates. Major WADSWORTH, of New-York, one of his aids, showed the utmost gallantry and devotion. He exerted himself to rally the forces when they first fell back, and towards the close, after having his horse shot under him, seized the colors of the wavering New-York Fourteenth, and called on the boys to rally once more to the glorious old flag. Private TYLER took hold of the colors with him, and the regiment rallied to another charge, but without success. Major WADSWORTH, as the Army retreated, remained at Fairfax Court-house, and devoted himself to purchasing everything needful for the wounded, of whom about a hundred and fifty were at that place.

Gov. SPRAGUE behaved with conspicuous gallantry, and insisted on making a stand for another fight at Centreville, but the men were too much demoralized by the panic which sprung up in the rear.

Col. BURNSIDE displayed great activity and courage at every stage of the fight, and is eager to renew it. Cols. HUNTER and HEINTZELMAN have sent word that, in spite of

Federal gun squad during training in Virginia. Photograph by Mathew Brady.

their wounds, they will take the field again in two days, if desired. When the Fourteenth New-York entered the field, they passed a wounded major of the rebel army, who begged for water. A private gave it to him, and he offered his gold watch in return. The private declined to take it, but the Major insisted, as he said some one else would get it if he did not. The testimony is universal to the barbarity and ferocity with which our wounded were treated by the rebels. Gen. SCOTT is in good spirits, and hard at work. RUSSELL got a report of the fight off in time for the Boston steamer. . . .

WASHINGTON, TUESDAY, JULY 23—2 P.M.

Among the dispatches received at Washington office to-day, was the following, addressed to a member of one of the regiments quartered at Arlington Heights, of course of the Sixty-ninth:

> NEW-YORK, JULY 23, 1861.
>
> Your wife wishes to know if you are dead, alive or wounded. If dead, please send the body on.

A spectator of the scene tells me that the Zouaves literally decimated the Black Horse Cavalry, the celebrated rebel troop. About the middle of the battle the Zouaves fired by platoons upon the rebel infantry stationed in the wood. After they had fired they discovered a troop of horse coming down on their rear. They carried the American flag, which deceived Col. HEINTZELMAN, and made him believe they were

United States Cavalry, and he so told the Zouaves. As they came nearer, their true character was discovered, but too late for all the Zouaves to reload. The regiment faced and received the cavalry as they came down, with leveled bayonets, which threw them into confusion. Then away went muskets, and the Zouaves went in with their knives and pistols. They seized horses and stabbed their riders. In this hand-to-hand conflict the Black Horse Troop were handled in their own professed way of fighting. The sequel showed the Zouaves to be the most expert handlers of the knife.

When the fight was over, there were not twenty of the four hundred cavalry left alive. Men and horses had been cut to pieces by the infuriated red-shirts. This troop of cavalry had boasted they would picket their horses in the grounds of the White House.

The telegraph office here is besieged by a crowd sending messages to friends. The capacity of the office is not equal to the extraordinary demand upon it, which will account for any delay in the receipt of answers to inquiries.

LEO.

INCIDENTS OF THE BATTLE.

Correction of Exaggerations—The Enemy in No Condition for Pursuit—Another Solferino Stampede—Straggling Soldiers—Treatment of the Wounded by the Rebels.

Editorial Correspondence of the New-York Times.

WASHINGTON, MONDAY EVENING.

Public feeling grows somewhat more settled and resolute in regard to the defeat of Sunday. The first reports brought by the stragglers and fugitives from the Army, and marked by all the exaggerations of men in a panic, created a feeling of consternation and intense alarm. Men were looking for the instant appearance of the rebel army against Washington—for an immediate uprising of the Secessionists of Baltimore, and for the immediate overthrow of the Government. Reflection and more accurate intelligence has modified this feeling very essentially—and the Washington public begin to realize that the American Government is not so near its end as they were inclined at first to suppose, and perhaps to hope. The earliest reports represented the defeat as an entire and disgraceful rout, which had completely broken up the Union Army.

It was asserted that the entire baggage train of the force, with all their horses, wagons and equipage of every kind collected at such an enormous cost, had fallen into the hands of the enemy, and that the rear of the Army was left without protection of any kind. It now appears that our Army retreated in very good order as far as Centreville, where it was protected from pursuit by the reserves, under Col. MILES; that no attempt was made to capture the baggage wagons which had nearly all been left between Centreville and Fairfax, and went back with the Army to the latter place, and that the only material which fell into the hands of the rebels was such as had been hastily, and not very creditably, abandoned on the road between Bull's Run and Centreville.

It is pretty evident that the enemy was in no condition for pursuit. A powerful force of cavalry might have done great execution upon the rear of our retreating columns; and they did make an attempt of this sort upon the Warrenton Road, but a volley from Col. BLENKER's regiment, which was sent out from Centreville to cover the retreat, soon put them to flight. The pursuit extended but a short distance, and was attended by no important result.

It will delight the heart of my excellent old friend of the *Herald*, to learn that I became involved in another stampede, not quite so extensive or disastrous as that of Solferino, but one sufficiently disgraceful to answer his purpose. As soon as it was understood in the crowd of teamsters, fugitive soldiers and miscellaneous hangers-on of the army at Centreville, that our columns were retreating, they became very considerably excited—and this feeling rose to panic when they heard the sound of cannon in the rear, as they supposed it to indicate that the enemy was pursuing in force. After I had driven something over a mile from the village on my way to Washington, the crowd in the rear became absolutely frenzied with fear, and an immense mass of wagons, horses, men on foot, and flying soldiers, came dashing down the hill at a rate which threatened destruction, instant and complete, to everything in their way. The panic spread as they proceeded, and gathering strength by its progress, the movement became absolutely terrific. The horses caught the frenzy of the moment, and became as wild as their masters. My driver attempting to check the speed of our carriage, found it suddenly crushed under the weight of an enormous Pennsylvania Army wagon which crushed it like an egg-shell. The opportune arrival of another carriage containing a couple of Congressmen, relieved me from the dilemma, and took me to Washington. Previous to my mishap I was overtaken and passed by a solitary horseman, who proved to be Mr. RUSSELL, of the London *Times,* who was profoundly disgusted with this movement, and was making all possible haste to get out of it.

The most discreditable feature of this stampede was the very large number of soldiers who had straggled away from their regiments during the battle, and who now threw away their muskets, blankets and knapsacks, and ran as if their lives depended on their speed. For a long time no attempt was made to stop them. But near Fairfax, a New-Jersey regiment had drawn up across the road, and compelled every soldier upon whom they could lay hands to go back to his regiment. They were dragged out of carriages and from the backs of horses, and turned backward with the greatest rigor. Many of them managed, however, to pass the guard, and the road all the way to Washington was crowded with these timid and fugacious warriors. How they were suffered to pass Long Bridge, having neither pass nor countersign, is among the mysteries which I have no thought of fathoming. But they made their appearance on the street corners and in the barrooms of the city with the early dawn—and each speedily be-

A telegraph communications station.

came the central point of a steadily swelling crowd, who learned the bloody history of this awful battle from the lips of these heroes, every one of whom had staid in the very thickest of the fight until his regiment was all cut to pieces, and he was left the sole survivor. It was these men who gave to the masses in Washington their knowledge of the terrible defeat the Union forces had sustained. Why Gen. MANSFIELD has suffered them thus to roam the streets all day, filling the public ear with their prodigious lies, and creating an intense and dangerous fever of the public mind, I cannot imagine. They ought either to be forced into the strict discipline of military life, or else sent home, where they will no longer be in the way of those who desire to do their duty.

The public must bear in mind this very large class of troops, when the list of killed, wounded and *missing* comes to be published. There must have been at least a thousand from the various regiments who thus ran away, and who will not be on hand to answer to their names when the master roll of their regiments is called. Their number must be deducted from the aggregate, in order to determine the real number of casualties.

I am told that a regiment of Southern Cavalry, called the Black Guards, from their riding black horses, received the special attention of the Fire Zouaves, who emptied a great number of their saddles before they were themselves cut up.

Capt. GILES, of the Sixty-ninth, who lives at the corner of Sixth-avenue and Thirteenth-street, had as narrow an escape as a man could well have. One bullet grazed and left its mark upon his windpipe, and another grazed the top of his head. Both marked without breaking the skin.

The treatment of our wounded by the rebels is reported as having been brutal to the last degree. Several soldiers assert that they saw them repeatedly draw their knives and cut the throats of our men as they lay upon the ground. Others stabbed them with their bayonets and inflicted every conceivable indignity upon them. In charging up the hill on the Warrenton road they set fire to the house used as a hospital for our men, some of whom escaped the flames by getting through the windows. A Massachusetts man passing a wounded rebel stopped and gave him water, but had not gone five rods when he saw him trying to stab another wounded man lying by his side. Such brutality would disgrace savages.

Gen. McClellan has been sent for to come to Washington immediately. It is conjectured that as he outranks McDowell, he will be put in command of the Department of Northern Virginia.

R.

BEFORE THE GREAT BATTLE.

INSTANCES OF COWARDICE AND HEROISM—THE BATTLE-GROUND BY MOONLIGHT—A SCENE OF ENCHANTMENT—PREPARATIONS FOR THE AFFRAY.

Editorial Correspondence of the New-York Times.

Centreville, Saturday Night,
10 o'clock, July 20, 1861.

We are on the eve of a great battle. Orders have been issued by Gen. McDowell for the columns to move at 2 o'clock to-morrow morning—each man leaving his blanket, haversack, &c., and taking three days' rations. The orders prescribing the several points at which the attack is to be made have been communicated to the Colonels and commanding officers. Each understands precisely what he is expected to do, and, so far as I am aware, all seem ready and determined to do it. A very serious difficulty has arisen from the fact that the time for which several of the regiments enlisted expired, or is held by them to have expired, to-day; and some of them insist upon retiring from the field. Among them, I regret to say, is the Eighth Regiment of New-York Militia, Col. Lyon.

They were mustered into the National service on the 25th of April, but as they were ready, and tendered themselves on the 20th, they insist that their term of three months must be dated from that day. Unless I am greatly mistaken, military usage is against them; but the point is one which ought to have been authoritatively settled long ago. Col. Lyon this morning wrote to Gen. McDowell, stating the fact, and claiming for his men the right to retire. Every possible appeal has been made to the regiment not to desert the Army on the very eve of an engagement, but I am sorry to say that it has not been properly seconded by the officers. Even those of them who profess a willingness to remain are exceedingly anxious that the men should be allowed to act upon their own opinions. I learn that, for two or three weeks past, there has been a good deal of disaffection in the regiment, and very many of both officers and men have shown a disinclination to go forward. They ought not to have postponed their decision until the very eve of the most important action of the whole war, thus far. They have a battery, with some 80 horses, which they are determined to take with them. This, I trust, the General will not in any case permit. I hope, indeed, that the regiment will decide not to inflict upon the Empire State, nor to incur for themselves, the disgrace and ignominy which will inevitably follow such a movement as they threaten to make.

Some of the Massachusetts regiments, among them, the Fifth, Col. LAWRENCE, are similarly situated—but I understand they claim the *right to remain,* if a battle is expected. Nothing can be more admirable than the spirit and conduct of the Massachusetts men thus far. One or two of their sick and wounded, in hospital here, learning that there was to be an action to-morrow, have begged to be permitted to rejoin their regiments—declaring their ability to do duty, and their disgust and aversion at the thought of being left behind. One of them begs to be taken in a baggage-wagon, that he may, at least, be within reach of his comrades. While in the woods, in the action at Bull's Run, on Thursday, they stood their ground admirably. Their Colonel (WELLS) went in with them, and was just as much exposed as the men. He says that one of them had just raised his rifle to fire, when a shot struck and shattered his right arm. He handed his gun to his comrade, and asked him to fire it for him.

A great many incidents are told of the action in the woods, which may or may not be true. Two of our Fire Zouaves, who strayed away from their own camp, went into the woods with the Massachusetts Regiment, wholly on their own hook. They wandered about coolly, seeking someone to fire at. One of them, seeing a rebel behind a tree, deliberately walked up to him, followed him round the tree, and shot him. It is said that the other crossed the ravine, and bayoneted a man at the guns of the battery—but, as I did not see it done, I take the liberty to doubt. Everybody says, however, that they behaved well, and that the regiment deserves a good place in the action to-morrow. They will certainly do good service if they have a chance.

This is one of the most beautiful nights that the imagination can conceive. The sky is perfectly clear, the moon is full and bright, and the air as still as if it were not within a few hours to be disturbed by the roar of cannon and the shouts of contending men. I am quartered at the extreme end of the village, towards the north. An hour ago I rode back to Gen. MCDOWELL's head-quarters, a mile and a half distant, at the foot of the sloping hill, along and beyond which the ten or fifteen regiments are encamped. As I rose over the crest of the hill, and caught a view of the scene in front, it seemed a picture of enchantment. The bright moon cast the woods which bound the field into deep shadows, through which the camp-fires shed a clear and brilliant glow.

On the extreme right, in the neighborhood of the Fire Zouaves, a party were singing the "Star-Spangled Banner," and from the left rose the sweet strains of a magnificent band, intermingling opera airs, like the beautiful serenade of "Don Pasquale," with the patriotic bursts of "Hail Columbia" and "Yankee Doodle." From far beyond the woods which bound the field came the hum of the hosts encamped in the extreme rear. The great mass of the Army is here, though four or five regiments are thrown far out on the roads in the other direction. Everything here is quiet, save the sounds of the music and the occasional shout of a soldier, or the lowing of the cattle, whose dark forms spot the broad meadow in the rear.

The rebels are in full force about four miles off, along the range of hills which bound the brook called Bull's Run. This is the real defence of Manassas Junction, and no pains have been spared to erect solid works which cover the entire front of their extended line. For a distance of six or eight miles they have fortified very strongly every defensible point. At the place where the action of Thursday occurred, the rebels have planted two or three new batteries, and, as can plainly be seen with glasses from an advanced position, they have collected very heavy reinforcements. On the road approaching Manassas, from a point further north, they have also planted batteries and mined a stone bridge, by which an intervening stream is crossed, so that it can be blown up as soon as our troops approach.

I do not intend to commit the possible indiscretion of revealing the means by which these obstacles will be overcome, if they are overcome at all; but everything is claimed to have been done which science and wise precaution can accomplish to open the way.

It is now 11 o'clock. I have been very kindly furnished with a saddle-horse by Major Wadsworth, and shall join the General's staff at 3 o'clock. What will happen to-morrow I hope to be able to tell you in my next.

H.J.R.

FROM ANOTHER CORRESPONDENT.

THE EVENTS PRECEDING AND SUCCEEDING THE BATTLE.

WASHINGTON, SUNDAY, JULY 21, 1861.

Yesterday, when upon a single oral information I ventured to criticize the ill-conducted demonstration at Bull's Run, I was only led to do it by the awkwardness of the movement, such as it appeared at the first glance. I was not then aware that this gross mistake proceeded from the fact, that a subordinate officer had taken upon himself to engage a battle with an invisible enemy, whom he knew to be concealed somewhere, without any knowledge as to its number and the strength of its intrenchments. This circumstance does not make this engagement look a bit better; for if it exonerates the Commander-in-Chief, it proves that subordination and military skill does not prevail among certain of our officers, precisely in the ranks of those where the public expects to find them.

According to the information I have been able to gather, it seems that when the division of Gen. TYLER came out from the route coming from Centreville, it entered into a wheat field, lined at its extremity with an undulating wood, girded all along by a small ravine. Arrived at a certain distance, some rare shots came from that point, as if to show that the enemy concealed beneath its impenetrable recesses was not numerous. However, Gen. TYLER had been advised previously that a masked battery was placed in that direction, and prudence which is also a part of the tactics of war, ought to have made him cautious in his advance towards the wood. He at first sent a few horsemen on a neighboring hill, exposing them purposely to the enemy's fire, so as to ascertain the number and position of its batteries. Unfortunately, this move, good in itself, was followed by another one quite incomprehensible. As Gen. TYLER'S Division was advancing, this General ordered four or five regiments to be placed in front of the enemy's hidden retreat, thus exposing them to receive its entire fire. Then, at a given time, and after a few cannon shots had been exchanged, several companies, led by Col. RICHARDSON, rushed into the wood in order to dislodge the rebels, none of whom had yet made their appearance. This act of imprudent rashness was attended by the most serious consequences. Our battery ceased its fire, the infantry laid down their arms, and during a certain time we remained in a complete inactivity, till our men, decimated by a raking fire, came out and fell back upon the second Michigan and Sixty-ninth Volunteers, which had been left outside. Such blunderings as these are hardly credible. There is no need to be a prophet to know that they will have for effect to lessen the confidence the public professes for our civilian officers, and worse, that of the soldiers. To give you an illustration of this—after the Massachusetts men who had born the brunt of the battle, went out of the woods, they exclaimed in the presence of several persons, "Give us officers and we will take the batteries!" These words speak volumes; they give you the key of the situation. Our army wants good officers!

But the most unfortunate occurrence of the day, if true, is undoubtedly the news we have just received of the junction of Gen. JOHNSTON with the Commander-in-chief of the rebels, Gen. BEAUREGARD, at Manassas. This movement is calculated to delay our success for the present, counteracts Gen. MCDOWELL'S plan, and places our Army in the ridiculous position of passing from the offensive to the defensive just as it begins to move. It seems that by means of false demonstrations upon Gen. PATTERSON'S line, Gen. JOHNSTON has caused him to believe that his Army was always facing his; and availing himself of this belief, he has, by an adroit maneuvering succeeded in escaping his sight, and reaching Manassas Junction. If this news if confirmed, you may look upon it as the most serious check we have yet experienced since the beginning of the campaign.

It is said that Gen. LANE, of Kansas, is leaving to-day for the West, to take command of his brigade. Secession seems to be on the increase in that quarter, hence his hurry.

Philanthrophy, a virtue which is to be found in all classes and is practiced by the lowly as well as the great, has just found a new adept in the person of Mr. FAY, Mayor of Chelsea, Massachusetts. That worthy citizen has just left the city whose Chief Magistrate he was, to come and take care of the sick and wounded soldiers. He brought with him, I believe, some metallic beds, and other implements used in hospitals. I have no doubt that his presence here will be highly appreciated by all, especially with the brave Massachusetts boys, to whose service he has devoted himself.

SUNDAY EVENING, 12 O'CLOCK AT NIGHT.

On Sunday evening, all the able-bodied inhabitants of Washington went out doors to look after the persons who had, in the morning, been on the other side of the Potomac, to get news from our Army. At an early hour in the afternoon, you could see, already, groups of persons standing at the corners of the streets leading to the ferry-boat, on the stoops of the hotels, in the neighborhood of the Departments—in a word, in every place where news was most accessible. Curiosity, it is said, is the mother of invention, and works upon the imagination as strongly as a romance. I had an evidence of this from the number of reports I heard in all directions. At 5 o'clock P.M., I was in possession of the long list of contradictory news hawked about by the newsmongers of this city, which would have put to shame the fertile genius of an Arabian tale-writer. According to this news, our Army was outflanked; Gen. LEE was threatening Washington, and MCDOWELL, surrounded by a circle of bayonets, had nothing else to do but to surrender at discretion. Another report said that we had taken Bull's Run Batteries, in the morning, but that they were retaken by the rebels in the afternoon; JOHNSTON, BEAUREGARD and LEE were concentrated, with 80,000 men, at Manassas; and, as God was on the side of the big battalions, we were likely to be whipped in the conflict. From the character of this rumor, it was easy to see that they had been begotten and spread by the Secessionists, who infect this city, and would rejoice, if they dared, over our defeat.

Later in the evening, however, we learned that the War Department had received dispatches announcing that three of the rebel batteries were taken, and that the New-York Firemen Zouaves, the Sixty-ninth, the Seventy-ninth and Thirteenth Regiments had shown in the attacks of these batteries as much *entrain* as French soldiers. From that moment you could see hope and joy beam upon the faces of the inhabitants of this city, the Secessionists excepted. It was evident, from their countenances, that the heart of the nation was suspended by a mysterious and sympathetic thread over the battle-field of Manassas. The satisfaction caused by the storming of Bull's Run was partially allayed by some further dispatches received by the War Department, later in the evening, announcing that HEINTZELMAN's brigade had met with some reverses.

It is 12 at night. The doors of several private citizens are still opened. Afar off the faint rolling of the drums of the regiments, hastening towards Gen. McDowell's headquarters is heard. The city is awake, but silent. Few persons, if any, will sleep this night. The rumbling on the pavements of wagons going to the camps, the trampling of the courier's horse galloping in the Avenue, and the conversations in the streets, is all that is heard. At 1 o'clock in the morning a regiment passes under my window. It is the Fifth, which I saw within this afternoon defiling on the other side of the Potomac. As it passes before Willard's Hotel, three cheers are exchanged between the civilians and the soldiers. The voice of the officers urge their men on. The regiment takes its run down Pennsylvania-avenue. I soon lose sight of it.

Monday Morning, July 22, 1861.

If the telegraph is as much frightened as the newsmongers who are hawking about news in the streets of Washington, you must by this time believe that Gen. McDowell has been routed, and that Washington is on the eve of being taken. Do not trust any of these rumors. True, two or three divisions of our Army—Burnside's, Heintzelman's and Richardson's—have experienced heavy losses—the consequence of which has been to urge them to retreat. But the *corps d'armée* is intact at Centreville. Consequently the panic caused by this encounter amounts to nothing else but a repulse by the rebels of a wing of our Army. It is not defeat—still less a route; it is a check.

The streets are full of soldiers belonging to the divisions alluded to. They are said to be fragments of the regiments who have been cut to pieces. As they are marching on towards the Department, it is difficult to address them questions. However, I take hold of a Fire Zouave, who tells me that they could have driven the enemy back had they been well supported by Sherman's Battery, whose fire was not to be compared to that of the rebels. His opinion was that if the artillery had been well served we could have been victorious. He says that what our troops had to suffer most of were cavalry charges. The rebels have drilled their negroes, and made excellent horsemen of them. He and his companions had to contend against a squadron entirely composed of black people. His regiment had suffered a great deal. In his opinion, out of eleven hundred Fire Zouaves six hundred only are alive.

Col. Burnside came in town this evening, and after an interview of a quarter of an hour with Gen. Mansfield returned to join his Brigade. His hat and coat were riddled by balls and his face grimed with dust. He did not say a word to the person who obstructed his passage in the lobby of Willard's Hotel.

The *Intelligencer* of this morning republished an article borrowed from a Louisiana paper, giving an account of the fortifications at Manassas Junction. If that account is true, it was a folly on the part of our Generals to attack, with an incomplete artillery and an unorganized army, a fortification which would baffle the efforts of the best European troops. I beg leave to call your attention to it.

PART TWO

1862

Nearly 6,500 soldiers died at Antietam on September 17, 1862, the bloodiest single day in American history. Two or three days after the fighting, Federal troops rested near the grave of Private John Marshall of the 28th Pennsylvania, whose headboard seemed to stand in for the thousands of others who lost their lives in the relentless gunfire. *(Library of Congress)*

The New-York Times.

VOL. XI—NO. 3247. NEW-YORK, TUESDAY, FEBRUARY 18, 1862.

GLORIOUS VICTORY.

THE FALL OF FORT DONELSON.

Johnston and Buckner, the Rebel Generals, Captured.

FIFTEEN THOUSAND OTHER PRISONERS.

Escape of Floyd and Pillow with Five Thousand Men.

Floyd Denounced by the Rebels as a Black Hearted Traitor and Coward.

Heavy Losses in Killed and Wounded on Both Sides.

Immense Amount of War Material Captured.

THE OFFICIAL DISPATCHES.

Flag-officer Foote Gone to Attack Clarksville.

AUTHENTIC PLAN OF FORT DONELSON.

The following brief telegrams announcing the surrender of Fort Donelson to the land forces under Gen. GRANT, were received in this City, yesterday, and appeared in "Extras" and in the afternoon papers.

CHICAGO, Monday, Feb. 17.

Fort Donelson surrendered yesterday forenoon.

Gen. BUCKNER and JOHNSTON, with 15,000 rebels, are prisoners.

Gen. FLOYD, by his great experience in the business, stole away with 5,000 men on Saturday night.

CINCINNATI, Monday, Feb. 17.

Fort Donelson surrendered yesterday forenoon. Fifteen thousand prisoners were taken, including Gens. BUCKNER and JOHNSTON.

ST. LOUIS, Monday, Feb. 17.

Dispatches from Gen. GRANT to Gen. HALLECK acknowledge the surrender of Fort Donelson with 15,000 prisoners, including Gens. J... and PILLOW.

Further official advices from F... that Gen. FLOYD escaped during ... rebels in the fort denounced him ... traitor and coward.

The enemy is known to have h... troops, fifteen thousand of whom ... Five thousand escaped, and the re... and wounded, or otherwise disable... stated, but the slaughter in our ran... terribly severe.

The casualties on the gunboats ... were as follows: On the *St. Louis* ... killed, including F. R. RILEY, ... wounded, among them Lieut. KEN...

On the *Louisville*, five sailors wer... slightly wounded, and two severely ... arms shot away.

On the *Carondelet* four were ... wounded, including WILLIAM HIN... two severely wounded.

On the *Pittsburgh* two were woun...

The force en route for Fort Do... came up, and were located on the ...

Gen. LEW WALLACE, with the sie... the Eleventh Indiana Regiment, ar...

NEWS RECEIVED IN WAS...

WASHINGTON, Monday, Feb. 17.

Gen. MCCLELLAN has received a dispatch fully confirming the capture of Fort Donelson.

NEWS RECEIVED FROM RICHMOND.

FORTRESS MONROE, Sunday, Feb. 16,
via BALTIMORE, Monday, Feb. 17.

...in this vicinity to be held in readiness for transportation of troops or Government stores.

CHICAGO, Monday, Feb. 17.

A special to the *Times*, dated Fort Donelson 16th, says:

"Fort Donelson surrendered at daylight this morning unconditionally. We have Gens. BUCKNER, JOHNSTON, BUSHROD and 15,000 prisoners, and 3,000 horses. Gens. PILLOW and FLOYD, with their brigade ran away on steamers without letting BUCKNER know their intentions.

Gen. SMITH led the charge on the lower end of the works, and was the first inside the fortifications. The Fort Henry runaways were bagged here.

The prisoners are loading on the steamers for Cairo.

Our loss is heavy—probably 400 killed and 800 wounded. We lose a large per centage of officers: Among them are Lieutenant-Colonels IRWIN of the Illinois Twentieth, WHITE of the Thirty-first, and SMITH of the Forty-eighth; Colonels JOHN A. LOGAN, SAWYER and RANSOM are wounded. Maj. POST, of the Eighth Illinois, with 200 privates, are prisoners, and have gone to Nashville, having been taken the night before the surrender. The enemy's loss is heavy, but not so large as ours, as they fought behind entrenchments.

We should have taken them by storming Saturday, if our ammunition had not given out in the night.

Gen. MCCLERNAND's Division, composed of Gens. OGLESBY's, WALLACE's and MCARTHUR's Brigades, suffered terribly. They were composed of the Eighth, Ninth, Eleventh, Eighteenth, Twentieth, Twenty-ninth, Thirtieth, Thirty-first, Forty-fifth, Forty-eighth and forty-ninth Illinois Regiments.

Gen. LEWIS WALLACE, with the Eleventh Indiana, Eighth Missouri, and some Ohio regiments, participated.

TAYLOR's, WILLARD's, MCALLISTER's, SCHWARTZ's and DRESSER's Batteries were in the fight from the commencement.

The enemy turned our right for half an hour, but our lost ground was more than regained.

Gen. LAUMAN's Brigade of Gen. SMITH's Division was the first in the lower end of the enemy's works, which was done by a charge of bayonets.

As nine-tenths of the rebels were pitted against our right, our forces on the right were ready all night to recommence the attack.

On Sunday morning they were met on their approach by a white flag, Gen. BUCKNER having sent early in the morning a dispatch to Gen. GRANT surrendering.

The works of the fort extend some five miles on the outside.

The rebels lost forty-eight field-pieces, seventeen heavy guns, twenty thousand stand of arms, beside a large quantity of commissary stores.

The rebel troops are completely demoralized, and have no confidence in their leaders, as they charge PILLOW and FLOYD with deserting them.

Our troops from the moment of the investment of the fort, on Wednesday, lay on their arms night and day, half the time without provisions, all the time without tents, and a portion in a heavy storm of rain and snow.

PLAN OF FORT DONELSON.

REPORT OF FLAG-OFFICER FOOTE.

CAIRO, Monday, Feb. 17, 1862.

Hon. Gideon Welles, Secretary of the Navy:

The *Carondelet* has just arrived from Fort Donelson, and ...

THE REBEL GENERALS CAPTURED.

GEN. ALBERT SIDNEY JOHNSTON.

Gen. JOHNSTON, who was captured at the fall of Fort Donelson, and is now in our hands as a prisoner of war, is one of the five "Generals" of the rebel army. The other four being BEAUREGARD, LEE, COOPER and J. G. JOHNSTON. He was in chief command of the rebel Department of Kentucky, to which he was appointed as the successor of BUCKNER, four months ago. He is considered by military men the ablest General in the rebel service.

He is a native of Mason County, Ky., was born in 1803, and is now consequently 60 years of age. His father was a native of Connecticut. He was a student at Transylvania University, and subsequently graduated at West Point in 1826. During eight years succeeding he served in the army as a Lieutenant and Adjutant of the Sixth Infantry, and engaged in the campaign against BLACK HAWK, in which he acted as Adjutant-General of the Illinois troops, with the rank of Colonel. He subsequently resigned his commission in the army, and in 1836 removed to Texas. He entered the Texan army as a private soldier, but Gen. RUSK soon discovered his strategic abilities and made him Adjutant-General of his command. He soon rose to be senior Brigadier-General of the Texan army, was promoted to succeed Gen FELIX HOUSTON, which led to a duel between them, wherein JOHNSTON was wounded. In 1837 he took the command-in-chief in Texas, and in 1839 he acted as Secretary of War of the new Republic, under President LAMAR. He participated also in the Indian fight on the River Neuces, in which the Cherokees, 700 strong, were defeated. In 1840 he retired from office and settled on his plantation near Galveston. He labored hard for the annexation of Texas. In 1846, at the request of Gen. TAYLOR he went to Mexico, and arrived there shortly after the battles of Resaca de la Palma and Palo Alto. He was elected Colonel of the First Texas Regiment, and served in that capacity for six months. He then served as Aid to Gen. BUTLER in the battle of Monterey; and for his conduct on that day he was recommended by Gen. TAYLOR for the appointment of Brigadier-General, but the position was bestowed upon Caleb Cushing. After this battle he retired to a plantation in Brazoria County, Texas, where he remained, until appointed by Gen. TAYLOR, in 1849, as Paymaster in the army. When the enrollment of four new regiments was proposed by the Pierce Administration, the Texas Legislature asked that he be appointed one of the Colonels; and he was accordingly appointed by JEFF. DAVIS, then Secretary of War, Colonel of the Second Cavalry, with his headquarters at San Antonio, Texas. There he remained till 1857, the greater part of the time in command of the Department of Texas. In the latter part of 1857 he received the command of the United States forces sent to coerce the Utah Mormons into obedience, and conducted the remarkable expedition across the Plains to Salt Lake City, in the Spring of the succeeding year. He was put in command of the Military District of Utah, and received the brevet rank of Brigadier-General. On the close of the Mormon troubles he was sent to California, and on the death of Gen. CLARKE, assumed the command of the Department of the Pacific. Shortly after the rebellion got under way, his loyalty was suspected, and Gen. SUMNER was sent out to supersede him. Before Gen. SUMNER reached California, JOHNSTON had left his command to join the rebels. For fear of being caught, he took the overland route, with three or four companions, on mules, and passed through Arizona and Texas, and thence to Richmond. At first he was appointed to a high command on the Potomac; but, upon the great importance of the Western Department being seen by JEFF. DAVIS, he was appointed to take chief command at Bowling Green. He then did every thing possible to strengthen that position, and ...

...in 1852, Commissary of Subsistence, with the rank of captain. When the secession movement began, he took an active but secret part with them, and as commander of the Kentucky State Guard, he exercised a powerful influence on the fighting element of his native State. Last Summer he visited Washington, represented himself there as loyal, ingratiated himself ...

On the hotels and principal buildings on Broadway the National Standard was also raised, making the City present as gay an appearance with regard to colors, as it did at the commencement of the war.

When the excitement was at its height Gen. SCOTT was seen in a carriage on Broadway. As soon as he was recognized cheer after cheer went up, and he was followed to a store where he was about to make some purchases. The crowd was so great, such an interest being taken in the General, that the Police were obliged to clear a passage through the people, in order to allow him to make his exit from the store.

From there the General drove to the Leather Manufacturers' Bank, on Wall-street, where he was immediately surrounded by brokers, merchants and others, who cheered him lustily. On the veteran General leaving the bank further enthusiasm was manifested, and continued until the General had entered his carriage, and was driven rapidly away.

In the evening BARNUM's Museum was brilliantly illuminated, every pane of glass in the building having a light behind it. The effect was most pretty, and it made that portion of Broadway almost as light as day.

The news of the capture occasioned great excitement in business circles, and gave unbounded satisfaction to all parties. At the Produce Exchange, the news was received with most enthusiastic cheering. Very few seemed surprised, though many were evidently pained to hear that FLOYD had stolen 5,000 men from the rebel ranks and gone to parts unknown.

THE UNION DEFENCE COMMITTEE.

The following communication has been sent in for publication:

OFFICE, No. 30 PINE-STREET,
NEW-YORK, Monday, Feb. 17, 1862.

At a special meeting of the Committee, held this day, Mr. DRAPER, Vice-Chairman, presiding, the following resolutions, submitted by the Chair, were unanimously adopted:

Resolved, That in further acknowledgment of the loyal and gallant conduct of the Union forces, now engaged in suppressing rebellion, this Committee desire to express their admiration of the strategic skill of the commanding Generals, the noble bravery and unflinching bravery of the officers, soldiers and seamen engaged in the investment, assault and capture of Fort Donelson, on the Cumberland River, in Tennessee.

Resolved, That the public heart of the country overflows with gratitude to the heroic men who have added a new glory to our national annals.

Resolved, That the memory of the patriots who have maintained the national honor at the sacrifice of their lives, becomes a sacred trust to a grateful country; and that the wounded and suffering defenders of the Union are entitled to the sympathy of all who appreciate principles of loyal duty and devoted patriotism.

Resolved, With the view to give public expression of the grateful sentiments cherished by the people in regard to the recent successes of the National arms, this Committee recommend that the citizens of New-York, Brooklyn and vicinity, be invited to assemble in mass meeting on the day made illustrious by the birth of WASHINGTON—the 22d of February, inst.

Resolved, That a Select Committee be appointed to make the necessary arrangements for the meeting, and to give public notice of the time and place; and that His Honor the Mayor be requested to preside.

REJOICING IN BROOKLYN.

The indefinite news in the morning papers of yesterday, as to the operations of our troops at Fort Donelson, caused great anxiety among all classes; they had not forgotten the events of the ever-remembered 21st of July; but when the semi-official announcement was made about noon that the Union troops had really gained a great victory over the rebels, it went like ... the whole people. The good news seemed to have been communicated simultaneously throughout the city, and great was the rejoicing thereat. The Stars and Stripes were displayed upon private and public buildings, and on ... docks, and the ferry-boats traversing the East River.

PHILADELPHIA, Monday, Feb. 17.

The news of the greatest victory of the war operates like sunshine, of which we are entirely destitute to-day. Crowds are gathering, under umbrellas, in the vicinity of Third and Chestnut streets, and "extras" find a ready demand.

The arrangements for the grand celebration of our ...

...ceived this morning, created the wildest ... Business of all kinds was temporarily ... The Boards of Trade adjourned at an ... The people claim the honor of the victory ... the troops there being twenty-five regime... fantry of Illinois, six of Iowa, and four ... There were also four regiments of Illino... and six companies of artillery from Wisco...

AUBURN, Monday.

One hundred guns were fired in this ... the Fort Donelson victory.

GENEVA, Monday.

The citizens of Geneva are all rejoi... are ringing, cannon are firing, and bonfire... over the great victory at Fort Donelson.

UTICA, Monday.

We share the universal war excitement ... are firing, flags flying, fireworks and bonfi...

BALTIMORE, Monday.

The Union men are overflowing with ... news is nowhere more acceptable than to ... cesh is overwhelmed at this Waterloo defe...

SAG HARBOR, N. Y., Monday.

The people here are rejoicing by the ... bells, firing of cannon and displaying of flag... schools are dismissed to participate in the ...

GREENPORT, Monday.

The news of the capture of Fort ... caused great rejoicing here. A salute of ... guns was fired.

The revenue-cutter *Agassiz*, Lieut.-Com... stationed in the harbor, is also firing a sal... gaily decorated with colors.

PROVIDENCE, R. I., Monday.

A citizens' salute of 100 guns, in hon... capture of Fort Donelson, was fired here ... noon, and a salute of 100 guns was also fir... of Gov. SPRAGUE.

BURLINGTON, Vt., Monday.

This village is wild with excitement ... capture of Fort Donelson. The bells are ... a National salute of 30 guns being fired.

DETROIT, Mich., Monday.

The news of the victory at Fort Donels... indescribable joy here. One hundred guns ... on receipt of the news, and to-night buildin... minated. The fire department, citizens an... are out in a grand procession, with banne... and rockets, to celebrate the grand event.

INDIANAPOLIS, Ind., Monday.

The greatest excitement prevailed ... the reception of the news of the captur... Donelson. A salute of 100 guns was fired, ... demonstration of joy exhibited.

A special train left at 7 P. M., for Fort ... with physicians, 25 volunteer nurses, an... quantity of hospital stores. A citizens' m... been called, to make arrangements for taki... the wounded that will be sent here.

Gov. MORTON leaves for Fort Donelson to...

IMPORTANT FROM MISSO...

The Pursuit of Price by Cur... Sigel.

Capture of a Portion of t... bel Supplies.

SPRINGFIELD, Sunday.

The following is a special to the *Democrat*:

"According to the latest advices the Fe... is in vigorous pursuit of the rebels. ...

...Baltimore, having on board the sub-mari... be laid across the Bay from this point to Ca...

The line has already been completed ... mington, Del., to Cape Charles, and als... headquarters of Gen. Wool, about a mile ...

After the Confederate victory at Manassas (Bull Run), the war see-sawed back and forth during the rest of 1861 with the Confederates winning small land battles in Missouri and Virginia which were offset by Union naval victories along the South Atlantic coast. In February 1862, however, a combined task force of Union soldiers commanded by Ulysses S. Grant and river gunboats commanded by Andrew Hull Foote captured Forts Henry and Donelson on the Tennessee and Cumberland Rivers along with the 13,000-man Confederate army at Fort Donelson, opening up the heartland of the Confederacy along these navigable rivers. These successes launched Grant's climb to eminence as the North's foremost military commander.

February 18, 1862.

GLORIOUS VICTORY.

THE FALL OF FORT DONELSON.

Johnston and Buckner, the Rebel Generals, Captured.

FIFTEEN THOUSAND OTHER PRISONERS.

Escape of Floyd and Pillow with Five Thousand Men.

Floyd Denounced by the Rebels as a Black Hearted Traitor and Coward.

Heavy Losses in Killed and Wounded on Both Sides.

Immense Amount of War Material Captured.

THE OFFICIAL DISPATCHES.

Flag-officer Foote Gone to Attack Clarkesville.

AUTHENTIC PLAN OF FORT DONELSON.

The following brief telegrams announcing the surrender of Fort Donelson to land forces under Gen. GRANT, were received in this City, yesterday, and appeared in the "Extras" and in the afternoon papers.

CHICAGO, MONDAY, FEB. 17.

Fort DONELSON surrendered yesterday forenoon.

Gens. BUCKNER and JOHNSTON, with 15,000 rebels, are prisoners.

Gen. FLOYD, by his great experience in the business, stole away with 5,000 men on Saturday night.

CINCINNATI, MONDAY, FEB. 17.

Fort Donelson surrendered yesterday forenoon. Fifteen thousand prisoners were taken, including Gens. BUCKNER and JOHNSTON.

ST. LOUIS, MONDAY, FEB. 17.

Dispatches from Gen. GRANT to Gen. HALLECK announce the surrender of Fort Donelson, with 15,000 prisoners, including Gens. JOHNSTON, BUCKNER and PILLOW.

Further official advices from Fort Donelson say that Gen. FLOYD escaped during the night, and the rebels in the fort denounced him as a black-hearted traitor and coward.

The enemy is known to have had thirty thousand troops, fifteen thousand of whom are our prisoners. Five thousand escaped, and the rest reported killed and wounded, or otherwise disabled. Our loss is not stated, but the slaughter in our ranks is mentioned as terribly severe.

The casualties on the gunboats at Fort Donelson were as follows: on the *St. Louis* there were three killed, including P. R. RILEY, of Cincinnati, two wounded, among them Lieut. KENDALL.

On the *Louisville,* five sailors were killed, four were slightly wounded, and two severely, each having both arms shot away.

On the *Carondelet* four were killed, six badly wounded, including WILLIAM HINTON, the pilot, and two severely wounded.

On the *Pittsburgh* two were wounded.

The force *en route* for Fort Donelson had mostly come up, and were located on the left.

Gen. LEW WALLACE, with the steamer *Missouri* and the Eleventh Indiana Regiment, arrived on Friday.

NEWS RECEIVED IN WASHINGTON.

WASHINGTON, MONDAY, FEB. 17.

Gen. MCCLELLAN has received a dispatch fully confirming the capture of Fort Donelson.

NEWS RECEIVED FROM RICHMOND.

FORTRESS MONROE, SUNDAY, FEB. 16,
VIA BALTIMORE, MONDAY, FEB. 17.

By a flag of truce to-day, we learn that Fort Donelson surrendered to Gen. GRANT yesterday.

Gens. PILLOW, FLOYD, JOHNSTON and BUCKNER were taken, together with 15,000 other prisoners.

DETAILS RECEIVED LAST NIGHT.

The following more detailed dispatches reached the City, last night, from the points indicated in the dates:

ST. LOUIS, MONDAY, FEB. 17.

Fort Donelson surrendered at 9 o'clock yesterday morning to the land forces. The gunboats were present at the time. *An immense amount of war material are among the trophies of victory.*

Gen. FLOYD skulked away the night before the surrender.

The gunboat *Carondelet* has arrived in Cairo with a large number of our wounded. Many have also been taken to the Paducah Hospital.

The city is wild with excitement and joy. The news was read at the Union Merchants' Exchange, creating the most intense enthusiasm. "The Star Spangled Banner" and the "Red, White and Blue" were sung by all present, after which they adjourned and marched to headquarters, twelve or fifteen hundred strong, where three rousing cheers were given for HALLECK and FOOTE. Gen. HALLECK appeared at the window, thanked the people for the hearty demonstration, and said:

"I promised when I came here, with your aid, to drive the enemies of the flag from your State. This has been done, and they are now virtually out of Kentucky, and soon will be out of Tennessee."

The "Star Spangled Banner" was repeated, and with louder cheers for the Union the crowd dispersed.

Judge HOLT wept for joy when he heard the news. Many of the stores were closed, and the city decorated with flags, and evidence of the greatest joy everywhere manifest.

Gov. YATES, Secretary HATCH and Auditor DUBOIS of Illinois, left for Fort Donelson this morning to look after the wounded Illinois troops.

A requisition has been made for all steamboats in this vicinity to be held in readiness for transportation of troops or Government stores.

CHICAGO, MONDAY, FEB. 17.

A special to the *Times,* dated Fort Donelson, 16th, says:

"Fort Donelson surrendered at daylight this morning unconditionally. We have Gens. BUCKNER, JOHNSTON, BUSHROD and 15,000 prisoners, and 3,000 horses. Gens. PILLOW and FLOYD, with their brigade ran away on steamers without letting BUCKNER know their intentions.

Gen. SMITH led the charge on the lower end of the works, and was the first inside the fortifications. The Fort Henry runaways were bagged here.

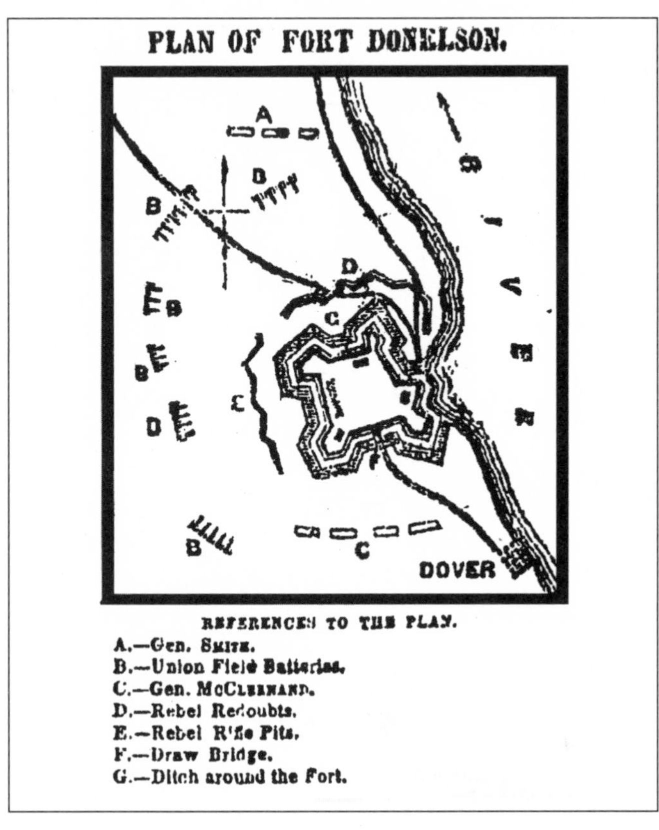

The prisoners are loading on the steamers for Cairo.

Our loss is heavy—probably 400 killed and 800 wounded. We lose a large percentage of officers: Among them are Lieutenant-Colonels Irwin of the Illinois Twentieth, White of the Thirty-first, and Smith of the Forty-eighth; Colonels John A. Logan, Sawyer and Ransom are wounded. Maj. Post, of the Eighth Illinois, with 200 privates, are prisoners, and have gone to Nashville, having been taken the night before the surrender. The enemy's loss is heavy, but not so large as ours, as they fought behind entrenchments.

We should have taken them by storming Saturday, if our ammunition had not given out in the night.

Gen. McClernand's Division, composed of Gens. Oglesby's, Wallace's and McArthur's Brigades, suffered terribly. They were composed of the Eighth, Ninth, Eleventh, Eighteenth, Twentieth, Twenty-ninth, Thirtieth, Thirty-first, Forty-fifth, Forty-eighth and Forty-ninth Illinois Regiments.

Gen. Lewis Wallace, with the Eleventh Indiana, Eighth Missouri, and some Ohio regiments, participated.

TAYLOR'S, WILLARD'S, MCALLISTER'S SCHWARTZ'S and RESSER'S Batteries were in the fight from the commencement.

The enemy turned our right for half an hour, but our lost ground was more than regained.

Gen. LANMAN'S Brigade of Gen. SMITH'S Division was the first in the lower end of the enemy's works, which was done by a charge of bayonets.

As nine-tenths of the rebels were pitted against our right, our forces on the right were ready all night to recommence the attack.

On Sunday morning they were met on their approach by a white flag, Gen. BUCKNER having sent early in the morning a dispatch to Gen. GRANT surrendering.

The works of the fort extend some five miles on the outside.

The rebels lose forty-eight field-pieces, seventeen heavy guns, twenty thousand stand of arms, beside a large quantity of commissary stores.

The rebel troops are completely demoralized, and have no confidence in their leaders, as they charge PILLOW and FLOYD with deserting them.

Our troops from the moment of the investment of the fort, on Wednesday, lay on their arms night and day, half the time without provisions, all the time without tents, and a portion in a heavy storm of rain and snow.

OFFICIAL BULLETINS OF THE VICTORY.

REPORT OF FLAG-OFFICER FOOTE.

CAIRO, MONDAY, FEB. 17, 1862.

Hon. Gideon Welles, Secretary of the Navy:

The *Carondelet* has just arrived from Fort Donelson, and brings information of the capture of that Fort by the land forces, yesterday morning, with fifteen thousand prisoners.

JOHNSTON and BUCKNER were taken prisoners.

The loss is heavy on both sides.

FLOYD escaped with 5,000 men during the night.

I go up with the gunboats, and as soon as possible will proceed up to Clarksville.

Eight mortar boats are on their way, *with which I hope to attack Clarksville.*

My foot is painful, but the wound is not dangerous.

The army has behaved gloriously.

I shall be able to take but two iron-clad gunboats with me, as the others are disabled.

The trophies are immense.

The particulars will soon be given.

A. H. FOOTE, Flag-Officer.

REPORT OF BRIG.-GEN. CULLUM.

CAIRO, FEB. 17, 1862.

To Major-Gen. McClellan:

The Union flag floats over Fort Donelson. The *Carondelet,* Capt. WALKER, brings the glorious intelligence.

The fort surrendered at 9 o'clock yesterday (Sunday) morning. Gens. JOHNSTON (A. SYDNEY) and BUCKNER, and fifteen thousand prisoners, and a large amount of material of war are the trophies of the victory. Loss heavy on both sides.

FLOYD, the thief, stole away during the night previous, with fire thousand men, and is denounced by the rebels as a traitor. I am happy to inform you that Flag-Officer FOOTE, though suffering with his foot, with the noble characteristic of our navy, notwithstanding his disability, will take up immediately two gunboats, and with the eight mortar boats which he will overtake, will make an immediate attack on Clarksville, if the state of the weather will permit. We are now firing a National salute from Fort Cairo, Gen. GRANT's late port, in honor of the glorious achievement.

(Signed) GEO. W. CULLUM,
BRIG.-GEN., VOLS. AND U.S.A.,
AND CHIEF OF STAFF AND ENGINEERS.

THE REBEL GENERALS CAPTURED.

GEN. ALBERT SIDNEY JOHNSTON.

Gen. JOHNSTON, who was captured at the fall of Fort Donelson, and is now in our hands as a prisoner of war, is one of the five "Generals" of the rebel army. The other four being BEAUREGARD, LEE, COOPER, and J. G. JOHNSTON. He was in chief command of the rebel Department of Kentucky, to which he was appointed as the successor of BUCKNER, four months ago. He is considered by military men the ablest General in the rebel service.

He is a native of Mason County, Ky., was born in 1802, and is now consequently 60 years of age. His father was a native of Connecticut. He was a student at Transylvania University, and subsequently graduated at West Point in 1826. During eight years succeeding he served in the army as Lieutenant and Adjutant of the Sixth Infantry, and engaged in the campaign against BLACK HAWK, in which he acted as Adjutant-General of the Illinois troops, with the rank of Colonel. He subsequently resigned his commission in the army, and in 1836 removed to Texas. He entered the Texan army as a private soldier, but Gen. RUSK soon discovered his strategic abilities and made him

Adjutant-General of his command. He soon rose to be senior Brigadier-General of the Texan army, was promoted to succeed Gen. FELIX HOUSTON, which led to a duel between them, wherein JOHNSTON was wounded. In 1837 he took the command-in-chief in Texas, and in 1839 he acted as Secretary of War of the new Republic, under President LAMAR. He participated also in the Indian fight on the River Neuces, in which the Cherokees, 700 strong, were defeated. In 1840 he retired from office and settled on his plantation near Galveston. He labored hard for the annexation of Texas. In 1846, at the request of Gen. TAYLOR he went to Mexico, and arrived there shortly after the battles of Resaca de la Palma and Palo Alto. He was elected Colonel of the First Texas Regiment, and served in that capacity for six months. He then served as Aid to Gen. BUTLER in the battle of Monterey; and for his conduct on that day he was recommended by Gen. TAYLOR for the appointment of Brigadier-General, but the position was bestowed upon CALEB CUSHING. After this battle he retired to a plantation in Brazoria County, Texas, where he remained, until appointed by Gen. TAYLOR, in 1849, as Paymaster in the army. When the enrollment of four new regiments was proposed by the Pierce Administration, the Texas Legislature asked that he be appointed one of the Colonels; and he was accordingly appointed by JEFF. DAVIS, then Secretary of War, Colonel of the Second Cavalry, with his headquarters at San Antonio, Texas. There he remained till 1857, the greater part of the time in command of the Department of Texas. In the latter part of 1857 he received the command of the United States forces sent to coerce the Utah Mormons into obedience, and conducted the remarkable expedition across the Plains to Salt Lake City, in the Spring of the succeeding year. He was put in command of the Military District of Utah, and received the brevet rank of Brigadier-General. On the close of the Mormon [troubles] he was sent to California, and on the death of Gen. CLARKE, assumed the command of the Department of the Pacific. Shortly after the rebellion got under way, his loyalty was suspected, and Gen. SUMNER was sent out to supersede him. Before Gen. SUMNER reached California, JOHNSTON had left his command to join the rebels. For fear of being caught, he took the overland route, with three of four companions, on mules, and passed through Arizona and Texas, and thereon to Richmond. At first he was appointed to a rebel command on the Potomac; but, upon the great importance of the Western Department being seen by Jeff. DAVIS, he was appointed to take [chief] command at Bowling Green. He then did everything possible to strengthen that position, and bring as large a force as could be got for its defense. Only a month ago, he issued an earnest appeal to Kentucky and Tennessee to furnish him with fifty thousand more men. But Gens. BUELL and HALLECK were "too much" for him. A week ago his position was outflanked, and the National army was in his rear; and last Monday, he and the greater part of his command left for Fort Donelson, to make a desperate stand against our advancing columns. He had just time to get his army in position for battle, when the fort was assaulted, and he and all his command there stationed taken prisoners. Gen. JOHNSTON stands a little over six feet high, is of a large body, sinewy frame, with a

The 36th Pennsylvania Infantry drilled at their winter quarters near Langley, Virginia, in preparation for the intense fighting that lay ahead. *(Library of Congress)*

grave, gaunt and thoughtful face; possesses quiet, unassuming manners—forming, in all, a soldier of very imposing appearance.

SIMON BOLIVAR BUCKNER.

Gen. BUCKNER, the second prisoner in rank captured at Fort Donelson, is a Brigadier-General in the rebel army, and for some months was in chief command in the rebel Western Department. He is a native of Kentucky, a graduate of West Point, and is now 38 years of age. In 1841, he was appointed, by brevet, Second Lieutenant in the Second Lieutenant in the Second Infantry, and next year he was Acting Assistant-Professor of Ethics at West Point. In 1846, he was transferred to the Sixth Infantry, in which he went to Mexico, and was brevetted First Lieutenant for gallant conduct at Contreras and Cherubusco, at which latter battle he was wounded. He was subsequently brevetted Captain for gallant conduct at Molino del Rey. In 1847 he was Regimental Quartermaster, subsequently Assistant Instructor in Infantry Tactics, and in 1852, Commissary of Subsistence, with the rank of captain. When the secession movement began, he took an active but secret part with them, and as commander of the Kentucky State Guard, he exercised a powerful influence on the fighting element of his native State. Last Summer he visited Washington, represented himself there as loyal, ingratiated himself into Gen. SCOTT's confidence, obtained permission to inspect all the fortifications in that vicinity, made Hon. ROBERT MALLORY and others believe that he wished to take active service in the army of the United States, returned to Louisville, and remained for a brief period, without giving public indication that he contemplated any disloyal movement, but all this time was holding conference with JEFF. DAVIS and the conspirators. Subsequently he managed to seduce a large part of the State Guard into the rebel service, and for this was appointed to command at Bowling Green. He is an adroit, skillful, bad man. The days of his active treason, however, are now ended.

GEN. BUSHROND.

Gen. BUSHROD, we believe, is a Kentucky Militia General. He is not a graduate of West Point, and is unknown to fame either in military or civil life.

HOW THE NEWS WAS RECEIVED.

REJOICING IN THE CITY—GEN. SCOTT ON BROADWAY.

Many were the anxious hearts carried to business yesterday. Over the matutinal [muffin] was read the fact that the right wing of the entrenchments at Fort Donelson had been carried, and that the Stars and Stripes waved over those works. In ferry-boats, omnibuses and cars men earnestly discussed the position of our troops, and confidently asserted that it was only a question of time with regard to the beleaguered fort. Yet, notwithstanding this confidence in the success of our troops, anxiety was depicted on many faces, and further news was looked for with the deepest interest.

Before noon the news arrived of the defeat of the rebels, and their surrender to the Union General. Every bulletin was soon surrounded with an eager crowd, who, with greedy eyes devoured the news. Newsboys were flying about with "Extras," and in an almost incredible short space of time the glorious news was all over town. Then came hand-shakings and congratulations that are impossible to describe, but which were fervent, honest and loyal.

At the City Hall, Custom-house, and other public buildings, the National flag was flung to the breeze. On the hotels and principal buildings on Broadway the National Standard was also raised, making the City present as gay an appearance with regard to colors, as it did at the commencement of the war.

When the excitement was at its height Gen. SCOTT was seen in a carriage on Broadway. As soon as he was recognized cheer after cheer went up, and he was followed to a store where he was about to make some purchases. The crowd was so great, such an interest being taken in the General, that the Police were obliged to clear a passage through the people, in order to allow him to make his exit from the store.

From there the General drove to the Leather Manufacturer's Bank, on Wall-street, where he was immediately surrounded by brokers, merchants and others, who cheered him lustily. On the veteran General leaving the bank further enthusiasm was manifested, and continued until the General had entered his carriage, and was driven rapidly away.

In the evening BARNUM'S Museum was brilliantly illuminated, every pane of glass in the building having a light behind it. The effect was most pretty, and it made that portion of Broadway almost as light as day.

The news of the capture occasioned great excitement in business circles, and gave unbounded satisfaction to all parties. At the Produce Exchange, the news was received with most enthusiastic cheering. Very few seemed surprised, though many were evidently pained to hear that FLOYD had stolen 5,000 men from the rebel ranks and fled to parts unknown.

REJOICING IN BROOKLYN.

The indefinite news in the morning papers of yesterday as to the operations of our troops at Fort Donelson, caused great anxiety among all classes, they had not forgotten the ever-to-be-remembered 21st of July; but when the semi-official announcement was made about noon, that the Union troops had really gained a great victory over the rebels, it [unintelligible] the whole people. The good news seemed to have been communicated simultaneously throughout the city, and great was the rejoicing there. The Stars and Stripes were displayed upon private and public buildings, and on line shipping at the docks, and the ferry-boats traversing the East River.

The news created a panic among the children in attendance at the public and private schools, and in several the scholars were so elated that they burst out into cheers, which could not be restrained, and the Principals were compelled to dismiss the scholars for the day. On the streets and in the public houses the last success of our arms was the subject under consideration, to the exclusion of all other topics. A gleam of satisfaction pervaded every countenance, and all seemed to feel that the rebellion, at last, was in a [unintelligible] way of being permanently crippled.

February 19, 1862.

THE GREAT VICTORY.

Further Particulars of the Capture of Fort Donelson.

Desperate Nature of the Fighting on Saturday.

Attempt of the Rebels to Cut Their Way Through Our Lines.

HOW THE SURRENDER WAS MADE.

Correspondence Between Gen. Buckner and Gen. Grant.

Some of the Names of the Killed and Wounded.

THE NATIONAL FORCES ENGAGED.

The End of the Rebellion in Tennessee at Hand.

The following dispatch, giving a somewhat detailed account of occurrences at Fort Donelson, on Saturday and Sunday, with the correspondence between the commanding officers of the opposing forces preceding the surrender, and the names of some of the National killed and wounded, appeared in but a portion of our morning edition yesterday, owing to the late hour at which it was received:

CHICAGO, MONDAY, FEB. 17.

A special from Fort Donelson says: The forces were about equal in numbers, but the rebels had all the advantage of position, being well fortified on two immense hills, with their fort near the river, on a lower piece of ground. From the foot of their entrenchments, rifle-pits and abatis extended up the river, behind the town of Dover. Their fortifications on the land side, back from the river, were at least four miles in length. Their water battery, in the centre of the fortifications, where it came down to the river, mounted nine heavy guns.

The rebels were sure of success. In any other cause and against less brave troops, they could easily have held the position against a hundred thousand men.

The business of getting the different brigades in position for attaching the new arrivals to the different divisions, took up the great portion of Friday night.

At daylight Saturday, the enemy opened on the Eighteenth Illinois, when Col. OGLESBY'S Brigade was soon engaged, and was soon followed by WALLACE'S and

McArthur's Brigades, the latter acting under Gen. McClernand, as the position of the troops had been changed during the night, and Gen. Grant had been called away during the night to the gunboats.

The movements of all the troops, except those attached to McClernand's Division, were made without anything except general orders.

At a suggestion from Gen. McClernand, Gen. Wallace sent up four regiments to support his division, who were nearly out of ammunition.

From the commencement till near 10 o'clock the fighting was terrific. The troops on the right were disposed as follows: McAuken's Brigade, composed of the Ninth, Twelfth, Forty-first, Seventeenth, and Nineteenth Illinois Regiments; next Gen. Oglesby's Brigade, consisting of the Eighth, Thirteenth, Twenty-ninth, Thirtieth, and Thirty-first Illinois Regiments, Schwartz's and Dresser's Batteries; next was Gen. Wallace's Brigade, of the Eleventh, Twentieth, Forty-fifth, and Forty-eighth Illinois Regiments. These three brigades composed Gen. McClernand's Division, and bore the brunt of the battle.

It was found that the enemy was concentrating his main force to turn our right, which was done by our men getting out of ammunition, and in the confusion of getting up reinforcements, retreating about half a mile. As soon as the division, which had stood its ground manfully for three hours, retired, the enemy occupied the field, when Gen. Grant ordered Gen. Smith to move forward his division and storm the enemy's works on our left. This order was obeyed with great alacrity, and soon the cheers of our daring soldiery were heard, and the old flag displayed from within the enemy's entrenchments.

Gen. Grant then sent word to Gen. McClernand that Gen. Smith was within the enemy's entrenchments and ordering their forces to move forward and renew the attack on the right. One of Gen. Wallace's Brigades—the Eleventh Indiana, Eighth Missouri and some Ohio Regiments—was rapidly thrown into position and Company A, of the Chicago Light Artillery, was planted in the road, and as the rebels, supposing we were in retreat, came, yelling, out of their works into the road, the Chicago boys poured a hailstorm of grape and canister into their ranks, slaughtering dozens of them.

Simultaneously with this the infantry commenced firing at will, and the rebels went pell-mell back into their works, our men advancing and taking possession of the ground lost, and a hill besides. Fresh troops who had not been in the action were then thrown forward, and as the shades of night drew on were in a strong position to participate in a simultaneous attack to be made on Sunday morning.

Gens. Oglesby, Wallace, and McArthur's brigades did the hardest fighting, and have suffered terribly. They would undoubtedly have held their first position but for the failure of their ammunition. The ammunition wagons were some distance off the hills preventing their being moved.

Some of our best officers and men have gone to their long homes.

Hardly a man that went over the field after the battle, but discovered some comrade who had fallen.

We lost three Lieutenant-Colonels, and at least one-quarter of all other officers were wounded or killed.

During Saturday night a contraction of all our lines was made for a simultaneous assault from every point, and orders were given by Gen. GRANT to take the enemy at the point of the bayonet. Every man was at his post. The Fifty-seventh Illinois was on the extreme right.

HOW THE SURRENDER WAS MADE.

At daylight the advance was made, and when the full light of day broke forth, white flags were hung in many places on the enemy's works.

An officer at a convenient point was informed that they had stacked their arms and surrendered early in the morning, the following correspondence having passed between the commanders:

GEN. BUCKNER TO GEN. GRANT.

HEAD-QUARTERS, Fort Donelson, Feb. 16.

SIR: In consideration of all the circumstances governing the present situation of affairs at this station, I propose to the commanding officer of the Federal forces the appointment of Commissioners to agree upon terms of capitulation of the forces at this post under my command. In that view I suggest an armistice until 12 o'clock to-day.

I am, very respectfully, your obedient servant,

S. B. BUCKNER, BRIG.-GEN., C.S.A.

To Brig.-Gen. U.S. GRANT, commanding United States forces near Fort Donelson.

GEN. GRANT TO GEN. BUCKNER.

Headquarters on the Field,
Fort Donelson, Feb. 16.

To Gen. S. B. BUCKNER—Sir: Yours, of this date, proposing an armistice and the appointment of Commissioners to settle the terms of capitulation is just received. *No terms except unconditional and immediate surrender can be accepted. I propose to move immediately on your works.*

I am, very respectfully, your obedient servant,

U.S. GRANT, BRIG.-GEN. COM'D'G.

GEN. BUCKNER TO GEN. GRANT.

HEADQUARTERS, DOVER, Tenn., Sunday, Feb. 19.
Brig.-Gen. U.S. Grant, U.S.A.:

SIR—The distribution of the forces under my command incident to an *unexpected change of commanders,* and the overwhelming force under your command compels me, *notwithstanding the brilliant success of the Confederate arms,* to accept the ungenerous and unchivalrous terms which you propose.

I am, Sir, your servant,

S. B. BUCKER, BRIG.-GEN., C.S.A.

Our force was soon in the enemy's works, when the rebel officers gave up their swords.

The bulk of the rebels are chagrined, as they knew of the surrender long before our men were apprised of it. PILLOW and FLOYD had planned and executed their escape during the night, taking with them FLOYD's Brigade and a few favorites, occupying what few small steamers they had. The prisoners are loud in their denunciations of the runaways.

Many of them acknowledged the hopelessness of their cause, and intimated a willingness to take an oath of allegiance, and return to their homes. To the question put to an officer, as to how many prisoners we had, he replied, *"You have all out of twenty-five thousand who were not killed, or did not escape."*

DISPATCHES RECEIVED LAST NIGHT.

REPORTS FROM CHICAGO.

CHICAGO, TUESDAY, FEB. 18.

The Chicago *Tribune*'s special dispatch from Fort Donelson, says that the position of the ground occupied by our troops in the attack on Fort Donelson, was such that not more than one regiment could operate at the same time, while the rebels could bring nearly their whole force to bear against us.

The first regiment to receive the rebels was the Eighteenth Illinois, which fought with desperate courage until their ammunition was exhausted, when they were forced to retire.

They were replaced by the Eighth Illinois, who were also driven back, after firing their last round.

Meanwhile the other regiments were lending such feeble assistance as their positions would admit.

Gen. Lew. Wallace was then ordered to reinforce Gen. McClernand, and he sent two brigades from the centre.

The Thirty-first Illinois Regiment, Col. Logan, fought like veterans, defending Schwartz's Battery under the most galling fire until every horse at the battery was killed, together with all the officers who had charge of the guns, as well as the Lieutenant-Colonel, the Acting-Major, seven Captains, and a number of Lieutenants of the Thirty-first Illinois Regiment had been killed, and the Colonel was wounded.

Being nearly surrounded, Capt. Cook, who was left in command, drew off what there was left of the regiment, not, however, until their last round was expended, and they had commenced driving the rebels before them.

The Second Brigade then came up and took the place of the retired one, and fought desperately, losing a great number of killed, but with the assistance of a portion of Wallace's Division, the Forty-ninth and Fifty-ninth Ohio Regiments, drove the rebels back to their entrenchments, gaining a portion of the ground lost.

The object of the rebels was, evidently, to cut their way through our troops.

The Gen. Johnson taken prisoner is Bushrod Johnson, a Brigadier-General from Tennessee.

REPORTS FROM CINCINNATI.

Cincinnati, Tuesday, Feb. 18.

The following is an account of Saturday's fighting at Fort Donelson.

On Saturday morning, the battle was resumed with unusual vigor and determination. The Eighth, Eighteenth, Twentieth, and Thirty-first Illinois occupied a position above the fort. They were about preparing a little food, when the rebels opened on them a fire of musketry. The line of battle was at once formed, and the storm of leaden hail returned, perceptibly thinning the rebel ranks. The rebels, from their advantageous positions, showered upon our ranks most murderous volleys, of musketry, grape and canister, killing and wounding our men almost by companies at every round; yet every man stood his ground bravely, determinedly and without flinching. These four regiments held their ground, dealing death, dying and fighting against appalling odds, and in the face of every disadvantage. The Eighteenth Regiment seems to have resisted the severest storm. Against their ranks the rebels directed their heaviest fire, but instead of falling back, *they advanced to the very face of the enemy, and there stood in the very jaws of death, with scarcely a prospect that a single one would escape.* For three hours these regiments, numbering scarcely 3,000 men, held their ground against the whole rebel garrison.

At one time the Eighteenth, being partially flanked, was exposed to a cross-fire of both musketry and artillery, but our right wing securing the rebels' left, at once relieved them. At this critical moment Col. Lawler fell. Capt. Bush, Acting

Confederate soldiers of the Third Georgia Infantry near Richmond, Virginia, during the winter of 1861–1862.

Lieutenant-Colonel, assumed command, but was soon wounded. Capt. CRANE was shot dead. Capt. LAWLER was mortally wounded. Lieuts. MANSFORD and THOMPSON killed. Capts. DILLON and WILSON, and Lieuts. KELLY and SCANLON wounded, so that the daring Egyptian regiment stood before an overwhelming fire almost without officers. They fell in heaps, dead and wounded. Companies were bereft of Captain and Lieutenants, Captains almost bereft of Companies.

The other three regiments did their duty nobly. Cols. OGLESBY, MARSH and LOGAN dashed along the ranks, waving their hats and cheering their men to the conflict. *"Suffer death, men,"* cried LOGAN, *"but disgrace never! Stand firm."* And well they heeded him. Many fell dead and wounded. Among the latter were Col. LOGAN and Lieut.-Col. WHITE.

OGLESBY'S and MARSH'S regiments fought desperately, losing, like other regiments, an undue proportion of officers. Col. OGLESBY displayed coolness and courage that have elicited the highest praise, and served well in stimulating his men. Never, perhaps, on the American Continent, has a more bloody battle been fought.

An officer who participated, and was wounded in the fight, says the scene beggars description. *So thickly was the battle-field strewn with dead and wounded that he could have traversed acres of it, taking at most every step upon a prostrate body.*

The rebels fought with desperation, their artillerists using their pieces with most fearful effect. On either side could be heard the voices of those in command, cheering on their men. The four Illinois regiments held their ground a full three hours.

Nearly one-third had been killed or wounded, yet the balance stood firm. Finally reinforcements arrived, and for an hour the slaughter continued.

About four o'clock our right wing turned their left, and the rebels fell back into the fortifications, and our flag was planted upon the position occupied by their left wing, and for a time the slaughter ceased.

DRESSER's and SCHWARTZ's Batteries were captured during the action, but the Eighteenth Illinois, with clubbed muskets, recovered DRESSER's, while the Thirty-first recovered SCHWARTZ's.

REPORTS FROM ST. LOUIS.

ST. LOUIS, TUESDAY, FEB. 18.

The *Republican*'s Fort Donelson correspondent gives the following account of the fighting on Saturday:

"Yesterday morning, just at daylight, a heavy sortie was made by the garrison from the left portion of their works. This attack was made upon the extreme right wing of the Union army, where it was the weakest. Part of Gen. MCCLERNAND's Division, under Col. OGLESBY, consisting of his brigade, which was stationed there; also, SCHWARTZ's and MCALLISTER's batteries. The point was upon a ridge leading into the right redoubt, and was situated just above the main fort.

During the night the enemy could be heard busily at work, but what at, it is impossible to tell, as a thicket and woods encompassed the Union troops on every side, rendering the view in almost any direction almost impossible. At daylight, a large body of the enemy suddenly appeared on the extreme right wing of Col. OGLESBY's command, and opened a terrible fire from cannon from their redoubts, playing at the same time on our forces from guns placed in position on the night previous.

The camp of the Twenty-ninth and Thirty-first was most exposed, and the whole brigade was at once formed into line as follows:

The Eighteenth Illinois held the extreme right.

The Eighth Illinois next.

The Thirteenth Illinois next.

Then the Twenty-ninth Illinois, supporting the right of Capt. SCHWARTZ's battery, and the Thirty-first defending the artillery on the left.

From the firing of the first gun till 9 o'clock the battle raged unremitting and with fearful loss on both sides. Again and again our troops drove the enemy back, but they were reinforced, while our troops had, owing to the extended lines of the army and also their position on the extreme right, to fight unassisted. More gallant fighting never took place than that of the Union troops. Exposed to the terrible firing of triple of their number, they stood their ground until *in some regiments every officer was killed or wounded.*

At last and reluctantly, regiment by regiment, they slowly fell back, leaving SCHWARTZ's batteries and three of MCALLISTER's guns in rebel hands. Retiring a few hundred yards, they all made a stand, and Gen. SMITH arrived with reinforcements, and at once drove the enemy into their works.

In the first of the battle was also Col. W.H.L. WALLACE's Brigade, the Eleventh, Twentieth, Seventeenth, and Forty-eighth; also, Col. MCARTHUR's Brigade, all of which troops suffered severely. Opposed to them were 12,000 rebels, supported by guns placed carefully in position.

Gen. GRANT, having command of the division, drove the enemy back with reinforcements, and gained the lost ground, at once ordered an advance by Gen. SMITH on the left, charging under a hot fire up the steep hill on which was the outer redoubt, our troops gained the high breastworks, and, with hardly a pause, went over them, *planting the Stars and Stripes over the walls.* Under a most galling fire, they formed, charged, and drove the rebels back, until they fell in to a new position behind some batteries.

When evening came, the Union troops had been victorious at every point, having gained back the ground lost in the morning, and got within one part of the enemy's works. Our troops held their position during the night, repelling the repeated assaults.

The scene within the captured fort, after the surrender, showed how terrible the rebel garrison had suffered. Everywhere were lying fragments of shells and round shot, half buried in the earth. Tents were torn to pieces, gun-carriages broken, and blood scattered around. In the left redoubt, where the assault had taken place, the dead bodies lay thickly, and abundant evidence of stern resistance and gallant attack were visible. On the extreme right, half a mile distant where the desperate *sortié* was made by the garrisons, similar scenes were visible.

The gallantry of the Union troops has been well and severely tested, *and they have proved more than equal to the task before them.*

As the fleet approached the fort this morning, a salute was fired, and three cheers went up where American flags were visible.

No officers in the army had an idea of Fort Donelson's defences, until they had been gained and examined.

Several regiments, when out of ammunition, rushed forward, and although exposed to the full fire of the rebel artillery, gallantly drove their foes back with the bayonet, and captured their guns.

The first battle between warships armor-plated with iron took place on March 9, 1862, at Hampton Roads, Virginia, where the James River empties into the Chesapeake Bay. The previous day the ten-gun C.S.S. *Virginia,* rebuilt as an ironclad from the hull of the steam frigate U.S.S. salvaged by the Confederates when they seized Norfolk in 1861, had steamed out to attack the Union blockade fleet at Hampton Roads. Union shot and shells bounced off the armor plate of the *Virginia.* In the worst day for the U.S. Navy until December 7, 1941, the *Virginia* (which both sides still tended to call the *Merrimac*) sank two wooden warships and ran another aground to be finished on the morrow, as everyone expected. Panic seized Washington, but in the nick of time the Union's own ironclad arrived that night and saved the rest of the fleet. This was the U.S.S. *Monitor,* built by the most innovative naval designer of the nineteenth century, John Ericsson, a native of Sweden who had become an American citizen. With low freeboard and a revolving gun turret, this "tin can on a shingle" slugged it out muzzle to muzzle with the *Virginia* on March 9, sending her limping back to Norfolk. It was the dawn of a new day in naval history; the "heart of oak" era was over.

March 10, 1862.

HIGHLY IMPORTANT NEWS.

Desperate Naval Engagements in Hampton Roads.

Attack Upon our Blockading Vessels by the Rebel Steamers Merrimac, Jamestown and Yorktown.

The Frigate Cumberland Run Into by the Merrimac and Sunk.

Part of Her Crew Reported to be Drowned.

SURRENDER OF THE FRIGATE CONGRESS.

Engagement of the Rebel Steamers with the Newport's News Batteries.

The Minnesota and Other Vessels Aground.

CESSATION OF FIRING AT NIGHT.

Opportune Arrival of the Iron-Clad Ericsson Battery Monitor.

A Five Hours' Engagement Between Her and the Merrimac.

The Rebel Vessel Forced to Haul Off.

THE MONITOR UNINJURED.

FORTRESS MONROE, SATURDAY, MARCH 8.

The dullness of Old Point was startled to-day by the announcement that a suspicious looking vessel; supposed to be the *Merrimac,* looking like a submerged house, with the roof only above water, was moving down the Norfolk by the channel in front of the Sewell's Point batteries. Signal guns were also fired by the *Cumberland* and *Congress,* to notify the *Minnesota, St. Lawrence* and *Roanoke* of the approaching danger, and all was excitement in and about Fortress Monroe.

There was nothing protruding above the water but a flagstaff flying the rebel flag, and a short smokestack. She moved along slowly, and turned into the channel leading to Newport's News, and steamed direct for the frigates *Cumberland* and *Congress*, which were lying at the mouth of James River.

As soon as she came within range of the *Cumberland,* the latter opened on her with her heavy guns, but the balls struck and glanced off, having no more effect than peas from a pop-gun. Her ports were all closed, and she moved on in silence, but with a full head of steam.

In the meantime, as the *Merrimac* was approaching the two frigates on the side, the rebel iron-clad steamers *Yorktown* and *Jamestown* came down James River, and engaged our frigates on the other side. The batteries at Newport's News also opened on the *Yorktown* and *Jamestown,* and did all in their power to assist the *Cumberland* and *Congress*, which, being sailing vessels, were at the mercy of the approaching steamers.

The *Merrimac,* in the meantime, kept steadily on her course, and slowly approached the *Cumberland,* when she and the *Congress,* at a distance of one hundred yards, rained full broadsides on the iron-clad monster, that took no effect, the balls glancing upwards, and flying off, having only the effect of checking her progress for a moment.

After receiving the first broadside of the two frigates, she ran on to the *Cumberland,* striking her about midships, and literally laying open her sides. She then drew off, and fired a broadside into the disabled ship, and again dashed against her with her iron-clad prow, and, knocking in her side, left her to sink, while she engaged the *Congress,* which laid about a quarter of a mile distant.

The *Congress* had, in the meantime, kept up shot engagement with the *Yorktown*

Federal sailors being entertained aboard ship in 1862.

and *Jamestown* and having no regular crew on board of her, and seeing the hopelessness of resisting the iron-clad steamer, at once struck her colors. Her crew had been disengaged several days since, and three companies of the Naval Brigade had been put on board temporarily, until she could be relieved by the *St. Lawrence,* which was to have gone up on Monday to take her position by one of the blockading vessels of the James River.

On the *Congress* striking her colors, the *Jamestown* approached and took from on board of her, all her officers as prisoners, but allowed the crew to escape in boats. The vessel being thus cleared, was fired by the rebels, when the *Merrimac* and her two iron-clad companions opened with shell and shot on the Newport's News batteries. The firing was briskly returned. Various reports have been received, principally from frightened sutler's clerks. Some of them represented that the garrison had been compelled to retreat from the batteries to the woods. Another was that the two smaller rebel steamers had been compelled to retreat from their guns.

In the meantime the steam-frigate *Minnesota* having partly got up steam, was being towed up to the relief of the two frigates, but did not get up until it was too late to assist them. She was also followed up by the frigate *St. Lawrence,* which was taken in tow by several of the small harbor steamers. It is rumored, however, that neither of these vessels had pilots on board them, and after a short engagement, both of them seemed to be, in the opinion of the pilots on the Point, aground. The *Minnesota* either intentionally or from necessity, engaged the rebel steamers at about a mile distance with only her two bow guns. The *St. Lawrence* also poured in shot from all guns she could bring to bear, and it was the impression of the most experienced naval officers on the point that both had been considerably damaged. These statements, it must be borne in mind, are all based on what could be seen by a glass at a distance of nearly eight miles, and from a few panic-stricken non-combatants, who fled at almost the first gun from Newport's News.

In the meantime darkness approached, though the moon shone out brightly, and nothing but the occasional flashing of guns could be seen. The *Merrimac* was also believed to be around, as she remained stationary, at a distance of a mile from the *Minnesota,* making no attempt to attack or molest her.

Previous to the departure of the steamer for Baltimore, no guns had been fired for half an hour, the last one being fired from the *Minnesota*. Some persons declared that immediately after this last gun was fired, a dense volume of vapor was seen to rise from the *Merrimac,* indicating the explosion of her boiler. Whether this is so or not, cannot be known, but it was the universal opinion that the rebel monster was hard aground.

Fears were of course entertained for the safety of the *Minnesota* and *St. Lawrence* in such an unequal contest; but if the *Merrimac* was really ashore, she could do no more damage. It was the intention of the *Minnesota,* with her picked and gallant crew, to run into close quarters with the *Merrimac,* avoid her iron prow, and board her. This the *Merrimac* seemed not inclined to give her an opportunity to do.

At 8 o'clock, when the Baltimore boat left, a fleet of steam-tugs were being sent up to the relief of the *Minnesota* and the *St. Lawrence,* and an endeavor was to be made to draw them off the bar on which they had grounded. In the meantime the firing had suspended, whether from mutual consent or necessity, could not be ascertained.

The rebel battery at Pig Point was also enabled to join in the combined attack on the *Minnesota,* and several guns were fired at her from Sewall's Point as she went up. None of them struck her, but one or two of them passed over her.

The Baltimore boat left Old Point at 8 o'clock last night. In about half-an-hour after she left the wharf, the iron-clad Ericsson steamer *Monitor* passed her, going in, towed by a large steamer. The *Monitor* undoubtedly reached Fortress Monroe by 9 o'clock, and may have immediately gone into service; if not, she would be ready to take a hand early on Sunday morning.

The foregoing are all the facts as far as can be at present ascertained, and are, probably, the worst possible version of the affair.

LATER AND BETTER NEWS.

A Five Hours' Engagement between the Ericsson Battery and the three Rebel Steamers.

The Rebel Vessels Driven Off—The *Merrimac* in a Sinking Condition.

WASHINGTON, SUNDAY, MARCH 9—5:45 P.M.

The telegraph line to Fortress Monroe is just completed, and a message from there states that after the arrival of the *Monitor,* last night, she was attacked by the *Merrimac Jamestown,* and *Yorktown. After a five hours' fight they were driven off and the Merrimac put back to Norfolk in a sinking condition.*

OFFICIAL.

[MY TELEGRAPH FROM FORTRESS MONROE.]

WASHINGTON, SUNDAY, MARCH 9—7 P.M.

The *Monitor* arrived at Fortress Monroe last night.

Early this morning she was attacked by three vessels—the *Merrimac,* the *Jamestown,* and the *Yorktown.*

After five hours' contest they were driven off—the *Merrimac* in sinking condition.

The above is official.

DISPATCH AUTHORIZED BY GEN. WOOL.

FORTRESS MONROE, SUNDAY, MARCH 9.

The *Monitor* arrived at 10 P.M. last night, and went immediately to the protection of the *Minnesota,* lying around just below Newport's News. At 7 A.M. to-day the *Merrimac,* accompanied by two wooden steamers, the *Yorktown* and *Jamestown,* and several tugs, stood out towards the *Minnesota,* and opened fire. The *Monitor* met them at once, and opened fire, when the enemy's vessels retired, excepting the *Merrimac. The two iron-clad vessels fought, part of the time touching each other, from 8 A.M. till noon, when the Merrimac retreated.* Whether she is injured, or not, it is impossible to say.

Lieut. J.L. WORDEN, who commanded the *Monitor,* handled her with great skill, assisted by Chief-Engineer STONERS.

The *Minnesota* kept up a continuous fire, and is herself somewhat injured. She was moved considerably to-day, and will probably be off to-night.

NORFOLK AND ITS NEIGHBORHOOD.

A Map Showing the Locality of the Great Maritime Action in Hampton Roads and the Railroad Connections of Norfolk with Richmond and Petersburgh. Reproduced from Our Sunday Edition.

The *Monitor* is uninjured, and ready at any moment to repel another attack. [Sent by order of Gen. Wool.]

Washington, Sunday, March 9.

The following was received to-night by Major-Gen. McClellan from Gen. Wool, dated Fortress Monroe, at 6 o'clock this evening:

"Two hours after my telegraphic dispatch to the Secretary of War last evening, the *Monitor* arrived. She immediately went to the assistance of the *Minnesota,* which was aground, and continued so until a few moments since. Early this morning she was attacked by the *Merrimac, Jamestown,* and *Yorktown*. After a five hours' contest they were driven off, the *Merrimac* in a sinking condition. She was towed by the

Jamestown, Yorktown and several smaller boats toward Norfolk, no doubt, if possible to get her in the dry-dock for repairs. The *Minnesota* is afloat and being towed toward Fortress Monroe."

THE VESSELS ENGAGED.

THE ERICSSON BATTERY *MONITOR*.

The new Ericsson battery, or, as she is now called, the *Monitor,* which left this port for Southern waters last Wednesday, has already had her first engagement with the enemy, and has come out the victor. It appears that she arrived in Hampton Roads last Saturday night, just after the rebel battery *Merrimac,* had been playing havoc with our blockaders. She came to the rescue precisely at the right moment. Yesterday morning she was set upon by the *Merrimac,* the *Jamestown* and the *Yorktown*. After a five hours' fight she drove them all off, the *Merrimac* putting back to Norfolk in a sinking condition. As the public will now be anxious to know something of the style and power of this iron-clad vessel, which has thus routed the famous rebel iron-clad floating battery, we append a full account of her, furnished by our correspondent, who accompanied her on a recent trial trip from this harbor.

DESCRIPTION OF THE VESSEL.

The designer and builder of the *Monitor* was Capt. ERICSSON, famous in connection with the invention of a mode of propelling vessels and working engines by the motor-power of caloric, or heated air. Capt. ERICSSON is a Swede by birth, but his remarkable and persevering scientific efforts have been carried on principally in this City for the last ten years.

By an act of Congress passed last Summer, the Secretary of the Navy was authorized to advertise for proposals to build one or more iron-clad vessels, all proposers to furnish their own plans. An appropriation of $1,500,000 was made to build such vessels, providing that the plans met with the approval of three commanding officers of the navy. The Board appointed consisted of Commodores JOSEPH SMITH, HIRAM PAULDING, and Capt. CHAS. H. DAVIS. Capt. ERICSSON sent in a plan which was accepted, with the understanding that the vessel was to be finished in one hundred days. The contract bears date the 4th of October, 1861.

The keel of this vessel was laid on the 25th of October, and so rapidly was the work performed, that the engines were put into the vessel and operated on the 31st of December last. The construction of the vessel was under the superindence of Engineer ALBAN C. STIMERS and Assistant Engineer ISAAC NEWTON, who were detailed from the frigate *Roanoke,* by the Government for that purpose.

THE ARMAMENT.

The armament consists of two 11-inch Dahlgren guns, which are the heaviest now used by the navy. The lower part of the gun-carriages upon which the upper part slides when the gun is run in or out, consists of solid, wrought iron beams, extending the whole diameter of the turret, with their ends secured to it in such a manner that they essentially form a part of it. These beams are planned perfectly true, are seven inches deep by four inches wide, and are placed perfectly parallel in the turret, both guns pointing in the same direction. This permits the officer working the guns to take his aim by sights fixed with the turret instead of with the guns, in the usual way, which requires personal exposure when taking the aim. The ports through the side of the turret are only sufficiently wide to permit the passage through them of the muzzle of the guns, and with just enough addition, vertically, for the elevation required. Inside of these swing iron pendulums, which close them against the enemy as soon as the gun recoils. The whole is made to revolve by a pair of steam engines placed beneath the deck; the handle which governs them passing up into the turret convenient to the hand of the officer who aims the gun.

THE AMMUNITION.

At the Novelty Iron Works a quantity of solid wrought iron shot was forged for the Monitor; each one weighing 187 pounds. These were intended for perforating and sinking iron-clad vessels of the enemy whose sides are the ordinary height above the water line. Besides these she carries a quantity of cast iron shots weighing 175 pounds each, and one hundred round of shells in weight 155 pounds each.

THE MACHINERY.

Mr. C. H. DELAMATER fitted this vessel with machinery. It consists of two horizontal tubular boilers, containing 3,000 square feet of fire surface, and two horizontal condensing engines, of forty inches diameter of cylinders, by twenty-two inches stroke of pistons. The propeller is nine feet diameter, sixteen feet pitch, and has four blades. Her speed is about six and a half knots an hour. All her machinery is below water-line.

THE *MONITOR'S* OFFICERS.

The following were the officers of the *Monitor* when she left this port, six days ago:

Lieutenant Commanding—John S. Worden.
Lieutenant and Executive Officer—S. D. Green.
Acting Masters—L. N. Stodder and J. W. Webber.
Acting Assistant Paymaster—Wm. F. Keeler.
Acting Assistant Surgeon—D. C. Logue.
Chief Engineer—A. C. Stimers.
Engineers—First Assistant, Isaac Newton; Second Assistant, Albert S. Campbell; Third Assistants, R. W. Sands and M. T. Sunstron.
Acting Master's Mate—George Frederickson.

THE SCIENTIFIC PLAN OF THE *MONITOR*.

Capt. Ericsson's idea in building the *Monitor* was to give the greatest buoyancy to the vessel, and as small a target as possible to the enemy, so as to enable him to completely protect every part, all its attachments and every person on board, when under the fire of an enemy. He conceived that to do this was to build a broad flat-bottomed vessel with vertical sides and pointed ends, so that it required but a shallow depth to displace water sufficient to buoy itself up, though loaded with an impregnable armor upon its sides, and a bomb-proof deck upon which is placed a shot-proof revolving turret containing two of the heaviest Dahlgren guns. To insure such a vessel the power of locomotion, it was only necessary to suspend beneath it a vessel of ordinary strength, sufficiently narrow and sloping at the sides, that if, as actual experiment has proven possible, the enemy's missile should pass below the shot-proof upper vessel, these sides can only be hit at such an acute angle that little harm is likely to ensue, and in its length approaching the bow only so nearly that its raking stem may receive the shot fired from directly ahead in the same way, and at the stern giving sufficient space to permit the dipping shot coming from directly aft to pass under the shot-proof end, directly on its course, without hitting the rudder, which is placed abaft the propeller.

The sides of the upper vessel are first formed of plate-iron, half an inch thick, outside of which is attached solid white oak, twenty-six inches thick, which again received the rolled iron armor of five inches thickness. The bomb-proof deck is supported by well-stanchioned and diagonally braced oak beams, ten inches square, placed with their faces twenty-six inches apart, upon which is laid planking seven inches thick, covered with rolled plate-iron one inch thick. As the bottoms of these beams are on a level with the water-line, the armor above water is supported by a backing of forty-one feet in depth. The lower vessel is of iron, one-half inch thick, made in the usual manner, and contains, in its after part, the steam machinery and coal, and in the forward part—the poop being divided by a wrought iron bulkhead—the quarters for the officers and crew, and the ammunition and stores. In describing

The deck of the Union monitor *Catskill,* which, like the others of its class, was tough and formidable, and just as infernally hot below decks. *(Library of Congress)*

the upper and lower vessel, it must not be imagined that they are constructed separately; they form, together, one vessel; it is only as respects form that they can be regarded as two.

THE PILOT-HOUSE AND ANCHOR.

The pilot is protected by a shot-proof pilot-house which alone weighs 22,000 pounds. The house stands five feet above the level of the deck. The anchor is suspended from a circular well, open at the bottom, situated in the extreme bow of the upper vessel, and connected with the capstan in the bow of the lower one. An arrangement is also provided for taking soundings below the water line.

THE TURRET.

The turret spoken of above is for the protection of the men while working the guns; in fact, no one is exposed or seen by the enemy. The turret revolves, and consists, first, of a rolled plate iron skeleton, one inch thick, to which is riveted two thicknesses, of one inch each, of rolled iron plates. Outside of these riveted plates are six thicknesses, of one inch each, of rolled plates bolted firmly to the first two thickness with screw bolts, having deep countersunk heads on the outside and nuts within, so that if in action the enemy's shot should loosen any of the plates they can easily be refastened. The seams are vertical, and these break joints with each other, consequently no shot can strike the seam of more than one thickness. The top is covered with a bomb-proof roof, placed six inches down within the turret, and perforated with holes. In addition to the above the gunners are protected by a shield, within the turret, of one and a half inch thickness.

FOR WHAT THE *MONITOR* WAS INTENDED.

The Ericsson Battery was not intended for an ordinary cruiser, but for the defence of our harbors and coast, and for operations such as those in which she has just achieved such a signal success. She is enabled to carry eight days' fuel, and thus can proceed easily from port to port along our seaboard. Provisions for three months can be stowed away in her, and a condensing apparatus for supplying fresh water to the officers and crew is fitted up on board.

THE LAST TRIAL TRIP OF THE *MONITOR* AND ITS RESULTS.

Last Monday the *Monitor* went on a trial trip down the Bay, about five miles beyond Fort Lafayette. Her steering qualities were found to be all that could be desired.

The guns were fired to test the question which had been mooted, of whether the concussion within the turret would not be so great as to injure seriously the ears of the men. First, a blank cartridge was fired with the hatches in the roof open. Then a charge of canister, weighing 135 pounds, with 15 pounds of powder, with the hatches still open, and finally the same charge with the hatches closed, as they will be under the fire of the enemy. It was found that in every case the concussion in every part of the interior of the turret was considerably less than when standing near such a gun fired in the open air. The sailors stationed at the guns, and who expected to handle them shortly against the enemy, all expressed themselves delighted at the success of the trial. The speed of the vessel by the ship log was 6¼ knots, the engines making 65 revolutions.

The last heard of the *Monitor* previous to the news of her success, was by a bark which arrived here yesterday morning. The bark reported that, on the 7th inst., at 10 P.M. off Barnegut, she passed the *Monitor* in tow, bound for Fortress Monroe.

This magnificent success in her first trial, will settle all questions as to her efficiency.

LIEUT. WERDEN.

Lieut. J. R. Werden, it will be recollected, at the commencement of the rebellion was captured by the rebels, after having conveyed dispatches from the Government

Fortified bridge of the Louisville & Nashville Railroad at Nashville, Tennessee.

to the National fleet off Pensacola, and imprisoned several months at Montgomery. He was exchanged a short time ago, and was immediately assigned to the *Monitor,* in which, as will be seen from the dispatches, he has done most effective service.

THE *MERRIMAC.*

The *Merrimac,* the iron-plated rebel steamer which attacked the Erickson Battery, was formerly the United States screw-frigate of the same name. She was built at the Navy-Yard at Charlestown, Mass., in 1855; and her last active service was in the Pacific Squadron. At the time of the rebel attack on the Norfolk Navy-Yard, she was lying there in ordinary, as a store and receiving ship. She was a ship of 3,200 tons burden, and was pierced for forty guns. When the Navy-yard was assailed, she was set fire to, scuttled and sunk, by the National officers, in preference to letting her fall into the hands of the rebels. A recent official report on the subject, made to the rebel authorities, stated that she was sunk and burned to her copper line and down through to her berth-deck, which, with her spacious gun-decks were also burned. After the rebels had got possession of the Yard, they proceeded to raise the hull of the *Merrimac,* and to convert her into a vessel of war for their own purpose. Her hull was cut down to within three feet of her water-work, and a bomb-proof house built on her gun-deck. She was then iron-plated and her bow and stern steel clad, with a projecting angle of iron for the purpose of piercing a vessel. She had no masts, and there was nothing to be seen over her gun-deck, with the exception of the pilot house and smoke-stack. The bomb-proof was three inches thick and made of wrought iron. Altogether she looked like a formidable war-ship. But when her iron sheeting was half on, it was tested by columbiads and found inefficient. She was then additionally strengthened, until she was so heavy that she came fair to become unmanageable, and even to sink by her own weight. In a description published some two or three months ago, her armament was stated as consisting of four 11-inch navy guns on each side and two 10-pounder Armstrong guns at the bow and stern. But no doubt great changes have been made in her armament before this time. The Norfolk *Day Book* of the 6th inst. had an article describing the attempt to convert the *Merrimac* into an impregnable iron-plated man-of-war as a failure. It began thus:

> "We have scarcely patience enough left to condemn in temperate language the reckless impropriety of two of our contemporaries, who have seen it, in their thirst for notoriety, to thrust before the public the fact the *Merrimac* had proved an abortion."

I was further said, that:

> "The calculation in displacement was erroneous. An error amounting to more than two hundred tons was discovered when the ship was floated off. The chief subject of regret is, that when she was shored up again the ship caught upon the blocks and received a considerable strain; consequently, some parts of the machinery have been taken up, and a quantity of dead-wood will have to be introduced to correct the tendency to log. Her great draught of water will prevent her taking part in active operations. This draught originally was about twenty-four feet, but it has been considerably increased."

The editor, however, comforted himself that at all events she could be used as a floating battery.

Her bow is armed with a steel plough, projecting six feet under water, to strike and sink the vessels of the blockading fleet. Her decks are protected by a covering of railroad iron, in the form of an arch, which it was hoped would be proof against shot and shell.

Perhaps this story of its failure was intended as a rebel ruse, to throw our naval force on the Potomac off its guard. The rebels had previously boasted of the immense power and strength of the *Merrimac* in the most extravagant manner. They had frequently averred that she was about to run out, sink the blockading vessels, and run along the Atlantic coast, and by destroying our men-of-war effectually raise the blockade. And indeed the first reports yesterday seemed as if the threat was actually about to be carried out. It was flashed over the wires that she had sunk the *Cumberland*, captured the *Congress*, and run the *Minnesota* ashore. The prospect seemed to be that she would rush along the Atlantic and Gulf coasts to the Rio Grande, sweeping the seas as she went. But she was no match for the *Monitor,* who has now effectually admonished her to keep out of the Road hereafter. . . .

THE NEWS IN WASHINGTON.

WASHINGTON, SUNDAY, MARCH 9.

The most intense excitement was created in Washington, to-day, by the news from Fortress Monroe, which came by the Baltimore boat. Visions were freely indulged in, of the *Merrimac* running the blockade of the fort, getting to sea, entering New-York harbor, and burning all the shipping at your docks, and holding your city itself at its mercy. The completion of the telegraph line to Fortress Monroe seems providential, in lifting these gloomy fears from the public mind. We only hope that the *Monitor* has done all that is claimed for her; but it is undeniable that yesterday's event in Hampton Roads is of the most exciting character, and should make New-York merchants and shipowners look instantly to their harbor defenses. The Stevens battery that the TIMES has in vain vindicated and urged to completion, might have been finished months ago, and could have sunk the *Merrimac* in twenty minutes; but she has been virtually abandoned by the Government, after the expenditure of half a million dollars on her. It is to be hoped that immediate action will be taken by Congress tomorrow to finish this iron velocipede and put her in commission.

Secretary STANTON gave orders this morning that the fullest reports of the Hampton Roads affair should be allowed to pass over the lines, so as to save the people of Northern cities from any vague fears.

The *Merrimac* is understood to have been under the command of Commandant BUCHANAN, late of the Navy-yard.

Two major Union victories took place on April 7, 1862. A combined task force of army troops under General John Pope and gunboats under Flag Officer Andrew Hull Foote captured Island No. 10 on the Mississippi River (so named because it was the tenth island downriver from the confluence of the Ohio and Mississippi Rivers at Cairo, Illinois) along with its 4,500 Confederate defenders, an important step toward gaining control of the entire Mississippi. On that same day, Union forces at Pittsburg Landing (often misspelled Pittsburgh) on the Tennessee River just north of the Tennessee-Mississippi state line counterattacked to regain the ground lost the previous day by a Confederate attack. This two-day bloodbath has gone down in history as the battle of Shiloh because the initial fighting on the morning of April 6 took place near a small Methodist church of that name. It was the largest battle of the war until that time, with a total of nearly 24,000 killed, wounded, and missing on both sides. One of the killed was Confederate commander Albert Sidney Johnston; the Union commander, Ulysses S. Grant, suffered a wounded reputation because of Union losses on the battle's first day and because of the contemporary belief that only General Don Carlos Buell's overnight reinforcement of Grant's army enabled the Federals to snatch victory from the jaws of defeat.

April 10, 1862.

THE BATTLE OF PITTSBURGH.

Important Particulars of the Terrible Struggle.

The Fight Continued Through Two Days.

Partial Success of the Enemy on Sunday.

Opportune Arrival of Gen. Buell's Forces.

Final Defeat and Flight of the Rebels.

Gen. Albert Sidney Johnston's Body Left on the Field.

Other Prominent Rebel Officers Killed.

Our Probable Loss in Killed, Wounded and Missing Five Thousand.

Gen. Wallace Killed and Gen. Prentiss Taken Prisoner.

Occupation of Corinth by Our Forces.

CAIRO, WEDNESDAY, APRIL 9.

Further advices from Pittsburgh Landing give the following about the battle: The enemy attacked at 4 o'clock Sunday morning, the brigades of Gens. SHERMAN and PRENTISS being first engaged. The attack was successful, and our entire force was driven back to the river, where the advance of the enemy was checked by the fire of the gunboats.

Our force was then increased by the arrival of Gen. GRANT, with the troops from Savanna, and inspirited by reports of the arrival of two divisions of Gen. BUELL's army.

Our loss this day was heavy, and, besides the killed and wounded, embraced our camp equipage and 36 field guns.

The next morning our forces, now amounting to 80,000, assumed the offensive, and by 2 o'clock P.M. had retaken our camp and batteries, together with some 40 of the enemy's guns and a number of prisoners, and the enemy were in full retreat, pursued by our victorious forces.

Our killed, wounded and missing are not less than 5,000.

CHICAGO, WEDNESDAY, APRIL 9.

The *Times*' account of the battle at Pittsburgh Landing on Sunday and Monday, says that the enemy surprised Gen. PRENTISS' Brigade, which was in the advance, five miles beyond Pittsburgh, at 5 o'clock on Sunday morning, taking two regiments prisoners and capturing the General. The fight continued during the entire day, the enemy driving our forces back to Pittsburgh with fearful loss.

Gen. BUELL, with Gen. NELSON's Division, arrived at 4 o'clock, and turned the tide of battle.

The enemy was commanded by Gens. POLK and BEAUREGARD, who suspended the attack about 5 o'clock.

On the morning of Monday, the troops having rested on the field, and being reinforced by Gen. NELSON's Division, supported by the gunboats, drove the enemy back and occupied their former position completely routing the rebels, who were immediately followed by several thousand cavalry, who at last accounts were some miles beyond Corinth.

The *Tribune* places our loss at from 500 to 1,000 killed and 3,000 to 4,000 wounded. The rebel loss is twice that number. *Six of our batteries were taken and retaken six times.*

The *Times* says that Gen. BEAUREGARD had given orders not to destroy any of the camp equipage taken on Sunday, as he *expected a complete victory the next day.*

CHICAGO, WEDNESDAY, APRIL 9.

The *Tribune*'s special from Cairo, 9th, gives the following summary of reports gathered from persons who witnessed the battle at Pittsburgh Landing:

The National army was posted between two streams, about four miles apart, that run into the Tennessee nearly at right angles, within about two miles from Pittsburgh. The left front was commanded by Gen. PRENTISS, who had several raw regiments. In his rear was Gen. SHERMAN, with his division, completely cutting it off from the main army.

Gen. MCCLERNAND put himself at the head of his troops and cut his way through the rebels, and rejoined the army.

The fight had now become desperate, and on Gen. GRANT's assuming command, the enemy were driven back, and the National forces occupied at night nearly the same position they did in the morning. The fight lasted 15 hours.

During the night, Maj.-Gen. LEW. WALLACE came up from Crump's Landing, with 19,000 troops, and in the morning the battle was renewed with great fury, neither party seeming disposed to yield. Between 11 and 12 o'clock the fight was terrific.

Soon after noon, Gen. BUELL had crossed the Tennessee, and attacked the enemy in flank with 40,000 men. The rebels were soon routed, Gen. BUELL pursuing them with 12,000 men, mostly cavalry, and *the latest rumors were that he had taken Corinth.*

Eight hundred wounded are reported to be on the steamer, on the way down. Gen. HALLECK is expected here in the morning *en route* for Tennessee. Several barges of ice are ordered to go up the Tennessee to-night for the use of the wounded.

THE FIRST DETAILED REPORTS.

The following dispatch reached us yesterday morning too late to be inserted in our regular morning edition, but was issued at an early hour in an "Extra:"

PITTSBURGH, *VIA* FORT HENRY,
WEDNESDAY, APRIL 9—3:20 A.M.

The greatest battle of the war has just closed, resulting in the complete rout of the enemy, who attacked us at daybreak Sunday morning. The battle lasted without intermission during the entire day, and was again renewed on Monday morning, and continued undecided until 4 o'clock in the afternoon, when the enemy commenced their retreat and are still flying toward Corinth, pursued by a large force of our cavalry. The slaughter on both sides is immense.

The fight was brought on by a body of three hundred of the Twenty-fifth Missouri Regiment, of Gen. PRENTISS' Division, attacking the advance guard of the rebels, which were supposed to be the pickets of the enemy in front of our camps. The rebels immediately advanced on Gen. PRENTISS' division on the left wing, pouring volley after volley of musketry, and riddling our camps with grape, cannister and shell. Our forces soon formed into line and returned their fire vigorously, and by the time we

THE FIELD OF CONFLICT IN THE SOUTHWEST.

Showing Number Ten, and the Rebel Defences on the River to Memphis; also, Pittsburg Landing, Corinth and the Line of the Tennessee River.

were prepared to receive them, had turned their heaviest fire on the left centre of SHERMAN's Division and drove our men back from their camps, and bringing up a fresh force, opened fire on our left wing, under Gen. MCCLERNAND. This fire was returned with terrible effect and determined spirit by both infantry and artillery, along the whole line for a distance of over four miles.

Gen. HURLBUT's Division was thrown forward to support the centre, when a desperate conflict ensued. The rebels were driven back with terrible slaughter, but soon rallied and drove back our men in turn. From about 9 o'clock, until night closed on the bloody scene, there was no determination of the result of the struggle. The enemy exhibited remarkably good generalship. At times engaging the left with apparently their whole strength, they would suddenly open a terrible and destructive fire on the right or centre. Even our heaviest and most destructive fire upon the enemy did not appear to discourage their solid columns. The fire of Maj. TAYLOR's Chicago Artillery raked them down in scores, but the smoke would no sooner be dispersed than the breach would again be filled.

The most desperate fighting took place late in the afternoon. The rebels knew that if they did not succeed in whipping us then, that their chances for success would be extremely doubtful, as a portion of Gen. BUELL's forces had by this time arrived on the opposite side of the river, and another portion was coming up the river from Savanna. They became aware that we were being reinforced, as they could see Gen. BUELL's troops from the river bank a short distance above us on the left, to which point they had forced their way.

In marked contrast to Grant, Gen. William T. Sherman was an intense, complex, sometimes ruthless soldier, who knew the brutality of war and often inflicted it himself upon the enemy. His unostentatious style provoked the nickname Uncle Billy from some of his men but his trademark steely gaze left no question as to who was in charge.

At five o'clock the rebels had forced our left wing back so as to occupy fully two-thirds of our camp, and were fighting their way forward with a desperate degree of confidence in their efforts to drive us into the river, and at the same time heavily engaged our right.

Up to this time we had received no reinforcements, Gen. LEW. WALLACE failing to come to our support until the day was over, having taken the wrong road from Crump's Landing, and being without other transports than those used for Quartermaster's and Commissary stores, which were too heavily laden to ferry any considerable number of Gen. BUELL's forces across the river, those that were here having been sent to bring up the troops from Savanna. We were, therefore, contesting against fearful odds, our force not exceeding thirty-eight thousand men, while that of the enemy was upwards of sixty thousand.

Our condition at this moment was extremely critical. Large numbers of men, had straggled toward the river, and could not be rallied. Gen GRANT and staff, who had been recklessly riding along the lines during the entire day, amid the unceasing storm of bullets, grape and shell, now rode from right to left, inciting the men to stand firm until our reinforcements could cross the river.

Col. WEBSTER, Chief of Staff, immediately got into position the heaviest pieces of artillery, pointing on the enemy's right, while a large number of the batteries were planted along the entire line, from the river bank northwest to our extreme right, some two and a half miles distant. About an hour before dusk a general cannonading was opened upon the enemy, from along our whole line, with a perpetual crack of musketry. For a short time the rebels replied with vigor and effect, but their return shots grew less frequent and destructive, while ours grew more rapid.

The gunboats *Lexington* and *Tyler,* which lay a short distance off, kept raining shell on the rebel hordes. This last effort was too much for the enemy and ere dusk had set in the firing had nearly ceased when, night coming on, all the combatants rested from their awful work of blood.

Our men rested on their arms in the positions they had at the close of the night, until the forces under Major-General WALLACE arrived and took position on the right, and General BUELL's forces from the opposite side and Savanna were now being conveyed to the battle-ground. The entire right of Gen. NELSON's Division was ordered to form on the right, and the forces under Gen. CRITTENDEN were ordered to his support early in the morning.

THE SECOND DAY'S BATTLE

Gen. BUELL having arrived on Sunday evening, in the morning the hail was opened at daylight, simultaneously by Gen. NELSON's Division on the left, and Major-Gen WALLACE's Division on the right. Gen. NELSON's force opened up a most galling fire on the rebels, and advanced rapidly as they fell back. The fire soon became general along the whole line, and begun to tell terrible effect on the enemy. Generals MCCLERNAND, SHERMAN and HURLBUT's men, though terribly jaded from the previous day's fighting still maintained their honors won at Donelson, but the resistance of the rebels at all points of the attack was worthy a better cause.

But they were not enough for our undaunted bravery, and the dreadful desolation produced by our artillery, which was sweeping them away like chaff before the wind. But knowing that a defeat here would be the death blow to their hopes, and that their all depended upon this great struggle, their Generals still urged them on in the face of destruction, hoping by flanking us on the right to turn the tide of battle. Their success was again for a time cheering, as they began to gain ground on us appearing to have been reinforced; but our left, under Gen. NELSON, was driving them, and with wonderful rapidity, and by eleven o'clock Gen. BUELL's' forces had succeeded in flanking them and capturing their batteries of artillery.

They however again rallied on the left, and recrossed, and the right forced themselves forward in another desperate effort. But reinforcements from Gen. WOOD and Gen. THOMAS were coming in, regiment after regiment, which were sent to Gen. BUELL, who had again commenced to drive the enemy.

About three o'clock in the afternoon Gen. GRANT rode to the left, where the fresh regiments had been ordered, and finding the rebels wavering, sent a portion of his bodyguard to the head of each of five regiments, and then ordered a charge across the field, himself leading, as he brandished his sword and waved them on to the crowning victory, while cannon balls were falling like hail around him.

The men followed with a shout that sounded above the roar and din of the artillery, and the rebels fled in dismay, as from a destroying avalanche, and never made another stand.

Gen. BUELL followed the retreating rebels, driving them in splendid style, and by 5½ o'clock the whole rebel army was in full retreat to Corinth, with our cavalry in hot pursuit, with what further result is not known, they not having returned up to this hour.

We have taken a large amount of their artillery and also a number of prisoners. We lost a number of our forces prisoners yesterday, among whom is Gen. PRENTISS. The number of our force taken has not been ascertained yet. It is reported at several hundred. Gen. PRENTISS was also reported as being wounded. Among the killed on the rebel side was their General-in-Chief, A. SYDNEY JOHNSTON, who was struck by a cannon ball on the afternoon of Sunday. It is further reported that Gen. BEAUREGARD had his arm shot off.

April 11, 1862.

THE BATTLE OF PITTSBURGH.

A Clear and Graphic Account of the Two Days Action.

Splendid Generalship Displayed on Both Sides.

Indomitable Bravery of Our Troops Against Great Odds.

Opportune Service of the Gunboats *Tyler* and *Lexington*.

The Movement of the Union Army Which Caused the Rebel Retreat.

Seventy Thousand Men Engaged on Each Side.

The Rebels Reinforced by Price and Van Dorn.

Reported Capture of John C. Breckinridge.

CINCINNATI, THURSDAY, APRIL 10.

A correspondent of the *Times* writes the following account of the Pittsburgh battle:

Our forces were stationed in the form of a semi-circle, the right resting on a point north of Crump's landing, our centre being in front of the main road to Corinth, and our left extending to the river in the direction of Hamburgh, four miles north of Pittsburgh Landing.

At 2 o'clock, on the morning of the 6th, 400 men of Gen. PRENTISS' Division were attacked by the enemy half a mile in advance of our lines. Our men fell back on the Twenty-fifth Missouri, swiftly pursued by the enemy. The advance of the rebels reached Col. PEABODY's Brigade just as the long roll was sounded, and the men were falling into line. Resistance was but short, and they retreated under a galling fire, until they reached the lines of the Second Division.

At 6 o'clock the attack had become general along our whole front. The enemy, in large numbers, drove in the pickets of Gen. SHERMAN's Division, and fell on the Forty-eighth, Fiftieth and Seventy-second Ohio Regiments. Those troops were never before in action, and being so unexpectedly attacked, made as able a resistance as possible, but were, in common with the forces of Gen. PRENTISS, forced to seek the support of the troops immediately in their rear.

At 10 o'clock the entire line on both sides was fully engaged—the roar of cannon and musketry was without intermission from the main centre to a point extending half way down the left wing. The rebels made a desperate charge on the Fourteenth Ohio battery, which not being sufficiently supported by infantry, fell into their hands. Another severe fight occurred for possession of the Fifth Ohio battery, and three of its guns were taken by the enemy.

By 11 o'clock, a number of commanders of regiments had fallen, and in some cases not a single field officer remained; yet the fighting continued with an earnestness which showed that the contest on both sides was for death or victory. Foot by foot the ground was contested, and finding it impossible to drive back our centre, the enemy slackened their fire, and made vigorous efforts on our left wing, endeavoring to outflank and drive it to the river bank. This wing was under Gen. HURLBUT, and was composed of the Fourteenth, Thirty-second, Forty-fourth and Fifty-seventh Indiana; Eighth, Eighteenth and Twenty-first Illinois. Fronting its line, however, was the Fourteenth, Fifty-seventh and Seventy-seventh Ohio, and Fifth Ohio Cavalry of Gen. SHERMAN's Division. For nearly two hours a sheet of fire blazed from both columns, the rebels fighting with a vigor that was only equaled by those contending with them.

While the contest raged the hottest, the gunboat *Tyler* passed up the river to a point opposite the enemy, and poured in broadsides from her immense guns, greatly aiding in forcing the enemy back.

Up to 3 o'clock the battle raged with a fury that defies description. The rebels had found every attempt to break our lines unavailing. They had striven to drive in our main column, and finding that impossible, had turned all their strength upon our left. Foiled in that quarter, they now made another attempt at our centre, and made every effort to rout our forces before the reinforcements, which had been sent for, should come up.

At 5 o'clock there was a short cessation in the fire of the enemy, their lines falling back for nearly half a mile, when they suddenly wheeled, and again threw their entire forces upon our left wing, determined to make a final struggle in that quarter, but the gunboats *Tyler* and *Lexington* poured in their shot thick and fast, with terrible effect.

Meanwhile Gen. WALLACE, who had taken a circuitous route from Crump's Landing, appeared suddenly on the enemy's right wing. In the face of this combination of circumstances, the rebels felt that their enterprise for the day was a failure, and as night was approaching, fell back until they reached an advantageous position somewhat in the rear, yet occupying the main road to Corinth. The gunboats continued to throw shells at them until out of range.

After a wearied watching of several hours of intense anxiety, the advance regiments of Gen. BUELL appeared on the opposite bank of the river. The work of passing the river began, the Thirty-sixth Indiana and Sixty-eighth Ohio being the first to cross, followed by the main portions of Gens. NELSON and BRUCE's Divisions. Cheer after cheer greeted their arrival, and they were immediately sent to the advance, where they rested on their arms for the night. All night long steamers were engaged

Battery Number 4, constructed by General George McClellan's engineers for the siege of Yorktown. *(Library of Congress)*

ferrying Gen. BUELL's force across, and *when daylight broke, it was evident the rebels, too, had been strongly reinforced.*

The battle was opened by the rebels at 7 o'clock, from the Corinth road, and in half an hour extended along the whole line. At 9 o'clock the sound of artillery and musketry fully equaled that of the previous day. The enemy was met by our reinforcements and the still unwearied soldiers of yesterday, with an energy they certainly could not have expected.

It became evident they were avoiding the extreme of our left wing, and endeavoring, with perseverance and determination, to find some weak point by which to turn our force. *They left one point but to return to it immediately, and then as suddenly would, by some masterly stroke of Generalship, direct a most vigorous attack upon some division where they fancied they would not be expected; but the fire of our lines was as steady as clock-work, and it soon became evident that the enemy considered the task they had undertaken a hopeless one.*

Further reinforcements now began to arrive, and took position on the right of the main centre, under Gen. WALLACE, Gens. GRANT, BUELL, NELSON, SHERMAN and CRITTENDEN were everywhere present, directing movements for a new stroke on the enemy. *Suddenly both wings of our army were turned upon the enemy, with the intention of driving them into an extensive ravine. At the same time a powerful battery, stationed in the open field poured volley after volley of canister into the rebel ranks.*

At 11½ o'clock the roar of the battle shook the earth. The Union guns were fired with all the energy that the prospect of the enemy's defeat inspired, while the rebels' fire was not so vigorous, and *they evinced a desire to withdraw.* They finally fell slowly back keeping up a fire from their artillery and musketry along their whole column as they retreated. They went in excellent order, battling at every advantageous point, and delivering their fire with considerable effect; but from all the divisions of our lines they were closely pursued, a galling fire being kept upon their rear.

The enemy had now been driven beyond our former lines, and were in full retreat for Corinth, pursued by our cavalry.

The forces engaged on both sides in this day's battle are estimated at about 70,000 each.

ACCOUNTS RECEIVED IN CAIRO.

CAIRO, THURSDAY, APRIL 10.

An arrival from Pittsburgh Landing says that the rebels, in making the attack on Sunday morning, carried the Stars and Stripes, and wore the Federal uniform.

General Bragg is reported to have been killed. Provisional Governor JOHNSON of Kentucky, is wounded, and was taken prisoner.

It is stated that Gen. PRENTISS escaped in the confusion of the rebels' retreat on the second day's fight.

Our total loss is about 7,000. This is the estimate of the military commanders who were in the engagement. Of this number 2,000 were taken prisoners, the balance are killed and wounded, in the usual proportions.

Gen. WALLACE of Illinois was reported dead, as it was thought impossible that he could live; he was however, living on Wednesday, and improving. He was shot in the back of the ear, the bullet coming out of his nose.

Gen. HALLECK passed Cairo to-day, *en route* for Pittsburgh Landing.

Five thousand prisoners are expected to arrive here tonight from Island No. 10.

Every preparation is being made here for the reception of our wounded from Pittsburgh.

ACCOUNTS RECEIVED IN CHICAGO

CHICAGO, THURSDAY, APRIL 10.

A special to the Chicago *Tribune,* from Cairo, says:

We are just beginning to get reliable details from the great battle of Pittsburgh. From several gentlemen who were on the field after the fight, the following is gathered:

Gen. PRENTISS' Brigade, consisting of the Sixty-first Illinois, Seventeenth Wisconsin, Twenty-fourth Indiana and Seventy-first Ohio, were attacked while eating their breakfast, by what seemed to be the entire rebel force. Gen. PRENTISS had no artillery, and his brigade was cut to pieces and forced to retire. PRENTISS and many of his men were taken prisoners.

At 12 o'clock, the entire line was engaged, but in full retreat. At 4 o'clock the enemy had taken SCHWARTZ's Battery of six guns, DRESSER's Battery of four guns, and WATERHOUSE's Battery, also, two Ohio batteries, names not known. Thousands of our soldiers who had taken refuge under the bank of the river utterly refused to fight, and in fact, they could not, as officers and men were mixed in inextricable confusion.

The army at this time seemed to be utterly defeated. At this juncture the gunboats *Lexington* and *Tyler* opened a tremendous fire of shot and shell upon the enemy, and kept it up every half hour during the night. Some of the shells set the woods on fire, and many dead rebels were burned.

At 7 in the evening the firing had generally ceased. About midnight the rebels attempted to plant a battery within 300 yards of our siege guns, but were driven away by the gunboats and siege guns, supported by three regiments of Gen. MITCHELL's Division, which had arrived and crossed the river about 6 in the evening.

Our informants persist in estimating our loss on Sunday at 3,000 killed and 6,000 wounded as being a low figure.

During the night the rebels were reinforced by Gen. Van Dorn and Price from Arkansas, with a very large force.

Gen. LEW WALLACE came up with the Eleventh and Twenty-third Indiana, Forty-fourth Illinois, and Eighth Missouri, and WILLARD's Battery, and in the morning fiercely attacked the enemy's left wing. They went into the fight at the double-quick with tremendous shouts, and did terrible execution. By 10 o'clock they had driven the rebels back two miles.

At about 10 o'clock the rebels were reinforced, and for a few minutes our men were forced to yield.

The other divisions of Gen. BUELL's army now appeared, and at once became fully engaged. For two hours all the destructive elements of the earth seemed to be striving for the mastery on this fatal field; but at last the Southern chivalry broke and fled in all directions.

Gen BUELL followed the flying foe with 12,000 troops, mostly cavalry, smiting without mercy, those who would not surrender. *He was reported to have taken Corinth with all its immense stores of arms and ammunition.*

The rebel troops were mostly from Texas, Mississippi and Louisiana, with many from Georgia and Alabama.

Our informants say that they could ride through the battle-field where our forces were posted, *but the dead was so thick in the enemy's lines that they could not do it there.* They assure us that the rebels occupied our camps on Sunday night, and took care of our sick and wounded, destroying nothing, *expecting confidently to have our entire army the next day. They thought the battle already fought and won.*

On Monday, Gen. McClernand cut his way through the enemy that had surrounded him. Most of his troops behaved with great gallantry, but the Fifty-third Ohio was ordered to the rear in disgrace for refusing to fight.

Our informants state that John C. Breckinridge is taken prisoner. They say they saw him pass to the general headquarters.

Chicago, Thursday, April 10.

The *Times*' special, in its account of the Pittsburgh battle says:

Gens. Prentiss and Sherman, with reinforcements from Gen. Hurlbut, maintained their position. The attack gradually extended to the centre, under McClernand, which soon became engaged with a superior force. Up to noon these four division, Prentiss, Sherman, Hurlbut and McClernand's held the entire rebel force in check. Although the enemy was constantly bringing up fresh troops, they gained no advantage until noon. Our lines were unbroken, except Gen. Prentiss' command. They being compelled to fall back, abandoned the camp.

Gens. Beauregard and Johnston commanded on the right, and Gen. Polk on the left.

Shortly after noon, the enemy made a grand attack on our whole line. Our force obstinately held their ground until the enemy hurled the entire force of 70,000 men against us.

Our line fell back, under the pressure, in good order, half or three-quarters of a mile, abandoning the camp to the enemy, taking a position in a semicircle on the bank of the river. Here they stood immovable, and fought obstinately five hours, the ground being fought over and over again.

The gunboats *Tyler* and *Lexington* had got within raking range, and, from their positions on the left, poured in a storm of shot and shell, which fairly annihilated them. Our immense siege guns had the same position on the right, so that, wherever the rebels turned they met iron hail, which scattered them like chaff. They advanced no more, but stubbornly held their position. Night came without any change.

In the meantime Gen. Buell arrived on the opposite bend of the river, having made a forced march all day. Eight regiments were crossed, took position in the centre, and immediately engaged the enemy. The fight continued with unparalleled obstinacy and appalling slaughter till darkness closed.

During the night Gen. Buell crossed with 39,000 men. Gen. Wilson took position on the left, and Gen McCook in the centre.

The battle was renewed in the morning by the rebels, after the arrival of 25,000 reinforcements, under Gen. Bragg, who were precipitated on Sherman's, McClernand's and Wallace's Divisions. They were held in check, however, and at the same time Gen. Nelson threw himself on their right with his division supported by Hurlburt and all the other available force.

The enemy, after maintaining their ground till 3 P.M., gave way. *The decisive blow was given by Gen. Grant, who headed a charge of six regiments in person, and precipitated his whole body on the enemy's centre with such desperate force, that they broke and ran.*

Retreat at once became general. Within half an hour the whole rebel army was falling back in dismay. Our rejoiced soldiers followed them, driving them through our camp in complete disorder. They were soon driven into broken country, where they would not form or fight.

There was no relaxation in the pursuit. At the last accounts the cavalry were eleven miles from the river, still following. The fugitives, exhausted, lay down and wait to be taken prisoner.

We can get no estimate of our loss. It is immense, however. *Some of our regiments had not above one hundred and sixty or two hundred left.*

Gen. PRENTISS displayed conspicuous bravery during the first part of the engagement, and before he was taken, he had just led a gallant charge of 1,000 men against a superior force of the enemy. He was repulsed and received a musket ball in the arm; at the same time his horse was killed. Before he could extricate himself the enemy were upon him.

I am informed on authority direct from the rebel camp, that BEAUREGARD made his advance on Friday to a point within a few miles of Gen. GRANT's position, here formed his line of battle, during the night resumed his march coming upon our forces before daybreak, completely surprising them. *The only wonder is that a rout of our army did not ensue at once.* Gen. HURLBUT, whose Division was in reserve, *made himself the main prop on which the fortunes of the day hung*. He acted with the utmost promptness.

Gen. A. S. JOHNSTON was killed in the forenoon of the second day's fight, during the attack on his position by our force, while endeavoring to rally his men. *Apparently fearless of danger, he rode along the entire front, waving his sword, shouting to his dismayed officers and frightened men.* When the rout was at its height, a cannon ball struck him, crushing his skull, killing him instantly. His body was found by the pursuers and brought to Gen. NELSON's tent.

The most spectacular Union victory in the string of successes for Northern arms in the winter and spring of 1862 was the capture of New Orleans, the South's largest city and port, on April 25, 1862. This feat was achieved entirely by the naval force under the command of David Glasgow Farragut, whose fleet ran the gauntlet of two Confederate forts seventy miles below New Orleans at dawn on April 24 and steamed upriver to subdue the city with eleven-inch guns trained on its streets. In subsequent weeks, Farragut's fleet moved up the river to Vicksburg while the Union river navy fought its way down to that Confederate bastion, which held out for another year.

April 29, 1862.

THE CAPTURE OF NEW-ORLEANS.

The City Occupied by Our Forces.

Additional Particulars from Rebel Sources.

A PANIC THROUGHOUT THE SOUTH.

Preliminary Operations of our Squadron in the Gulf.

The Entrance of Our Flotilla into the Mississippi Passes.

GREAT OBSTACLES OVERCOME.

Reconnaissance Toward the Rebel Forts.

FULL DETAILS OF THE EXPEDITION.

Our Dispatch From Fortress Monroe.

FORTRESS MONROE, SUNDAY, APRIL 27,
VIA BALTIMORE, MONDAY, APRIL 28.

Five contrabands left Portsmouth, opposite Norfolk, at 1 o'clock last night, and arrived here this morning. They bring several late papers and much valuable information. They are intelligent men, and give interesting accounts of affairs in the vicinity of Norfolk. They confirm the reported capture of New-Orleans by our forces, and state that much excitement prevails in the South regarding it.

I send extracts from the Richmond *Enquirer* of the 26th, in which the appearance of the National gunboats before New-Orleans is announced.

[The following telegram announcing the fall of New-Orleans was embodied in Gen. WOOL's dispatch published yesterday, but we reproduce it for the sake of completeness.—Ed. TIMES.]

THE FALL OF NEW-ORLEANS

From the Richmond Enquirer, April 26.

The following telegram from Mobile, dated April 25, was received in Richmond at 11 o'clock P.M.:

> "The enemy passed Fort Jackson at 4 o'clock yesterday morning.
>
> When the news reached New-Orleans the excitement was boundless. Martial law was put in full force, and business was completely suspended.
>
> All the cotton and steamboats, excepting such as were necessary to transport coin, ammunition, etc., were destroyed. At 1 o'clock to-day, the operators bade us good-bye, saying that the enemy had appeared before the city, and this is the last we heard from the Crescent City.
>
> This is all we know regarding the fall. Will send particulars as soon as they can be had."

EDITORIAL COMMENTS.

From the Richmond Enquirer April 26.

Affairs were critical at New-Orleans at this time. On Thursday, according to intelligence received here, two of the enemy's gunboats passed Fort Jackson, and commenced to make cautious observations in the river above. The same information stated that the *Louisiana,* the iron-clad battery, was in position to resist them.

On yesterday, there were reports that an additional number of the enemy's vessels had run by the forts. Telegraphic intercourse with the city of New-Orleans was very difficult, on account, it was stated, of the excitement prevailing there, which had caused a general interruption of business.

THE NEWS FULLY CONFIRMED.

The City of New-Orleans Occupied by the National Forces.

FORTRESS MONROE, APRIL 28, 1862.

The Hon. E. M. Stanton:

News of the occupation of New-Orleans by our forces is confirmed to-day.

No further news. (Signed,)

JOHN E. WOOL, MAJOR-GENERAL COM'G.

To the Associated Press:

A flag of truce to-day took dispatches and letters to prisoners. No papers were received.

The telegraph operators having left New Orleans, there is no news from there. The operators attempted to return, but *found the city occupied by the National forces.*

There is no other news.

WASHINGTON, MONDAY, APRIL 28.

The President has received a special dispatch, to-night, from a source altogether different from that through which the information came yesterday, of the fall of New-Orleans, confirming the same. The President thinks it is a mistake, however, in announcing the city as fallen. He says it fell when it went down with rebeldom; and that now it has risen.

IMPORTANT FROM THE GULF.

Preparations for the Expedition Against New-Orleans.

Full Details of the Movements of the National Forces.

The United States steamer *Connecticut,* Commander WOODHULL, from the blockading squadron, arrived at this port yesterday, bringing the mails and about two hundred sick and wounded seamen, from the various ships of the blockading squadron. She has also several refugees from Texas, who were taken from Matamoras by the United States gunboat *Montgomery.*

The *Connecticut* left the Southwest Pass April 12. The ships of the expedition to New-Orleans were all inside the Passes, and were making preparations to move.

They had their decks sanded, and were all ready for action. The crews of the ships along the coast are all in very good health.

LETTERS FROM OUR SPECIAL CORRESPONDENT.

OFF PILOTTOWN,
SOUTHWEST PASS OF THE MISSISSIPPI,
SATURDAY, MARCH 29, 1862.

The destination of Commodore PORTER's mortar flotilla is no longer a secret. It is bound to the Crescent City. The bomb-schooners are now anchored within the Mississippi Passes, and the large naval fleet of Commodore FARRAGUT, which is to operate conjointly with them, is also here, or hovering along the coast not far away, in readiness for entering the river at the shortest notice.

I last wrote from Ship Island, just after the arrival there of the flotilla from Key West, when none but the leaders of the expedition knew how long we should tarry nor whither our departure would take us. But there was no undue curiosity manifested. Seafaring men seem to be contended creatures, and Captains and crews settled themselves down to routine life, as though unceasing drills with mortar, cannon and small arms were the height of happiness. Without warning, however, on Saturday morning, the 15th inst. after the flotilla had been at Ship Island four days, a signal was made by the flagship to get under weigh, and the signs of prompt obedience were immediately to be seen. Sails were unloosed, the windlasses were manned, and in twenty minutes the twenty-one vessels were bowling along with a fair wind for Pass à l'Outre. As they swept from the roadstead, in a single line, equidistant, the beauty of the scene must have partially recompensed the soldiers on the sand island for their disappointment at the sudden departure. They had confidently hoped, poor fellows, that the advent of the flotilla augured a move for themselves from their dreary post, and their grief must have been poignant when the vessels, like specters, disappeared from their sight.

The next morning the fleet was close to the uninviting mud-banks which mark the entrance to the Mississippi. But there was no wind, and the larger number of the vessels could not make headway against the current, which set them seaward again, and Tuesday morning dawned before they had reassembled. It has been evident from the beginning that Commodore PORTER does not wish to spend time in idleness. While awaiting the concentration of the fleet at Pass à l'Outre, he kept his flagship, the graceful *Harriet Lane,* which had preceded the flotilla from Ship Island, flitting about continually. Now, she generously caught hold of a helpless schooner and dragged her into line; and again, relaxing her man-of-war dignity, she would seize three of the little vixens and dash off with them up the river, as easily as a regular tugboat. After three days' labor, which was often interrupted by the densest of fogs, all the schooners were anchored within the Pass. This result was hastened by the arrival of the steamers *Clifton* and *Westfield,* both of which are gunboats attached to the expedition.

Meanwhile, the schooners had been making their warlike toilettes, and it was interesting to observe the rapidity with which the change was effected in their dress. The flotilla is divided into three divisions of seven vessels in each, and each division prepared itself for action at a given signal. Now you looked upon the little craft and saw the graceful rig and trim looks of pleasure yachts, and in a few moments more they would present the saucy mien of vessels of war. There is a spirit of friendly emulation, a healthy rivalry, existing in the flotilla with reference to rapidity in executing orders, and this manoeuvre of metamorphosing the hound into the bulldog, afforded one of the best opportunities it had had for exhibition. The men were put to their trumps. In less than ten minutes after each division had been signalized to "house topmasts," the sails were stripped from the masts, the rigging cast loose, running gear unrove, and the spars upon the decks of every vessel. Some of the crews were three or four minutes ahead of the others, but all did more than well.

But with the "housing" of the topmasts, this work of preparation was not entirely done. The heavy standing rigging of the foremasts was brought in to the masts and "frapped" around them, the forebooms and gaffs were unshipped and secured with the topmasts on the outside of the vessels, in a manner which is likely to prevent accidents from splinters in case a shot should strike them, and the main decks were cleared of everything which could impeded the rapid handling of the guns. These precautionary measures having been adopted, the fleet is now in fighting trim, fierce and formidable.

The stay at Pass à l'Outre was short. The hind-most vessels had scarcely taken position within the entrance, when another order was given to get under way. An opinion prevailed, naturally enough, that the flotilla was to pass up the river until it encountered rebel obstructions; but such was not the plan or procedure. Some of the vessels (as many as the steamers could manage) were taken in tow, and the rest, with a favorable wind, followed under sail. After reaching the head of the Passes, where the frigates *Hartford* and *Brooklyn,* with five or six gunboats, have stationed themselves as grim sentinels, the flotilla was directed down stream again, and is now anchored about four miles from the entrance of the Southwest Pass, opposite Pilottown.

This Pilottown is a hamlet of about a dozen houses, which, as the name signifies, was formerly the abiding place of the Mississippi Pilots. Months since the rebel rulers in Louisiana made these people desert their homes, and the sole occupants of the place, until within a week or two, have been a family of Germans, who live by oystering and fishing, and who refused to obey the mandate which called upon them to relinquish their possessions. The town is located upon a mudbank, and consists of one street, which runs perhaps half a mile, along the margin of a bayou. The houses, one of which is of considerable size, and had been used as a hotel, are generally well constructed, and superior in every respect to what one might look for in such a locality. Each of them contains some of the heavier kind of household furniture, which could not be conveniently removed in the hurry of the proprietors' departure. But it is a very odd village. It is not founded upon a rock nor upon the sand, but upon the water. The buildings are supported upon piles, driven into the mud, and the Mississippi flows beneath them. There is but one promenade, a plank walk, a few feet wide, which also rests upon piles, and extends the length of the village. Some water is fenced in in front of each house, and some water is fenced in the rear of each house, but for what purpose it is difficult to imagine, except that the inhabitants wished to delude passers-by into the belief that they owned flower and kitchen gardens. I can only think of one class of persons whom living here would please, and that is sportsmen of indolent propensities. They could sit at the upper-story windows, and pop away at canvas-back, widgeon, teal, and other waterfowl, which at early morning, seek minnows and shrimp in these watery enclosures. During my visit to this aquatic region, I tried to find points of resemblance to the description of the deserted "Sweet Auburn," but was not successful in a solitary instance.

The town is now garrisoned by a squad of marines under Lieut. HEISLER of the flagship *Hartford*, and the Stars and Stripes float once more from the staff on the pilot's look-out, where, before secession times the brave flag always floated. Commodore FARRAGUT has made the place a spar-yard, and the sheds and jetties at the easterly end are piled with spare booms, top-masts and other materials, belonging to vessels-of-war, which would be in the way during a battle. In a fight, there is always more danger on ship-board from splinters than from all other causes, and it is fortunate that a convenient place has been found for storing the hamper from which they are produced.

The flotilla has now been here nearly two weeks, and there are no means of telling how much longer it may be delayed. Two causes, I am informed, hinder our advance. The first is, that all the gunboats have not arrived, and without their aid the dismantled schooners could not stem the current and get into line of battle; and the second, that all the steam vessels must replenish their coal-bunkers before they are ready for action. Tugs and colliers are hourly expected. Until they come, we must cultivate patience.

This detention, however, will not be without advantages. On the mortar vessels the crews in a great degree are novices in the use of guns of any description, and the drilling is necessary. For the past few days the exercises of this kind have been almost incessant, and the men work with commendable zeal. Much of my time is passed on board the schooner *Para,* Capt HOOD, (to whom I am indebted for many courtesies,) and in witnessing the drills the hours are relieved of much of the tediousness, which would otherwise mark them. Capt HOOD and his officers do much by their example in the way of instructing the men. A very animating scene is often presented when drilling is in progress simultaneously upon all the vessels, and the air is resonant again and again with sturdy cheering, which tells of victory over the imaginary foe.

But the drilling of the crew is not all that entertains one. There are a hundred little

Admiral Farragut and his fleet captain, Drayton (left to right), on board the USS *Hartford*.

things in the daily routine of life on board a war-vessel which make time pass quickly to an interested observer. Listening to the strange and comical calling and piping of the boatswains is a perennial pleasure. They whistle shrilly through a silver pipe upon the slightest pretence, and follow usually with an order uttered in the hoarsest and harshest tones which vocal organs may make. The Captain of the *Para* wants his gig, and SIMPSON, the boatswain, gives a series of chirps and twitters, and then comes in measured cadence from the cavernous depths of his lungs a sound, which is interpreted "away, there gigsmen, away!" He pipes for everything. There is piping to shorten sail, and piping to make sail; piping to wash clothes and to hang them up to dry; to quarters, and to dismiss from quarters; when a boat comes alongside, and when a boat leaves. But SIMPSON's most elaborate pipes are for dinner and liquor. Upon these occasions he fairly exhausts himself with his whistle, and it is with difficulty that he manages to jerk out the one word, "grub," or "grog," which follows. The "grog" call is made twice a day—at 8 A.M. and 12 M. It is thought so musical, that if we had an Ixion on board I am sure his wheel would stop, or a Sisyphus, his stone would cease rolling. At its sound all work is suspended, and the crew march up to the Master-at-Arms. This functionary has previously stationed himself upon deck with a few half-gill measures and a tub of whisky. As each man files along he receives a measure full of the liquor, which he drinks upon the spot. But these calls and growls of the boatswain are useful in spite of their comicality. His pipes can be heard far above the roaring of the sea and the howling of the wind, where lungs alone would be unable to make orders understood.

I had very nearly forgotten to mention that the gunboat *Owasco,* on her trip from Ship Island to the Passes, a few nights since, captured two rebel schooners, laden with cotton, which had run the blockade from New Orleans. They were concealed under Chandeleur Island, Mississippi Sound, when discovered, and sought to elude detection by lowering their sails. Their names, I believe, are the *President* and *Eugenia*. Prize crews are sent on board, with orders to go to Key West. The sailors and officers of the prizes were distributed among the flotilla. I have conversed with some of them respecting matters at New-Orleans, but I do not place sufficient reliance on the statements to warrant me in repeating them.

Off Pilottown, S. W. Pass of the Mississippi River
Wednesday, April 2, 1862.

Only those who have spent three weeks as we have, in strict isolation from the world, can understand how profound was the feeling of joy which yesterday afternoon pulsated through every heart in the Western Gulf Squadron, at the announcement that the steamer *Connecticut,* with mails from home, was off the bar. She had been expected several days earlier, and the anxiety to receive her news had been greater than usual, in consequence of our latest advices, papers of the 5th of March, having left affairs in that interesting state which augured the quick approach of important movements. We are now in a measure relieved of this tantalizing suspense. For, although the mails have not yet been distributed, the substance of the news has passed from mouth to mouth until all have heard it, and await with keener zest the delivery of the newspapers containing the particular accounts. I have not been able to ascertain what are the latest dates brought down, but I shall long remember the eagerness with which I glanced through a well-worn copy of the Times of the 10th ultimo, giving the news of the disastrous attack upon our vessels in Hampton Roads by the *Merrimac,* and the gallant fighting of the *Monitor.* I was not able to retain the paper long enough to inform myself respecting the evacuation of Manassas, and the proposal before Congress of gradual emancipation of the slaves, but had to be satisfied with the bare fact that such was the news. To-day, if the mail shall have been distributed, I will know all.

This matter of distributing mails in the navy causes much complaint. There seems to be no system about it, and often letters or newspapers remain for weeks within a stone's throw of their destination before being delivered. The most flagrant instance of carelessness of this kind was made known a day or two since. The gunboat *Owasco*, on leaving New-York early in February, brought with her a mail for the fleet. Most of it should have been distributed at Key West six weeks ago, but those to whom the bags were entrusted stowed them away in the vessel's sailroom, where they remained forgotten until last week. Even then they were found by accident. But a truce to grumbling, if I would send the news.

Five weeks since, when I attached myself to the mortar flotilla, its destination was a secret which I made no effort to learn. I determined to follow wherever it went, leaving time to make its developments. In a previous letter I have said that we are bound to New-Orleans. Now, I have to furnish information respecting the forces which are to operate with us. The glory of the achievement is not to rest entirely upon us. It has to be shared with a large and powerful squadron of war vessels under Commodore FARRAGUT, to whose general control the conduct of operations is confided. But the motor fleet still holds its position as the main stay and prominent feature of the expedition.

During the three weeks that I have been at the Passes, the time has been exclusively devoted to preparing for the attack upon the rebel strongholds, with whose reduction rebellion will have been annihilated. Forts St. Phillip and Jackson are nearly opposite each other, about thirty miles from the entrance of the river, and seventeen from the Head of the Passes, where our advanced vessels are anchored. Both these works were unfinished when the rebellion commenced, but the rebels have since had ample time to strengthen them, and they have not failed to render them as nearly impregnable as possible. Fort Jackson only has a tier of casemated guns. All the others are mounted *en barbette.* As the river between the two forts is not more than 700 yards wide, an idea may be formed of the proximity at which the fighting will be done when the vessels attempt to pass up. Recent reconnaissances have been determined that the rebels have probably 175 guns bearing upon the channel. Some of these are of heavy caliber, but nothing can long resist the force which will be brought to oppose them. There is always one advantage on the side of ships against forts. The former can concentrate their fire upon one object, and at the same time be so diffused themselves as to disconcert the garrison. . . .

This is a terrible force to be arrayed against the recusant people of Louisiana; almost double the number of guns and vessels which Commodore DUPONT used so gloriously at Port Royal. But that was a pigmy affair in comparison with the gigantic character of the obstacles to be overcome here. Imagine the storm of destruction which these guns alone can raise, and then think of the fury which can be added to it when 21 mortars simultaneously hurl their missiles. Each mortar shell weighs 200 pounds, (the weight of a barrel of flour,) and five of these shells can be thrown from the entire fleet each minute. Their flight may be gauged with the utmost accuracy. Is it not right to believe that this weight of metal will prove irresistible? When the attack will be made cannot even be conjectured. Commodore FARRAGUT is determined not to move until all his vessels are here. The *Pensacola* and *Mississippi,* two of the largest, are aground on the bar, where they will remain until a heavy southwest gale comes to deepen the water.

The *Hartford* and *Brooklyn*, with from three to four gunboats, form the vanguard of the squadron. They are anchored at the Head of the Passes, in the very place where HOLLINS' ram last summer bore down upon the *Richmond, Preble* and *Vincennes*. Four days since I went up as a guest of the officers of the gunboat *Kinco* to visit this place. There is not so much to interest there as down at Pilottown. For a week or two a pleasant excitement was furnished by expecting a second call from HOLLINS, for whom a reception had been prepared. He, however, has not chosen to come, and our vessels, though unrelaxing in their vigilance, have almost given up the idea of his coming. Every day a little tug leaves the forts and comes within sight of our ships, but she is so fleet that our boats have no chance of getting her within range of their guns.

While I was at the Head of the Passes a reconnaissance was made in the gunboats *Kennebec* and *Wissahickon*, under the direction of Fleet Captain BELL. The vessels approached within two miles of the forts, and remained exposed to their fire for some minutes. The rebels have cut down the trees on the river banks, which obstructed the view. As soon as our vessels appeared Fort St. Phillip opened fire upon them with two rifled guns, which are supposed to be each of 100-pound calibre. Twenty-five or thirty shots were fired, and a shell exploded within twenty yards of the *Kennebec*. She changed her position and another shell burst directly in her wake, showing that the rebels have practiced sufficiently to have the exact range of the channel. Below Fort St. Philip, and opposite a line of eight schooners,

which are moored across the stream, is a small earthwork, probably protecting one end of a chain cable, which the schooners support. This obstruction will not prove formidable, however. We have ways of overcoming it. It is supposed that the vessels may be prepared as fireships, but preparations have been made to meet that contingency. There is a rumor that the enemy has secured quantities of heavy driftwood, which is to be let loose upon our vessels with the force of an avalanche when they arrive opposite the forts. The only thing that gives color to the statement is the fact that very little drift-wood is seen floating down the stream. It is scarcely among the possibilities to hold drifting trees and heavy logs sufficiently long against the force of the current for such a purpose. If the plan were tried it would prove only a temporary obstruction, and none of our vessels except the two or three paddle-wheel steamers would suffer injury.

I observe that each of the large steam vessels belonging to the squadron has taken a very prudent course for protecting their machinery. Heavy chain cables have been securely bolted upon their sides, forming a perfect armor for that part of the ship in which the engine is located. Of course other measures have been taken for putting the vessels in fighting trim. Everything which is unserviceable during a fight has been removed and placed ashore at Pilottown. Thus denuded of their topmasts and other light hamper, they have an air of strength and massiveness, which is simply terrible.

I mentioned that the *Mississippi* and *Pensacola* were aground on the bar. They have been there more than a week attempting its passage. The armament of both has been removed, but neither has been lightened sufficiently to cross until the water becomes higher. Fogs down at the bar seem to be perennial, and impede operations greatly. The steamers *Clifton* and *Westfield* have both been at work upon the helpless vessels, but having exhausted coal, they have had to suspend operations.

The health of the entire squadron is excellent. The mortar captains, a jolly set of fellows, may become ill, however, if something is not done soon. They begin to fret at the lack of opportunity for ridding themselves of the large amount of superfluous energy with which they are imbued.

R. J. W.

For the Confederacy the news from February to June 1862 was mostly bad, as Union naval forces gained control of the interior river networks and Union armies conquered much of Tennessee, northern Mississippi, and southern Louisiana while General George B. McClellan's large Army of the Potomac moved up the peninsula of Virginia formed by the York and James Rivers to within six miles of Richmond. The otherwise indecisive battle of Seven Pines east of Richmond on May 31-June 1 did have one decisive result: Robert E. Lee replaced the wounded Joseph E. Johnston as commander of the Army of Northern Virginia. Lee immediately began planning a counteroffensive, which he carried out in a series of attacks beginning June 26 that came to be known as the Seven Days Battles. At a cost of 20,000 Confederate casualties (compared with 16,000 for McClellan's army), Lee drove the Army of the Potomac away from Richmond to a new base at Harrison's Landing on the James River. Although McClellan tried to save face by calling this retreat a "change of base," everybody else recognized it as a defeat, even though Northern newspapers including *The Times* tried to put the best face on these battles. In the South, Lee emerged as a hero.

July 3, 1862.

HIGHLY IMPORTANT.

A Reliable History of Events Before Richmond from Our Special Correspondents.

FULL DETAILS TO MONDAY NIGHT.

Five Days of Almost Continuous Fighting.

Repulse of the Enemy Near Mechanicsville on Thursday.

Desperate Battle at Gaines' Hill on Friday.

Retreat of Our Forces Across the Chickahominy.

Repulse of the Enemy in Front on Saturday.

Continuous Skirmishing Along the Rear on Sunday.

Another Desperate Battle on Our New Position on Monday.

OUR GUNBOATS ON JAMES RIVER IN ACTION.

The Position of Affairs on Monday Night.

From the Special Correspondents of the New-York Times.

ARMY OF THE POTOMAC, ON THE JAMES RIVER,
MONDAY EVENING, JUNE 30, 1862.

Events of the gravest character have transpired within the last five days, touching the condition and prospects of the army on the Peninsula. Acting under the necessity which the Commanding General has long foreseen, the widely-extended lines of the army, with its miles of well-constructed defences, stretching almost from the James River on the left, to, and beyond the Chickahominy on the right, have been abandoned, and the army before Richmond has fallen back to a more practicable line of defence and attack, upon the James River. Hither the grand army, with its immense artillery and wagon train; its Commissary and Quartermaster's stores; its ammunition; its cattle-drove, of 2,549 head; in fact, its entire *materiel*, horse, foot and dragoons, bag and baggage, have been transferred. This manoeuvre, however—one of the most difficult and dangerous for a commander to execute in the face of the enemy—has been accomplished safely, though under circumstances of difficulty and trial which would have taxed the genius of a Napoleon. *The army has been engaged in constant conflict with the enemy for six days,* during which their highest energies have been taxed to the uttermost. We have had no moment of repose—no opportunity scarcely to properly care for the wounded and to bury the dead. The enemy have closely watched every movement and, with an army more than double that of our own, have had the ability to constantly launch fresh troops upon our rear, an advantage which they have been quick to discover, and remorseless in improving. Their perfect knowledge of the roads, paths and bridges, and the topography of the country, which has taken us time to learn, has placed an immense advantage in their hands. Heaven grant that here under the shadow of these hills, and with the cooperation of the gunboats, our overtaxed soldiers and officers may have that brief repose which is so essential to them. And to the existence of the army itself.

The interruption of all communications with the Government has, no doubt, convulsed the country with anxiety and alarm. A knowledge of the facts, however, will relieve this feeling, while any effort to conceal the truth will not only be fruitless, but will leave the public to imagine a thousand evils which do not exist.

Beginning with the fight at Mechanicsville on Thursday, our advance forces, while steadily falling back, have had a continuous running fight.

On Friday one of the severest battles which was ever fought on this continent occurred on the right of the Chickahominy, near Gaines' Hill. On Saturday, after our forces had retired in good order across the creek and destroyed the bridges, we were attacked in front of our encampments, but Gen. SMITH repulsed the enemy, leaving the ground strewn with his dead.

On Saturday morning, the arrangements have been completed, the wagon train was started on its way to James River and was followed on Sunday morning by the artillery and Commissary train.

Meantime the enemy, getting scent of our movement, strongly reconnoitered our front, and finding that several of our positions had been abandoned, pushed in and attacked us vigorously. Gens. HOOKER and RICHARDSON drove them back, and Gen. MEAGHER's Brigade, always on hand at the right time, charged, and captured two of their guns. The rebels paid a dear price for the information which they obtained. The chief struggle was near Savage's Station.

Anticipating a movement on our right flank, the railroad bridge over the Chickahominy was destroyed on Saturday morning. The rebels, supposing we had fallen back on the White House, sent a large force of infantry, cavalry and artillery in that direction, but after a long, rapid and weary march discovered they had gone on a wild goose chase in the wrong direction. They only found a small force of our infantry and cavalry scattered down to guard the rear, who fell back and escaped from White House Landing. The rest was one of those "howling wildernesses," which the rebels intend to leave for us. All the quartermaster and commissary stores had been removed two days before, and the rubbish burned.

Gen. McCLELLAN and Staff left the headquarters at Savage's Station at daylight on Sunday morning, with a body guard of the Fourth United States Cavalry, and halted some five miles out, after crossing the White Oak Creek.

There were, on Saturday, about one thousand of the wounded and sick, chiefly accumulated from the battle of Friday, many of whom it was found impossible to remove, owing to the nature and severity of their wounds, and as a matter of humanity, as well as of necessity, they were left behind. A great many, however, who could walk slowly followed the track of the army, and the ambulances brought away a great many others.

WITHDRAWING FROM THE FRONT.

Gen. HOOKER's Division broke camp in the entrenchments at 3 o'clock Sunday morning, and Gen. SICKLES' and GROVER's Brigades proceeded to the outposts to relieve Gen. PATTERSON's New-Jersey Brigade. At 5 o'clock A.M. the three brigades fell back to the second line of redouts, where they formed a line of battle with RICHARDSON's and KEARNY's Divisions, and remained until 8 o'clock P.M. On discovering that Gen. HOOKER had fallen back, the enemy advanced his scouts with two field-pieces, and opened a brisk fire upon his rear, along the line of the railroad. Gen. MEAGHER's Brigade made a movement on both the enemy's flanks, while the Eighty-eighth New-York charged in front, and captured two of the guns. The enemy then fell back under cover of the wood. None were killed in HOOKER's Division. In the Twenty-sixth Pennsylvania three were wounded; the First Massachusetts lost two prisoners. One man lost both legs by a shell. KEARNY's and RICHARDSON's Divisions were the last off the field.

On the approach of the rebel force to the Savage's Station, where the hospital was established, a white flag was sent out, and it was met by a Lieutenant Colonel of the Confederates, who gave assurance that the hospital should be respected. There was no firing, purposely, in that direction, and if an occasional shell exploded near the house, it is believed to have been accidental.

When Gen. Robert E. Lee took command of the Confederate forces in June 1862, Northern troops were poised to capture Richmond, the very capital of the Confederacy. Rapidly strengthening and reorganizing a dispirited army, Lee developed a bold and brilliant plan of attack which was to give the South its greatest chance of victory.

About 120 rebel prisoners, who were captured on Friday, accompanied us under guard. On Sunday forenoon an advance body of our cavalry, who were reconnoitering in front, discovered a body of rebel cavalry near a small church, and, after a sharp engagement, put them to flight, killing a considerable number of horses and capturing some twenty-five prisoners, who were added to the group already in hand.

SEDGWICK's Division left the front at daylight, and were engaged by the enemy half way to Savage's Station, which they reached at 5 P.M. Here the enemy's infantry, with a battery, came out of the woods on the right, and attacked them.

The First Maine were advanced on the left, with a line of skirmishers in front. They had twelve wounded, three mortally, viz: SMITH, WREN and TAYLOR. C. W. HASKELL, Company C, was slightly wounded in the hand by a shell.

SEDGWICK's Division crossed the creek at white Oak Swamp about 4 o'clock A.M., Monday. His rear was not annoyed during the night.

KEYES' and PORTER's Divisions had already preceded us on the march, and had reached a position on the James River, near Turkey Island, which is about ten or twelve miles above City Point.

The Engineer Brigade of Gen. WOODBURY preceded the army, and constructed corduroy roads where they were necessary. At the Four-mile Creek, a bridge was built across the run. At the White Oak Swamp Creek two bridges were also constructed by the same valuable corps. One for the passage of the main army train, and the other to accommodate Gen. HEINTZELMAN's Division, who, with HOOKER and RICHARDSON, covered the retreat.

DESTRUCTION OF THE BRIDGES

As the army resumed its march on Monday morning, information was received, through Gen. RICHARDSON, that the enemy was pursuing, and orders were given to destroy the bridges.

The Engineer Corps was detailed for this duty, and also to defend the approach to the place. A wide space of trees had been felled across the creek, and the brigade was deployed as skirmishers at the right and left of the passage. AYRES' battery of six guns was also left to hold the position, and was stationed on the hill overlooking the swamp.

HOW THE RETREAT WAS CONDUCTED

The retreat was conducted in the most perfect order. There was no trepidation or haste; no smashing up of wagons by careless or fast driving, and not a single accident of any consequence is believed to have occurred. A drove of 2,500 fat cattle, under the charge of Col. CLARK, Chief Commissary, and Capt. E. M. BUCHANAN, Commissary of Subsistence on Gen. MCCLELLAN's Staff, were successfully driven along. They had been brought up from the White House, and narrowly escaped stampeding by the rebels.

The country through which we passed contained some of the finest farming lands I had seen in Virginia. Broad farms, with well-grown crops of oats and wheat, were passed along the roads, in which the horses and cattle found abundant forage. The forage of the army had all been consumed the day before, thus relieving the train of an immense burden. Instead of the expected swamps and impassable roads, we found well-traveled country roads in excellent condition, along which the immense artillery and wagon train passed with the greatest ease. After approaching within about five miles of the river, the train was divided, part being sent by each of three roads which converged near the landing. An occasional halt was ordered, to enable the advance to examine the roads and woods in front for a concealed force or masked batteries, but nothing of the kind interrupted our progress. A teamster or some mischievous person would occasionally report that we were attacked in front, which would produce a temporary scare, but beyond this, nothing delayed the movement. The soldiers regarded it as the carrying out of part of a necessary plan—the only dissatisfaction expressed being at the leaving behind of so many of the sick and wounded.

Plenty of provisions and medicines were left for them, however, and if they were permitted to use them, their situation for some time to come will be much better there than with the army in the midst of conflict and alarm.

CARE OF THE SICK AND WOUNDED.

At Savage's Station the Government had made arrangements for the sick and wounded as they were brought from the field. It was under the care of Dr. JOHN SWINBURNE. Dr. BRUNOT, of Pittsburgh, Penn., arrived on Monday with a corps of surgeons and nurses. How many of these remained with the patients I am not able to state. There is a report that a large part of them ran away when the army left. It was certainly a severe test of their philanthropy to be left in rebel hands. The demand for nursing and surgical attendance was so great that large numbers were obliged to wait for long hours before their cases could be reached. The worst cases were attended to first, but there was and have been a great many who never received attentions at all. The entire area in the back and on both sides of the house was covered with the wounded, and there were also some twenty large tents pitched in the garden at the east of the house, filled with sick and wounded. The stores for Mrs. HARRIS, the benevolent lady, who assisted by Mrs. SAMPSON, are devoting themselves to the sick, were delayed at White House, and if they reached Savage's at all, it is doubtful whether the good things were not appropriated by the rebels as soon as they got possession of the place.

Many poor fellows who were scarcely able to drag themselves along, clung to the skirts of their comrades, or hobbled on crutches, apparently dreading more than death itself, falling into the hands of the rebels. Many became so exhausted that they fell by the wayside, and could only be roused and helped forward by the greatest exertion.

THE APPROACH TO JAMES RIVER.

When an aid of Gen. MCCLELLAN rode back and reported that *the way was all open to James River,* a thrill of relief ran through the whole line, and the sight of the green fields skirting its banks was indeed an oasis in the terrible desert of suspense and apprehension through which they had passed. The teams were now put upon a lively trot in order to relieve the pressure upon that portion still in the rear.

Gen. MCCLELLAN and Staff rode ahead and took possession of the old estate known as Malvern Hills, owned by B. F. DEW, one mile back from "Turkey Island Bend." It is a large, old-fashioned estate, originally built by the French, and has near it, in front, an old earthwork constructed by Gen. WASHINGTON during the Revolutionary war. It has a spacious yard shaded by venerable elms and other trees. A fine view of the river can be had from this elevated position. Gen. MCCLELLAN expressed the opinion that *with a brief time to prepare, the position could be held against any force the enemy can bring against us.*

Exhausted by long watching and fatigue, and covered thickly with the dust of the road over which we had passed, many of the officers threw themselves upon the

Company K of the First Pennsylvania Reserves. (Medford Historical Society)

shady and grassy lawn to rest. The soldiers also attracted by the shady trees, surrounded the house, or bivouacked in fields near by.

Gen. McClellan immediately addressed himself to the task of preparing dispatches for the Government.

THE FIRE IN OUR REAR.

At 2 o'clock P.M. firing was heard in the direction of White Oak Swamp, where it was supposed Ayres was holding in check the rebel force who were attempting to cross. This continued for nearly two hours, when sudden and heavy firing began farther to the left, in the direction of Charles City Cross Roads. At this point an immense body of fresh troops, with artillery and cavalry, had made their appearance direct from Richmond, and were engaging our batteries still left to guard the road.

Orders were sent immediately to put the troops in line of battle; and Gens. Porter's and Keyes' commands were soon on the way up the hill, returning from their comfortable encampment beyond Malvern Hills. By 4½ o'clock P.M. the road was thronged with these troops, with artillery and cavalry, hastening to resist the advance of the enemy.

The firing now became more and more rapid, and was evidently approaching our line. The roar of the cannon was incessant, and the dust of the contest swept upward and whirled in eddying clouds above the forest trees, which concealed friend and foe from view.

Members of the Staff and messengers hurriedly mounted and rode to and fro with important orders to the commanding officers. The wagons were drawn up on the right of the field as a kind of temporary breastwork, and the troops were disposed in line of battle at the westward, from which direction the enemy was advancing.

The firing now became incessant, the explosion of shells constant and most terrific from both lines, and the roar of musketry, mingled with the shouts and cheers of the contending forces. If we could have seen them, and estimated their strength or number, it would have been some relief, but they were advancing, apparently, to within less than a mile of our position, under cover of woods. It was very evident that *our men were being driven in, and that, too, by an overwhelming force.* At this juncture two of our gunboats, the *Galena* and *Aroostook* moved forward some half a mile and opened fire upon the left with their 54-pounders, the shells exploding in the edge of the woods along the line of hills where it was supposed the enemy would attempt to turn our left. No doubt these terrific missiles had an excellent effect in deterring them from this enterprise, and in retarding their advance. In so long a range there was danger that some of our own men might be hit, and a signal station was established on the top of an old house overlooking the field, and also commanding a view of the river. The firing from the *Galena* was directed in front by these signals. The *Jacob Bell* and also the *Aroostook* fired several shells during the last part of the battle.

During the evening, and while the fight was going on, crowds of dusty men rushed down to the river, and plunged in to bathe. Considering the circumstances of the army, this was hardly the time to adjust one's toilet.

Meantime the contest raged with terrible fury along our whole front and right. Exploding shells filled the air, and rifled shot screamed overhead. So thick was the cloud of dust enveloping the field, it was impossible, except from the sound, to determine which way the tide of battle ebbed or flowed. The gunboats kept up a discharge of their heavy shells upon the enemy's position. Provost-Marshal PORTER meantime took charge of the disabled and sick soldiers, and conducted them to the rear. A large number of stragglers filled the road, who seemed to have business in an opposite direction from that in which the enemy was coming.

The Prince DE JOINVILLE, with the Duke DE CHARTRES and Count DE PARIS, took charge of dispatches for the Government, and Gen. MCCLELLAN accompanied them as far as the gunboat *Jacob Bell,* on board of which he bade them a final adieu toward evening. The crew manned the rigging, and cheered as the General returned to headquarters.

The day's contest wound up by a diminuendo of musketry, and by dark all firing, except an occasional shot, had ceased. It was too late to obtain any list of killed and wounded, or in fact to learn definitely the result of the fight. The *Jacob Bell* went down to City Point ordering up the *Southfield,* and all the other vessels lying below.

It should be borne in mind that the wide bottoms along the river separate the gunboats in many places, some two miles from the forces operating on the hills. The gunboats *Galena, Maratanza, Aroostook, Maraska* and *Port Royal,* are near by, and ought to be able to render valuable assistance to the army until it can be placed in position to operate. The indications are that the *enemy will continue to harass our positions, and give the troops no rest, day or night, until they have been dislodged or compelled to embark.* Should affairs reach the latter crisis, where are the transports to receive such an army on board, with its immense *materiel* of war? There are scarcely vessels enough now in the James River to take on board the wounded and sick, to say nothing of the army.

The *Jacob Bell* having returned from City Point, was dispatched, about 10 o'clock P.M., to Fortress Monroe, with the Prince De Joinville and companions, who, it was understood, carried dispatches to the War Department.

When the steamer left, all was quiet along the river, and it was supposed that our forces were holding their position at Malvern Hills.

The results of the contest are not known. The fight was a most determined one on both sides.

Transports and steamers were proceeding up the river; among them the *Wilson Small,* of the Sanitary Commission. All their vessels will be needed to remove the sick and wounded. Early arrangements will no doubt be made by the Government for the recovery of the wounded from Savage's Station and from the battle-field of Gaines' Hill.

THE BATTLE OF GAINES' HILL.

Full Details of the Desperate Battle of Friday.

Had the enemy possessed full information of the purpose of our Commanding General they could not have taken better advantage of our position than they did. The fact that our front gave way at Mechanicsville on Thursday, after making a successful stand, and fell back toward Gaines' Hill, seem to have suggested to them that a general retrograde movement was contemplated, and it became their policy to follow and fight us on the retreat. With the Chickahominy in our rear, it was, of course, impossible for our army to cross, successfully, under the enemy's fire; and there is no doubt but that they expected to overtake and compel us to fight or be cut to pieces at the bridge.

On Thursday nearly all the wagons were sent across, to have them out of the way. This movement was going on all day and night, and, if known to the enemy, must have revealed the fact that our army was either about to retreat or to change its position. This was too valuable an opportunity to be lost, and was improved to the best advantage. Our troops had been engaged in an exhausting contest at Mechanicsville the day before. They had plenty of fresh soldiers, and were near their base of operations, from which whole masses could be drawn at an hour's notice. We were separated from our centre by the bridges of the Chickahominy, from which we could obtain reinforcements only by a comparatively tardy and uncertain process. That they brought nearly their whole force against us on that side of the river shows that a determined effort was to be made to compel us to cross the river, and then to pass to the rear and turn our right.

Foreseeing this plan, and without the necessary force to guard against the movement, *the only expedient left was adopted by the Commander of the Union forces. The enemy were to be held in check as long as possible, to enable him to safely withdraw his whole force to the James River, and take up a new position.* Another day and night would, no doubt, have found our entire right abandoned, and the commands of PORTER MCCALL and STONEMAN withdrawn safely to the left of the Chickahominy, and the bridges destroyed, without a battle. That this was not permitted was owing to the watchfulness of the enemy, or to the treason of some one within our lines who possessed a knowledge of our plans.

A precipitate retreat was out of the question. It would have resulted in the sacrifice of the entire right wing. With our retreating forces massed in front of the Woodbury and Grapevine Bridges, along the river bottoms, a pursuing force commanding the eminence at Dr. WILLIAMS' house, would be able to cut them to pieces, or compel a surrender. From the attacking party we here, for the first time, took a position of defence, and accepted the battle which was offered.

THE ATTACK IN THE MORNING.

The enemy skirmishers made their appearance beyond Gen. MORRELL's encampment at an early hour in the morning, and were met by the advance pickets of the Ninth Massachusetts, who engaged them sharply, steadily retiring toward Gaines Hill. During this hour's contest, the Ninth Massachusetts lost a considerable number of their men. They fell back slowly and in good order on the road toward Cold Harbor.

Meantime, MCCALL's Brigade of Pennsylvania reserves, and SYKES' Brigade of regulars took up a position upon the high land overlooking the valley of the Chickahominy, eastward of and near the roads leading from Gaines' Hill to Cold Harbor. Your correspondent arriving at this place just as the troops were coming up, watched with much care the forming of the line of battle, and the disposition of the troops.

SYKES' Brigade, consisting of the Third, Fourth, Twelfth and Thirteenth United States Infantry, DURYEE's Zouaves and WELL's Battery, commanded by Lieut.-Col. R.C. BUCHANAN, were disposed on both sides of the road leading north from Gaines' Hill and parallel to the road to Cold Harbor. The Zouaves were drawn up in the open field, facing the line of the enemy's approach, while the regulars were placed to the right, left and rear. In the game field and along the road, Capt. WEED, in anticipation of the attempt of the enemy to push their lines up the Cold Harbor road to our right, found an admirable position for his battery of 3-inch Parrots, in a wheatfield about forty rods to the right of his original position, on a slight eminence which commanded a cross-road intersecting that to Cold Harbor. Here he could sweep a mile of the cross-road, and effectually prevent the passage of any considerable body of the rebels to the right. Experience soon showed that this position was well chosen, for it proved, during the day, one of the hottest in the fight. Capt. De Hart's Battery was posted further to the left, and directly confronted the rebel line, whose position, though not as yet precisely known, was partially revealed by the sound of his artillery and musketry beyond a belt of woods toward Gaines' Hill. Capt. De Hart's Battery consisted of six 12-pounder Napoleon guns, besides which there was a battery of 3-inch rifled guns, of wrought iron, belonging to the reserves. Capt. Eaton's Battery was on this left, and Capt. Keen's further to his left.

This Capt. Eaton, of Drainsville memory, was killed; Capt. Kerns was wounded; Capts. Whiting, Chambliss, Lieut. Sweet killed, and Lieuts. Arnold, Watkins and one other officer were all wounded during the day. Lieut. Hayden, of Edwards' Battery, and Lieut. Piper were also wounded.

McCall's troops came rather wearily into line. They had been fighting nearly all of the previous day and night, and did not relish being called so soon to the repetition of the entertainment.

Morell's division were disposed in the centre and to the left of the hospital, nearly abreast of Gen. Porter's headquarters.

There was now an intermission of the fire beyond the woods lasting for half an hour—an ominous silence—and all eyes were directed toward the enemy's position to detect, if possible, any movement right or left. The field of conflict about to take place was bounded by the road leading to Cold Harbor, on the west; the meadow or bottom of the Chickahominy on the south and east, and a belt of woods stretching northward nearly parallel with the river. The land is elevated, somewhat undulating, and near the centre contains a thinned growth of pine. Near the north line of this space, and along the road leading to the military bridges are three houses, the first Sally McGee's; the second, Joseph McGee's, at first taken for a hospital, and the third, Dr. Williams' house on the hill, to which all the wounded who were brought off the field were conveyed. Gen. Porter's headquarters was at Adams' house, about a third of a mile distant.

About 10 o'clock the pickets at our right were driven back from the woods skirting the field, and shortly afterward those stationed on the Cross Roads toward the Cold Harbor road, were also driven in. The enemy were silently creeping up to the right. Simultaneously he made his appearance in a green field, directly in front, drawn up in line of battle, and in five minutes their batteries opened on our lines with shell. Following this the enemy had also placed a battery in position, fronting that of Capt. Weed's and commenced fire—the fire of the two rebel batteries being at an angle of 45 degrees to our position, enfilading the troops. There was a temporary panic among horses, men and servants, who plunged, dodged, scampered and skedaddled to get out of range. Your reporter, perfectly cool himself—of course—was twice tossed nearly out of his saddle or thrown over the horse's head, as he raced uncontrolled about the field. A small party of cavalry disgracefully started down the road to get under cover of the woods, but your reporter hailed and brought them to by a word of gentle admonition. They turned and took a short path out to McGee's. Here we found the rifled shot of the rebels flying overhead, and going nearly a mile beyond, close up to Williams' house. Capt. Weed opened his battery, as did those of Tidball's, which was stationed near the same position. The battery of Capt. De Hart also replied vigorously. The Zouaves, who were drawn up in line nearest to the enemy, stood motionless and stern awaiting the onset, while the regulars occupied the field and road, ready to receive and return the rebel fire as soon as they should get within range. The whiz-z-z of Minie bullets, and scream of shell and shot from a dozen different directions, now showed that the work had begun in earnest. The people, old, young, white and black, male and female, occupying the houses near the field, now ran across the field to get under cover of the woods.

The force of the enemy could not be ascertained, as they kept concealed to a great extent, and fired across a small ravine at our line. As they advanced, the Zouaves and regulars also met them, and sturdily maintained their ground.

The position of these batteries and of Sykes' command was not essentially changed during the day. They held their own under a most terrific fire, and to Weed's and Tidball's Batteries is unquestionably due the credit of preventing the flanking of our right.

As the contest thickened, the enemy showed themselves in constantly augmenting numbers. The tide of battle swayed to the left, and finally covered the entire rolling land overlooking the river valley. Details from the Zouaves and other ambulance corps began to bring in the wounded from the field, and soon the hospital was full of the badly wounded. One man whose arm had been torn from his shoulder by a shell, cried with vexation because he could not have time to discharge his musket.

By 2 o'clock, the woods covering the hill were thronged by the two contending armies. The enemy generally advanced in three lines, the first firing and falling down while that behind repeated the same movement. By the time the third line had discharged their pieces, the first had loaded and were ready to rise and fire again.

Thus the battle raged, the enemy at times giving way before the impetuous charges of our men, and again recovering and advancing. The fiercest portion of the fight was near the brow of the hill. Batteries thundered, musketry roared, and the din and noise of the contending forces were terrific.

It was apparent that the rebels were constantly bringing fresh troops upon the field, and there was literally no end to their number.

As soon as it could be done, orders were sent back for reinforcements, and Slocum's Division came over the bridge and marched to the support of our hard-pressed forces. About 5 o'clock the Irish Brigade of Gen. Meagher came upon the field, and with a shout of defiance went in and for a few moments staggered the rebel lines by their persistent and courageous conduct. A few thousand more of such desperate heroes would have turned the tide of battle. The rebels who fell into our hands were furiously drunk, having got a supply of whisky from one of our encampments, where it had been carelessly left by a Commissary.

At this point I find myself obliged to stop writing in order to send forward my copy by my brother reporter. I will finish the account by the next conveyance.

E. S.

July 4, 1862.

FROM GEN. M'CLELLAN.

The Great Battle Continued Through Seven Days.

IMMENSE LOSSES ON BOTH SIDES.

Terrific Onslaught of the Rebels on Our New Position.

Final and Overwhelming Defeat of the Enemy.

Death of Stonewall Jackson and Gen. Barnwell Rhett.

Gen. Magruder Reported to be a Prisoner.

Gen. McClellan Safe and Confident in His New Position.

Arrival of Considerable Reinforcements.

OFFICIAL ADVICES FROM GEN. McCLELLAN.

WASHINGTON, THURSDAY, JULY 3—3:12 P.M.

A dispatch from Gen. MCCLELLAN, just received at the War Department, dated "from Berkley, Harrison's Landing, July 2, 5:30 P.M.," states that he has succeeded in getting his army to that place, on the banks of the James River, and *had lost but one gun,* which had to be abandoned last night, (Tuesday,) because it broke down; that an hour and half ago *the rear of the wagon train was within a mile of the camp, and only one wagon abandoned;* that we had a severe battle yesterday (Tuesday,) *that we beat the enemy today,* the men fighting even better than before; that all the men are in good spirits and that *the reinforcements from Washington have arrived.*

ADVICES FROM FORTRESS MONROE.

FORTRESS MONROE, TUESDAY, JULY 1.

A gun boat has just arrived here from the scene of action yesterday, ten miles above City Point.

That division of our army has been fighting three days, and has retreated about 17 miles.

The fight of yesterday was most terrific, the enemy having three to our one.

The battle commenced with our land forces, and after about four hours' fighting, our gunboats got in range and poured into the rebels a heavy and incessant fire.

This fire the rebels stood about two hours and then retreated.

Our troops have captured, not withstanding their disadvantages, a large number of artillery pieces and 2,000 prisoners.

Among the prisoners captured is the Rebel General MAGRUDER.

The place where this last action took place is near Turkey Creek.

The retreat of the rebels last evening was with great disorder, and their loss has been very heavy, much greater, it is thought, than ours.

There is nothing definite, however, in regard to losses.

In the retreat forced upon Gen. MCCLELLAN by the superior numbers of the enemy, I learned that he had to spike his siege guns and leave them on the field, after burning the carriages. The nature of the ground rendered it impossible to move them.

[This it will be seen, is denied by Gen. MCCLELLAN himself.]

In the retreat many of our sick and wounded were necessarily left behind. There are, of course, innumerable reports and rumors here, but I send only what appears to be authentic.

FORTRESS MONROE, TUESDAY, JULY 1.

The loss of the enemy in killed and wounded alone yesterday (Monday) is said not to have been less than four thousand, but we hear nothing definite of the loss on either side.

Gen. SHIELD's army arrived here this morning and have proceeded up the James River. They came [unintelligible] Annapolis.

FORTRESS MONROE, WEDNESDAY, JULY 2—9 P.M.

The steamer *Daniel Webster* has just arrived here from City Point with upwards of three hundred wounded on board.

A gentlemen, who came down, in charge of them informed me that *yesterday was the sixth day that the battle has been going on, with the most terrific fighting the sun ever shone upon.* It has extended the whole length of our line.

We have lost a great many men in killed, wounded and missing, *probably fifteen to twenty thousand.*

He informed me that Gen. MCCLELLAN's headquarters at Harrison's Landing today and his lines extend five miles above toward Richmond. This move of the right wing of the army was predetermined upon and planned ten days ago and would have been carried out sooner, but for certain reasons well known in the army, but which it would not be proper to state. The enemy's forces have greatly outnumbered ours in almost every action, *but not withstanding that they have been repulsed oftener than not and their loss far exceeds ours.*

Yesterday Gen. MCCLELLAN is said to have *captured a whole rebel brigade, and took from them several rifle cannon, and other pieces.*

It is now said that we have lost very few of our siege guns, most of them having been recovered in safety.

There have been a great many wounded prisoners taken on both sides.

Our informant says that Gen. McClellan and his Staff all agree that the present position of our army is *far more advantageous as a base of operations against Richmond than that hitherto occupied.*

The gunboats can now be brought to bear, and materially aid in carrying on the work.

Some of our regiments have suffered terribly while others have but little. The New-York Fifth, suffered terribly. They made a most heroic struggle, and made great havoc among the enemy. About one-half their number are killed, wounded, and taken prisoners. They were in the fight at Cold Harbor, and fought against desperate odds.

Our left wing was engaged yesterday, July 1 up to 2 o'clock, with the enemy, mostly with artillery.

The enemy's force, gathered from prisoners, who were members of Beauregard's Western army, was 185,000 men, whilst our effective force did not exceed 95,000.

The Richmond *Dispatch,* on Monday, announced the death of Gen. "Stonewall" Jackson and of Gen. Barnwell Rhett, of South Carolina.

ADVICES RECEIVED IN THIS CITY.

A person arrived in this City last evening from the field of battle before Richmond, having left there on Tuesday evening, July 1, at 9 P.M.

At that time Gen. McClellan's advance was three miles northwest of Harrison's Landing, and within fifteen miles of Richmond.

The enemy was terribly repulsed in the battle of Monday, which was sanguinary in the extreme. We were attacked at four different points, and summarily repulsed the enemy three, when they pressed Heintzelman's left very hard, but Sumner went to his relief, and they were finally repulsed with great slaughter. Heintzelman captured eight guns and a whole brigade of rebels, 1,600 including their Colonels—Pendleton, of Louisiana, ex-Congressman Lamar, of Georgia and McGowan, of South Carolina.

Our transportation was all safely removed but seventy-five wagons, which were burned in camp.

The enemy's attack, on Monday, was fierce in the extreme. Kearny, Hooker, Richardson, Sedgwick, Smith, and McClellan participated.

The reserve under McCall suffered severely, and Gens. McCall and Reynolds were probably taken prisoners, as they were missing Tuesday night. Gen. Meade is severely wounded and Gens. Burns and Brooks slightly.

Stonewall Jackson is undoubtedly killed. Gen.McClellan, after the fullest investigation, credits the report: all the prisoners corroborating it.

THE RECENT GREAT BATTLES.

Map Showing Richmond, Fort Darling, the Line of the James River, the Present Location of Gen. McClellan, and the Scene of the Recent Great Battles.

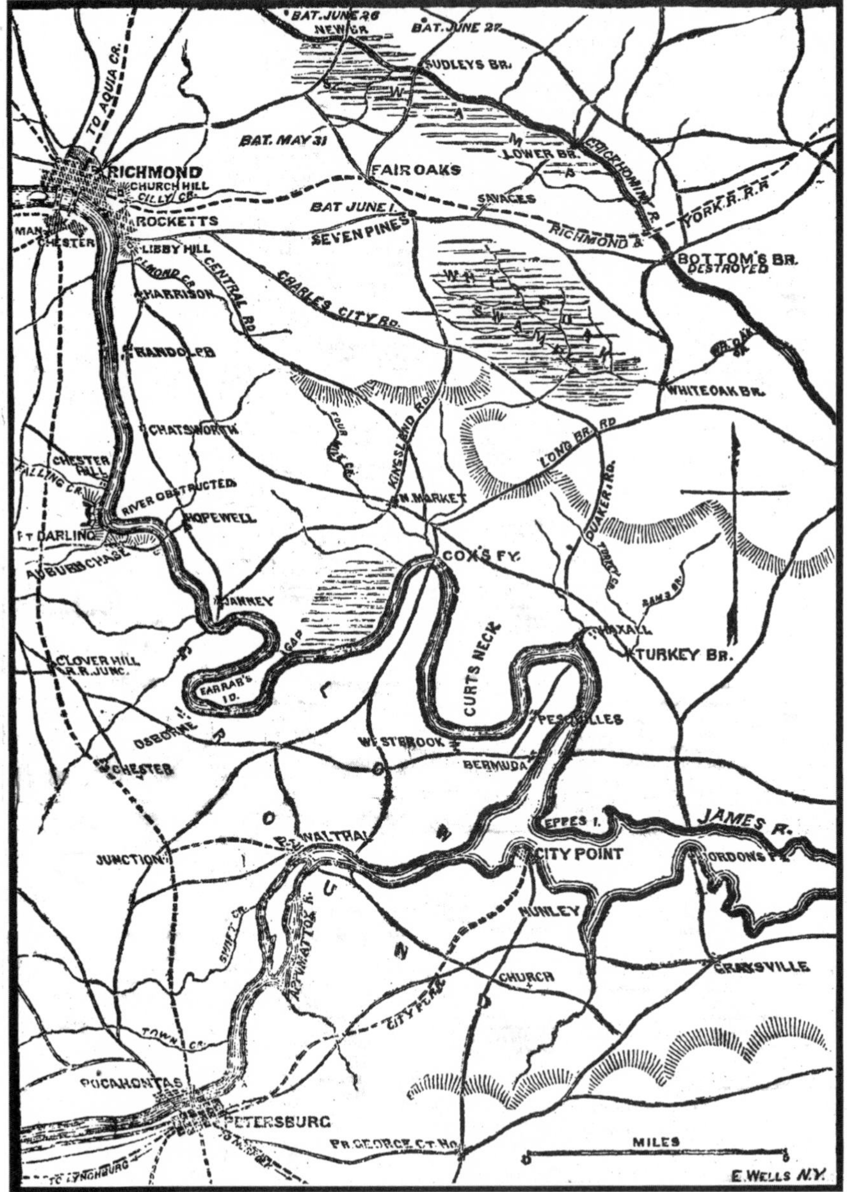

The rebel General S. R. ANDERSON was mortally wounded in the action at Savage's Station on Sunday.

On Monday night entrenchments were begun and prosecuted as rapidly as possible. The first boat of reinforcements arrived just as our correspondent left. Supplies were also coming in abundance.

Our total loss in the whole six days terrible fighting, from Wednesday up to Monday night is about twelve thousand, seven thousand five hundred of which were lost in the battle of Friday on the right.

Col. MCQUAID of New-York, Col. CASS, of Massachusetts, Maj. PATTERSON of Pennsylvania, and all the field officers of the DURYEE Zouaves heretofore reported killed or wounded and many others, are alive and well.

OUR FORTRESS MONROE CORRESPONDENCE

CITY POINT, WEDNESDAY, JULY 2, 1862.

I did not write you yesterday, because the reports were coming in so thick and contradictory, that without having time to thoroughly sift them, you would be just as likely to receive wrong as right information. What little I am now permitted to tell you is, therefore reliable for I have taken pains to obtain it from trustworthy eyewitnesses or from parties who ought to be thoroughly well posted.

Whatever may be the impression in New-York, there is but one conclusion arrived at here by all intelligent people in spite of all that the army peddlers and other skidaddling croakers have to say, and that is that the terrible battle which has been raging for the last four or five days has exhibited the most masterly strategy on the part of MCCLELLAN, and bravery in himself, his officers and his men. So far from there being anything like defeat in his position, it is eminent success, and the enemy, without intending it, could not have better contrived to play into his hands.

I have just been on board the *George Washington,* which arrived this morning with 821 sick and wounded; among others, Gen. MEADE, and Brig.-Gen. W. A. GORMAN of SEDGWICK'S Division—the former wounded very severely by the fragment of a shell passing through his body, and the latter prostrate by sickness. I have had a long and interesting conversation with one of the patients—a Captain of the Twenty-third Pennsylvanian, and a man of great intelligence—and I was glad to find, not only in the facts he advanced, but in the cheerful and confident view he took of the dreadful struggle now going on, a full corroboration of the opinion so earnestly sustained by the TIMES and its correspondents.

The whole affair is simply this: As soon as MCCLELLAN discovered—by the bold raid of STUART near the White House, and other indications—that the enemy had an intent upon that point, he at once came to the conclusion to turn that to account; and, by moving on to a spot that could be of no significance [unintelligible] and order removed from his own base [unintelligible] concentrated his forces on the James River where he could have the aid of our gunboats of the rebels. For this reason—[unintelligible] was made upon [unintelligible] Gen. McClellan had cause to be [reserved] army stores, provisions, [unintelligible] and all the rest by train [unintelligible?], leaving but a small portion [unintelligible] at from $5,000 to $50,000 (though probably nearer the first sum) to be destroyed, in the event of any enemy approaching sooner than they could remove it.

So certain is this, that many days elapsed before there was any demonstration at the White House, loaded vessels were seen coming down the York River and up the James with what intent people did not *then* know, though they do *now.* All this being arranged, orders were given for Porter's wing to fall back, and *he was doing so when attacked by the rebels.* The result was that, after great slaughter on both sides, McClellan has reached the very spot he intended on the James River, with all his equipments and allowed the rebels to go into the very trap he had prepared for them. Does this look like defeat?

Much excitement prevailed here yesterday (Monday) when news came of the bloody work of the last two days, and the information that our army was on rations which must soon be exhausted. This fear is now, however, entirely removed. Boats, loaded with provisions, are rapidly going up the James River in abundance, and twelve vessels had already unloaded when my informant left, which was at 6 o'clock last evening. I was also informed that Gen. McClellan is in a strong position, under cover from gunboats, and able to hold his own until reinforcements come. The latter we know are rapidly on the way to him—though whence and in what number I am not at liberty to say. Well sustained in the position he now holds, there can be no doubting his success.

Some people here are contemplating not only the possibility but the probability of the rebels venturing down the peninsula as far as Yorktown, and even further. It is almost to be hoped they will have the foolhardiness to do so. They might thereby gain the glory of shedding more human blood, but they will only be rushing on their own destruction. Shut up between the York and James rivers, without a plank afloat to confront our gunboats on them, it is difficult to see how they could either hold anything or sustain themselves there, while every man taken from their forces to go there is only increasing McClellan's chances of entering Richmond.

It is the province of those of your correspondents who were on the battle-field to give the details of what passed under their own eyes. I am merely giving you impressions derived from those who actually took a part in the fights, and who betray not the remotest symptoms of despondence. They all assured me that never did a General live who commanded more thoroughly the love of his men, and one of them said, with deep emotion, that there was not a man in his army who would not die for him. Should calamity befall our noble [unintelligible] chieftain before Richmond, through lack of strength before overwhelming numbers—and under all other circumstances

Federal gunners en route to Cedar Mountain, Virginia, August 1862.

could he fail—God help the truckling politicians, who will have brought him and his country to such extremity! He has done all that man can do. He has the endorsement of men, both at home and from abroad, who stand high in the ranks of war; and if disaster attends him, the responsibility not only should, but *will* be placed upon other shoulders than his. To know how deeply the army feel upon this subject, one should mix with them, as we correspondents are compelled to do; and you may depend up it, a long account is being scored up against some political marplots of the Press and Congress.

Amongst the reports here which I have heard, but know not whether to credit or not, is that Gen. McCall was wounded in the neck on Sunday, and is now a prisoner in Richmond; also that "Stonewall" Jackson is killed. . . .

We are awaiting, with intense excitement, the result of the next two or three days; but unless something worse arrives than we would have yet heard, Richmond must and will be ours in a few days.

NEMO

After the Seven Days Battles, the opposing armies in Virginia skirmished warily for several weeks. In August President Lincoln decided to withdraw McClellan's inactive force from the James River to northern Virginia to reinforce the newly formed Union Army of Virginia under General John Pope for a renewed campaign against Richmond from that direction. McClellan was slow to carry out this operation, while Lee shifted his army to meet the new threat. On August 29 Pope attacked Stonewall Jackson's corps of the Army of Northern Virginia near the Bull Run battlefield of the previous year; next day General James Longstreet's corps reinforced Jackson and led a smashing counterattack that once again defeated the Federals, driving them back to Washington. Overoptimistic dispatches from Pope on August 29 and the morning of the 30th misled the Northern press into initial claims of a Union victory, as in these stories in *The Times.*

August 31, 1862.

HIGHLY IMPORTANT.

Defeat of the Rebels on the Old Bull Run Battle-Ground.

DISPATCH FROM GEN. POPE.

A Terrific Battle on Friday, Lasting All Day.

The Combined Forces of the Enemy Engaged.

The Rebels Driven from the Field.

Our Losses Not Less than Eight Thousand Killed and Wounded.

The Rebel Losses Probably Double.

Important Capture Made by our Forces.

Retreat of the Rebels Toward the Mountains on Friday Morning.

PROMPT PURSUIT BY GEN. POPE.

ANOTHER GREAT BATTLE YESTERDAY.

OFFICIAL DISPATCH FROM GEN. POPE.

HEADQUARTERS FIELD OF BATTLE.
GROVETON NEAR GAINESVILLE, AUG. 30, 1862.

To Major-Gen. Halleck, General-in-Chief, Washington, D.C:

We fought a terrific battle here yesterday, *with the combined forces of the enemy,* which lasted with continuous fury from daylight until after dark, by which time *the enemy was driven from the field,* which we now occupy.

Our troops are too much exhausted to push matters, but I shall do so in the course of the morning, as soon as FITZ-JOHN PORTER's corps come up from Manassas.

The enemy is still in our front, but badly used up.

We have lost not less than *eight thousand men killed and wounded,* and from the appearance of the field, *the enemy have lost at least two to our one.* He stood strictly on the defensive, and *every assault was made by ourselves.*

Our troops have behaved splendidly.

The Battle was fought on the identical battle-field of Bull Run which greatly increased the enthusiasm of our men.

The news just reached me from the front that the *enemy is retreating toward the mountains.* I go forward at once to see.

We have made great captures, but I am not able yet to form an idea of their extent.

JOHN POPE, MAJOR-GENERAL COMMANDING

THE SECOND BULL RUN BATTLE

WASHINGTON, SATURDAY, AUG. 30.

To-day's *Evening Star*, speaking of the battle of yesterday says:

"The battle was continued by the army corps of Generals HEINTZELMAN, MCDOWELL and SIGEL [*unintelli*gible] against a [rebel force] believed to number near fifty to sixty thousand strong that is against the army corps of JAMES LONGSTREET. We defeated a portion of the rest of LEE's army that has succeeded in making its way down from White Plains through Thorough-fare Gap.

The location of the battle of the day was in the vicinity of Haymarket, and from Haymarket off in the direction of Sudley Church, or, in other words but a few miles northwest of the scene of the never-to-be-forgotten battle of Bull Run.

HEINTZELMAN's Corps, if we are correctly informed, came up with the enemy's rear about 10 A.M., seven miles from Centreville, which point he left at daybreak.

He found STONEWALL JACKSON fighting with MCDOWELL or SIGEL, or both, on the right, in the direction of Haymarket, the position they took by going north from Gainsville, to command the entrance to and exit from Thorough-fare Gap.

Our own informant, who left Centreville at 4 o'clock in the afternoon, a cool and clear-headed man, says that up to that hour, the impression prevailed there that nothing had definitely resulted from the day's fighting, which, though continuous, had not been a very bloody battle.

Persons subsequently arriving, who were on the field of action themselves until 4 P.M., however, represent that the tide of success was decidedly with the Union army, which pushed the rebels successfully on both sides.

An impression prevails that the reserve of LEE's army, supposed to be from twenty to forty thousand strong, might suddenly appear near the field, and we know that the heavy corps under FITZ-JOHN PORTER was so posted that it could instantly move upon LEE with equal ease, whether attacking MCDOWELL, SIGEL or HEINTZELMAN.

The railroad, we are happy to say, has already been repaired quite up to Bull Run, and supplies, etc., are now being transported over it to that point.

By midnight we have every reason to believe that the Bull Run bridge will again be passable, when the trains can run again to Manassas.

Ere evacuating Manassas, the rebels paroled the 700 Union prisoners they had taken since the commencement of the movement for which they are paying so dearly.

The rebels realized that prisoners in their present strait were an elephant in their hands, and wisely thus got rid of them.

These 700 prisoners covered all the stragglers they had taken, as well as the 500 of TAYLOR's Brigade.

WASHINGTON, SATURDAY, AUG. 30.

The following is gathered from private sources:

On Wednesday morning, or rather on Tuesday night, a report reached Warrenton Junction that JACKSON was again in our rear, and that, instead of making an attack and retiring, as his cavalry did on Friday night last, at Catlett's Station, he had taken up a position on the railroad near Bristor, four miles south of Manassas; had burned two railroad trains, torn up the railroad tracks, cut the telegraph, and took prisoners all the guards along the road.

These reports prove to have been true, and the events of Wednesday showed his determination not to be easily driven from the neighborhood.

It seems from what can be learned from the rebel wounded in our hands, that JACKSON and EWELL started from the vicinity of Warrenton Springs on Sunday, with three divisions, crossed the Rappahancock some six miles south of Blue Ridge, and proceeded by way of Orleans and Salem to Bristor, making the distance in about two and a half days.

On reaching this point their first object of attack was the house of MR. LIPSCOMBE, where ten officers were stopping, and who were on the back porch at the time, smoking.

The house was attacked both front and rear, and the bullet holes in the wood and plaster, with the fact that none of the party were wounded, showed what poor marksmen these rebel cavalry were. The entire party, however, with the exception of Capt. O. A. TILDENMORE, were taken prisoners.

The next attack of the rebels was upon a company of the One Hundred and Fifth Pennsylvania Infantry and some dozen of Pennsylvania Cavalry, left to guard the road, two or three of whom were killed, and the remainder are supposed to be captured.

A train of empty cars then came along from Warrenton, and was fired into by a regiment of infantry and one of cavalry, but escaped without serious injury.

Orders were then issued by JACKSON to tear up the railroad tracks, which was done, and a second train coming along, ran off the track, and was fired into.

A third train following ran into the second and was also fired into, and some persons on board were taken prisoners.

A fourth train made its appearance, but the Engineer suspected something wrong, stopped at a distance and blew a whistle, and being answered by one of the others, backed and returned toward Warrenton.

Two trains were then fired, under the direction of JACKSON, and entirely consumed, excepting the iron-work.

The rebels then proceeded a mile down the tracks, burned the bridge of Cattle Run, tore up some thirty feet of the track, and cut the telegraph.

They also burned the bridge across Broad Run, at Bristor.

On Wednesday morning, EWELL's Rebel Division were placed in position on each side of the railroad, having three batteries, one on the right, one on the left, and the other near the railroad, with infantry and cavalry between, the entire force being concealed behind bush-woods and the artillery with an open field in front.

Our troops sent down from Warrenton Junction to attack them consisted of HOOKER's Division, with a portion of KEARNY's, but the latter, it is said, did not get a chance to enter into the contest.

General HOOKER was in command, and not expecting the enemy to be in any large force, ordered a charge through a piece of woods and into the cleared space, when a most thunderous fire was opened upon him from the entire line of the rebels, their batteries firing grape and canister the most of which, however, went over the heads of our troops. But the fire from the rebel line of infantry was very destructive and some of HOOKER's regiments were commanded to fall back to the woods but on being [surprised?] [they?] retreated, our boys pursuing them, shouting and yelling.

The Third New-Jersey Brigade was commanded by Col. CARR, who had his horse shot under him while urging his men on to an attack. This is the Brigade, though somewhat changed, which so nobly held the extreme left in the battle of Williamsburgh for four hours, sustaining a loss there of over six hundred killed and wounded.

Adjutant BENEDICT's horse was also shot during the action.

Lieut.-Col. POTTER, of the Second Regiment, Excelsior Brigade, was shot in the head while leading his men.

The pursuit continued till dark, the enemy retreating towards Manassas.

The result of this action was that the enemy was beaten and driven from the field, sustaining a loss about equal to our own.

Our loss was about fifty killed and over two hundred wounded, a complete list of which was collected, but stolen.

The Second New-York regiment lost about ten officers and some ninety or one hundred killed and wounded.

The Excelsior Brigade suffered severely.

The physicians on the ground (Dr. MORROW of the Second New Hampshire being the only named I can now recollect) exerted themselves to relieve the wounded; and although the accommodations to operate were very poor, they succeeded during the afternoon and night in attending to all.

Gen. POPE arrived on the ground in the evening and proceeded towards the scene of action, but the fighting was then over and the enemy in full retreat.

JACKSON had left for Manassas during the day with his division, where he pillaged the place, capturing a large number of prisoners, and burning every building, except the telegraph building and a few shanties, after taking off their own old rags, and putting on our good clothing, and helping themselves to food of all kinds, arms, equipments, and whatever else they could carry away out of the cars, about a hundred of which were at that place, for the greater part loaded with supplies for our army.

The rebels then set fire to all the cars, and they now present a mass of bleached ruins.

On their arrival, they found a portion of two New-Jersey Regiments of Infantry, which had arrived there during the forenoon. They immediately attacked them, our troops defending themselves for some time, but finding the number of the enemy so great, and that they were being flanked, they retreated towards Centreville, and got away with the loss of some forty wounded and about twelve killed. The rebels captured six hundred and twenty-five of them, but they were paroled yesterday morning just before the battle commenced.

The pursuit was continued towards Centreville on Thursday afternoon, and a squadron of the Second Pennsylvania Cavalry, with Gen. BIRNEY, was in the advance, and stopped at Centreville to inquire the route taken by the enemy. While there a woman waved a flag from the back window, at which signal a force of rebel cavalry, about 2,000 strong, under Gen. LEE, emerged from the woods. Our men had scarcely time to mount their horses and escape, coming down the road at full speed, the enemy in swift pursuit. They were followed until they came to where our infantry were drawn in line of battle on each side of the road, at which point, the rebels received a volley which caused them to retreat at more than a double-quick.

Our troops took up the line of march, and followed the rebels during the night on the Gainesville or Warrenton road, and soon came in sight of the old Bull Run battleground in strong position, and under cover of the.

The action commenced about 9 o'clock, our batteries having been placed in position, and MILROY's Brigade having the advance, was ordered to charge the rebels through the woods, and to cross toward the railroad switch, when the enemy poured into our troops a perfect storm of grape and canister.

This caused them to fall back, but they soon rallied, and paid the enemy with interest.

The rebels here rose *en masse* behind the railroad track, and again caused our men to fall back, which they did behind HAMPTON's Pittsburgh Battery, which opened upon the rebels terrifically. The enemy were at the time only about thirty yards distant, and the effect of the fire destroyed at least 600 of them. In this action, however, HAMPTON lost one of his guns. He had to change his position to the left, as he was unable to maintain himself under the fire which the rebels poured into him.

The battle in other quarters raged furiously, the general result of which has already been stated from other sources.

The position of the forces on Thursday night remained about the same as it was at the commencement of the action.

The loss on both sides is heavy.

Gen. DURYEE, when engaged in making a reconnaissance to-day, was wounded in the hand.

The fighting up to 12 o'clock to-day was of a desultory character.

We occupy the ground where the rebels had buried their dead.

FIGHTING STOPPED AT NOON YESTERDAY.

PHILADELPHIA, SATURDAY, AUG, 30.

The Washington *Star* says:

"At 12½ o'clock this afternoon. The fighting that has been heard all day stopped, as we learn from parties just down from Fairfax County. We trust this fact means the surrender of the rebels, and we don't see how it can mean aught else."

The *Star* also contains some severe statements on the slow movements of Gen. FRANKLIN's Division which were open to criticism in Washington to-day.

According to the accounts of those last from the battle-field, the belief there was that Jackson was aiming to get off from POPE in the direction of Aldie.

The *Star* doubts this.

A dispatch is published from Capt. MASSER, late Commissary in charge of Centreville, announcing his arrival there with 624 paroled prisoners.

The *Star* contains an urgent call for nurses, for whom prompt railroad transmission has been ordered by the War Department.

PREVIOUS NEWS IN WASHINGTON.

From the Washington Star on Friday Evening.

PHILADELPHIA, SATURDAY, AUG, 30.

We have information that satisfies us that the rebel force that suddenly appeared between the position of the army of Gen. POPE, and at Bristor and Manassas, on Tuesday night last, was the army corps of JACKSON, and STUART's independent cavalry corps. They consisted of infantry and artillery, and marched about thirty thousand strong from near Waterloo, on the head waters of the Rappahannock, around by White Plains to Manassas, about forty miles in two days, without wagons, tents, blankets, or even knapsacks, thus leaving their baggage of every description to be transported by wagons, with the other army corps of LEE's following behind them.

Instead of fighting merely a portion of STUART's Cavalry at Manassas, on the day before yesterday, TAYLOR's brigade were actually confronted by a greater portion of Jackson's *corps d'armée*, Maj. Gens. JACKSON, EWELL, TALIAFERRO, A. P. HILL, and STUART, and the General and Chief, Robert LEE, and his son, Brig. Gen. FITZHUGH LEE, being present at Manassas during the [unintelligible].

Yesterday, at 1 o'clock P.M. JACKSON's advance on [words?] of cavalry and had collected their own wounded of the action of the day before with TAYLOR, if not their wounded of the engagement on the same day with HOOKER, and also the prisoners they took from TAYLOR.

In the afternoon, about 800 of this cavalry force under STUART in person, moved down from Fairfax Court-house to Vienna.

HOOKER's battle, of the day before yesterday, was with EWELL's division, and was a gratifying success.

Maj. Gen. POPE, by 9½ o'clock yesterday morning, had concentrated his very large army, so as to badly interfere with the calculations upon which the rebel Generals must have ventured their bold and extraordinary movement.

At 4 P.M. yesterday an engagement commenced between POPE and JACKSON's rear or LONGSTREET's advance, somewhere about Manassas. If with the former, then HEINTZELMAN's *corps d'armée,* or a portion of it, were engaged on our side. If with the latter, then MCDOWELL or SIGEL, or both, commenced it. It continued through the balance of the afternoon.

We had gotten MCDOWELL's force, including SIGEL's probably, between JACKSON's rear and LONGSTREET's front, and had also all the rest of his army well up within supporting distance. Thus it continued through the balance of the afternoon.

Facts within our knowledge lead to the impression that in twenty-four hours direct communication will have been established between Washington and Maj.-Gen. POPE's army; more especially as there are signs that JACKSON's army corps is endeavoring to proceed northwardly, as though making for the experiment of opposing the reestablishment of such communications with his immediate front, with Pope's army practically between him and the other rebel *corps d'armée.*

We may add that Gen. McClellan is disposing of his heavy Union force around Washington and Alexandria, and the fortifications, so as to make it play an important part in the eventful drama of the hour.

In the battle of yesterday, the attack certainly came from our side.

OUR CORRESPONDENCE FROM THE FIELD.

THE GUERRILLA RAID UPON THE ORANGE AND ALEXANDRIA RAILROAD—THE ATTACK NEAR WHITE PLAINS—CAPTURE OF A NEW-YORK BATTERY AT MANASSAS—THE FIGHT AT BULL RUN, &C.

Headquarters in the Field Between Alexandria and Bristor Station,
Thursday, P.M., Aug. 28, 1862.

I have fortunately been able to obtain some reliable and interesting details of the transactions during Tuesday night and a portion of yesterday (Wednesday,) on the line of the Orange and Alexandria Railroad and vicinity. Tuesday evening, between 5 and 8 o'clock, five trains of empty cars were captured and mostly destroyed by a rebel cavalry force on the road between Bristor Station and Manassas Junction, and on the same evening the enemy destroyed a bridge across Broad River, and subsequently the bridges across other small creeks on the railroad. There were stationed at Manassas Junction, Tuesday, the Twelfth Pennsylvania Cavalry, numbering between 500 and 600 men, Col. White, and the First New-York Battery—10 pieces—with about 300 men to serve them. At 6 o'clock, a dispatch was received by telegraph from Warrenton Junction, directing the cavalry to proceed immediately to White Plains, (15 miles,) on the Manassas road, and keep a sharp look out for the enemy, who, it was understood, had crossed the Rappahannock in force on Sunday, and by the way of Jeffersonton and Little Washington, was making his way for some point on the line of the Orange and Alexandria Railroad, with a view, no doubt, to divide our forces and isolate the command of Gen. Pope—a position which the commander of the Union forces desired him to take, and a fatal one to the enemy it is certainly believed to be. The Pennsylvania cavalry left for the point directed, but finding none of the enemy at White Plains, at a late hour the corps started to return to the Junction. When within eight or nine miles of the latter place, they found a corps of about 1,000 cavalry, supposed to be commanded by Fitzhugh Lee, drawn up to dispute their further progress. A brisk skirmish took place, when our cavalry cut their way through the rebel ranks, losing a number in killed, wounded and prisoners. There was a kind of running fight kept up until the Junction was reached, at about 1 o'clock A.M. of

Wednesday, when the rebels apparently retired satisfied. The cavalry fell back to a position one mile north of the Junction, knows as BEAUREGARD's Headquarters, and were under arms all night, without knowing what had transpired at the Junction during their absence at White Plains. In this interval the rebels had fallen upon the First New-York Artillery by surprise—the officer in command supposing the approaching force to be our own cavalry until too late—and captured eight of their guns. This was not done, however until after a test of sanguinary resistance, resulting in the killing and wounding of [unintelligible] on both sides. A member of the Pennsylvania Cavalry, not knowing that the Junction was in the hands of the rebels, walked very deliberately to the [unintelligible] and finding himself in a trap, coolly asked the first rebel he met "how things were going," and in reply the rebel soldier said, "All right—we have had lots of fun and plunder." Our soldier then attempted to set loose a number of Government horses tied in a stable, when an officer said, "That is not one of our men—shoot him." At about this time the two guns saved from the New-York Battery commenced throwing shell, and this soldier escaped and reached his own command. It was now 7 o'clock Wednesday morning. The rebels occupied the earthworks near the Junction, but after a time advanced from their position and made an unsuccessful attempt to take the remaining guns of the New-York Battery. A running fight was kept up along the line of the railroad, our troops gradually falling back until near mid-day, when at a point one mile south of Fairfax Station, they were met by a force of infantry and artillery under the command of Brig.-Gen. TAYLOR, of New Jersey, and the rebels were driven back to Manassas Junction forthwith. A fact especially worthy of notice in this connection is, that upon the person of a prisoner captured was found a copy of the identical dispatch sent by telegraph from Warrenton Junction, between 4 and 5 o'clock P.M. of Tuesday, directing the cavalry at Manassas Junction to leave for White Plains, so that they were enabled to attack the place when the least resistance could be offered. It is believed by many that this dispatch could not have been obtained in any other way than through the agency of some employe of the Government.

Of the fight that took place Wednesday afternoon with Gen. TAYLOR's force, on the road between Manassas Junction and Bull Run, and at the latter place, but little reliable information can be obtained at this time. The engagement was a sharp and deadly one—the rebels holding their position at night; but those who ought to know what occurred this morning look very good-natured, and hence we, who are in the dark, draw the inference that the rebels got their dessert this morning. The rebel force in action at Bull Run, Wednesday evening, is believed to have been about 5,000 men, principally cavalry and artillery. Our force consisted of ten regiments of infantry, and ten guns. Gen. TAYLOR was so badly wounded in one of his legs, by the explosion of a shell, that the leg was amputated to-day. The Eleventh and Twelfth Ohio Regiments, it is said, suffered the most—the latter having, according to a statement of a member, eighty wounded and twelve killed. The wildest rumor was circulated in

Alexandria to-day about the result of the fight yesterday and this morning, but there is no occasion for any alarm. A force of ____ men, left the vicinity of Alexandria early this morning for the scene of action—a force which, with that under Gen. POPE's immediate command, is sufficient to crush a very respectable force of the enemy. I shall send forth additional details as soon as anything reliable can be obtained. The excitement was somewhat intensified in Alexandria last night, by the 12th Virginia Cavalry rushing into the city in a panic; and the excitement was again renewed this morning by the return of a train of cars that started for Manassas Junction. The train was fired upon when fifteen miles out and returned.

I escaped from the Rappahannock just at the right moment. Had I been 20 minutes later on Tuesday night, I should have been captured by the rebels. The train that kept us company all the way up was nabbed. It is supposed that JACKSON had nearly his whole force near White Plains. If so there is no escape for them as far as I can see. POPE must have 200,000 well-disciplined troops south of JACKSON. There are 75,000 fresh troops encamped about Washington, and then there is an immense force of tried men—say 50,000 men—between this point and JACKSON's position. Gen. MCCLELLAND reached Alexandria Wednesday morning, and was at the telegraph office writing dispatches—orders—nearly all night. He can write with facility with either hand. To-day he is confined to his room by reason of slight indisposition. The rebels captured a saddle of mine at Manassas Junction, and a small bundle of papers and clothing. They were placed on the train just behind the one in which I took passage, by mistake. I hope that HALLECK's infamous order about correspondents will be modified soon. It is very unsatisfactory to be compelled to obtain information as we do now. The Tenth New-York Cavalry, 750 men (new corps), is now passing to the front. They are the finest set of men, and best mounted, in the service. They elicit the admiration of every one.

New regiments are rolling in upon us here almost every hour in the day—quite as fast as they can be accommodated. Three hundred paroled prisoners, I suppose, left Washington yesterday for Dixie, and Fortress Monroe. But these matters you get by telegraph.

The report in the *Tribune* of the fighting on the Rappahannock are, for the most part, grossly erroneous.

THE OPERATIONS OF GEN. TAYLOR'S BRIGADE AT BULL RUN AND VICINITY WEDNESDAY AUG. 27—JACKSON COMPLETELY CUT OFF ON THURSDAY, BY GENERAL HOOKER AND KEARNY

FAIRFAX COURT HOUSE, FRIDAY, AUG. 29, 1862.

In my last I gave you a correct and somewhat detailed account of the operations of the Twentieth Pennsylvania Cavalry, and First New-York Battery at Manassas Junction and vicinity, on Wednesday, the 27th inst., down to the time when they were relieved by reinforcements. To continue in order as the events occurred, Brig.-Gen. TAYLOR, in command of the New Jersey Brigade, 1,600 strong—*all infantry*—left Alexandria early on Wednesday morning, to reinforce the command at Manassas Junction. When one mile north of Bull Run Bridge, they found the track obstructed by the debris of a destroyed train of cars, and, disembarking, proceeded on foot toward Manassas Junction. Upon arriving in sight of the latter place, they saw the Stars and Stripes flying, and heard the roar of cannon; as the flag was there and no shots were directed toward Gen. TAYLOR's column, that officer concluded that our forces were firing upon a force of the enemy beyond, and consequently pressed forward at a double-quick. Too late the discovery was made that the troops at the Junction were rebels, and that the raising of the Stars and Stripes, and the aiming of their guns in an opposite direction was a ruse of the enemy. When within half gunshot distance, the rebels opened upon Gen. TAYLOR's command, right, left, and front, with the eight 32-pound cannon which they had captured a few hours before from the New-York Battery. Their cavalry immediately fired a volley and charged at the same time, which for a moment created a panic in our ranks. Gen. TAYLOR speedily obtained order, and gradually fell back to Bull Run Bridge, he having no artillery or cavalry to use against the rebels. At the latter place Gen. TAYLOR was reinforced by the arrival of the Eleventh and Twelfth Ohio Volunteers—the latter a cavalry corps—and quite a brisk fight took place, when the rebels were finally repulsed. Gen. TAYLOR was wounded in the leg while gallantly rallying his men against a superior force of the enemy, composed of cavalry and artillery. Late at night, the commander of our forces, learning that the rebels had received large reinforcements, fell back to Fairfax Station, and at 11 o'clock at night moved on to this place, as the advance of a large force which left Alexandria on Thursday morning. The rebels had disappeared.

It is alleged that the Twelfth Pennsylvania Cavalry acted in the most scandalous manner at Bull Run, and the bulk of the regiment made a rapid retreat toward Alexandria. To the truth of this, however, I cannot vouch.

JACKSON CUT OFF.

The movements on Thursday, the 28th, were more important than any that have taken place line during the present conflict. Gen. POPE having developed. Gens. HOOKER and KEARNY with their thoroughly [unintelligible] commands advance upon the rear of JACKSON and have forced him to where he is completely cut off, and must, with his whole force, be captured and destroyed unless some stupendous error is made on our side. JACKSON will probably get into Washington somewhat sooner than he expected, and in a manner less agreeable than he anticipated.

There is heavy firing northwest of this place this morning, and it is supposed that our force have compelled Jackson to face about and fight.

IMPORTANT FROM WASHINGTON.

The Significance of the Second Battle of Bull Run.

The Fate of the Bogus Confederacy to be Determined.

THE BULK OF THE REBEL ARMY ENGAGED.

Richmond Almost Deserted.

The Great Struggle Still Proceeding.

Arrangements for the Care of the Wounded.

OUR SPECIAL WASHINGTON DISPATCHES.

WASHINGTON, SATURDAY, AUG. 30.

THE SECOND BATTLE OF BULL RUN.

The Battle of Bull Run substantially began the war—has been the common remark on the streets this morning—and the new battle of Bull Run is now ending it. The rebels have staked everything on this die. They know they must defeat us before the new levies become effective, or their last opportunity is gone; and so, abandoning baggage, and with only such rations as they can carry, they have attempted to fight their way into Washington or Maryland. Four days have been spent in this attempt—three of them in hard fighting. They are in a country utterly barren of supplies, and have been too busy to forage for them, if the country did afford them. The rations they carried with them must be exhausted, and the opinion therefore begins to be suggested as probable, in well informed circles, that to-day's battle, or at least tomorrow's, must exhaust their resources and compel either a surrender or a hasty retreat.

Officials likely to be well informed as to the recent progress of affairs express the utmost confidence both as to the results of the engagement thus far, and the prospects for to-morrow. The cannonading continued up to dark, and unless one party or the other retire under cover of the darkness, it must be renewed with dawn.

There are rumors that the rebels have been heavily reinforced, but they probably arise from the pretty well ascertained fact *that the bulk of the rebel army has been engaged.*

The first definite news of yesterday's engagement reached here early this afternoon. The War Department speedily communicated the facts to the different Departments, and made requests for volunteer nurses to proceed immediately to the battle-field. Most of the bureaus in several Departments were at once left almost destitute of clerks. The following regulations were issued for persons proposing to go down:

Volunteers for attending to the wounded on the battle-field will observe the following directions:

First—The volunteers of each department will be enrolled by one of their own number as chief, and for each division a surgeon will be furnished by the Surgeon-General, under whose directions they will act.

Second—Each volunteer will provide himself with a bucket and tin cup, to supply water, and also a bottle of brandy.

Third—Transportation will be furnished for all as rapidly as possible at the rendezvous, by Capt. Danas, corner of Twenty-second and G streets. Those who can, should provide their own transportation.

Shortly after these regulations were issued, the Government began impressing the hacks and all other means of conveyance. The Street Railroad Company tendered their omnibuses, recently bought from the late omnibus line, and a large number were accepted. Large numbers of citizens began preparing to go down. Many of them have gone already, and many more start out at daybreak.

Trains are running out to Manassas again, and telegraphing communication is restored.

The wounded have already begun to come in from the battle-field of the previous days. Provision can be made to move in the Hospitals already fitted up here for several thousand more—many of the wards having been lately emptied by the return of convalescents to their regiments. Besides these, the hospital accommodations in Baltimore are to be brought into requisition immediately, and some of the wounded have already begun to be sent over. It is also stated that the capitol itself is to be occupied.

THE SOUND OF THE BATTLE.

The *Star* says: "Not only was the sound of the cannonading of the great battle near Centreville to-day, distinctly heard here, but the smell of the gun powder was quite perceptible at times when the wind freshened from that quarter.

Lee's victory at Second Manassas persuaded him to follow up with an invasion of Maryland. At the same time the Confederacy's other major army, the Army of Tennessee, moved north into Kentucky. These dual invasions were the Confederacy's supreme bid to win control of these key border states, earn diplomatic recognition by foreign powers, and conquer a peace by defeating Union armies in their own back yard. But both invasions ran into difficulty from the start. Few Marylanders or Kentuckians rallied to the Confederate cause. Union forces refused to evacuate their garrison at Harpers Ferry, as Lee had expected them to do. He therefore divided his army into four parts, three of them to converge on Harpers Ferry and capture it. A careless courier lost one copy of Lee's order for this operation; four days later a Union corporal found it in a field near Frederick. Learning of Lee's plans from this lucky find, McClellan ordered three corps to fight their way through the gaps in the South Mountain range on September 14 hoping to destroy the enemy forces before they could unite. McClellan moved too slowly to accomplish this goal or to prevent the capture of Harpers Ferry, but in a day-long battle along the ridges between Antietam Creek and the village of Sharpsburg on September 17, the Army of the Potomc stopped the invasion and forced Lee to retreat across the Potomac to Virginia with most of his objectives unachieved. The battle of Antietam was the bloodiest single day of the entire Civil War with 23,000 casualties on both sides, more than 6,000 of them killed or mortally wounded. Three weeks later the Confederate Army of Tennessee was stopped at the battle of Perryville and forced to withdraw from Kentucky.

September 19, 1862.

THE GREAT BATTLES.

The Fighting Continued Through Wednesday.

The Advantages on the Side of the National Army.

THE BATTLE NOT RENEWED YESTERDAY.

Great Extent and Magnitude of the Struggle.

The Entire Rebel Army in Maryland.

A Dispatch from the Gallant General Hooker.

He Claims a Great Victory on Wednesday.

DREADFUL CARNAGE ON BOTH SIDES.

Our Losses Estimated at Ten Thousand Killed and Wounded.

DISPATCH FROM GEN. HOOKER.

CENTREVILLE, MD., WEDNESDAY, SEPT. 17.

A great battle has been fought, and we are victorious. I had the honor to open it yesterday afternoon, and it continued until 10 o'clock this morning, when I was wounded, and compelled to quit the field.

The battle was fought with great violence on both sides.

The carnage has been awful.

I only regret that I was not permitted to take part in the operations until they were concluded, for I had counted on either capturing their army or driving them into the Potomac.

My wound has been painful, but it is not one that will be likely to hold me up. I was shot through the foot.

J. HOOKER, BRIG.-GEN.

NEWS BY WAY OF HARRISBURGH.

HARRISBURGH, PENN., THURSDAY, SEPT. 18.

The news received during last night indicates that the result of yesterday's fight was decidedly in our favor; but still another battle is necessary to determine who shall finally be the victor.

It was expected that the battle would be again renewed this morning, but no firing has been heard, and it is supposed that burying of the dead is the order of the day.

Gen. MCCLELLAN's headquarters are at Sharpsburgh.

Surgeon-Gen. SMITH dispatched a special train to Hagerstown yesterday to attend our wounded.

The number of wounded in Gen. MCCLELLAN's army is very large; most of them will probably be brought into Pennsylvania.

The rebel prisoners taken have been sent to Fort Delaware.

HARRISBURGH, THURSDAY, SEPT. 18—P.M.

Information received here this morning direct from the battlefield, represented that the battle would undoubtedly be resumed to-day, but up to this hour no firing had been heard at Hagerstown. The forces remain about in the same position as in yesterday's fight.

FIELD OF THE LATE AND PENDING BATTLES.

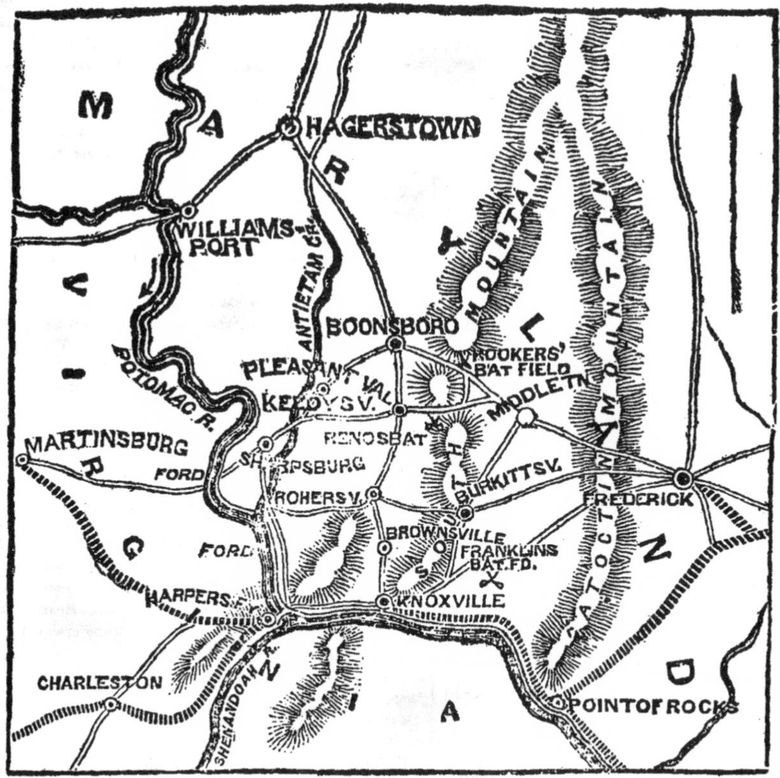

Preparations are now being made here for receiving the sick and wounded from the late battle. Citizens are anxious to do all in their power for the comfort of those who are fighting for the support of the National Government.

Troops are still coming in by thousands and are immediately forwarded. The Government having complete control of the road to Chambersburgh and Hagerstown. The regular trains to these points were suspended to-day, but will be resumed in a few days.

NEWS BY WAY OF PHILADELPHIA.

PHILADELPHIA, THURSDAY, SEPT. 18.

A special dispatch, dated Hagerstown, yesterday, to the *Press,* says of the fight on Tuesday:

The battle raged with great spirit. The firing on either side was very heavy, until toward sundown, when the rebels were flanked by HOOKER and PORTER, and severely punished. Their fire became desultory, and it was evident that their ammunition was giving out.

This morning the battle was renewed by the rebels with renewed vigor. They acted as if they had been reinforced and furnished with fresh ammunition. The battle lasted until 4 o'clock this afternoon, when the rebels retreated, leaving Gen. LONGSTREET and the remnant of his division in our hands as prisoners.

The entire rebel army will be captured or killed. There is no chance left for them to cross the Potomac, as the river is rising and our troops are pushing them continually and sending prisoners to the rear.

Six batteries of artillery belonging to Gen. LONGSTREET's Division were captured yesterday and to-day, and it is said that we have taken nearly 15,000 prisoners since. Sunday.

STONEWALL JACKSON's army is with Gen. LEE and other distinguished officers will be forced to surrender within a day or two at furthest.

Our immense army is in motion, and our Generals are certain of ultimate decisive success.

Stores for our army are coming by way of Harrisburgh and Baltimore.

Gen. BURNSIDE has retaken the position of Harper's Ferry, and is advancing on a special mission with his troops.

NEWS BY WAY OF BALTIMORE.

BALTIMORE, THURSDAY, SEPT. 18.

I was on the battle-field up to 10 o'clock yesterday morning, and left with confidence that all was going on right. It was a grand battle—the most severe of the war—every division of the rebel army being on the field.

From Harrisburgh dispatches and other movements, I think there has been some change in the position of the armies at the close of the day, but have no doubt all is well. Army trains were moving forward from Frederick this morning.

September 20, 1862.

GREAT VICTORY.

The Rebel Army in Full Flight Out of Maryland.

The Dead and Wounded Left Behind.

Our Cavalry Pushing Them Across the Potomac.

The Whole National Army in Good Condition.

Further Details of the Great Battle of Wednesday.

No Fighting of Consequence on Thursday.

Official Dispatches from Gen. McClellan.

HE ANNOUNCES A COMPLETE VICTORY.

DISPATCHES FROM GEN. MCCLELLAN.

FIRST DISPATCH.

HEADQUARTERS ARMY OF POTOMAC,
SEPT. 19—8:30 A.M.

Maj.-Gen. H. W. Halleck, General-in-Chief:

But little occurred yesterday, except skirmishing.

Last night the enemy abandoned his position, leaving his dead and wounded on the field.

We are again in pursuit.

I do not yet know whether he is falling back on an interior position, or crossing the river.

We may safely claim a victory.

GEORGE B. MCCLELLAN,
MAJOR-GENERAL.

SECOND DISPATCH.

HEADQUARTERS ARMY OF POTOMAC,
FRIDAY, SEPT. 19—10½ A.M.

Maj.-Gen. H. W. Halleck, General-in-Chief:

PLEASANTON is driving the enemy across the river.

Our victory was complete.

The enemy is driven back into Virginia. Maryland and Pennsylvania are now safe.

GEO. B. MCCLELLAN, MAJOR-GENERAL.

OUR LATEST WASHINGTON DISPATCHES.

WASHINGTON, FRIDAY, SEPT. 19—11½ P.M.

A special dispatch from the Times' Baltimore correspondent says that Gen. MCCLELLAN's bulletins have greatly discouraged the rebels there. They are inclined to believe that the Confederate combinations have failed, and that their cause is ruined.

WASHINGTON, FRIDAY, SEPT. 19—12 MIDNIGHT.

It is now clearly apparent that the rebel army is repelled from Maryland. Probably nearly or quite the whole has succeeded in crossing the Potomac, with slight additional loss of men, wagons and artillery. It is believed that the rebels can sufficiently defend the most important crossings to allow the bulk of their forces successfully to retreat to Winchester which is probably their base, or to any point they choose.

LATEST REPORTS FROM HEADQUARTERS.

HEADQUARTERS OF THE ARMY OF THE POTOMAC
FRIDAY MORNING, SEPT. 19, 1862.

At daylight, this morning, it was discovered that the enemy had changed their position. Whether their whole force has crossed the river or taken a new position, nearer the river, is not at present known.

Had the rebels remained, a general engagement between both armies would have taken place this morning.

OUR DISPATCHES FROM HARRISBURGH.

HARRISBURGH, FRIDAY, SEPT. 19—1 P.M.

A dispatch just in from Gov. CURTIN, on the battle-field, says that the battle is raging fearfully, and progressing favorably for our side.

McClellan has been largely reinforced. The Pennsylvania militia were also advancing to the field, under Gen. Reynolds.

Surgeon-Gen. Smith has telegraphed to prepare for the wounded to be brought here, and all the churches and other buildings are being got ready.

There is intense excitement, but every one is full of hope.

Harrisburgh, Friday, Sept. 19—3 P.M.

By an official telegram just received, we learn that our victory is complete. The enemy is in full retreat, and our forces are driving them to the river.

No details at present.

FROM THE ASSOCIATED PRESS CORRESPONDENT.

Harrisburgh, Friday, Sept. 19.

Information just received from the battle-field says our victory is complete, and that Gen. Pleasonton is in hot pursuit of the enemy, and driving them across the Potomac. The whole Federal army is in good condition, and the enemy has been badly punished.

THE GREAT BATTLE OF WEDNESDAY.

Baltimore, Friday, Sept. 19.

A gentleman who left the battle-field at 9 o'clock on Wednesday night, confirms the statement of the reporter of the Associated Press at headquarters, in every particular.

He says that our forces occupied the position chosen by the enemy at the commencement of the battle, and that the rebels were driven back a mile and a half at all points, except upon our extreme right, which they still held at the close of the day.

Our informant was all day within a hundred yards of Gen. McClellan, and says that the results of the day were regarded by him and his Staff as a glorious victory, though not a final one.

There was no faltering at any point of the line of our whole army.

Our soldiers were exultant at the results of the day's fight, and Gen. McClellan was in the highest spirits.

The opinion of Gen. McClelland and those around him was that the final result would depend on who got reinforcements first.

Our informant says that nothing had been heard on the field of the capture of Gen. Longstreet or the killing of Gen. Hill, and that there is no truth in either report.

Twenty thousand more reinforcements were expected to reach the field yesterday from Harrisburgh.

Our informant thinks the loss of the rebels fully equal to ours.

The gentleman who furnished us with the fore-going intelligence is one of our most respectable and intelligent citizens, and says that the battle of Wednesday was not a decisive one. It was a contest in which all the advantages were with Gen. McCLELLAN, who occupied the field of battle at the close of the day.

GEN. MANSFIELD.

Brig.-Gen. J. K. F. MANSFIELD, killed at the battle of Sharpsburgh on Wednesday, was a native of Connecticut, from which State he was appointed a cadet to the West Point Military Academy in Oct., 1817. He was at the time of his death about sixty years of age. He graduated on the 30th of June, 1822, standing No. 2 in a class of forty members, among whom are the Gens. HUNTER, McCALL and others noted during the present war. On the 1st of July, 1822, he was brevetted a Second Lieutenant of a corps of Engineers and received his full rank the same day. On the 5th of March, 1832, he was promoted to a First Lieutenancy, and on the 7th of July, 1838, became Captain. He served in the Texan and Mexican wars, and on the 9th of May, 1846, was brevetted Major for gallant and distinguished services in the defense of Fort Browne, in Texas. On the 23rd of the following September, he was brevetted Lieutenant-Colonel for gallant and meritorious conduct in the several battles of Monterey, in Mexico, on the 21st, 22d and 23d of September, 1846.

On the first of those days he was severely wounded. He was brevetted Colonel on the 23d of February 1847, for gallant and meritorious conduct at Buena Vista. During the campaigns of 1846 and 1847 of the war with Mexico he held the position of Chief Engineer of the army under Gen. TAYLOR. Previous to the war he had been appointed as member of the Board of Engineers, viz.: From Dec. 8, 1842, to Sept. 8, 1845, and after the war he resumed this same position, which he kept for some time. On the 18th of May, 1853, he was appointed as Inspector-General of the United States Army, with the rank of Colonel. This position he held at the breaking out of the rebellion. On the 6th day of May, 1861, he was brevetted a Brigadier-General of the Regular United States Army, and on the 14th of May, 1861, he was commissioned a full Brigadier-General. He was placed in command of the position at Newport News, which he held until the advance upon Norfolk transferred his services to the other shore of the James River.

He was next placed in command at Suffolk, Va. When Gen. POPE met with his reverses in Virginia, and demanded a Court of Inquiry to examine into the conduct of certain of his officers, Gen. MANSFIELD was ordered to proceed to Washington to sit as one of the Court. The inquiry having been postponed, by order of the President, at the request of Gen. McCLELLAN, Gen. MANSFIELD was assigned a post of duty in the field. In the discharge of that duty he fell, at the post of honor.

COL. MCNEIL.

Among the killed in this week's terrible battles in Maryland, is Col. McNeil, the commander of the justly celebrated "Bucktail" Regiment, while leading a charge at the head of his men, near Antietam Creek. Hugh Watson McNeal was a son of Rev. A. McNeal, a Cameronian clergyman, and was born in Seneca County, New-York, in 1830. He was educated at Yale College, and entered upon the study of the law in the office of Clarence W. Seward at Auburn.

In 1857 he commenced practice in this city but was obliged to abandon his profession two years afterward by reason of ill health. He removed to [unintelligible] and engaged in [unintelligible] upon the breaking out of the rebellion he enlisted as a private in a company known as "Wild Cats," commanded by Capt. Stone, whereby he was afterwards posted with the famous "Bucktail" Regiment. In a short time he was comissioned Lieutenant and then Captain. In this capacity he led the regiment in a magnificent bayonet charge at Drainesville. The exploits of the regiment are familiar to all. While with McDowell on the Rappahannock; while in pursuit of Stonewall Jackson up the Shenandoah Valley, under Fremont, and particularly at the spirited battle of Cross Keys, the Bucktails gained the foremost name for valor and vigor. And since then they have not ceased for a day to harass the enemy. They accompanied Gen. Hooker in the recent expedition up the Potomac in quest of Stonewall Jackson. On Tuesday they came up with the enemy under Lee, near Sharpsburgh. The National troops were disposed in order of battle. The Bucktails were at the front. The action commenced at dark and lasted two hours. Col. McNeil had just charged upon the rebel forces, driving them back half a mile, when he received his death wound.

He was a daring and intrepid officer, a generous friend and kinsman, the idol of his family and regiment, and his loss cannot be replaced.

BATTLE OF ANTIETAM CREEK.

Full Particulars from Our Special Correspondent.

The Most Stupendous Struggle of Modern Times.

The Battle Won by Consummate Generalship.

The Rebel Losses Estimated as High as Thirty Thousand.

A GREAT NUMBER OF PRISONERS CAPTURED.

BATTLE-FIELD OF ANTIETAM CREEK,
THURSDAY, SEPTEMBER 18, 1862.

Another great battle has been fought, and the cause of the Union has once more been vindicated upon one of the most bloody and well-contested fields known to ancient or modern times. Wednesday, Sept. 17, 1862, will, we predict, hereafter be looked upon as an epoch in the history of the rebellion, from which will date the inauguration of its downfall. On that day about one hundred and sixty thousand men met in deadly strife upon the field of Antietam—a name which will occupy a leading position in the history of the war—and there, marshaled by brave and able men, fought with a desperation and courage never before excelled and rarely, if ever equaled, for twelve hours, leaving the Union army in possession of the contested ground. This victory was not gained, however, without the sacrifice of many valuable lives, and the maiming of thousands of individuals.

PRECEDING EVENTS.

Before attempting to present even a glance at this battle, let us first prepare the reader
192 for a correct understanding of it by relating—in continuation of my last letter—the events immediately preceding the great contest. My last brought Gen. MCCLELLAN's advance into Maryland up to midday on Tuesday, Sept. 16, at which time the army occupied a position in close proximity to the road leading from Boonesville to Sharpsburgh, and upon and near the left bank of the little creek known by the name of Antietam, which rises in Central Pennsylvania, and, after running in a southerly direction, its waters are mingled with the turgid waters of the Potomac, and about five miles above Harper's Ferry.

The enemy occupied a position on the right bank of the Antietam, favorably located for both offensive and defensive operations, and in this respect had the advantage. To circumvent the enemy, and secure an equally favorable position, was the first object to be obtained. That this required the genius of a great leader, needed no military man to elucidate, for the whole position of affairs could be taken in at a glance. How well and successfully this object was accomplished, the success of our army is abundant evidence. Of some of the details of the movement to this end we shall give in the proper place. Just across the creek, in plain view from the eastern bank, the enemy's skirmishers could be distinctly seen, and from elevated positions massed forces of infantry and cavalry could be discovered in every little valley and ravine for miles on either hand. Two hundred thousand men was what the enemy pretended to have within the scope of the eye, and from repeated personal inspection, aided by an excellent glass, while standing in a favorable position, I should judge the figure named not an exaggerated one.

PREPARATIONS FOR A MOVEMENT.

Between 12 and 2 o'clock P.M. all was silent along the lines. The German Battery of sixteen 20-pound Parrott guns, upon the eminence overlooking the river's bank were silent. Major ARNDT had fallen, and the infantry battalions were quietly resting upon the ground under the hill, upon the tops of which were planted our artillery. This quietness was like the quietness that precedes the storm. The Commanding General had arrived upon the ground at an early hour the day before, and had made himself familiar with the position, and at the time of which we write was busily engaged in giving the necessary instructions to the Commanders of Corps, so as to render our success in the impending conflict as much a matter of certainty as possible.

THE MOVEMENT.

Soon after 2 o'clock P.M. the Parrott guns to which allusion has been made before, were opened upon the enemy and worked with great rapidity, and nearly every shell thrown, as I afterward ascertained, did fearful execution in the massed columns of the enemy. In a brief space after this terrible fire had been opened, there was a movement of the troops inexplicable to the uninitiated at the movement but the object of which was soon revealed to the careful observer. The Antietam was to be crossed! Gen. HOOKER's Corps, by a flank movement, gained a [point?] to the north of between two or three miles, and changing direction to the left reached the river at Kelly's Ford. A portion of the Pennsylvania Reserve, under command of Brig. Gen. MEADE were thrown across the river and were deployed as Skirmishers, and under their cover and the gunnery of the German New York Battery, Gen. HOOKER and most of the missiles were thrown too high, hence our loss at this point was comparatively trifling. This battery was speedily silenced, and the rapid movements of Gen. HOOKER's column soon placed it in jeopardy; but the enemy, always on the alert, managed to get their pieces out of the way before a battery could be thrown across to sustain the infantry column in its local movements. The enemy's skirmishers were forced back step by step by the Reserves to their main body, by which time the whole of the advancing column was in position, and ready for more decisive offensive operations. The enemy rushed forward seemingly bent upon annihilating the comparatively small force sent against them, and several times there was some wavering under the terrible and impetuous resistance—but the troops quickly rallied, and, under the lead of their able commander, secured the much coveted and necessary position to secure success. This movement across the river was one for which Gen. HOOKER was peculiarly qualified, and he executed it in a manner highly creditable to his skill as a General. Here the battle of Antietam commenced in earnest. Until nightfall set in Gen. Hooker pressed the enemy back, and every step was gained by hard fighting.

THE DEMONSTRATION TO THE LEFT.

Tuesday afternoon Gen. Burnside's column was brought up to the river and directed to make a demonstration on the enemy's right, by crossing the stream three or four miles below the point where Gen. Hooker had crossed, with a view to secure a stone bridge—to facilitate the crossing of artillery and munitions—and also to threaten the enemy's right flank, to correspond with the demonstrations of Gen. Hooker on his (the enemy's) left, which was to be the real point of attack. This order was promptly obeyed, and carried out with alacrity. Gen. Burnside, by dark, had arrived at the point of crossing, and on the following morning forced the enemy back from the bridge, and rendered important aid with his artillery.

TUESDAY NIGHT.

194 During the night of Tuesday, Gen. Banks' Corps, then under the command of Gen. Mansfield, who was killed early the following day, Gen. Franklin's Corps and two divisions of Gen. Sumner's Corps—Sedgwick's and French's—were thrown across the river at the ford to sustain Gen. Hooker, when the line of battle was formed in the following order: Gen. Hooker on the right; Gen. Sumner—the line running nearly north and south—the left, inclining toward the river and in a direction a little to the east of south. Gen. Franklin's force was placed in a reserve on the right. On Wednesday morning early the balance of Gen. Sumner's Corps—Gen. Richardson's Division—was thrown across the creek and extended the line to the left; the commands of Gens. Morell, Fitz-John Porter and Couch were brought on to the field later in the day, but were not required, and were therefore held in reserve.

THE BATTLE OF ANTIETAM.

On Wednesday morning, Sept. 17, the sun rose in a cloudless sky, and all nature seemed to smile as if the world were filled with the elect of God. But its splendors were soon dimmed with the smoke rising from the battle-field.

To enable the reader to understand the events of this day, he should look at a map which had laid out the principal roads throughout the State of Maryland. With a pencil follow the road of "pike" from Boonsboro' direct to Sharpsburgh—which is nearly three miles west of the river, at the point where the road crosses it; the battle-field is on both sides of that road—between the river and Sharpsburgh—the bulk of it being north of the Boonsboro' road, and in the triangle formed by the roads connecting Bakersville and Middletown and Bakersville and Sharpsburgh. The surface is interspersed with hill and vale, and covered with cornfields and grassland, and skimming and stretching toward the centre from different points are thin belts of forest trees—all of which gives advantage to the enemy acting on the defensive, he having an opportunity to select his position for defensive operations, and when forced from one position he had only to fall back a short distance to find a position naturally as strong as the first. The engagement was opened early Wednesday morning by the advance of a strong line of our skirmishers. They were met by a similar movement on the part of the enemy. The latter were forced back onto the right of our line. Gen. HOOKER came into action with the enemy's left, commanded by Gen. HILL who commanded a portion of LONGSTREET's Corps. BANK's corps was, within that hour, at work, and was followed soon after by Gen. PATTERSON's command. The first fire was at about 5 o'clock and at 6 o'clock the infantry arm entered upon its work. The line [unintelligible].

THE ENEMY'S LEFT WAS FORCED BACK.

For nearly three miles from the ford, where the bulk of our troops crossed the creek before 9 o'clock, when they were relieved by Gen. SEDGWICK's coming to the front. Just previous to this, MORRIS' Brigade, of HOOKER's command, had advanced from a belt of timber across a plowed field, into a place of woods, where the enemy, massed in great force, was repulsed, and the troops fell back to the belt of timber in some disorder, but soon rallied again, and regained the field in front. It was at this moment that Gen. MANSFIELD, in command of Gen. BANK's corps, was mortally wounded, carried from the field and died soon afterward. Gen. WILLIAMS succeeded to the command of the corps, and Gen. CRAWFORD took command of WILLIAMS's Division until he was wounded and taken from the field. The repulse of MORRIS' Brigade was accomplished by an old and contemptible trick of the enemy. As the corps advanced to the woods across the plowed field, the rebels unfurled the Stars and Stripes, and waving them, cried out "What the h—are you doing? Don't fire upon your friends!" Our troops, deceived by this ruse, ceased firing, when the rebels opened upon them a thunderous volley of musketry and cross fire, and creating a temporary panic. They rallied and drove the enemy back, but it was done at a great sacrifice of life. These troops were relieved by:

GEN. SEDGWICK'S COMMAND

coming up on their left. The enemy who had gained a point of extending some distance in front of our line, at the left of Gen. BANKS' corps, were drawn out, and across a plowed field in front, to the center beyond, with terrible slaughter AYER's battery opening upon them with grapeshot, strewing the ground with the dead. At one point, just on the brow of a little roll of the ground that the infantry, emerging suddenly upon the open field, supposed that it was a rebel company coming for them and the dead rebels got an extra volley. This corps came into action by brigades, between 8 and 9 o'clock—GORMAN's, DANA's and HOWARD's. While preparing for action, the enemy appeared from an unexpected quarter, and opened a terrific fire with a view of breaking the line by a sudden attack with musketry and artillery, he believing that it was composed of raw troops. But they soon discovered their mistake; these veterans, notwithstanding the sudden attack, though their lines were broken for a moment, were not disconcerted, but received it with cheers. While under this galling fire the Fifteenth Regiment Massachusetts Volunteers made a dash forward and seized the battle-flag of one of Gen. HILL's regiments, and now have it to show to their friends as a trophy of the day. In this connection it should be mentioned that Capt. HOWE and Lieut. WHITTIER, of Gen. SEDGWICK's Staff, distinguished themselves in the action by rallying the left of Gen. SEDGWICK's division, and on several occasions, by their example, they encouraged the men in discharging their duties faithfully. Gen. SEDGWICK's horse was killed, and he was wounded twice, but remained on the field until he was ordered to the rear with his command.

FRENCH'S DIVISION.

The division under Gen. FRENCH occupied a position to the left of SEDGWICK's, and was fairly engaged by 10½ o'clock. The fighting on the extreme right at this time was confined mostly to artillery, while the tide of infantry fighting swept along toward the left of our line. The left of this division gave way and fell back from the superior force they had to contend against—the rebel hordes making pell mell after them. The left fell back in pretty good order, and upon a walk, under as galling a fire of musketry as is often experienced. This movement was evidently no fault of the men. The rebels advanced, and as they ventured a little to the rear of our line at that point, Col. BURKE (acting Brigadier-General in Gen. RICHARDSON's Division,) changed his front, and poured in several volleys upon their flank, strewing the ground with dead. The balance, hastened somewhat by a crossfire from AYER's battery, fled in utter dismay. The left of FRENCH's Division advanced again, and fought like heroes until ordered to the rear.

RICHARDSON'S DIVISION.

Three Brigades of this Division, commanded by Gen. MEAGHER, Gen. CALDWELL and Col. BURKE's Tenth Pennsylvania, did not cross the creek until Wednesday morning, when Gen. RICHARDSON was ordered to form on the left of FRENCH's Division. The Division, crossed the river and moved up with alacrity near the line of battle, ready for action. Having filed about through the valleys to avoid letting the enemy know of the movement, the Division laid down under the brow of a hill, just in rear of the line of battle, until wanted. It was now about 9 o'clock.

THE IRISH BRIGADE

In less than half an hour after taking this position Gen. MEAGHER was ordered to enter the line with the Irish Brigade. They marched up to the brow of the hill, cheering as they went, let by Gen. MEAGHER in person, and were welcomed with cheers by FRENCH's Brigade. The musketry fighting at this point was the severest and most deadly ever witnessed before—so acknowledged by veterans in the service. Men on both sides fell in large numbers every moment, and those who were eye-witnesses of the struggle did not suppose it possible for a single man to escape. The enemy here, at first, were concealed behind a knoll, so that only their heads were exposed. The brigade advanced up the slope with a cheer, when a most deadly fire was poured in by a second line of the enemy concealed in the Sharpsburgh road, which at this place is several feet lower than the surrounding surface, forming a complete rifle-pit, and also from a force partially concealed still further to the rear.

At this time the color-bearer in the right wing advanced several paces to the front, and defiantly waved his flag in the face of the enemy; as if by a miracle, he escaped without serious injury.

The line of the brigade, in its advance up the hill, was broken in the center temporarily by an obstruction, the right wing having advanced to keep up with the center and fell back a short distance, when Gen. MEAGHER directed then that a rail fence which the enemy a few minutes before had been fighting behind should be torn down. His men, in face of a galling fire, obeyed the order when the whole brigade advanced to the brow the hill, cheering as they went and causing the enemy to fall back to the second line—the Strasburgh road, which is about three feet lower than the surrounding surface. In this road was massed a large force of infantry, here was the most hotly contested point of the day. Each brigade of this Division was in turn brought into action at this point and the struggle was truly terrific for more than four hours—the enemy finally, however, were forced from their position. In this work the New-York German Battery, stationed on the hill across the Creek, rendered efficient service by pouring in upon their massed forces a constant stream of 20-pound shells.

Gen. CALDWELL's Brigade was next ordered into action by Gen. RICHARDSON in person. They two advanced in good order, cheering, and were received with cheers by the Irish Brigade. It was at about this time that the left of FRENCH's Division, commanded by Col. BROOKS of the Tenth Pennsylvania, was directed by Gen. RICHARDSON to wheel to the right, and a murderous flanking fire was poured into the flank of an advancing division of the enemy, causing him to recoil, and fall back in disorder.

This division was actively engaged for nearly five hours, and lost nearly half of the men taken into action. The fight, which had opened by five o'clock in the morning, gradually swept down to the left of the main line, where it opened at about 9 o'clock. Soon after this time, Gen. BURNSIDE's guns were heard on the extreme left, on the flank of the enemy, he having obtained possession of the stone bridge across the creek on the Strasburgh road. This seemed to surprise the rebels, and a desperate effort was made to change their line of battle so as to repel the flanking movement on their right. To this end their line was extended, and large [unintelligible] were thrown off to meet Gen. BURNSIDE so that by 12 o'clock the rebel line of battle, having been forced back on the right, was [unintelligible]. Toward night our infantry got to work on the extreme left, the rebel ranks gave way at all points—but in good order, and the day's fighting was brought to a close by a heavy artillery fire—and the enemy, in the language of the cannonading General, were just where he wanted them.

It was undoubtedly the intention of Gen. LEE to repeat here what he accomplished at Richmond—crush our right wing by throwing upon it the bulk of the force at his disposal; and nothing but the most consummate generalship prevented him from succeeding in his pet scheme. In selecting Gen. HOOKER to take the initiative in this important movement, the right man was put in the right place. He soon discovered the intended movement, and he was heavily reinforced during Tuesday night, so that when the enemy marched down his massed columns upon our right, they were everywhere repulsed with great slaughter.

On Wednesday afternoon as the storm of battle passed to the left, Gen. McCLELLAN rode along the lines at the right and was received with the greatest enthusiasm by the forces at that point. While Gen. SUMNER actually had charge of the field operations, Gen. McCLELLAN visited every part of the field in person, and by his presence encouraged the troops to deeds of valor. Gen. SUMNER more particularly paid attention to the right, for he saw Gen. RICHARDSON was on the left with his own (SUMNER's) old corps and his services were not particularly needed there.

As a whole, officers and men all did their duty. As there are exceptions to all rules, so there is to this. Two regiments, at least, marched from the field during the hottest of the conflict; and, in one instance, at least, the officers with the lead in this apparently disgraceful movement. We refrain from indicating these regiments until such time as their conduct is officially noticed. . . .

THE BATTLE OF WEDNESDAY.

Another Detailed Account of the Great Struggle.

From the Tribune Extra.

BATTLE-FIELD OF SHARPSBURGH,
WEDNESDAY EVENING, SEPT 17, 1862.

Fierce and desperate battle between 200,000 men has raged since daylight, yet night closes on an uncertain field. It is the greatest fight since Waterloo—all over the field contested with an obstinacy equal even to Waterloo. If not wholly a victory to-night, I believe it is the prelude to a victory to-morrow. But what can be foretold of the future of a fight in which from 5 in the morning till 7 at night the best troops of the continent have fought without decisive result?

I have no time for speculation—no time even to gather details of the battle—only time to state its broadest features—then mount and spur for New-York.

After the brilliant victory near Middletown, Gen. McCLELLAN pushed forward his army rapidly, and reached Keedysville with three corps on Monday night. That march has already been described. On the day following, the two armies faced each other idly, until night. Artillery was busy at intervals; once in the morning, opening with spirit, and continuing for half an hour with vigor, till the rebel battery, as usual, was silenced.

McCLELLAN was on the hill where BENJAMIN's battery was stationed, and found himself suddenly under a rather heavy fire. It was still uncertain whether the rebels were retreating or reinforcing—their batteries would remain in position in either case, and as they had withdrawn nearly all their troops from view, there was only the doubtful indication of columns of dust to the rear.

On the evening of Tuesday, HOOKER was ordered to cross the Antietam Creek with his corps, and, feeling the left of the enemy, be ready to attack next morning. During the day of apparent inactivity, McCLELLAN had been maturing his plan of battle, of which HOOKER's movement was one development.

The position on either side was peculiar. When RICHARDSON advanced on Monday he found the enemy deployed and displayed in force on a crescent-shaped ridge, the outline of which followed more or less exactly the course of Antietam Creek. Their lines were then forming, and the revelation of force in front of the ground which they really intended to hold, was probably meant to delay our attack until their arrangements to receive it were complete.

During the day they kept their troops exposed and did not move them, even to avoid the artillery fire, which must have been occasionally annoying. Next morning the lines and columns which had darkened cornfields and hill crests, had been withdrawn. Broken and wooded ground behind the sheltering hills concealed the rebel masses. What from our front looked like only a narrow summit fringed with woods, was a broad table-land of forest and ravine, cover for troops everywhere, nowhere easy access for an enemy. The smoothly-sloping surface in front and the sweeping crescent of slowly mingling lines was all a delusion. It was all a rebel stronghold beyond.

Under the base of these hills runs the deep stream called Antietam Creek, fordable only at distant points. Three bridges cross it, one on the Hagerstown road, one on the Sharpsburgh pike, one to the left in a deep recess of sleepy falling hills. HOOKER passed the first to reach the ford by which he crossed, and it was held by PLEASONTON with a reserve of cavalry during the battle. The second was close under the rebel centre, and no way important to yesterday's fight. At the third BURNSIDE attacked and finally crossed. Between the first and third lay most of the battle lines. They stretched four miles from right to left. . . .

September 21, 1862.

THE GREAT VICTORY.

Latest Reports from the Headquarters of the Army.

The Flight of the Rebel Army into Virginia.

A Portion of our Army Across the Potomac in Pursuit.

Heavy Losses of the Rebels on Wednesday.

The Reoccupation of Harper's Ferry by Our Forces.

Rumored Capture of Stonewall Jackson and His Entire Army.

Army Supplies and Hospital Stores Going Forward from Washington.

LATEST REPORTS FROM HEADQUARTERS

HEADQUARTERS ARMY OF THE POTOMAC,
SATURDAY MORNING, SEPT. 20.

The rebel army has succeeded in making its escape from Maryland. They commenced to leave about dusk on Thursday evening, and by daylight yesterday morning were all over, except a small rear-guard. They saved all their transportation, and carried off all their wounded but about 300. And 400 rebel stragglers were taken during the day by Gen. PLEASONTON's cavalry, who took the advance.

Nearly every house in Sharpsburgh was struck by our shells. Two were burnt, and also a large barn located in the centre of the town. The citizens who remained escaped injury by staying in their cellars. One child was killed. Two rebels, while cooking their supper on Tuesday, were killed by one of our shots passing through the kitchen.

The name given to this battle is the Antietam.

After our forces occupied the whole field, the rebel loss was found to be far greater, particularly in killed than was at first supposed. Fully 2,500 were found lying on the field, while a larger number had been buried the day before by their friends.

Their loss in killed and wounded will not come far from 18,000 to 20,000.

THE BATTLE OF ANTIETAM.

Further Particulars from Our Special Correspondent.

INCIDENTS OF THE BATTLE-FIELD.

Effect of the Rebel Raid into Maryland—Swindling the People—Shooting at Women—Jackson's Losses—The Battle-ground—Shocking Scenes—The New Hampshire Fifth—A Daring Act—The 9th New-York—The 63d New-York—Death at the Post of Duty—A Death Struggle, &c.

NEAR THE BATTLE-FIELD OF ANTIETAM,
FRIDAY, SEPTEMBER 19, 1862.

The smoke of the battle has cleared away; the Grand Army, which, in this campaign, at least, has not been thwarted in one single contemplated movement, is moving on to fulfill the object of its mission, and the enemy having fled in confusion before it have a moment's leisure to survey the scene of the late conflict, relate some interesting particulars, omitted in the hurry attending the preparation of my letter giving a general description of the battle, and more calmly look at the results of the campaign in Maryland.

Of the advance of the army but little need be said at this time—only that it is marching as fast as circumstances permit, and that the first great object—the driving of the enemy from Maryland—has been accomplished.

The visit of STONEWALL JACKSON to this State, while attended with much evil, has not been entirely unproductive of good. There has been a deep secession current operating upon the people of this State ever since the heresy of secession assumed a tangible shape. Her people have been wheddled and cajoled with the bauble, until a large number of them were anxiously looking forward to the precious moment when they could fairly clutch it. The day which had long been deferred at length arrived, and JACKSON, with his dirty ragged, and shoeless followers, entered this—to them—Paradise. The land was overflowing with milk and honey—or, to a more practical figure—the land was full of just what Jackson's army stood most in need of—something to eat, and something to wear, and he and they luxuriated to their heart's' content. They played the *rôle* of gentlemanly robbers to perfection, and were so polite in their robberies that some of the people did not discover they had been dealing with swindlers until it was too late to correct the error they had made. The block-headed dueler dies a gentleman and the wanton asks to be treated like a lady, so JACKSON and his horde committed the most wanton and cruel acts with a bland smile and as graceful a bow as the original BEAU BRUMMELL could have made, and asked it to be borne in mind that he was polite and courteous. But with the retreating form of the rebel chief the illusion which the secession bauble had thrown around the people began to be dispelled. They began to realize that they had been stripped of everything, and only received in return a worthless mess of pottage, otherwise, confederate "I.O.U.'s" worth, perhaps, in good time, when rags are scarce, two cents per pound. Those from whose eyes the scales did not drop at once, found their sight when McClellan's army came along for what the first did not steal the latter borrowed, and the upshot of the matter is, some of Maryland's more fortunate neighbors will have to supply her people with something to eat.

Rely upon it, that the raid of Jackson into this State has forever squelched all that there was before of secession. The masses have tasted the tempting fruit, and found it to be like a green persimmon—very puckery and unpleasant to taste. Gen. Wool can remove his army, destroy his earthworks, and turn the guns of Fort McHenry seaward, without any fear of a rising in Baltimore. You cannot insult a Marylander now more thoroughly than to ask him if there are any secessionists in this State. He at once sees two large armies passing through his fields, stripping his cornfields, butchering his cows and hogs and robbing his hen-roost.

The effect upon the rebel army must be disheartening. They had been assured that all that was necessary to drag Maryland into the whirlpool of secession was to march a large army into the State, and the people would *en masse* fall into the rebellion. This was what the rank and file of the rebel army believed, whether Jackson believed it or not. He, perhaps, only thought of obtaining supplies for his army; but his soldiers talk bitterly against him for practicing deception, and threaten to deprive him of a worthless life. So that the result of this raid, as affecting the rebel cause, must be, in any event, most disastrous. Instead of obtaining 60,000 undisciplined troops and a cordial welcome, Jackson got less than 5,000 recruits, lost at least 30,000 men, and finally has had his half demoralized army kicked out of the State. Perhaps the devil's praying friend on earth, after this experience, will desire to make a raid into some Free State—but we do not believe it. He will endeavor to fall back where, upon familiar ground, his soldiers can fight behind something, instead of meeting our troops in a manly, fair field fight.

In this connection we will state that Frederick City did have several citizens who largely sympathized with the rebellion. Two of these individuals were largely engaged in the boot and shoe business. Now, shoe leather is one of the articles Stuart's soldiers stand most in need of, and when he entered the fair city of Frederick he put a severe test to his sympathizers in that locality, by buying out whole stocks at different stores. The boot and shoe dealers mentioned were the first to put their professions into practice, and succeeded in parting with—much against their will—between them, about $20,000 worth of boots and shoes, and received in payment therefore Confederate and Richmond bank notes. While dealing out their stocks freely, and biting their lips in vexation, but not daring to remonstrate, some of their loyal neighbors, who had concealed their stocks, enjoyed themselves hugely at the expense of the Secession sympathizers, by congratulating them upon the sudden increase of their business.

Lincoln visiting the generals of the Army of the Potomac in the field shortly after the bloody battle of Antietam, September, 1862.

But this was not the worst the rebels did in Maryland. Just upon the eastern bank of the Antietam Creek, opposite the battle-ground, resides a highly respectable family, whose head is named ALFRED N. COST. This family were peaceably engaged in their usual household duties and necessarily had to pass occasionally to a spring of water near at hand. On several occasions the women of this family were fired at by the rebel skirmishers while at this Spring, and to the credit of Gen. MCCLELLAN be it said, when his attention was called to the fact, he promptly sent a sufficient force to the vicinity to punish such outrages if repeated.

THE BATTLE-GROUND

Late last night and early this morning I visited the scene of the most deadly conflicts during the battle yesterday, and examined particularly the plowed field where Hooker's, SEDGWICK's and BANKS' troops in turn contended against the rebel hosts, and the sidehill, the cornfield and the road where FRENCH's left was repulsed, and where RICHARDSON's Division gained so signal a triumph, and MEAGHER's, CALDWELL's and BROOKES' brigades made such terrific slaughter in the enemy's ranks, and gained imperishable renown. The dead and wounded were strewn upon the places indicated, in hideous confusion. Here was a perfect winnow of Butternuts and Graybacks interlanded with Uncle Sam's blue coats; at another point the dead and wounded rebel and Union troops were in heaps, as if designedly placed so for a funeral pyre or an *auto da fé*, without the combustible material; and everywhere could be seen stern, unmistakable evidence of the desperate struggle which always characterizes civil war among the whole human family, be it between a savage or civilized people. Here was the pile made by KIRBY's Battery, there was a heap by THOMPSON's and HAZZARD's grape and canister, when the real leader, maddened to desperation by the exigencies of the hour, hurled his massed columns upon certain destruction. Scattered here and there were groups of blackened corpses indicating but too plainly the deadly certainty with which the German New-York Battery hurled its thunderbolts from the hill east of the Antietam. Mangled humanity in all its ghastly forms could be seen upon this field; to the left, to the right, behind and before, on every hand the eye beheld the horrors of the field. Mingled with the dead came up to the ear the groans of those in whose breasts there yet remained a spark of vitality, but whose lamp had nearly expired; the hopeful cases, so far as possible, were removed for medical assistance before midnight of Wednesday; the hopeless cases were allowed to remain upon the field. Some in a perfectly conscious, others in a half conscious state, while more were insensible to all worldly affairs. One of the latter class—a rebel soldier—while we were walking over the field at night, vainly attempted to rise; he had received a wound upon the temple from which the brain protracted; he clutched at the air and a helping hand was extended to him and words of sympathy were spoken but no sign of recognition followed, and in a moment more the helpless victim fell over upon his face and was numbered with the dead. God grant that we may never witness another such scene. Thursday morning none of the dead had been removed and our forces held undisputed possession of the field, so that an approximate estimate could be made of the number actually killed on either side at one point, the bodies of 110 dead rebels were counted, while there were only 12 bodies of Union soldiers—and with one single exception—where the Irish Brigade and the left of FRENCH's Division had the hardest fight—this proportion would hold good everywhere on the battle-field. The enemy acknowledge a loss of two men killed to our one, but it would be nearer the truth to say that *they had five men killed where we had one.*

During the war's first year, President Lincoln repeatedly maintained that his goal was restoration of the Union and was not the emancipation of slaves. He rescinded orders by two of his commanders emancipating slaves in their military districts. Although personally antislavery, Lincoln was concerned about retaining the support of border-state Unionists and Northern Democrats for the war, and he knew they would be alienated if it became a war against slavery. But Republicans insisted that a blow against slavery would help win the war by striking at the labor system that sustained the South's economy, and that a war begun by the South to defend slavery could not be won without striking *against* slavery. As the war dragged on into its second year, Lincoln was converted to this conviction. In July 1862 he decided to issue a proclamation freeing the slaves in enemy territory by invoking his war powers as commander in chief to seize enemy property (in this case, slaves) being used to wage war against the United States. Secretary of State William H. Seward persuaded Lincoln to withhold the proclamation until a Union victory could give it more force and legitimacy. Lincoln decided that Antietam was enough of a victory for that purpose, and on September 22 he issued the following preliminary proclamation warning that he would issue a final proclamation on January 1, 1863, affecting all sates or portions of state then in rebellion.

September 23, 1862.

HIGHLY IMPORTANT.

A Proclamation by the President of the United States.

The War Still to be Prosecuted for the Restoration of the Union.

A DECREE OF EMANCIPATION.

All Slaves in States in Rebellion on the First of January Next to be Free.

The Gradual Abolition and Colonization Schemes Adhered to.

Loyal Citizens to be Remunerated for Losses, Including Slaves.

WASHINGTON, MONDAY, SEPT. 22.

By the President of the United States of America:

A PROCLAMATION.

I, Abraham Lincoln, President of the United States of America, and Commander-in-chief of the Army and Navy thereof, do hereby proclaim and declare, that hereafter, as heretofore, the war will be prosecuted for the object of practically restoring the constitutional relation between the United States and the People thereof in which States that relation is, or may be suspended or disturbed; that it is my purpose, upon the next meeting of Congress, to again recommend the adoption of a practical measure tendering pecuniary aid to the free acceptance of rejection of all the Slave States so called, the people whereof may not then be in rebellion against the United States, and which States may then have voluntarily adopted, or thereafter may voluntarily adopt, the immediate or gradual abolishment of Slavery within their respective limits; and that the efforts to colonize persons of African descent with their consent upon the Continent or elsewhere, with the previously obtained consent of the governments existing there, will be continued.

That on the first day of January, in the year of our Lord one thousand eight hundred and sixty-three, all persons held as slaves within any State, or any designated part of a State, the people whereof shall then be in rebellion against the United States shall be then, thenceforward, and forever, free; and the Executive Government of the United States, including the military and naval authority thereof, will recognize and maintain the freedom of such persons, and will do no act or acts to repress such persons, or any of them, in any efforts they may make for their actual freedom.

That the Executive will, on the first day of January aforesaid, by proclamation, designate the States and parts of States, if any, in which the people thereof, respectively, shall then be in rebellion against the United States; and the fact that any State, or the people thereof, shall on that day be in good faith represented in the Congress of the United States by members chosen thereto at elections wherein a majority of the qualified voters of such State shall have participated, shall, in the absence of strong countervailing testimony, be deemed conclusive evidence that such State and the people thereof have not been in rebellion against the United States.

That attention is hereby called to an act of Congress entitled "An act to make an additional article of war," approved March 13, 1862, and which act is in the words and figure following:

> Be it enacted by the Senate and House of Representatives of the United States of America in Congress assembled, That hereafter the following shall be promulgated as an additional article of war for the government of the army of the United States, and shall be obeyed and observed as such.

"ARTICLE—All officers or persons in the military or naval service of the United States are prohibited from employing any of the forces under their respective commands for the purpose of returning fugitives from service or labor who may have escaped from any persons to whom such service or labor is claimed to be due, and any officer who shall be found guilty by a Court-martial of violating this article shall be dismissed from the service.

"SECTION 2 And be it further enacted, that this act shall take effect from and after its passage."

Also the ninth and tenth sections of an act entitled "An act to suppress insurrection, to punish treason and rebellion, to seize and confiscate property of rebels, and for other purposes," approved July 17, 1862. and which sections are in the words and figures following:

"Sec. 9. And be it further enacted, That all slaves of persons who shall hereafter be engaged in rebellion against the government of the United States, or who shall in any way give aid or comfort thereto, escaping from such persons and taking refuge within the lines of the army; and all slaves captured from such persons or deserted by them and coming under the control of the government of the United States; and all slaves of such persons found on (or) being within any place occupied by rebel forces and afterwards occupied by the forces of the United States, shall be deemed captives of war, and shall be forever free of their servitude and not again held as slaves.

"Sec. 10. And be it further enacted, That no slave escaping into any State, Territory, or the district of Columbia, from any of the States, shall be delivered up, or in any way impeded or hindered of his liberty, except for crime or some offence against the laws, unless the person claiming said fugitive shall first make oath that the person to whom the labor or service of such fugitive is alleged to be due, is his lawful owner, and has not been in arms against the United States in the present rebellion, nor in any way given aid and comfort thereto, and no persons engaged in the military or naval service of the United States shall, under any pretence whatever, assume to decide on the validity of the claim of any person to the service or labor of any other person, or surrender up any such person the claimant, or pain of being dismissed from service."

And I do hereby enjoin upon and order all persons engaged in the military and naval service of the Unites States, to observe, obey and enforce, within their respective spheres of service, the act and sections above recited.

And the Executive will in due time recommend that all citizens of the United States who shall have remained loyal thereto throughout the rebellion, shall (upon the restoration of the constitutional relation between the United States and their respective States and people, if the relation shall have been suspended or disturbed,) be compensated for all losses by acts of the United States, *including the loss of slaves.*

In witness whereof, I have hereunto set my hand, and caused the seal of the United States to be affixed.

Done at the City of Washington, this Twenty-second day of September, in the year of our Lord one thousand eight hundred and sixty-two, and of the Independence of the United States the eighty-seventh.

ABRAHAM LINCOLN.
BY THE PRESIDENT.
WILLIAM H. SEWARD, SECRETARY OF STATE.

After the battle of Antietam, Lincoln repeatedly urged and then ordered General McClellan to cross the Potomac and attack the retreating Army of Northern Virginia before it could recover. McClellan dawdled and complained of shortages, and did not cross the river for six weeks. Fed up with "trying to bore with an augur too dull to take hold," as Lincoln expressed it to one of McClellan's supporters, the president removed him from command on November 7 and put General Ambrose Burnside in his place.

November 10, 1862.

IMPORTANT NEWS.

Gen. McClellan Relieved of the Command of the Army of the Potomac.

Gen. Burnside Appointed in his Place.

The Order of Displacement Delivered on Friday Night.

A FAREWELL ADDRESS TO THE SOLDIERS.

General McClellan on His Way to Trenton, N.J.

How the News was Received in Washington.

HEADQUARTERS OF THE ARMY OF THE POTOMAC. SALEM, VA.,
SATURDAY, NOV. 8—12 O'CLOCK, NOON.

The order relieving Major-Gen. MCCLELLAN from the command of the army of the Potomac was received at headquarters at 11 o'clock last night. It was entirely unexpected to all, and therefore every one was taken by surprise.

On its receipt, the command was immediately turned over to Gen. BURNSIDE.

Gen. MCCLELLAN and his Staff will leave tomorrow for Trenton, where he is ordered to report.

The order was delivered to him by Gen. BUCKINGHAM, in person.

His last official act was the issuing of an address to his soldiers, informing them in a few words that the command had devolved on Gen. Burnside, and taking an affectionate leave of them.

Lincoln met with General George McClellan after the bloody battle of Antietam and urged him to pursue the retreating Confederate troops under the command of Robert E. Lee. The preternaturally conservative McClellan refused to do so, citing the need for his men to rest and regroup after the struggle. Soon thereafter, describing McClellan as having "the slows," Lincoln fired the diminutive commander and replaced him with General Ambrose Burnside. *(Library of Congress)*

THE NEWS IN WASHINGTON.

Special Dispatch to the New-York Times.

WASHINGTON, SUNDAY, NOV. 9.

The removal of Gen. MCCLELLAN, and the significant fact of his being ordered to report to his family at Trenton, have produced some excitement here to-day. At the hotels, crowds have been discussing the subject, and occasionally the feelings of some have found expression in language disrespectful to the President and disloyal to the Government. The truly loyal and more sensible of Gen. McClellan's friends, however, whilst they regret his removal, acquiesce in the action of the President, as the friends and admirers of other Generals have done on like occasions. It is certain that Mr. LINCOLN never performed a duty which gave him so much pain as did the removal of MCCLELLAN just at this time; but facts recently presented in an official shape by the General-in-Chief made it clear to the President that he had but one course to pursue, and when these facts are given to the public, as they will be soon, all true supporters of the Government will not hesitate to concede the wisdom of the act, whilst those who are blinded by prejudice, and those animated by spirit of disloyalty, will, of course, seize this occasion as an opportunity for renewing their expressions of hostility to the administration.

A few gentlemen, wearing shoulder straps, have been rendering themselves, today, fit subjects for the Old Capitol Prison, by talking loudly against the act of relieving MCCLELLAN of his command. A Lieutenant-Colonel said publicly, tonight, that if by fighting another hour he could put down the rebellion, he would not do so.

It is understood that Judge HOLT has written a long letter to a gentleman of your City, strongly condemnatory of Gen. MCCLELLAN's course, which it is said will be made public.

Dispatch to the Associated Press.

WASHINGTON, SUNDAY, NOV. 9.

The first information the public received of the relief of Gen. MCCLELLAN from the command of the Army of the Potomac, was through the telegram published this morning. It affords a general theme of conversation and comment, and excites surprise, the event occurring unexpectedly. The cause of the Executive action in the premises does not appear to be known outside of official circles, and hence the absence of facts gives rise to conflicting speculations.

Gen. MCCLELLAN, it is said, passed through Washington to-day, on his way to Trenton.

THE ELEVATION OF BURNSIDE.
REJOICING IN PROVIDENCE.

PROVIDENCE, SUNDAY, NOV. 9.

By order of Gov. SPRAGUE, a salute of 100 guns is to be fired here to-morrow noon, in honor of the appointment of the Rhode Island General, Burnside, to the command of the Army of the Potomac.

THE NEWS IN PHILADELPHIA.

PHILADELPHIA, SUNDAY, NOV. 9.

The removal of General MCCLELLAN has caused much excitement throughout the city, and is the universal topic of conversation. Among the rumors as to the cause, it is said that some instructions from the General-in-Chief were not followed, and that the escape of LEE followed as a consequence.

FORNEY's Press of to-morrow, in speaking of the removal says:

It was purely a military act, and was the result of a military consultation and decision, although recommended to the President and approved by him some time ago. It was only finally resolved upon after the change became inevitable. No act of the present Administration, we might say no Executive act since the beginning of the Government, has been the subject of more careful deliberation.

After taking command of the Army of the Potomac, General Burnside moved quickly to cross the Rappahannock River at Fredericksburg in a new "On to Richmond" campaign. Delay in the arrival of pontoon bridges frustrated his initial plans, but Burnside went ahead and finally bridged the river on December 11. On the 13th he launched an attack against the Confederates holding a strong defensive position on the heights behind Fredericksburg and to the south of the town. The result was a slaughter, especially in front of a sunken road at the base of Marye's Heights. A potential breakthrough on the Confederate right was frustrated by General William B. Franklin's failure to reinforce success and a timely counterattack by Jackson's troops. The Army of the Potomac retreated back across the Rappahanoock, demoralized by their heavy casualties (more than 12,000) with no result. When Lincoln received the news, he exclaimed: "If there is a worse place than hell, I am in it." As usual with newspapers in both North and South, *The Times* put the best face on a defeat.

December 15, 1862.

IMPORTANT FROM VIRGINIA.

The Great Battle Fought on Saturday at Fredericksburgh.

Storming of the First Lien of the Enemy's Works.

FAILURE TO CARRY THE POSITION.

TERRIFIC FIGHTING UNTIL DARK.

Splendid Success of Gen. Franklin on the Left.

Stonewall Jackson Driven Back About a Mile.

Several Hundred Prisoners Captured.

A Number of Our General Officers Killed and Wounded.

NO GENERAL ENGAGEMENT YESTERDAY.

THE OPERATIONS OF SATURDAY.

HEADQUARTERS OF THE ARMY OF POTOMAC,
SATURDAY, DEC. 13, 1862.
IN THE FIELD—11 O'CLOCK, A.M.

The great battle, so long anticipated between the two contending armies, is now progressing.

The morning opened with a dense fog, which has not entirely disappeared.

Gen. REYNOLDS' Corps, on the left, advanced at an early hour, and at 9:15 A.M., engaged the enemy's infantry. Seven minutes afterward the rebels opened a heavy fire of artillery, which has continued so far without intermission.

Their artillery fire must be at random, as the fog obstructs all view of almost everything.

Our heavy guns are answering them rapidly.

At this writing, no results are known.

HEADQUARTERS OF THE ARMY OF THE POTOMAC,
SATURDAY DEC. 13—11 P.M.

The fog began to disappear early in the fore-noon, affording an unobstructed view of our own and rebel positions.

It being evident that the first ridge of hills, in the rear of the city, on which the enemy had their guns posted behind works, could not be carried, except by a charge of infantry, Gen. SUMNER assigned that duty to Gen. FRENCH's Division, which was supported by Gen. HOWARD's.

The troops advanced to their work at ten minutes before 12 o'clock at a brisk run, the enemy's guns opening upon them a very rapid fire. When within musket range, at the base of the ridge, our troops were met by a terrible fire from the rebel infantry, who were posted behind a stone wall and some houses on the right of the line. This checked the advance of our men, and they fell back to a small ravine, but not out of musket range.

At this time another body of troops moved their assistance In splendid style, notwithstanding large gaps were made in their ranks by the rebel artillery. When our troops arrived at the first line of the rebel defenses, they "double quicked," and with "fixed bayonets" endeavored to dislodge the rebels from their hiding places. The concentrated fire of the rebel artillery and infantry, which our men were forced to face, was too much for them, and the centre gave way to disorder, but afterwards they were rallied and brought back.

From that time the fire was spiritedly carried on, and never ceased until after dark.

Gen. FRANKLIN, who commanded the attack on the left, met with better success. He succeeded after a hard day's fight, in driving the rebels about one mile. At one time the rebels advanced to attack him, but were handsomely repulsed with terrible slaughter and loss of between four and five hundred prisoners belonging to Gen. A. P. HILL's command. Gen. FRANKLIN's movement was directed down the river, and his troops are encamped tonight not far from the Massaponox Creek.

Our troops sleep to-night where they fought to-day. The dead and wounded are being carried from the field.

The firing of musketry ceased about 6 o'clock this evening, but the Rebels continued throwing shell in to the city until 8 o'clock.

The position of the rebels was as follows:

Gen. Longstreet on the left, and holding the main works.

Gen. A. P. Hill and "Stonewall" Jackson were in front of Gen. Franklin, with Jackson's right resting on the Rappahannock, and Hill's forces acting as a reserve.

The troops are in good spirits and not the least disheartened.

From Another Correspondent.

Headquarters Army of the Potomac,
Saturday, Dec. 13—10 P.M.

Last night our troops were rapidly pushed across the river, and every preparation made for a battle. Gen. Franklin's Division crossed two miles below the city, while Gen. Sumner's troops occupied a portion of the town. Gen. Franklin's line was moved forward at sunrise, with his right resting on Fredericksburgh, his centre advanced a mile from the river, and his left resting on the river three miles below.

Skirmishing commenced on the left about daylight. Soon after a rebel battery opened on our lines, and the Ninth New York Militia was ordered to charge, but after a fierce struggle was compelled to retire. The remainder of the Brigade, under Gen. Tyler, then charged the enemy's guns, when the fight became general on the extreme left.

Gen. Meade's and Gen. Gibbon's Divisions encountered the right of Gen. A. P. Hill's command.

The cannonading was terrific, though our troops suffered but little from the enemy's artillery. Gradually the fight extended around to the right. Gen. Howe's division went in, and then Gen. Brooks' division. About 10 o'clock A.M. Gen. Sumner's troops engaged the enemy back of the city, since which time the battle has raged furiously along the whole line. The enemy, occupying the woods and hills, had a much more advantageous position, but were driven back on their right a mile and a half early in the day.

About noon Gen. Gibbon was relieved by Gen. Doubleday, and Gen. Meade by Gen. Stoneman. Afterward Gen. Newton's Division moved round to the support of the left, when the firing ceased in that portion of the field for a short time, and broke out with greater fierceness in the centre, where our troops were exposed to a plunging fire from the enemy's guns and earthworks from the hills.

Along the whole line the battle has been fierce all day, with great loss on both sides. To-night each army holds its first position, with the exception of a slight advance of our left. Cannonading is still going on, and the musketry breaks out at intervals quite fiercely.

Gens. GIBBON, VINTON, BAYARD and CAMPBELL are wounded. Gen. BAYARD was struck in the hip by a solid shot, while conversing with Gen. FRANKLIN and his Staff, and cannot survive. His right leg has been amputated, but the operation will only serve to prolong his life a short time.

Several hundred prisoners have been taken, who report that Gen. LEE's entire army is in the immediate vicinity. Gen. HILL's troops were withdrawn this morning and started down the river, but afterwards returned. Gen. FRANKLIN is to-night opposed to STONEWALL JACKSON.

It is impossible to form an accurate idea of the loss on either side, as the firing is still going on rendering it extremely difficult to remove the killed and wounded.

The city suffered terribly from the enemy's artillery, and is crowded with our troops, the front extending but a short distance beyond.

The balloon has been up all day. During the morning but little could be seen, owing to the dense fog; but the afternoon was remarkably clear.

This evening the rebels have been shelling Fredericksburgh, endeavoring to drive our troops out of the place, but without success.

THE OPERATIONS OF SUNDAY.

HEADQUARTERS ARMY OF POTOMAC
DEC. 14—11:30 A.M.

There is no fog to-day, the sun shining brightly, with a strong breeze. At daylight this morning there was a heavy fire of artillery and infantry in front of the first line of works, where Gens. SUMNER and HOOKER were engaged yesterday. The fire slacked about an hour afterward, and was heard only at intervals until now. The same occurred in front of Gen. FRANKLIN's Division down the river. The object of both parties was evidently to feel the other.

During last night and this forenoon the rebels have considerably extended their works and strengthened their position. Large bodies of troops are now to be seen where but few were to be seen yesterday.

Our dead which were killed yesterday, while charging in front of the enemy's works, still remain where they fell. When attempting their removal last night, the rebels would open fire with infantry, but the wounded have all been removed from the field, and all the dead obtained are now buried.

Both Union and Confederate troops used balloons for aerial reconnaissance.

The indications are that no decisive battle will be fought to-day, unless the rebels should bring on the engagement, which they will not probably do.

REPORTS BY WAY OF WASHINGTON

WASHINGTON, SUNDAY, DEC. 14.

It is thought here that about 40,000 of our troops were engaged in yesterday's battle.

From information received early this morning, preparations were making all night for a conflict to-day, Gen. BURNSIDE remaining on the field, giving orders, looking to the position and conditions of his forces.

Additional surgeons, and everything which the necessities of the wounded require, have been dispatched from Washington to the battle-ground.

It is proper to caution the public against hastily crediting the many unsupported rumors concerning yesterday's battle. Some of them here prevalent have no other basis than surmise, and are mere inventions in the absence of facts. Rebel sympathizers are responsible for not a few of these fictions.

Gentlemen in high public positions repeat the assertions, as coming from Gen. BURNSIDE, that *he has men enough, and, therefore, desires no further reinforcements.*

OUR SPECIAL ARMY CORRESPONDENCE.

Details of Operations to Saturday Morning.

The Crossing of the Rappahannock—The Movement Splendidly Performed—Preponderance of the Union Forces—Condition of Fredericksburgh, &c., &c.

CAMP OPPOSITE FREDERICKSBURGH,
SATURDAY, DEC. 13, 1862.

Affairs are rapidly culminating here, and the crisis of battle, the grandest—probably the most decisive—of the war, approaches apace.

The nation may well pause and hold its breath, in the terrible suspense now impending. The prelude of the conflict has passed. The taking of the town by assault, and after a determined fight with the enemy's sharpshooters and skirmishers, and the crossing of the river by a considerable portion of the Union force, are fast bringing the two great armies face to face. To-day—to-morrow at furthest—must witness events which will long live in history. May we hope that the battle will be as decisive as it now promises to be bloody and terrible.

The events of yesterday may be briefly summed up as follows:

Gen. SUMNER's Corps, the Right Grand Division, were across and occupied the town; one division took possession the first night, and the remainder of the column passed across the upper bridges in the morning. They filled the whole length of Caroline or Main-street to the lines of the railroad, and by degrees extended their front to Commerce-street, and the streets running up from the river, until the body of the town was filled up. They remained under cover of the houses, the streets running nearly North and South being parallel to the line of the enemies' batteries behind the town. The completion of a second pontoon bridge during the first night greatly facilitated the passage of the troops. The first artillery thrown across were the Napoleon batteries attached to Gen. SUMNER's Division.

The enemy's pickets stubbornly occupied the outskirts of the town, and a fusilade between them and our own advance pickets was kept up during the day. The remainder of FRANKLIN's column crossed their two pontoon bridges during the forenoon, two miles below the centre of the town. Their passage, as well as that of Gen. SUMNER's Corps, was disputed by occasional but not very persistent firing from the rebel batteries which are chiefly to the south and rear of the town, so as to command the line of the railroad, and also the Bowling Green.

Gen. REYNOLDS' First Corps brought up the rear of FRANKLIN's column, and occupied the broad plateau South of the town, extending for miles down the river.

Gen. HOOKER's Grand Division, which had been on foot since Thursday, when

Clara Barton's work in Fredricksburg, Virgina, hospitals caring for the wounded of the Wilderness campaign attracted national attention. Twenty years later she would found the American Red Cross. Portrait by Mathew Brady. *(U.S. Army Signal Corps)*

they broke camp, remained with the head of its column pointed toward the upper bridges, but up to 3 o'clock awaited Gen. BURNSIDE's orders to advance.

Three times during the day the enemy's battery commanding this crossing opened fire upon the troops which came down, their shells exploding with uncomfortable accuracy just at the hither end of the bridge, on the slope of the hill, and even beyond on the level plain by which they approached.

Shortly after 3 P.M. HOOKER's column began to move down the river, as if with the design of crossing on the bridges below, where FRANKLIN crossed. Up to a late hour, however, they had not gone over. It is believed they passed the river during the night.

This change in the line was no doubt occasioned by the extraordinary activity displayed by the rebel batteries southeast of the town.

At 2½ P.M. The whole semi-circle of batteries in that direction opened fire upon the pontoon bridges, and upon the lower part of the town, where our troops were quartered. Their other batteries, north of the plank-road, and toward Falmouth, simultaneously poured in their contribution upon the upper crossing, and that part of the town lying in front of it.

Five separate batteries below, working ten or twelve guns, and four above, with eight or ten kept up a fire of shot and shell until near sundown. Many of their shells fell short, but some took effect in the town, and near the river. What damage they did to the troops I could not learn at that late hour.

Several shells burst near the LACEY House, and one close by the north end of the building while I was getting the names of the wounded lying in that place. One man, a few minutes afterward, was brought in with his arm terribly shattered by a piece of shell. A considerable body of cavalry and infantry were partially sheltered behind these buildings, which are of brick. It being used as a hospital, and occupied by the rebels in common with the Union wounded soldiers is a guarantee that it will be respected. Its position being only a little to the left of the crossing and nearly in line of one of the main rebel batteries, probably accounts for these shells bursting so near it.

We must presume that they were accidental shots, as I believe there is no well authenticated instance of their intentionally firing upon a hospital. It is situated only two hundred yards north of Lieut. MILLER's battery, which is protected by earthworks, and very prominent on the high land below the house. These circumstances render the place unsafe, and it will only be used as a temporary hospital. The wounded will, for the present, be carried to the rear, where tents have been established for their accommodation.

The main body of the rebel army is believed to be in position some five or six, perhaps ten miles west, with a strong rear guard for cooperating with and supporting their batteries.

If estimates which I have heard be correct, we have an aggregate of over sixty thousand men more than the estimated strength of the rebel army. Our artillery figures up over five hundred guns. Considering the difficulties of the situation, the completion of six pontoon bridges, and the crossing of such an army in twenty-four hours, is worthy of all military achievement. The events of the last two days have increased the enthusiasm of the whole army toward its Commander, and strengthened confidence in the generals leading the Grand Divisions. With town and river behind we must fight—there is no backing out.

THE TOWN—ITS CONDITION.

Our shot and shell have riddled a great many of the houses in town; and most of the churches, from foundation to steeple, have been *accidentally* perforated by the storm of missiles which were sent into the town. As the monuments and representatives of a priesthood and people thoroughly baptized in treason, they deserved no exemption from the common doom, but being larger than any other buildings, and very prominently in the range of our fire, they naturally received their full share of the iron storm. The clock in the steeple of the Episcopal church was untouched, and continues to toll of the eventful hours for the benefit of the Union forces in the town.

In spite of prompt and general efforts to guard the houses from intrusion and pillage, by the establishment of guards, a good many residences have suffered more or less spoliation. Household articles, such as cooking utensils and crockery, pickles, sweetmeats and flitches of bacon, were observed among the troops, as I passed through the different streets. The latter, taken from the meat houses of the first families, no doubt, were generally transfixed on the end of bayonets, and carried in triumph on their shoulders.

There has been, as yet, no general pillaging of the town, and it will not be permitted. The principal stores have each a strong guard to protect the small stock of goods left behind in the flight of their proprietors.

Not over twenty houses all told, have been burned, and the total damage to the place, by the bombardment and flames, I estimate at not over two hundred thousand dollars.

The few dead who were shot in the streets, have been buried, necessarily in the town near where they fell. Considering all the terrible circumstances of provocation, the preservation of the town from total destruction, and its wholesale pillage by the army, are in the highest degree creditable to the Union troops, and to their discipline. Enclosed is a list of the killed and wounded as far as ascertained.

In haste to send the mail.

E. S.

PART THREE

1863

Approximately 180,000 African Americans comprising 163 units served in the Union Army during the Civil War.

The New-York Times, Saturday, January 3, 1863.

EMANCIPATION.

President Lincoln's Proclamation.

The Slaves in Arkansas, Texas, Mississippi, Alabama, Florida, Georgia, South Carolina and North Carolina Declared to be Free.

Parts of Louisiana and Virginia Excepted.

The Negroes to be Received into the Armed Service of the United States.

WASHINGTON, Thursday, Jan. 1, 1863.

By the President of the United States of America—a Proclamation:

Whereas, on the twenty-second day of September, in the year of our Lord one thousand eight hundred and sixty-two, a Proclamation was issued by the President of the United States containing among other things the following, to wit:

That on the first day of January, in the year of our Lord, one thousand eight hundred and sixty-three, all persons held as slaves within any State or designated part of a State, the people whereof shall then be in rebellion against the United States, shall be then, thenceforth, and *forever free*; and the Executive Government of the United States, including the Military and Naval authority thereof will recognize and maintain the freedom of such persons, and will do no act or acts to repress such persons or any of them in any effort they may make for their actual freedom. That the Executive will, on the first day of January aforesaid, by Proclamation, designate the States and parts of States, if any, in which the people therein, respectively, shall then be in rebellion against the United States, and the fact that any State or the people thereof, shall on that day be in good faith represented in the Congress of the United States by Members chosen thereto at elections wherein a majority of the qualified voters of such State shall have participated, shall in the absence of strong countervailing testimony, be deemed conclusive evidence that such State and the people thereof, are not then in rebellion against the United States."

Now, therefore, I, ABRAHAM LINCOLN, President of the United States, by virtue of the power in me vested, as Commander-in-Chief of the Army and Navy of the United States, in time of actual armed rebellion against the authority and Government of the United States, and as a fit and necessary war measure for suppressing said rebellion, do, on this first day of January, in the year of our L[illegible] one thousand eight hundred and sixty-th[illegible] purpose so to do, [illegible] period of one hu[illegible] first above-mentio[illegible] States and parts [illegible] thereof respectiv[illegible] against the United [illegible]

ARKANSAS, T[illegible] the Parishes of [illegible] son, St. John, St. [illegible] Assumption, Terr[illegible] St. Martin, and [illegible] of New-Orleans [illegible] FLORIDA, GEO[illegible] NORTH CAROL[illegible] forty-eight count[illegible] and also the co[illegible] Northampton, Eli[illegible] and Norfolk, incl[illegible] Portsmouth, and [illegible] present, left precisely as if this proclamation were not issued.

And, by virtue of the power, and for the purpose aforesaid, I do order and declare that all persons held as slaves within said designated States and parts of States are, and henceforward, shall

NEWS FROM WASHINGTON.

Arrival of General Butler and Staff.

His Views on the Conduct of the War.

The West Virginia Bill Signed by the President.

OUR SPECIAL WASHINGTON DISPATCHES.

WASHINGTON, Friday, Jan. 2.

THE ARRIVAL OF GEN. BUTLER.

The arrival of Gen. BUTLER this evening, accompanied by Col. SHAFFER and other members of his Staff, caused a very decided sensation, and his rooms at the National Hotel were immediately besieged by numbers of people anxious to see and hear the man who succored Washington, captured Baltimore, and evangelized New-Orleans. He was visible to very few, however, as his duty called him early in the evening to wait on President LINCOLN at the White House. Gen. BUTLER seems in excellent health, and is apparently all the better for the severe labors of his late command. He is entirely uninformed of the intentions of the Government as regards himself, but says that, on the arrival of Gen. BANKS at New-Orleans as his successor, he was convinced that he was not wanted there, and he thought he would come to Washington. It is needless to say that he is ready and anxious to serve his country, in whatever way his labors can be made most useful.

The intimations which have reached the public occasionally, in regard to the Anti-Slavery convictions of Gen. BUTLER, have done him no injustice. He is satisfied, he says, that in *this* war the whole property of the South is against the *Government*; that it is a revolt of the upper classes against the people; that so long as these upper classes retain their property, it will be used to aid the rebellion. It is a war of three hundred thousand property holders against the Union, or even less than this number, for they are not all fools. In depriving these class rebels of their property in slaves, they, of course, are weakened. The rich slaveholders must be extinguished as a class. He does not say "exterminated," but "extinguished." Their property must change owners. This done, they may go to Mexico, or to Cuba, or stay here, as they choose, for they will then be harmless. His expressions are equally strong in affirming the sincere loyalty of the poorer classes. Entertaining these opinions, he confesses to some chagrin on reading Gen. BANKS' disclaimer, in his proclamation, of any designs against Slavery; and had almost feared that in giving frank expression to his own views in his farewell address, he had gone counter to the policy of the rulers from whose counsels Gen. BANKS had so lately come.

Gen. BUTLER'S interview with the President was prolonged till a late hour, and took place in the presence of Secretary SEWARD and Senator BROWNING, the former being sent for on the General's arrival.

THE TENNESSEE BATTLE.

The city is filled with rumors in regard to the late battle in Tennessee—some favorable and some adverse. The latest dispatches known to the Presi-

THE PORTER COURT-MARTIAL.

Testimony of Gen. McClellan, for the Defence.

WASHINGTON, Friday, Jan. 2.

There was a crowded attendance at the Porter Court-Martial, to-day, including privileged ladies, all anxious to see McClellan and hear his testimony in favor of Gen. Porter. At the request of Gen. Porter,

life and death. Report what progress is made, and when will you be through. See me before you sail.
G. B. McCLELLAN.

To Maj.-Gen. F. J. PORTER.

That order was executed by him to my satisfaction entirely. His first movement to Newport's News was departing from the letter of my instructions. I should say in explanation that Porter sent me a dispatch stating that he should go at a certain hour, if I did not object. By some delay of the telegraph, I did not receive this dispatch until after he started, but I fully approved of his course. The effect of that movement was very decidedly to expedite his arrival at Aquia Creek at least one day, if not more. I saw him next at Aquia Creek. I think he was twenty-four to thirty-six hours between there and Falmouth. Did not see him after he left Falmouth. From what I saw of his conduct, and from what I heard from him after he knew he was to go to the assistance of Gen. Pope, I think he did all a zealous, energetic and patriotic officer should have done. At any time after he received notice that he was to go to the assistance of Gen. Pope, I had no reason whatever to suppose that he would fail Pope or his country in the discharge of his duties.

Gen. McClellan identified Porter's dispatches to Burnside, already in evidence.

I did not receive the impression from those telegrams that Gen. Porter would not be true to Gen. Pope.

Gen. McClellan identified a dispatch sent by him to Gen. Porter, requesting Porter to give Pope full support. This dispatch, it will be recollected, is dated Sept. 1, after alleged disobedience of Pope's orders by Porter, already published.

Q.—As you have stated, Gen. McClellan, that you never entertained a doubt that Gen. Porter would be true to Gen. Pope, how came you to send him such a dispatch as that?

A.—I sent that in accordance with the request of the President of the United States, who sent for me that day and told me he had understood that there was an unkind feeling on the part of the Army of the Potomac toward Gen. Pope, and requested me to use my personal influence to correct it, by telegraphing through to Gen. Porter, or to any other of my friends there. I told him that I did not consider it necessary, but was perfectly willing to do it. I had no doubt, then, in my own mind, that the Army of the Potomac and all connected with it would do their duty without any such action on my part.

Q.—I understand you to say you sent that telegram to quiet the apprehensions of the President—not apprehensions of your own?

A.—Entirely so, Sir.

To Judge-Advocate Holt—On the morning that dispatch is dated I was placed in command of the defences of Washington. I was placed in command that morning by a verbal order. The order for Gen. Pope to fall back to the defences of Washington did not emanate from me, but my recollection is, that it was sent at a very early hour of the morning of Tuesday, Sept. 2. I was directed not to assume command over the active troops commanded by Gen. Pope until they reached the immediate vicinity of the defences of Washington. I was expressly excluded from all control over them until that time.

To the Court—I cannot give the exact date when the order came directing Gen. Porter to join Pope's command. The order came direct from Gen. Halleck, and had been received by Gen. Porter when I reached Acquia Creek.

Question by the Court—Are your own feelings toward Gen. Pope of a friendly character?

A.—My acquaintance with Gen. Pope——

This question was objected to by the Court, and withdrawn.

Q.—When the accused was making his efforts to leave the Peninsula, did he know that he was to be placed under the command of Gen. Pope?

A.—No. It was only known that the Army of the Potomac was to move to Aquia, to reinforce and assist the Army of Virginia. The question of command had not been decided, so far as I know.

John Tucker, who was Assistant Secretary of War in Aug. 18th, 1862, testified to the activity and zealousness of Gen. Porter in embarking his command at Old Point Comfort. Witness did not see anything in Porter's conduct, or hear anything in his language, giving any indication that he would fail to do his whole duty in cooperating with and supporting Gen. Pope. Witness did not know whether Porter knew at the time referred to that he was to be placed under command of Pope.

Lieut. Geo. T. Ingham, of Gen. Sykes' Staff, testified that the order brought by Capt. Pope from Gen.

A train, with supplies, would leave Memphis yesterday for Holly Springs.

When Island No. 10 was evacuated lately, sixty-nine cannon were spiked, and 10,000 rounds of ammunition thrown into the river.

JEFFERSON DAVIS addressed the Mississippi Legislature at Jackson on the 26th ult.

MARRIED.

DIED.

Although rumors swirled through Washington in December 1862 that Lincoln would not issue the final Emancipation Proclamation on January 1 because Democratic gains in the 1862 congressional elections were interpreted in some quarters as a repudiation of the Proclamation, Lincoln never wavered. On January 1 he signed the Proclamation in the presence of a few colleagues, telling them: "I never, in my life, felt more certain that I was doing right than I do in signing this paper. If my name ever goes into history it will be for this act, and my whole soul is in it."

January 3, 1863.

EMANCIPATION.

President Lincoln's Proclamation.

The Slaves in Arkansas, Texas, Mississippi, Alabama, Florida, Georgia, South Carolina and North Carolina Declared to be Free.

Parts of Louisiana and Virginia Excepted.

The Negroes to be Received into the Armed Services of the United States.

WASHINGTON, THURSDAY, JANUARY 1, 1983.

By the President of the United States of America—a Proclamation:

Whereas, on the twenty-second day of September, in the year of our Lord one thousand eight hundred and sixty-two, a Proclamation was issued by the President of the United States containing among other things the following, to wit:

"That on the first day of January, in the year of our Lord, one thousand eight hundred and sixty-three, all persons held as slaves within any state or designated part of a state, the people whereof shall there be in rebellion against the United States, shall be then, thenceforth, and *forever free*; and the Executive government of the United States, including the Military and Naval authority thereof will recognize and maintain the freedom of such persons, and will do no act or acts to repress such persons or any of them in any effort they may make for their actual freedom. That the Executive will, on the first day of January aforesaid, by Proclamation, designate the States and parts of States, if any, in which the people therein, respectively, shall then be in rebellion against the United States, and the fact that any State or the People thereof, shall on that day be in good faith represented in the Congress of the United States by Members chosen thereto at elections wherein a majority of the qualified voters of such States shall have participated, shall in the absence of strong countervailing testimony, be deemed conclusive evidence that such State and the people thereof, are not then in rebellion against the United States."

Now, therefore, I, Abraham Lincoln, President of the United States, by virtue of the power in me vested, as Commander-in-Chief of the Army and Navy of the United States, in time of actual armed rebellion against the authority and Government of the United States, and as a fit and necessary war measure for suppressing said rebellion, do, on this first day of January, in the year of our Lord, one thousand eight hundred and sixty-three, and in accordance with my purpose so to do publicly proclaimed for the full period of one hundred days from the day of the first above-mentioned, order and designate as the States and parts of States wherein the people thereof respectively are this day in rebellion against the United States, the following, to wit:

ARKANSAS, TEXAS, LOUISIANA—except the Parishes of St. Bernard, Picquemines, Jefferson, St. John, St. Charles, St. James, Ascension, Assumption, Terrebonne, Lafourche, St. Mary, St. Martin, and Orleans, including the City of New-Orleans—MISSISSIPPI, ALABAMA, FLORIDA, GEORGIA, SOUTH CAROLINA, NORTH CAROLINA and VIRGINIA—except the forty-eight counties designated as West Virginia, and also the counties of Berkley, Accomac, Northampton, Elizabeth City, York, Princess Ann and Norfolk, including the cities of Norfolk and Portsmouth, and which excepted parts, are for the present, left precisely as if this proclamation were not issued.

And, by virtue of the power, and for the purpose aforesaid, I do order and declare that all persons held as slaves within said designated States and parts of States are, and henceforward, shall be FREE, and that the Executive Government of the United States, including the military and naval authorities thereof, will recognize and maintain the freedom of said persons.

And I hereby enjoin upon the people so declared to be free, to abstain from all violence unless in necessary self-defence, and I recommend to them that in all cases, when allowed, they labor faithfully for reasonable wages.

And I further declare and make known that such persons of suitable condition, will be received into the armed service of the United States to garrison forts, positions, stations, and other places, and to man vessels of all sorts in said service.

And, upon this act—sincerely believed to be an act of justice, warranted by the Constitution—upon military necessity—I invoke the considerable judgment of mankind and the gracious favor of Almighty God.

In witness whereof I have hereunto set my hand and caused the seal of the United States to be affixed.

[Seal]

DONE AT THE CITY OF WASHINGTON, THIS FIRST DAY OF JANUARY, IN THE YEAR OF OUR LORD ONE THOUSAND EIGHT HUNDRED AND SIXTY-THREE, AND OF THE INDEPENDENCE OF THE UNITED STATES OF AMERICA THE EIGHTY-SEVENTH.

(Signed) ABRAHAM LINCOLN

BY THE PRESIDENT, WM. H. SEWARD, SECRETARY OF STATE.

General Joseph Hooker succeeded Burnside as commander of the Army of the Potomac in January 1863 and soon infused new spirit into what Hooker began calling "the finest army on the planet." At the end of April Hooker stole a march on Lee and got much of his army across the Rappahannock in Lee's rear. After this promising start, however, Hooker lost his nerve and Lee seized the initiative. On May 2, after a long flanking march, Jackson's corps hit the 11th Corps of the Army of the Potomac end-on and rolled it up just west of the crossroads hostelry of Chancellorsville. Although Jackson was wounded, Lee next day continued the attack at Chancellorsville while the Union forces left at Fredericksburg fought their way through Confederate defenses in a bid to come up on Lee's rear. The following dispatches in *The Times* were filed while the battle still raged and the Union outlook was still promising. On the night of May 5–6, however, the demoralized Hooker acknowledged defeat by pulling the whole army back across the Rappahannock. "My God, my God! What will the country say?" exclaimed Lincoln when he heard the news. It was a low point in the war for the North.

May 5, 1863.

FROM THE ARMY OF THE POTOMAC.

Details of the Important Operations to Sunday Night.

Letters from Our Special Correspondents.

Terrible Battles Fought on Saturday and Sunday at Chancellorsville.

Unsuccessful Attempt of Stonewall Jackson to Turn General Hooker's Right.

A Terrific and Successful Night Attack upon the Enemy.

A Fierce Battle of Six Hours' Duration on Sunday.

A FAIR STAND-UP FIGHT.

The Results in Our Favor, but Undecisive.

THE OPERATIONS AT FREDERICKSBURGH.

The Two Ridges Behind the City in Our Possession.

OUR FORCES ADVANCED FOUR MILES.

About Four Thousand Prisoners Captured.

TERRIBLE LOSSES OF THE ENEMY.

CHANCELORSVILLE, VA., TEN MILES WEST BY SOUTH OF FREDERICKSBURGH,
SATURDAY, MIDNIGHT, MAY 2, 1863.

The Military operations which have been in progress on the line of the Rappahannock for a week past, have to-day culminated in what, if not precisely a great battle, only escapes that designation because we all feel that greater, by far, remains behind.

Gen. HOOKER, by a series of brilliantly audacious maneuvers and movements, of a celerity wholly unmatched in this war, has succeeded in crossing the Rappahannock River, and gaining for his army a position ten miles west by south, and in the rear of Fredericksburgh.

Gen. LEE, at first completely surprised by this move, and utterly puzzled as to his antagonist's intentions, has, however, had time to recover himself, and with a hand almost equally bold in the grand game of strategy—abandoning his position in Fredericksburgh, and the line of twenty miles down the Rappahannock which he has held for months—has changed his front, and stands opposite us in the horrid gage of battle.

We have secured a strong position, *completely turning the enemy line of rebel defensive heights in the rear of Fredericksburgh,* against which our army on the 13th of last December madly dashed itself. This, as Gen. HOOKER expresses in his inspiriting order of Thursday, gives us the advantage of compelling the enemy to fight us on ground of our own choosing.

The battle which must ensue to-morrow must be bloody, though it may not be decisive, for the enemy will fight with desperation, feeling that he risks everything on this tremendous throw. But if it be with one battle, two battles, or a dozen battles, Gen. HOOKER will not stop short until he is either himself destroyed, or has destroyed the army of the rebellion and follows their flying columns into Richmond.

WILLIAM SWINTON.

THE GREAT BATTLE OF SUNDAY.

HEADQUARTERS IN THE FIELD, NEAR CHANCELLORSVILLE, VA.,
SUNDAY, MAY 3, 1863—5 P.M.

Another bloody day has been added to the calendar of this rebellion. Another terrible battle has been fought, and more fields crimsoned with human blood. Few more such days as this will find no armies left on either side to fight battles.

Group of Signal Corps officers.

My last letter brought up the situation to Saturday morning. It was then certainly expected that the enemy would begin the attack as soon as it was day, and our dispositions were made accordingly. But the attack did not begin. Events proved that the enemy did design to attack, but he chose to make that attack in a manner and at a point different from what was generally anticipated by us on Saturday morning. Daylight grew broader and yet no guns. Finally about 6 o'clock, a brass Napoleon, looking down the plank road in front of the Chancellor House, saw a regiment come into the road in column and attempt to deploy. One or two doses of canister caused them to deploy rather irregularly, and more like skirmishers on the retreat.

Soon after, Gen. HOOKER and Staff began an inspection of our lines, which occupied full two hours. Every portion was visited, and the work of the night was closely inspected. On the extreme left new lines were chosen, and the engineer officers soon marked out the line and character of the defenses to be erected. When the inspection closed, the entrenchments were pronounced to be of the very best character, especially those on the right, where the columns of SLOCUM and HOWARD were posted.

There had been only slight disturbances during the night, as both forces had been busy with their axes rather than their muskets. From Gen. HOWARD's front came a report that the enemy was engaged all night in cutting a road past his picket line to the right. How much attention was paid to this fact at the time I do not know, but subsequent events proved that it was very significant.

The day continued to pass in a very dull manner for a day of battle, and only here and there was there anything more even than desultory skirmishing and picket firing.

About 3 o'clock the pickets on the right of Gen. SLOCUM's front reported that from a certain position wagons had been seen moving in a westerly direction nearly all day. It was at once surmised that this might be a retreat, but subsequent events proved that it was a part of an affair of altogether another nature. To ascertain, however, what it really was Gen. SICKLES, who was still in reserve, was ordered to make a reconnaissance in heavy force in that direction. This was done with great promptness, and the divisions of

Gens. BIRNEY and WHIPPLE, with Gen. BARLOW's brigade, from HOWARD's corps, were pushed out to the front, BERDAN's brigade of sharpshooters having the advance, and supporting RANDOLPH's battery. Our troops moved rapidly and soon became more or less engaged, especially with the artillery and the sharpshooters as skirmishers. BERDAN soon sent in some sixty prisoners, belonging to the Twenty-third Georgia, including one Major, two Captains and three Lieutenants. Being upon the ground, I examined these prisoners, and soon found that the "wagontrain" which we had seen moving during the day was composed mainly of ordnance wagons and ambulances, and that STONEWALL JACKSON and Staff were at the head of a column of troops which the wagons followed.

Nothing more was needed to convince us that this daring opponent was executing another of his sudden movements, and it was at once resolved to checkmate him. Gen. SICKLES was ordered to push on and Gen. WILLIAMS' division of SLOCUM's column was ordered to cooperate. BIRNEY pushed ahead with great vigor, and with RANDOLPH's battery soon sent to the rear as prisoners of war the entire remnant of the Twenty-third Georgia regiment, numbering over four hundred officers and men. The column of the enemy which had been moving up this road was now literally cut in two, and Gen. WILLIAMS had commenced a flank movement on the enemy's right, which promised the most auspicious results.

But at 5 o'clock a terrific crash of musketry on our extreme right, announced that JACKSON had commenced his operations. This had been anticipated but it was supposed that after his column was cut, the corps of Gen. HOWARD (formerly Gen. SIGEL's), with its supports, would be sufficient to resist his approach, and finding that he was himself assailed in the rear, he would turn about and retreat to escape capture.

But to the disgrace of the Eleventh Corps be it said, that the division of Gen. SCHURZ, which was the first assailed, almost instantly gave way. Threats, entreaties and orders of commanders were of no avail. Thousands of these cowards threw down their guns and soon streamed down the road toward headquarters. The enemy pressed his advantage, Gen. DEVENS' division, disaffected by the demoralization of the forces in front of him, soon followed suit, and the brave General was for the second time severely wounded in the foot, while endeavoring to rally his men. Gen. HOWARD, with all his daring and resolution and vigor, could not stem the tide of the retreating and cowardly poltroons. The brigades of Cols. BUSHDECK and MCLEAN only remained fighting, and maintained themselves nobly as long as possible. But they too, gave way, though in good order, before vastly superior numbers.

Gen. HOOKER now sent his aid of Gen. HOWARD the choicest division of his army, the creation of his own hand—the famous Second Division of the Third Corps, commanded by Major-Gen. BERRY. Capt. BEST soon moved his batteries on a ridge running across the road, and after a short, but sanguinary contest the further advance of the enemy was stayed.

Of course this disaster compelled the recall of the SICKLES and SLOCUM who had been pursuing their work with remarkable vigor. Gen. WILLIAM's division returned only to find a portion of their works filled with the enemy. SICKLES' division could not communicate with the rest of the army at all by the way they advanced, and only at great risk by any other route.

This was the position at dark, and it did not look very promising. But our energetic commander was more than equal to the emergency. New dispositions to repair this disaster were at once resolved upon. Communication was at once had with Gens. BIRNEY and WHIPPLE, and a night attack ordered, to restore the connection of the lines. Gen. WARD's brigade, of Gen. BIRNEY's division, made the attack at 11 at night, aided by Capt. BEST's guns, massed on the ridge in front of the enemy. BIRNEY's position was on the extreme left of this new line of battle, but WARD's terrific attack was entirely successful, communication was restored, and in a charge made by the brigade, a portion of the artillery lost by HOWARD was gallantly retaken by Gen. HOBART WARD.

This night attack was the most grand and terrific thing of the war. The moon shone bright, and an enemy could be seen at good musket range. The air was very still, and the roar and reverberation of the musketry and artillery past all conception. Malvern Hill was a skirmish compared with this, save in the degree of slaughter. But it was successful—the enemy were driven back nearly half a mile, and our tired men once more slept on their arms. That night's work was ended.

Now I come to Sunday. It was perfectly evident from the position of affairs on Saturday night, that there must be a change of our lines, which would throw the enemy out of our rear and into our front again. It will be seen by what skillful generalship the enemy was fought and checked on front, and flank, and rear, while this was being done.

Gen. REYNOLDS' First Army Corps arrived at United States Ford on Saturday afternoon. It was immediately put into positions on our right, which was withdrawn from the plank road to the Ely's Ford turnpike. This line was immediately formed by Gens. REYNOLDS and MEADE, the latter's position, on the left, having been relieved by Gen. HOWARD's Eleventh Corps, which notwithstanding its disorganized condition was so far reorganized during the night as to be fit for duty again this morning. They were assigned the position on the left, where it was probable there would be little or no fighting, and were protected by the strong works built the day before by Gen. MEADE's corps. Our new line now assumed the shape of a triangle, prolonged at the apex, the right of the line being somewhat longer than the left. As the portion of the line on the right was new, time was necessary to fortify and entrench it, and the work was carried on vigorously by the Fifth and First army corps.

It was very evident at daylight this morning that the day would bring forth a terrific battle. We know that the enemy had been re-enforcing his line all night, at the expense undoubtedly of the strength of his force on our left. His intention was evidently to fight for the possession of the plank road, which it was perfectly apparent he must have, as that portion of it which we then held, was subject to the enemy's assaults in front and on both flanks.

But the possession of this road was not obtained by the enemy save at our own time, at his severest cost and after one of the most desperate, tenacious and bloody conflicts, for its short duration, of the whole war. At 5 o'clock A.M. the rebels could be plainly seen up the plank road, about a mile and a half from the Chancellor House, which Gen. HOOKER still retained at his headquarters, though a shell had gone through it the evening before, and another had cut down a tree directly in front of it.

Our line of battle was formed with Gen. BERRY's gallant division on the right. Gen. BIRNEY next on the left, Gen. WHIPPLE and Gen. WILLIAMS supporting. At 5½ A.M. the advance became engaged in the ravine, just beyond the ridge where Capt. BEST's guns had made their terrific onslaught the night before, and where they still frowned upon the enemy and threatened his destruction.

The rattle of musketry soon became a long continued crash, and in a few moments, as battalion after battalion became engaged, the roar surpassed all conception, and indicated that the fight would be one of the most terrible nature. Gen. BERRY's division, which had checked the enemy's advance the night before, engaging him again, and if it were possible for them to add more laurels to their fame, then they did it thrice over again. The enemy advanced his infantry in overwhelming numbers, and seemed determined to crush our forces. But the brave men of SICKLES and SLOCUM, who fought their columns with desperate gallantry, held the rebels in check, and inflicted dreadful slaughter among them. Gen. FRENCH's division was sent in on the right flank of our line at about 7 A.M., and in a short time a horde of ragged, streaming rebels running down the road, indicated that that portion of the enemy's line had been crushed. At 8 o'clock A.M., Gen. FRENCH sent his compliments to Gen. HOOKER, with the information that he had charged the enemy and was driving him before him.

SICKLES maintained the attack upon his line with great endurance. The enemy seemed determined to crush him with the immensity of his forces, and, as subsequently shown from the statements of prisoners, five whole divisions of the rebel army were precipitated upon this portion of the line, for from these five divisions we took during the day an aggregate of over two thousand prisoners.

The exploits of our gallant troops in those dark, tangled, gloomy woods may never be brought to light; but they would fill a hundred volumes. It was a deliberate, desperate hand-to-hand conflict, and the carnage was perfectly frightful. Cool officers say that the dead and wounded of the enemy covered the ground in heaps, and that the rebels seemed utterly regardless of their lives, and literally threw themselves upon the muzzles of our guns. Many desperate charges were made during the fight, particularly by BERRY's division. MOTT's brigade made fifteen distinct charges, and captured seven stands of colors, the Seventh New-Jersey, Col. FRANCINE, alone capturing four stands of colors and five hundred prisoners.

Gen. COUCH's Second Army Corps, though only in part present, did excellent work. It was Gen. FRENCH who charged and drove the enemy on the flank, and it was the indomitable HANCOCK who gallantly went to the relief of the hard-pressed SICKLES.

The engagement lasted without the slightest intermission from 5½ A.M. to 8:45 A.M., when there was a temporary cessation on our part, occasioned by getting out of ammunition. We held our position for nearly an hour with the bayonet, and then being resupplied, an order was given to fall back to the vicinity of the Chancellor House, which we did in good order. Here the contest was maintained for an hour or more, not so severely as before, but with great havoc to the enemy, and considerable loss to ourselves.

The vicinity of the Chancellor House was now the theatre of the fight, and my visits to that spot became less frequent. Gen. HOOKER maintained his headquarters there until 10 A.M., when it was set on fire by the enemy's shells, and is now in ruins. Chancellorsville is no longer in existence, having perished with the flame, but Chancellorsville is in history, never to be effaced.

Our new line was now so far established as to render it safe to withdraw all our forces on that front, which was accordingly done, and at 11:30 A.M. the musketry firing ceased.

The engagement had lasted six hours, but had been the most terrific of the war. Our artillery had literally slaughtered the enemy, and many of the companies had lost heavily in men themselves, but the guns were all saved.

The enemy was now no longer in our rear, but had been shoved down directly in our front, and is now directly between us and our forces in Fredericksburgh, and we were again in an entrenched and formidably fortified position. The enemy has gained some ground, it is true, but at the sacrifice of the flower of his force, five of his seven divisions having been cut to pieces in the effort, and over 2,000 of them have fallen into our hands.

Our right wing, under Gens. REYNOLDS and MEADE was not engaged, save the division of Gen. HUMPHREYS, which went into the woods on the enemy's left flank, and fought valiantly under their brilliant leader, until their ammunition was exhausted.

During the afternoon the enemy has made several attempts to force our lines, particularly at the apex of our position, near the Chancellor House, but Capt. WEED has massed a large quantity of artillery in such a position as to repulse with great loss everything placed within its range. The enemy tried several batteries and regiments at that point at different times during the afternoon, and they were literally destroyed by the fire of our terrible guns. Nothing can live within their range.

Our present position is impregnable if our troops continue to fight as they have today. Gen. LEE, the prisoners say, has issued an order that our lines must be broken at all hazards. Let them try it again with what they have left. They can, and perhaps will destroy themselves by attacks upon this position.

Our troops are perfectly cool and confident. They have fought with great spirit and enthusiasm and will continue to do so.

L.L. CROUNSE.

After the attack on Chancellorsville had ground to a halt in the gathering darkness of May 2, 1863, Stonewall Jackson rode ahead to scout the possibility of following up with a night attack, and as he returned was shot by his own men who mistook his escort for Union cavalry. Jackson's arm was amputated, and eight days later he died of pneumonia that set in after he was wounded.

May 14, 1863.

The Death of Stonewall Jackson.

In the death of STONEWALL JACKSON, the rebels have unquestionably lost by far their greatest military leader, in the peculiar style of strategy which has made his name famous. Immediately after the secession of Virginia he appeared on the scene, and ever since then he has been one of the foremost figures. He was the leader in the first hostile act of the Secessionists of Virginia—the march upon Harper's Ferry. In the first great action of the war, the battle of Manassas Plains, he took part, and one of his characteristic personal and military qualities, expressed in his title of "STONEWALL," here first appeared. In every great battle fought since that time by the main rebel army, and in many minor affairs, he has been a leading actor—in the Peninsular battles, where he was the first to attack our right; in the second battle of Manassas; at the battle of Antietam; at the battle of Fredericksburgh, and lastly at the battle of Chancellorsville, on the 3rd, in which engagement he received his death-wound—inflicted accidentally, it is said, by one of his own men. His campaign up and down the Shenandoah Valley, in the Spring of last year, and his series of engagements with Gens. BAINES and FREMONT, were only inferior in importance to the six or seven first-class battles in which he played his part. In each of the battles in which he acted subordinately, he was generally assigned to the peculiar and critical duties of opening the assault, making a dashing movement upon the flank or rear, or seizing and holding a point which might be called the key of the situation. In a short letter, written by him about a year ago, in reply to the accusation of having written a piece of sentimental poetry, he denied the poetical imputation, and said that the only ambition of his life was to serve the South, and "give a practical illustration of some of the simplest rules of war." These rules seem to have been celerity of movement, concentration of force, and rapid, persistent and heavy blows on his adversary's most vulnerable point—while the body with which he operated he kept in an extraordinary state of mobility. The numerical strength of that force seems to have varied from the twelve or fifteen thousand he commanded in the Shenandoah Valley to the forty thousand he was usually credited with in the great actions.

The traits of STONEWALL JACKSON's personal character are nearly as familiar to the public as his military feats. He was a man of narrow mind, but of tremendous will and indomitable purpose; and he flung the great energy of his nature into all that he undertook. He was strictly moral and fanatically religious; and the fact that he was a ruling elder in the Presbyterian Church shows that he stood well with his brethren. He was an acute political speculator and an ardent devotee of the Southern State Rights school. Like Gen. LEE himself, he was, however, a theoretical Unionist up to the very date of Virginia's secession; and, like LEE, he is said to have struggled long in deciding between his duty to his country and his devotion to Virginia; and it was only when his own State drew the sword, that he at last determined to follow her fortunes. He was but 37 years of age at the time of his death—was a graduate of West Point, and actor in the Mexican war, and at the time of the breaking out of secession, was a Professor in the Military Institute in Lexington, Va. His death is a tremendous and irreparable loss to the secession cause, as no other rebel of like character has been developed during the war. He will figure in history as one of the ablest of modern military leaders; and it will only be the brand of *traitor* on his brow that will consign him to infamy, as it has brought him to an untimely grave.

Perhaps the most celebrated battlefield hero of the Confederacy, Gen. Stonewall Jackson was a deeply religious man who declared that he wanted his troops to be "an army of the living God" and regularly distributed religious tracts to his men. He was also a brilliant military tactician and motivator, driving his men in May 1862 to travel 340 miles in 24 days while fighting in three battles and numerous skirmishes. When Jackson died after being accidentally wounded by one of his men, General Robert E. Lee declared, "It is a terrible loss. I do not know how to replace him."

Even as the Army of the Potomac retreated in frustration after the battle of Chancellorsville, Ulysses S. Grant's Army of the Tennessee (the Union named its armies after rivers) was making progress in its campaign against Vicksburg after a winter of frustration. In December 1862, Grant and his foremost lieutenant, General William T. Sherman, had been forced to call off their first campaign against Vicksburg when cavalry raids destroyed Grant's supply base at Holly Springs, Mississippi and Sherman's attack on Chickasaw Bluff north of Vicksburg was repulsed. During the rest of the winter, Grant and Acting Rear Admiral David Dixon Porter, commander of the gunboat fleet on the Mississippi, tried several ways of moving through the maze of bayous and swamps west and north of Vicksburg to get across the big river for a campaign on dry ground east of what the Confederates proudly described as their "Gibraltar of the West" at Vicksburg. Finally in April, Porter ran the fleet past Vicksburg's big guns on the swift current to a point downriver where he could ferry Grant's army across to higher ground. From May 1 through May 17, Grant cut loose from his base, marched 130 miles and won five battles, and penned Vicksburg's 30,000 Confederate defenders into their works, which Union assaults on May 19 and 22 failed to carry—despite the initial overoptimistic reports in the dispatches reprinted here that Vicksburg had fallen. Grant settled down for a siege that would last six weeks.

May 26, 1863.

VICKSBURGH.

News from Gen. Grant's Army to Friday Night, 22d.

Our Centre Within One Mile of Vicksburgh Court-house.

The Right and Left Wings Within a Mile and a Half.

Six Thousand Prisoners Already Captured.

REPORTS OF PREVIOUS OPERATIONS.

The Part Taken by Admiral Porter's Fleet.

Occupations of the Works at Haines' Bluff.

The Fortifications Very Strong and Extensive.

Details of the Battles of Baker's Creek and Black River Bridge.

WASHINGTON, MONDAY, MAY 25.

The latest advices from our army at Vicksburgh are up to 9 o'clock on Friday night.

Our centre corps had then fought its way to within one mile of Vicksburgh Courthouse.

Our right wing, under SHERMAN, was about a mile and a half from the Courthouse.

Our left wing, under MCCERNAND was also about a mile and a half from the Courthouse.

Six thousand prisoners had already been taken.

An official report has been received from Admiral PORTER, announcing the capture of Haines' Bluff, with 14 pieces of heavy artillery.

A dispatch from Gen. HURLBUT, who is thoroughly familiar with the situation, expresses the most perfect confidence in our complete success.

FROM ANOTHER CORRESPONDENT.

Up to 11 P.M. no official dispatches had been received warranting the statement of the fall of Vicksburgh—everything thus far resting on the declarations that the place must fall next day. At the latest official advices Gen. GRANT's line of battle was near a mile and a half from the city.

THE GREAT BATTLE OF BAKER'S CREEK.

CINCINNATI, MONDAY, MAY 25.

Special dispatches from the army of Gen. GRANT contain full accounts of the battles in Mississippi, representing them as a series of bloody and desperate engagements, in which our soldiers immortalized themselves.

The *Commercial's* special dispatch is as follows:

BATTLEFIELD OF BAKER'S CREEK,
SATURDAY, MAY 16, 1863.

The Federal army under Gen. GRANT has won another glorious victory.

A furious battle has been fought, lasting nearly five hours, and resulting in the defeat of the enemy at all points, with a loss of 3,000 killed and wounded, and three complete batteries of heavy rifled cannon, besides single pieces, 2,000 prisoners, large quantities of small arms and camp equipage.

Our success was signal and complete.

Early in the morning of the 16th inst., Gen. MCCLERNAND's corps were put in motion, while Gen. HOVEY's division advanced across the open field to the foot of Champion Hill.

At 11 o'clock the battle was commenced.

Champion Hill was covered with timber, flanked on both sides with ravines and gullies, and in many places covered with an almost impenetrable growth of scrubby bushes.

The rebels opened with a heavy fire from their four-gun battery, and from their sharpshooters in the woods.

The battle raged terribly from 11 A.M. to 3 P.M.

Gen. HOVEY's division carried the heights in gallant style, making a dash on the first battery and captured it from the rebels. Lying thick in the vicinity were guns, gun-carriages broken, caissons overturned, knapsacks, blankets, small arms and other debris—all attesting the terrific struggle for the ground.

At this juncture the rebels were reinforced, and Gen. HOVEY, was slowly driven back.

Gen. QUINBY, with a brigade, went to the support of Gen. HOVEY, and the ground was speedily reoccupied and the rebels finally repulsed.

At the commencement of the engagement Gen. LOGAN's division marched to the brow of the hill, forming in line of battle on the right of Gen. HOVEY, and advanced in gallant style, sweeping everything before them to the edge of the woods.

In the front of Gen. LOGAN the battle was of the most desperate character imaginable.

The rattle of musketry was incessant and continued, and the reports were so blended that a single discharge was rarely heard.

Gen. LOGAN captured two batteries, a large portion of prisoners, small arms, &c.

CHICAGO, MONDAY, MAY 25.

Specials contain the following:

CHAMPION HILLS, TWENTY-SIX MILES EAST OF
VICKSBURGH, SATURDAY, MAY 16

Early this morning Gen. MCCLERNAND's corps was put in motion. HOVEY's division was on the main road from Jackson to Vicksburgh, but the balance of the corps was a few miles to the southward, on a parallel road, and MCPHERSON's corps followed HOVEY's division closely.

At 9 o'clock HOVEY discovered the enemy in front of Champion Hill, to the left of the road, near Baker's Creek, apparently in force. Skirmishers were thrown out and the division advanced cautiously and slowly to give MCPHERSON's advance division under LOGAN time to come within supporting distance. Gen. HOVEY's division advanced across the open field at the foot of Champion Hill, in line of battle. At 11 o'clock the battle commenced. The hill itself was covered with timber, and is in fact but an abrupt terminus of a high ridge running north and south, flanked both sides by deep ravines and gullies, and in many places covered with an impenetrable growth of scrubby white oak brush. The rebels appeared deficient in artillery throughout the battle, but opened with rather a heavy fire from a four-gun battery of rifled 6-pounders, planted about 400 yards back from the brow of the hill.

The woods on both sides of the road leading up the face of the hill, and winding back on the ridge a mile or more, were filled with sharpshooters, supported by infantry. Here the battle began, just as our men entered the edge of the timber, and raged terribly from 11 till between 3 and 4 o'clock. Gen. HOVEY's division carried the heights in a gallant style, and, making a dash on the first battery, drove the gunners from their posts and captured the pieces. The rebels lay thick in the vicinity of the guns. Their horses were more than half killed. Gun-carriages and caissons were broken, and knapsacks, blankets, small arms and other *debris,* attested the deadly struggle. The colors of the Thirty-first Alabama regiment were captured there. At this juncture MITCHELL's Ohio battery was opened, at about eighty yards from the brow of the hill. The rebels made a dash for it, but the fleetness of the horses prevented its capture. At the same time the rebels appeared with fresh troops on that wing, and redoubled their efforts to hold their position, and dislodge our troops on the hill. HOVEY was slowly driven back to the brow; but a brigade from Gen. QUINBY was ordered to his support, and the ground was speedily recovered, and the rebels finally repulsed.

At the commencement of the engagement, Gen. LOGAN's division marched past the brow of the hill, and forming in line of battle on the right of HOVEY, advanced in grand style, sweeping everything before them. At the edge of the wood in front of LOGAN the battle was most desperate. Not a man flinched or a line wavered in this division. All behaved like veterans, and moved to new positions with a conscious tread of victory. Two batteries were captured by this division, and enough hard fighting done to immortalize it. They also captured a large portion of the prisoners, small arms, &c.

Between 3 and 4 o'clock Gen. OSTERHAUS' and Gen. MCARTHUR's divisions came into action on the extreme left, and completed what had been so auspiciously carried forward. They were both miles away when the engagement began, but were brought forward with all dispatch possible. The enemy were in full retreat soon after, and three divisions pursued till 9 o'clock, and are now encamped at Ward's Station, eight miles beyond the battle-ground.

From rebel prisoners I learn that PEMBERTON commanded in person. FITZHUGH LEE and GREGG, who commanded at the battle near Raymond, and others of note, had subordinate commands. I also learn that great dissatisfaction exists toward PEMBERTON. He is accused by many of selling out to GRANT; also of planning military operations for the last four weeks so as to insure the latter's success.

It is impossible yet to do more than approximate our loss. I think it will be about 1,000 killed and wounded. It may prove less, but it cannot be much more. But few officers of distinction are injured. The Twenty-fourth Indiana lost one hundred men. Lieut.-Col. SWAIN, commanding, was killed. Not a General or staff officer on our

The unassuming Gen. Ulysses S. Grant—diminutive in stature, reticent in demeanor, and informal in his dealings with subordinates—was an aggressive, popular commander. General William Sherman, one of his friends, described him as "the greatest soldier of our time if not all time." Photograph by Mathew Brady. (U.S. Army Signal Corps)

side was hurt. This has been the hottest and most brilliant fight in the Southwest for several months. The men are enthusiastic whenever Gen. GRANT appears. His reckless exposure of himself on the field begets unbounded admiration among the privates.

Well-authenticated cases of rebel barbarity to our wounded men can be enumerated. Three different men, who were shot down in the battle, were subsequently sabred by the rebels when they temporarily retook the ground. The men lived to narrate the atrocity, but will scarcely recover.

BATTLE OF BLACK RIVER BRIDGE.

BLACK RIVER BRIDGE, TWELVE MILES EAST OF VICKSBURGH, SUNDAY, MAY 17.

MCCLERNAND's corps marched to this place early this morning. OSTERHAUS was in the advance, and found the rebels strongly entrenched on the east bank of the river. Batteries were soon in position, playing on the enemy's works. At 10 o'clock Gen. LAWLER's brigadee in CARR's division, charged across the open fields, two hundred yards in width, wading the bayou in front, and swarming over into the entrenchments. Seventeen cannon were taken inside the earthworks, and from 500 to 2,000 prisoners captured. No description can do justice to the intrepidity of the regiments comprising this brigade. The rebel fire from artillery and musketry was appalling, but they rushed on to victory, regardless of death, and literally swept everything before them. Gen. MART GREEN's Missouri brigade, (rebels,) over twelve hundred strong, was cut off by the Eleventh Wisconsin, and surrendered. Gen. VAUGHN's brigade was also principally captured. The losses of the eleventh Wisconsin was slight. The Twenty first and Twenty-third Iowa led in the charge, and sustained the principal loss. The Eleventh Wisconsin also captured a stand of colors.

Furious cannonading continued all day from the rebel batteries on the other side of the river. They fired the bridge, to prevent our crossing. Pontoons have been sent to SHERMAN's corps. He will probably cross a few miles above here, and attack in flank. The force opposite is thought to number 25,000. Our army is in excellent fighting condition, and think themselves invincible. As Gen. GRANT rode to the front to-day, he was everywhere greeted with tremendous and uproarious cheering.

This morning two 4-pound howitzers and two 6-pounder rifled-guns were surrendered, with horses, harness and ammunition complete without a shot, a few miles back on the road. These guns became separated from the main body of the rebel army yesterday in the retreat, and were cut off by our advance.

Our loss in to-day's fighting is not heavy. The rebel killed and wounded is unknown. Their troops did not fight as obstinately to-day as yesterday. They seemed to expect a defeat. The wonder is they were not wholly withdrawn to the other side without an engagement.

Gen. OSTERHAUS was slightly wounded, but rode on the field again.

REBEL VIEWS OF THE SITUATION.

WASHINGTON, MONDAY, MAY 25.

Richmond papers of yesterday morning, received here to-night, lie vigorously in their efforts to conceal their disasters at Vicksburgh. Witness the following extracts:

From the Richmond Examiner, 23d.

"A telegram dated Jackson, from the reporter of the Mobile *Advertiser* and *Register*, published in another column, was received here yesterday morning. It was at first received without criticism, and believed, and occasioned no little gloom, especially among the weak-minded individuals of the community; but when reread it was found that the dispatch would not stand inspection, and in the course of the day the whole account became pretty generally discredited. The reporter tells of a battle on Sunday, and, further on, states—which perhaps is the only authentic information he gives—

that Gen. LORING is in command at Jackson. That LORING is at Jackson, and has not informed the Department here of the Sunday's battle, is *pretty good proof that there was no such battle*. It is to be presumed that he enjoys, at least in an equal degree with the reporter, facilities for acquiring and transmitting intelligence relative to the movements of our troops. Jackson and the country around are in a high state of excitement, and, doubtless, the theatre of countless rumors. Out of these rumors the reporter has made his story. As to the statements of our tremendous loss of artillery, there may be something in that, though that should be received with caution.

To the further discredit of the dispatch, we may add that it was not believed in official circles, and that up to the late hour last night, no information had been received later than Gen. JOHNSTON's dispatch of the 18th, which conveyed the information that Gen. PEMBERTON had been attacked at Edward's Depot, and been compelled to fall back behind the Big Black. We have authentic information that Gen. PEMBERTON, in anticipation of this movement of GRANT upon Jackson, *has for a month past been removing medical and commissary stores from that place to Vicksburgh.*

From the Richmond Examiner, 23d

The news that thirty cannon were spiked on the retreat from Jackson, which still rests on very slight authority, and that Vicksburgh has been besieged on the land, has caused considerable sensation; but the imagination of the worthy public on this, as on very many other occasions, has far out run the reality. *Vicksburgh has not fallen—is not going to fall.* It is not in so much danger now as it has often been before, and the Federal army, struggling to complete the long siege, is in a very dangerous situation. The Confederate forces have undisputed possession of Jackson and the railroad. The Federal army is working between that point and Vicksburgh, and *Gen. Johnston is at the head of a rapidly increasing column, which will soon make a terrible apparition upon the scene of action.* In the town of Vicksburgh provisions have been accumulated which will last for months. The defenses on the side of the land are ample. The conformation of the ground gives an overwhelming advantage to the garrison in case of an assault. There is no reason whatsoever for despair about Vicksburgh. It is a lucky point for the Confederate army. It has already cost the invader many a thousand of men, many millions of dollars, and will cost twice as much more before many weeks are over.

The crisis in the military situation around Vicksburgh has long been impending, and will now soon be decided for the season. The division of our forces, and some bad management of the batteries commanding the river before the town, have lost us the first engagements. Both of those engagements were far from being decisive, either of the fate of the town or of the campaign in the State. It is far more probable than otherwise, that Gen. Johnston will be able to recover the ground lost by the mistakes made in the military command. *There is really no occasion for panic about*

Vicksburgh. Whatever may be the result of the military operations around it, *their interest will soon be eclipsed by far greater events elsewhere*. Within the next fortnight the campaign of 1863 will be pretty well decided. *The most important movements of the war will probably be made in that time*. If the Confederate standard is again victorious, as may be hoped with much and solid reason—although mere victory will not end the war, it will destroy the efficiency of the enemy's army for the rest of this year. *If we gain all that is now fairly possible, an entirely new character will be given to future operations, which will relieve the country of half the suffering it has hitherto endured*. Now is the noble day, the fortunate hour, for the Confederate army. At this time, if ever, let every man be at his post.

The good news of Grant's victories in the campaign leading up to the siege of Vicksburg was not sufficient to offset the bad news that demoralized Northern public opinion starting with the defeat at Fredricksburg in December and continuing into June as reports arrived that Lee had decided to use the Confederate victory at Chancellorsville as a springboard for a second invasion of the North. Then came the first week of July 1863, which brought the best news for any single week of the war until the fall of Richmond and the surrender at Appomattox in April 1865. The Army of the Potomac had shadowed the Confederate invaders into Pennsylvania as General Hooker began acting as though he were afraid to fight Lee again. On June 28 Lincoln replaced Hooker with General George Gordon Meade, and three days later the advance units of the opposing armies clashed near Gettysburg, Pennsylvania. An epic three-day battle built up from this initial clash is chronicled in the following dispatches. On July 4 the crippled Army of Northern Virginia began limping back to its namesake state. Then came news from the West of the surrender of Vicksburg, also on the Fourth of July. Although the war would continue for almost two more years, these twin Confederate defeats foretokened ultimate Union victory.

July 6, 1863.

THE GREAT BATTLES.

Splendid Triumph of the Army of the Potomac.

ROUT OF LEE'S FORCES ON FRIDAY.

The Most Terrible Struggle of the War.

TREMENDOUS ARTILLERY DUEL.

Repeated Charges of the Rebel Columns Upon Our Position.

Every Charge Repulsed with Great Slaughter.

The Death of Longstreet and Hill.

Our Cavalry Active on the Enemy's Flank.

THE REBEL RETREAT CUT OFF.

Chambersburgh in our Possession.

Advance of the Militia under Gen. Smith to Important Positions.

The Rebel Pontoon Bridge at Williamsport Destroyed.

The Contents of the Captured Dispatches from Jeff. Davis to Lee.

A Peremptory Order for the Rebel Army to Return to Virginia.

OFFICIAL DISPATCHES FROM GEN. MEADE.

WASHINGTON, SATURDAY, JULY 4—10:10 A.M.

The following has just been received:

HEADQUARTERS ARMY OF POTOMAC,
NEAR GETTYSBURGH, Friday, July 3—8½ P.M.

Major-Gen. Halleck, General-in-Chief:

The enemy opened at 1 P.M., from about one hundred and fifty guns, concentrated upon my left center, continuing without intermission for about three hours, at the expiration of which time, he assaulted my left center twice, being, upon both occasions, handsomely repulsed, with severe loss to him, leaving in our hands nearly three thousand prisoners.

Among the prisoners is Brig.-Gen. ARMSTEAD and many Colonels and officers of lesser rank.

The enemy left many dead upon the field, and a large number of wounded in our hands.

The loss upon our side has been considerable. Maj.-Gen. HANCOCK, and Brig.-Gen. GIBSON were wounded.

After the repelling of the assault, indications leading to the belief that the enemy might be withdrawing, a reconnaissance was pushed forward from the left and the enemy found to be in force.

At the present hour all is quiet.

My cavalry have been engaged all day on both flanks of the enemy, harassing and vigorously attacking him with great success, notwithstanding they encountered superior numbers both of cavalry and infantry.

The army is in fine spirit.

GEORGE MEADE,
MAJ.-GEN. COMMANDING.

THE PRESIDENT TO THE COUNTRY.

WASHINGTON, D.C., JULY 4—10:30 A.M.

The President announces to the country that news from the Army of Potomac, up to 10 P.M. of the 3rd, is such as to cover that army with the highest honor; to promise a great success to the cause of the Union, and to claim the condolence of all for the many gallant fallen; and for this, he especially desires that on this day He, whose will, not ours, should ever be done, be everywhere remembered and reverenced with profoundest gratitude.

(Signed) A. LINCOLN.

THE GREAT BATTLE OF FRIDAY.

Our Special Telegrams from the Battle-Field.

NEAR GETTYSBURGH, SATURDAY, JULY 4.

Another great battle was fought yesterday afternoon, resulting in a magnificent success to the National arms.

At 2 o'clock P.M., LONGSTREET's whole corps advanced from the rebel center against our center. The enemy's forces were hurled upon our position by columns in mass, and also in lines of battle. Our center was held by Gen. HANCOCK, with the noble old Second army corps, aided by Gen. DOUBLEDAY's division of the First corps.

The rebels first opened a terrific artillery bombardment to demoralize our men and then moved their forces with great impetuosity upon our position. HANCOCK received the attack with great firmness, and after a furious battle, lasting until 5 o'clock, the enemy were driven from the field, LONGSTREET's corps being almost annihilated.

The battle was a most magnificent spectacle. It was fought on an open plain, just south of Gettysburgh, with not a tree to interrupt the view. The courage of our men was perfectly sublime.

At 5 P.M. what was left of the enemy *retreated in utter confusion,* leaving dozens of flags, and Gen. HANCOCK estimated *at least five thousand killed and wounded on the field.*

The battle was fought by Gen. HANCOCK with splendid valor. He won imperishable honor, and Gen. MEADE thanked him in the name of the army and the country. He was wounded in the thigh, but remained on the field.

The number of prisoners taken is estimated at 3,000, including at least two Brigadier-Generals—OLMSTEAD, of Georgia, and another—both wounded.

The conduct of our veterans was perfectly magnificent. More than twenty battle flags were taken by our troops. Nearly every regiment has one. The Nineteenth Masschusetts captured four. The repulse was so disastrous to the enemy, that LONGSTREET's corps is perfectly used up. Gen. GIBBON was wounded in the shoulder. Gen. WEBB was wounded and remained on the field. Col. HAMMELL, of the Sixty-sixth New-York, was wounded in the arm.

At 7 o'clock last evening, Gen. MEADE ordered the Third corps, supported by the Sixth, to attack the enemy's right, which was done, and the battle lasted until dark, when a good deal of ground has been gained.

During the day EWELL's corps kept up a desultory attack upon SLOCUM on the right, but was repulsed.

Our cavalry is to-day playing savagely upon the enemy's flank and rear.

L. L. CROUNSE

FROM ANOTHER CORRESPONDENT.

GETTYSBURGH, FRIDAY, JULY 3.

The experience of all the tried and veteran officers of the Army of the Potomac tells of no such desperate conflict as has been in progress during this day. The cannonading of Chancelorsville, Malvern and Manassas were pastimes compared with this. At the headquarters, where I write, sixteen of the horses of Gen. MEADE's staff officers were killed by shell. The house was completely riddled. The Chief of Staff, Gen. BUTTERFIELD, was knocked down by a fragment of case-shot. Col. DICKINSON, Assistant Adjutant-General, had the bone of his wrist pierced through by a piece of shell. Lieut. OLIVER, of Gen. BUTTERFIELD's Staff, was struck in the head; and Capt. CARPENTER, of Gen. MEADE's escort, was wounded in the eye.

While I write the ground about me is covered thick with rebel dead, mingled with our own. Thousand of prisoners have been sent to the rear, and yet the conflict still continues.

The losses on both sides are heavy. Among our wounded officers are HANCOCK, GIBBON, and a great many others whose names I feel restrained from publishing without being assured that they are positively in the list of casualties.

It is near sunset. Our troops hold the field with many rebel prisoners in their hands. The enemy has been magnificently repulsed for three days—repulsed on all sides—most magnificently to-day. Every effort made by him since Wednesday morning to

This famous photograph by Alexander Gardner of a dead Confederate sharpshooter in the Devil's Den, Gettysburg, Pa., July 1863, is believed to have been posed.

penetrate MEADE's lines has been foiled. The final results of the action, I hope to be able to give you at a later hour this evening.

S. WILKESON.

DETAILS FROM OUR SPECIAL CORRESPONDENT.

HEADQUARTERS ARMY OF POTOMAC,
SATURDAY NIGHT, JULY 4.

Who can write the history of a battle whose eyes are immovably fastened upon a central figure of transcendingly absorbing interest—the dead body of an oldest born, crushed by a shell in a position where a battery should never have been sent, and abandoned to death in a building where surgeons dared not to stay?

The battle of Gettysburgh! I am told that it commenced on the 1st of July, a mile north of the town between two weak brigades of infantry and some doomed artillery and the whole force of the rebel army. Among other costs of this error was the death of REYNOLDS. Its value was priceless, however, though priceless was the young and the old blood with which it was bought. The error put us on the defensive, and gave us the choice of position. From the moment that our artillery and infantry rolled back through the main street of Gettysburgh and rolled out of the town to the circle of eminences south of it. We were not to attack but to be attacked. The risks, the difficulties and the disadvantages of the coming battle were the enemy's. Our were the heights for artillery; ours the short, inside lines for manoeuvreing the reinforcing; ours the cover of stonewalls, fences and the crests of hills. The ground upon which we were driven to accept battle was wonderfully favorable to us. A popular description of it would be to say that it was in form an elongated and somewhat sharpened horseshoe, with the toe to Gettysburgh and the heel to the south.

LEE's plan of battle was simple. He massed his troops upon the east side of this shoe of position, and thundered on it obstinately to break it. The shelling of our batteries from the nearest overlooking hill, and the unflinching courage and complete discipline of the army of the Potomac repelled the attack. It was renewed at the point of the shoe—renewed desperately at the southwest heel—renewed on the western side with an effort consecrated to success by EWELL's earnest oaths, and on which the fate of the invasion of Pennsylvania was fully put at stake. Only a perfect infantry and an artillery educated in the midst of charges of hostile brigades could possibly have sustained this assault. HANCOCK's corps did sustain it, and has covered itself with immortal honors by its constancy and courage. The total wreck of CUSHING's battery—the list of its killed and wounded—the losses of officers, men and horses COWEN sustained—and the marvelous outspread upon the board of death of dead soldiers and dead animals—of dead soldiers in blue, and dead soldiers in gray—more marvelous to me than anything I have ever seen in war—are a ghastly and shocking testimony to the terrible fight of the Second corps that none will gainsay. That corps will ever have the distinction of breaking the pride and power of the rebel invasion.

For such details I have the heart for. The battle commenced at daylight, on the side of the horse-shoe position, exactly opposite to that which EWELL had sworn to crush through. Musketry preceded the rising of the sun. A thick wood veiled this fight, but out of its leafy darkness arose the smoke and the surging and swelling of the fire, from intermittent to continuous, and crushing, told of the wise tactics of the rebels of attacking in force and changing their troops. Seemingly the attack of the day was to be made through that wood. The demonstration was protected—it was absolutely preparative; but there was no artillery fire accompanying the musketry, and shrewd officers in our western front mentioned, with the gravity due to the fact, that the rebels had felled trees at intervals upon the edge of the wood they occupied in face of our position. Those were breastworks for the protection of artillery men.

Suddenly, and about 10 in the forenoon, the firing on the east side, and everywhere about our lines ceased. A silence as of deep sleep fell upon the field of battle. Our army cooked, ate and slumbered. The rebel army moved 120 guns to the west and messed there LONGSTREET's corps and HILL's corps, to hurl them upon the really weakest point of our entire position.

Eleven o'clock—twelve o'clock—one o'clock. In the shadow cast by the tiny farm house 16 by 20, which Gen. MEADE had made his Headquarters, lay wearied Staff officers and tired reporters. There was not wanting to the peacefulness of the scene the singing of a bird, which had a nest in a peach tree within the tiny yard of the whitewashed cottage. In the midst of its warbling, a shell screamed over the house, instantly followed by another, and another, and in a moment the air was full of the most complete artillery prelude to an infantry battle that was ever exhibited. Every size and form of shell known to British and to American gunnery shrieked, whirled, moaned, whistled and wrathfully fluttered over our ground. As many as six in a second, constantly two in a second, bursting and screaming over and around the headquarters, made a very hell of fire that amazed the oldest officers. They burst in the yard—burst next to the fence on both sides, garnished as usual with the hitched horses of aids and orderlies. The fastened animals reared and plunged with terror. Then one fell, then another—sixteen laid dead and mangled before the fire ceased, still fastened by their halters, which gave the expression of being wickedly tied up to die painfully. These brute victims of cruel war touched all hearts. Through the midst of the storm of screaming and exploding shells, an ambulance, driven by its frenzied conductor at full speed, presented to all of us the marvelous spectacle of a horse going rapidly on three legs. A hinder one had been shot off at the hock. A shell tore up the little step of the Headquarters Cottage, and ripped bags of oats as with a knife. Another soon carried off one of its two pillars. Soon a spherical case burst opposite the open door—another ripped through the low garret. The remaining pillar went almost immediately to the howl of a fixed shot that WHITWORTH must have made. During this fire the houses at twenty and thirty feet distant, were receiving their death, and soldiers in Federal blue were torn to pieces in the road and died with the peculiar yells that blend the extorted cry of pain with horror and despair. Not an orderly—not an ambulance—not a straggler was to be seen upon the plain swept by this tempest of orchestral death thirty minutes after it commenced. Were not one hundred and twenty pieces of artillery, trying to cut from the field every battery we had in position to resist their purposed infantry attack, and to sweep away the slight defenses behind which our Infantry were waiting? Forty minutes—fifty minutes—counted on watches that ran! Oh so languidly. Shells through the two lower rooms. A shell into the chimney that daringly did not explode. Shells in the yard. The air thicker and fuller and more deafening with the howling and whirring of these infernal missiles. The chief of staff struck—SETH WILLIAMS—loved and respected through the army, separated from instant death by two inches of space vertically measured. An Aide bored with a fragment of iron through the bone of the arm. Another, cut with an exploded piece. And the time measured on the sluggish watches was one hour and forty minutes.

Then there was a lull, and we knew that the rebel infantry was charging. And splendidly they did this work—the highest and severest test of the stuff that soldiers are made of. HILL's division, in line of battle, came first on the double-quick. Their muskets at the "right-shoulder-shift." LONGSTREET's came as the support, at the

Confederate soldiers at Gettysburg, 1863.

usual distance, with war cries and a savage insolence as yet untutored by defeat. They rushed in perfect order across the open field up to the very muzzles of the guns, which tore lanes through them as they came. But they met men who were equal in spirit, and their superiors in tenacity. There never was better fighting since Thermopyalæ than was done yesterday by our infantry and artillery. The rebels were over our defenses. They had cleaned cannoniers and horses from one of the guns, and were whirling it around to use upon us. The bayonet drove them back. But so hard pressed was this brave infantry that at one time, from the exhaustion of their ammunition, every battery upon the principal crest of attack was silent, except CROWEN's. His services of grape and cannister was awful. It enabled our line, outnumbered two to one, first to beat back LONGSTREET, and then to charge upon him, and take a great number of his men and himself prisoners. Strange sight! So terrible was our musketry and artillery fire, that when ARMSTEAD's brigade was checked in its charge, and stood reeling, all of its men dropped their muskets and crawled on their hands and knees underneath the stream of shot till close to our troops, where they made signs of surrendering. They passed through our ranks scarcely noticed, and slowly went down the slope to the road in the rear.

Before they got there the grand charge of EWELL solemnly sworn to and carefully prepared, had failed.

The rebels had retreated to their lines, and opened anew the storm of shell and shot from their 120 guns. Those who remained at the riddled headquarters will never forget the crouching, and dodging, and running, of the Butternut-colored captives when they got under this, their friends, fire. It was appalling to us as good soldiers even as they were.

What remains to say of the fight! It staggled [unintelligible] on the middle of the horse shoe on the west, grew big and angry on the heel at the southwest, lasted there till 6 o'clock in the evening, when the fighting Sixth corps went joyously by as a reinforcement through the wood, bright with coffee pots on the fire.

I leave details to my excellent friend and associate Mr. HENRY. My pen is heavy. Oh, you dead, who at Gettysburgh have baptized with your blood the second birth of Freedom in America, how you are to be envied! I rise from a grave where wet clay I have passionately kissed, and I look up and see Christ spanning this battle-field with his feet and reaching fraternal and lovingly up to heaven. His right hand opens the gates of Paradise—with his left he beckons to these mutilated, bloody, swollen forms to ascend.

INCIDENTS OF THE BATTLE.

Capt. CUSHING, Company A, Fourth Regular.

Rebel officers with whom I have conversed frankly admit that the result of the last two days has been most disastrous to their cause, which depended, they say, upon the success of LEE's attempt to transfer the seat of war from Virginia to the Northern Border States. A sounded rebel Colonel told me that, in the first and second days' fight, the rebel losses were between ten and eleven thousand. Yesterday they were greater still. In one part of the field, in a space not more than twenty feet in circumference, in front of Gen. GIBBONS' divisions, I counted seven dead rebels, three of whom were piled on top of each other. And close by in a spot not more than fifteen feet square lay fifteen "graybacks," stretched in death. These were the adventurous spirits, who in the face of the horrible stream of canister, shell and musketry, scaled the fence wall in their attempt upon our batteries. Very large numbers of wounded were also strewn around not to mention more who had crawled away or been taken away. The field in front of the stonewall was literally covered with dead and wounded, a large proportion of whom were rebels. Where our musketry and artillery took effect they lay in swaths, as if mown down by a scythe. This field presented a horrible sight—such as never yet been witnessed during the war. Not less than one thousand dead and wounded laid in a space of less than four acres in extent, and that, too, after numbers had crawled away to places of shelter.

The enemy's infantry, saving a small force of sharpshooters, was wholly out of sight at daylight on Saturday morning. There was talk on Friday night, after battle, of organizing a column of pursuit.

Before the fighting was over—before sunset, considerably—the Signal Officers reported that an immense train of army wagons was going out of Gettysburgh northwest, on the road to Cashtown. Oh! That they could have run against the stonewall of the Harrisburgh army.

July 8, 1863.

THE RETREAT OF LEE.

The Whole Rebel Army Pushing for the Potomac.

The Route of Retreat Via Hagerstown and Williamsport.

The Army of the Potomac Pressing Closely Behind.

Desperate Efforts of the Rebels to Save Their Trains.

THE POTOMAC VERY HIGH.

Rumor of the Commencement of Another Battle Near Williamsport.

MOVEMENTS OF OUR CAVALRY.

Terrible Losses of the Enemy at Gettysburgh.

NEWS RECEIVED IN HARRISBURGH.

HARRISBURGH, PENN., TUESDAY, JULY 7.

Gen. COUCH received information to-day, which is considered reliable, that Gen. LEE intends occupying and holding Maryland Heights until his army can recross the Potomac.

There is no news here to-day from the Army of the Potomac.

HARRISBURGH, TUESDAY, JULY 7—6 P.M.

Information received here proves beyond a doubt the continued retreat of the rebels toward Hagerstown and Williamsport, with the intention of crossing the Potomac. Their wagon trains are all in front, and are being ferried across slowly in two flatboats.

The Potomac is very high—bank-full—and they cannot cross, their only pontoon bridge having been destroyed.

A large force of infantry prevented the capture of Williamsport by Gen. BUFORD, with his cavalry.

Our army is fast following them up, and a great battle will be fought before they succeed in getting away. This fight, it is hoped, will result in the capture or dispersion of the whole of LEE's army. . . .

HARRISBURGH, TUESDAY, JULY 7—10:20 P.M.

The latest report here is that the whole rebel army is routed in utter panic.

They are fleeing in all directions, throwing away arms, abandoning guns, trains and everything for life.

TELEGRAM FROM FREDERICK, MD.

WASHINGTON, TUESDAY, JULY 7.

Mr. HENRY sends the following to this bureau from Frederick:

The rebels are known to be fortifying several gaps in the South Mountain, to cover their retreat across the Potomac. The main body of LEE's army will probably attempt to cross the Potomac at Hancock, for which point they are making in a disorganized, demoralized condition.

Our cavalry is operating vigorously on the rebel flanks and rear, capturing large numbers of prisoners. Several hundred wagons loaded with plunder, obtained in Pennsylvania, have been captured by our forces, and the prospect is that much of their ammunition and supply trains will be gobbled before they reach the Potomac.

Among the prisoners thus far captured are twenty-three Colonels, and a host of officers of inferior grades.

The rebels in the late battles lost thirteen General officers, killed, wounded or prisoners. A rebel Colonel, with whom I conversed, says that LEE's invading force did not exceed seventy-five thousand men. He had 180 pieces of artillery with him.

The rebel losses, as estimated by themselves, foot up thirty thousand. We have taken about twelve thousand prisoners, not including their wounded, who have all fallen into our hands.

Stirring news from PLEASONTON's cavalry may be expected within the next twenty-four hours. His forces are harassing the rebels in their retreat, playing havoc with their trains, &c.

Upward of fifty stand of colors were captured from the enemy.

OUR SPECIAL ARMY CORRESPONDENCE.

FURTHER DETAILS OF THE GREAT BATTLES OF FRIDAY.

GETTYSBURGH, PENN., SUNDAY, JULY 5.

As the details, the incidents and the general history of the great victory were brought to light, it is clearly defined as the most hotly contested and destructive engagement of the great rebellion. The peculiar feature of the battle is the ferocity and desperation with which it was fought by both armies, and the glorious issue places

Union Army construction corps in action.

the luster of the National arms, and the valor of the Army of the Potomac in the imperishable annals of brilliant history.

The battle occupied three days. Six hours fighting on Wednesday, four hours on Thursday, and including the artillery firing on Friday, thirteen hours that day, making a total of twenty-three hours, during which the battle raged with extreme fury.

The momentous and decisive part of the battle was that on Friday. It began really at daylight, and continued until 10 o'clock, the principal part of the musketry fighting being on the right, with SLOCUM's corps. A lull of three hours followed, during which the enemy massed his artillery on our centre, held by HANCOCK with the Second, and NEWTON with the First corps. At 1 o'clock one hundred and twenty guns opened on that position, and raised shot and shell in a perfect deluge for one hour and forty minutes. A graphic description of this awful period has already been furnished to the TIMES by an abler pen than mine, for that writer and one of the TIMES' messengers had the exciting felicity of enduring that storm of iron during the whole time. Mr. WILKESON is to-day engaged in the mournful duty of obtaining the remains and effects of his eldest son, the gallant young BAYARD, who was mortally wounded on Wednesday, left on the field, and dying finally, after ten hours suffering, without a friend or a word to soothe the dying agonies of his soul. Lieut. WILKESON was but nineteen years old, yet had command of Battery G, Fourth regular artillery. His death adds another noble soul to the holocaust of this terrible war.

I rode this morning over the entire length of the battle-field, and it is not too much to say, for I have seen nearly every other battle-field in Maryland and Virginia, that the slaughter was perfectly unparalleled. Our details were busily engaged in collecting and burying the dead, and the ghastly, terrible sights were enough to shock a heart of adamant.

The vast number of dead lying in front of SLOCUM's line, on the right, and of HANCOCK's and NEWTON's on the centre, attracted much comment. They had been literally mown down by whole ranks at a single discharge. SLOCUM accomplished a bloody repulse of EWELL's corps on Friday morning, sustaining but small loss himself, his position being very formidable, against which the enemy insanely charged.

But the field, full of the greatest incidents and the scene of the most desperate fighting, was on the centre, in front of HANCOCK and NEWTON, against whom LONGSTREET's corps was precipitated. The enemy's front was that of one division in line of battle; there were two such lines, and a very heavy line of the skirmishers, almost equal to another line of battle. Out of their concealment in the woods they came across the open fields and up the gentle crest, on the top of which was our line—a weak line of men behind a line of defenses hastily thrown up and composed partly of stone walls, partly of rifle-pits, and partly of natural projections of soil and rock. The first charge was repulsed; the line broke and fell back before it had reached a point two-thirds the way over. A second line was formed; the officers came to the front, and with the onset of fierce and brutal hearts they rushed. Our men looked with astonishment, while fighting with great vigor; their line was dangerously weak; the defenses were not formidable. A few men temporarily gave way; our advance, in some instances, slightly faltered. The artillery engaged was small in force, having been seriously weakened during the early part of the fight. The rebels came on so close that their expressions of fierce rage were plainly distinguished; some of them actually gained the inside of the first wall—but they never returned. Our immortal men, nerved to a degree of desperation never before equaled, poured forth such a devastating fire, and the artillery joining with its terrible canister, that the two long lines of the foe literally sank into the earth. Of the divisions of PICKETT and HETH, who made that charge, composed of eight brigades, positively not two brigades returned uninjured across the field. *The color-bearers of thirty-five rebel regiments,* who were in that charge, were shot down, the colors fell on the field, and were gathered by the victorious veterans of the Second corps. Being repulsed, large numbers of the enemy started back on the retreat, but our fire was so destructive that they fell flat on their faces, or again rushed about and implored mercy at our hands as prisoners of war. Seven Colonels of rebel regiments were buried on that field this morning; eight more were captured, beside those who were wounded and crawled or were taken off. Among the rebel officers killed and captured on that front were BARKSDALE on Thursday; GARNETT killed, and ARMISTEAD wounded on Friday;—these general officers; Col. MAGRUDER, brother of Gen. MAGRUDER, killed; Col. LEE, of the Forty-eighth Virginia is a prisoner; Col. ALLEN, of the Forty-eighth Georgia is killed; Col. MILLER, of the Forty-second Mississippi is a prisoner and wounded; Col. FRYE, of the Thirteenth Alabama, and Col. ASHBORN, of Virginia are both prisoners. All these captured or destroyed by the brigade of Gen. WEBB, a most intrepid officer, who won, with many others, the highest plaudits for his conduct.

A peculiar fact concerning our position is contained in the expression of surprise which the rebel officers uttered when they crossed our lines as prisoners of war. One of the Colonels said, as he looked at our thin line, "Where are the men who fought us?" "Here," said a Captain. "My God!" exclaimed the Colonel, "if we only had another line we could have whipped you;" and then, still gazing about him with astonishment, he continued, with great emphasis, *"By G-d, we could have whipped you as it was!"* This is a positive fact, and illustrates how the noble Army of the Potomac can yet fight, after all the imputations of demoralization and inefficiency which have been heaped upon it.

The Second division of the Second corps loses 42 officers killed and wounded, and 1,786 enlisted men killed and wounded.

The highest praise is awarded to Gens. HANCOCK and NEWTON, for their distinguished conduct on this portion of the field. HANCOCK was severely wounded in the thigh, but remained, laying on his back on the field, and giving the orders. Gen. NEWTON was especially active in supporting the line on the right with reinforcements.

History will never chronicle a tenth part of the gallant deeds performed during these bloody days; but the satisfaction of having nobly performed his duty shall be the sweet recompense of every patriot's heart.

The enemy, by a partially secret and ignominious retreat, has awarded to this gallant army the acknowledgment of victory. His forces are now on their way back to Virginia, beaten, weakened and demoralized by a terrible defeat; he is hotly pursued, a victorious army on his rear, a strong local force on his flank, and a swollen river in his front, are the obstacles to his successful retreat.

L. L. CROUNSE

Following hard upon the elation caused by victories at Gettysburg and Vicksburg came panic and outrage caused by the draft riots in New York City. The Union Congress had passed a conscription law in March 1863 over the almost unanimous opposition of Democrats. Party leaders told their followers, especially Irish Americans in New York City, that they would be drafted to fight in a war to free the slaves who would come north and take away their jobs. The hiring of black stevedores to replace striking Irish dockworkers in June 1863 lent credence to the charge. The provision in the conscription law that a drafted man could hire a substitute or pay a $300 commutation fee to avoid serving gave rise to the accusation of class bias against the poor. When the drawing of names of draftees began in mid-July, mobs composed mainly of Irish Americans burned draft offices, attacked the premises of *The New York Times* and *New York Tribune* (Republican papers that supported the draft), burned the Colored Orphan Asylum, lynched several black men, and destroyed the homes or business places of prominent Republicans. The sheer number of rioters overwhelmed the police, and the militia had gone to Pennsylvania because of the Confederate invasion that culminated at Gettysburg. On the fourth day of the riot (July 16), returning militia and the police finally brought the riot to an end. At least 120 people, mostly rioters, had been killed. It was the worst urban violence in American history.

July 15, 1863.

THE REIGN OF THE RABBLE.

Continuation of the Riot—The Mob Increased in Numbers.

DEMONSTRATIONS IN THE UPPER WARDS.

Encounters Between the Mob, the Metropolitans and the Military.

Large Numbers of the Rioters Killed.

COLONEL O'BRIEN MURDERED AND HUNG.

Streets Barricaded, Buildings Burned, Stores Sacked, and Private Dwellings Plundered.

Gov. Seymour in the City—He Addresses the Mob and Issues a Proclamation.

Increased Preparations on the Part of the Authorities.

The Mercantile Community Aroused—Citizens Volunteering en Masse.

REPORTED SUSPENSION OF THE DRAFT.

The reign of the mob which was inaugurated on Monday morning has not yet ceased, although today will probably witness the end of the infamous usurpation. All Monday night the rioters, unchecked, prosecuted their depredations, and yesterday morning found the lawless spirit not a whit abated. On the contrary, the malignant originators of the disturbance grew bolder at the impunity with which they were necessarily permitted to indulge in their first day's career, and at one time more serious consequences than any which have yet occurred were threatened. Happily, however, the military and police authorities early in the day recovered from the partial paralysis into which the sudden demonstrations of the mob had thrown them, and in sufficient force were able to contend with the truly formidable organization of lawless men. A few wholesome but severe lessons were administered to the rioters during the day wherever they showed themselves most turbulent, and toward evening there seemed to be unmistakable indications that the supremacy of law would soon be acknowledged even by the most rabid of the offenders. Perhaps, however, the mere fact that a score or more of the rioters were killed in the various conflicts with the military and the police was not solely the cause of this abatement of the spirit of violence. The proclamation of Gov. HORATIO SEYMOUR, and the announcement made early in the afternoon, that President LINCOLN had ordered the draft in this City to be suspended, may also have had something to do with restoring the malcontents to reason. At any rate, after nightfall the streets were comparatively quiet.

There is no question that the rioting yesterday was engaged in by vastly larger numbers than on Monday, and the spectators of the disorderly scenes were increased also by many thousands. This may be accounted for by the fact that all the large manufacturing establishments were closed, labor on the docks and at the ship-yards was suspended, and every branch of business was arrested, leaving thousands of persons at liberty to participate in the excesses, either passively as spectators, or in an active manner.

In the movement of the mob yesterday, moreover, there was no mistaking the fact that pillage was the prime incentive of the majority. "Resistance to the draft" was the flimsiest of veils to cover the wholesale plundering which characterized the operations of the day.

Our reporters record their observations and the incidents they have been able to collect, as follows:

The Riot in Second-avenue.

EIGHTEEN PERSONS REPORTED KILLED, SEVERAL FATALLY INJURED.

Between 12 and 1 o'clock yesterday, the rioters commenced their attack upon the Union Steam Works, situated on the corner of Twenty-second-street and Second-avenue. The guns taken from the armory on Monday were stored in this building, and the most active efforts were made by the insurgents to secure them.

The rioters turned out in large force, numbering from 4,000 to 5,000 people—including children. The shops and stores for half a mile around were closed, and the streets were filled with crowds of excited men, women and children.

At 2 P.M. three hundred Policemen, under the command of one of the Inspectors, arrived upon the ground. The rioters had in the meantime taken possession of the building, and, when the officials made their appearance, they attempted to escape by the rear windows; but too late to escape the notice of the Police. Finding themselves caught in a tight place, they made an attack on the Police. This assault the Officers met by a volley from their revolvers, and five of the mob were shot.

About twenty rioters remained in the building; there was but one way for them to make their exit. The police filled the door, and each had, in addition to his usual weapons, a loaded revolver. The mob became desperate and made a deadly assault upon the police; they in turn used their weapons so effectually that fourteen of the mob were almost instantly killed. A scene, which defies all powers of description, then followed. Men, women and children rushed through the streets in the most frantic state of mind, and as the dead and wounded were borne from the place, the wild howlings of the bereaved, were truly sad to hear.

Four persons were killed and quite a number were injured by jumping from the second story windows of the building.

When the rioters were dispersed, the Police took possession of the Union Steam Works building, and at late hour last night they still held the place. A collision between the authorities and the mob is liable to take place at any moment. The Police and military are fully prepared to meet them.

THE RIOTERS IN THE SECOND-AVENUE

At about 8½ o'clock yesterday morning a telegraph dispatch was received that a large crowd of rioters were gathering all along the Second-avenue, in the neighborhood of Thirty-fourth-street, threatening all the houses along that thoroughfare. A strong force of police, about 300, were immediately detailed under Inspector CARPENTER to break up the crowd. The rioters had gathered in formidable numbers, and for a time committed no overt acts. It was then ascertained that Col. H. F. O'BRIEN, of the Eleventh New York Volunteers, who lives in the immediate neighborhood, had tendered his services, and those of his command, for the purpose of suppressing the riot. The mob, becoming incensed, proceeded to the residence of the Colonel and warning his family to leave, completely gutted the entire house. They were about to set it on fire, but finding that the house was not his property, they desisted. The police, under Inspector CARPENTER and Capt. COPEL then marched from the Central office, preceded by the Broadway Squad, to the Bowery, where they took possession of a sufficient number of the Third-avenue cars, and proceeded up the avenue. On arriving at Thirty-second-street, the railroad track was found obstructed, and the police then formed in a solid column and marched down to Second-avenue. They were met by the assembled mob with silence. When the whole force had got in the block between Thirty-fourth and Thirty-fifth streets, they were closed in upon by the mob and assailed by a thick shower of bricks and stones, which rained from the houses and windows in the neighborhood. For some moments the men wavered and the peril was imminent, when the reassuring voices of the officers in command recalled them, who then returned the shower of stones with their revolvers. The order was then given to charge, and a most furious onset was made on the rioters, driving them into the houses, the officers chasing them all over the buildings and driving them into the streets, where they were scattered by a most vigorous application of clubs. All the side streets were then cleared, and the police marched over the battle-ground victorious. The police then marched through the infected district, meeting nothing but lowering looks, the mob being thoroughly beaten. While marching through the Third-avenue, they met a detachment of the Eleventh regiment N. Y. S. V., headed by Col. O'BRIEN, and a couple of field-pieces, under command of Lieut. EAGELSON, coming down the avenue on a trot. They formed a junction with the police force, and then countermarched through Second-avenue.

THE DEATH OF COL. O'BRIEN.

After the detachment of military under Col. O'BRIEN had succeeded in dispersing the mob, they fell back at some distance from the Colonel, who went forward near the crowd, having his sword and a revolver in his hands, when he was immediately set upon, surrounded, and so dreadfully maltreated that he expired a short time after. His body lay dead on the sidewalk for some time, and some of the more fiendish in the crowd amused themselves by firing several pistol-shots at his head, after which the body was strung up to the nearest lamp-post, where it remained for some time. It was afterward taken down and thrown again in the street, and had not been moved up to 8 o'clock last night. The reasons given by some of the rioters for such treatment were that the military had shot a mother and her child.

DOINGS OF THE MILITARY.

At an early hour the military began to assemble at Police Headquarters, and were in readiness to proceed to the performance of any duty to which they might be assigned. A company of United States regulars from Governor's Island, under the command of Lieut. Wood, formed in line in front of the Headquarters.

At 10½ o'clock this company was sent to the Seventh Ward, where the rioters had begun to tear down a number of buildings, and were also setting them on fire. The following order was issued by Gen. Sandford:

NEW-YORK, July 14, 1863.

The whole military force now at the Police Headquarters will forthwith return to the Seventh-avenue arsenal and report to Maj. Gen. Sandford.

CHAS. W SANDFORD, Major-General.
Headquarters Department of the East.

New-York, July 14, 1863.

Special Order—All the troops called out for the protection of the City are placed under the command of Maj.-Gen. Sandford, whose orders they will implicitly obey.

C. T. CHRISTIANSEN
Assistant Adjutant-General

In pursuance of these orders all the available military force, with the exception of Lieut. wood's company of United States regulars, were sent to Thirty-fourth-street, where the mob was carrying on their work of destruction, tearing down buildings and seting them on fire. About 10 o'clock the military were drawn up in line, and orders given to fire.

The orders were promptly obeyed, many persons being wounded, and a large number (it is reported), were killed. The muskets were loaded with Minié balls.

About the same time, Lieut. Wood's company encountered a large crowd in Delancy-street, which attempted to obstruct their passage, and made an attack upon the soldiers. The brave fellows, however, were not to be frightened, and Lieut. Wood immediately gave the order to fire, which was obeyed with the greatest promptitude. A large number of the mob fell, some killed and others seriously wounded. Those who escaped the galling fire of ball scattered, and the soldiers were left in possession of the field.

At about 10½ o'clock yesterday morning, as a Company of United States infantry from Forts Lafayette, Hamilton and Richmond, under the command of Lieut. Wood, were marching through Pitt-street, they were assailed with volleys of bricks and stones, and at length, having been ordered to disperse the rioters at all hazards, fired upon the crowd, and several persons are said to have been killed.

In Thirty-fourth-street, at about the same time, three detachments of United States Marines, one company of Zouaves, and one company of regulars from Fort Schuyler, together with a company of artillery, and two pieces of ordinance from Staten Island, arrived on the ground where the mob had strongly posted themselves. Col. O'Brien had command of these forces, and marched his men straight through the crowd down the Third-avenue. He also fired his revolver into the crowd, which resulted in death to some and wounded many.

The crowd, continuing to increase, the two howitzers were placed in position on the corner of Thirtieth-street, and three rounds of blank cartridges were fired among the rioters. This dispersed them but for a few moments, for they again shortly after appeared in full force, menacing the military with threats of speedy retaliation. Many of them had, by this time, obtained arms, and threatened to overpower the troops.

Col. O'Brien of the Eleventh New-York, was afterward beaten to death by the crowd on Second-avenue, and then hung.

At the Seventh regiment Armory a guard of 400 men were stationed, under Lieut. Kempe. They had two howitzers loaded with grape and canister.

Col. Henry E. Davies was busily engaged during the day organizing a volunteer force at the same armory. Volunteering seemed to go on briskly, and the Colonel expected to have a force of 10,000 men organized before morning.

At the Eighth regiment Armory there were over 100 men guarding the premises.

Col. Jardine, of the old Hawkins Zouaves, was engaged in reorganizing the old regiment of the Hawkins Zouaves.

At the Arsenal and the Division Armory cannon were trained and ready for use, and any attack upon them would be repulsed with great loss to the rioters.

The military force under the command of Gens. Brown and Sandford, were strongly posted at the arsenal in Thirty-seventh-street.

Miscellaneous Movements.

BARRICADES ON THE FIRST-AVENUE.

Late in the afternoon the rioters commenced to barricade First-avenue, near Eleventh-street, and First-avenue, near Fourteenth-street. The telegraph poles, which they had torn down, were used for these barricades, together with numerous carts, which had been picked up in the adjacent streets. At Thirteenth-street two street-sweeping machines, which had been captured the previous evening were burned amid the shouts of the men, women and boys who thronged the avenue. The especial spite the rioters had against these machines was that they were labor-saving, and to their ignorant minds, they appeared their prime enemies. The moving spirit in the riotous conduct was a man who announced himself a returned soldier, but who declared that his sympathy had been aroused for the South by the emancipation of the "niggers." He made excited speeches to crowds of people, and seemed particularly desirous of stirring up a fight with any one who should have the hardi-hood to combat his sentiments. He and others inveighed bitterly against grain-elevators as labor-saving machines—as inimical to the poor man, and intimated a purpose to destroy them as they had destroyed the street-sweepers. Upon the adjacent tenement houses were numbers of men, some of them armed with guns in anticipation of an attack by the soldiers. A gun-store in Fifth-street near Avenue A had been broken open in the morning and completely gutted of its contents. The mob were in a great state of fear, the false alarms of mischievous boys causing a general scampering.

ATTACK ON THE MAYOR'S RESIDENCE.

Early in the morning the rioters had assembled *en masse* on Fifth-avenue, in front of the residence of Mayor OPDYKE, and commenced a violent assault upon his house, and succeeded in forcing the front door, and in breaking the costly plate glass in the second and third story windows. One of the lamps on the front stoop was entirely demolished. The riot here was mainly conducted by boys between the ages of eighteen and twenty years.

Col. B. F. MANIERRE seeing that things were likely to take a serious shape, organized a few friends into a platoon, and with clubs and revolvers succeeded for a time in holding the rioters in check. They were finally relieved by a strong detachment of police, who held the position unmolested until they in turn were relieved by a detachment of the United States soldiers from Governor's Island, under command of Capt. WILKINS. This detachment numbered 84 men and four Sergeants, and now hold the place without opposition. It will be necessary to keep a strong detachment of police or military around the house of Mayor OPDYKE, as it is, if possible, the sincere intention of the rioters to gut and burn the building.

Before we left this scene of action a man named PETER DOLAN, who lives in the upper part of the City, was arrested and taken into custody by the police on the charge of being one of the ringleaders in the assault upon Mayor OPDYKE's house.

STOPPAGE OF CITY CARS

The cars on most of the City railroads suspended their trips early in the day, so that it was found difficult to obtain access to different parts of the City. The Third-avenue cars did not run at all during the day, a portion of their tracks up town having been torn up by the mob on Monday. The Fourth-avenue ran cars till noon, when they were obliged to stop from the same cause. The Sixth and Eighth-avenue cars also ran during the forenoon, but stopped early in the day. The reason of the mob tearing up the railroad tracks is said to have been to prevent the cars from conveying troops up town. The track of the Hudson River Railroad, between Fifty-third and Fifty-ninth street was torn up by the rioters early in the morning. The horse cars of this road were stopped during the morning at the corner of Twenty-sixth-street and Eleventh-avenue, probably for the purpose of plundering the passengers, but after being detained awhile, they were permitted to pass on. Some of the City railroad lines stopped running on account of the mob threatening the drivers and conductors. They also threatened to burn the depots unless the railroads suspended their trips.

Many of the stages running through Broadway, were taken possession of by the Police Commissioners to be used in transferring the police from place to place. One of the drivers of these stages having taken it into his head that he would not carry Policemen, his place was very summarily filled by a member of the force, and himself turned loose upon the street.

BUSINESS GENERALLY SUSPENDED.

The rioters, in large numbers, at early in the morning went to the docks and ordered the longshoremen to join them, under threats of violence. The New-Orleans and other lines of steamers have in consequence been compelled to cease loading. Jewelry stores, money brokers' offices and other establishments containing property of a valuable character, were not opened at all, and after 3 o'clock, as a general thing, all business places were shut up. The Custom-House and Assay-office were closed at an early hour in the afternoon.

BURNING OF A GAS-HOUSE AND FERRY-HOUSE.

After perpetrating several acts of brutality in the vicinity of the North-river, the mob proceeded to the gas-house on Forty-second-street, and in a few moments the building was in flames. They then went to the ferry-house at the foot of Forty-second-street, North River, and after meeting with some opposition by the police, which proved of no avail whatever, they set fire to the building, and it is now in ruins. The crowd at this point was probably the largest ever seen in this City congregated in one place. It may be safely asserted that there were over 6,000 people assembled in that neighborhood. Some were armed with clubs, some with pistols, and a few muskets. The police were powerless, and were obliged, from sheer exhaustion, to let the rioters for a time take their own way.

BURNING OF CAPT. DUFFY'S HEADQUARTERS.

About 1 o'clock yesterday morning the headquarters of Capt. DUFFY, Provost-Marshal of the Fifth Congressional District, corner of Grand and Ridge streets, was surrounded by a mob of about five hundred persons, who applied the incendiary torch and burned it to the ground.

The papers and documents had, however, been previously removed.

THE RIOTERS IN CATHERINE-STREET.

About 10 o'clock, last evening, a barber-shop and a shoe-store in Catherine-street, near East Broadway, were set on fire by a mob of about 500 men and boys. The buildings were entirely destroyed. The large clothing store of BROOKS BROTHERS, situated in the same street, was also visited by the insurgents. A great amount of plunder was secured by the mob in the shape of clothing, boots and shoes, and goods from a grocery store adjoining the burned buildings.

ONSLAUGHT ON NEGRO DWELLINGS.

At Thirty-fifth-street there are a number of Negro dwellings. An onslaught was next made upon them; fortunately, however, all the Negro women and children had been secretly conveyed by the Police to the Twentieth Precinct Station-house, where they were made secure in cells. Learning this, and with a purpose, if possible, not to lose their prey, the rioters next made a charge on the Station-house, but by the untiring exertion of Capt. WALLING and his brave men they were prevented from gaining admission. They were at last dispersed by the military, who, firing upon the crowd, soon set them to flight.

ORGANIZATION OF MINUTE MEN.

The organization of Minute men by Col. DAVIS, under order of Gen. SANDFORD, proceeded yesterday with great vigor at the Seventh Regiment Armory at the Tompkins Market. A complete regiment was raised and command given by Col. DAVIS to Col. CLEVELAND WINSLOW, Duryee's Zouaves. A large number of the old regiment volunteered their services. The organization of Minute men will be continued to-day at the same place by Col. DAVIS. A brigade will probably be completed by this evening. It is the duty as well as the immediate interest of every citizen to organize. The services of the members of the old regiment are particularly desired to command drill the new levies. All law-abiding citizens are most urgently requested to report at the Seventh Regiment Armory without a moments delay, when every man will be immediately equipped. Every man in arms to-day will be worth ten to-morrow.

After Civil War battles the dead were hastily buried on the battlefield, sometimes in mass graves. A lawyer in Gettysburg, David Wills, wanted to reinter Union soldiers killed in that battle with dignity and honor in a military cemetery. With the support of governors of Northern states, Wills purchased land for this purpose adjacent to the local cemetery on the hill south of town where part of the battle had been fought. The cemetery for the Union dead, which became the model for other national military cemeteries established during and after the war, was dedicated on November 19, 1863. The main speaker was Edward Everett, America's most celebrated orator, who gave a two-hour speech that lived up to expectations. President Lincoln then rose and spoke for two minutes. Few at the time appreciated the power of Lincoln's words, printed here, but one who did was Edward Everett, who wrote to Lincoln the next day: "I should be glad, if I could flatter myself that I came as near to the central idea of the occasion, in two hours, as you did in two minutes."

November 20, 1863.

THE HEROES OF JULY.

A Solemn and Imposing Event.

Dedication of the National Cemetery at Gettysburgh.

IMMENSE NUMBER OF VISITORS.

Oration by Hon. Edward Everett—Speeches of President Lincoln, Mr. Seward and Governor Seymor.

The ceremonies attending the dedication of the National Cemetery commenced this morning by a grand military and civic display, under command of Maj.-Gen. COUCH. The line of march was taken up at 10 o'clock, and the procession marched through the principal streets to the Cemetery, where the military formed in line and saluted the President. At 11½ the head of the procession arrived at the main stand. The President and members of the Cabinet, together with the chief military and civic dignitaries, took possession on the stand. The President seated himself between Mr. SEWARD and Mr. EVERETT after a reception marked with the respect and perfect silence due to the solemnity of the occasion, every man in the immense gathering uncovering on his appearance. . . .

Federal troops marched through the streets of Gettysburg, Pennsylvania, during the dedication of the National Cemetery on November 19, 1863. The occasion provided the setting for Lincoln's "few appropriate remarks" which became known forever as the Gettysburg Address.
(*U.S. Army Signal Corps*)

PRESIDENT LINCOLN'S ADDRESS.

The President then delivered the following dedication speech:

Fourscore and seven years ago our Fathers brought forth upon this Continent a new nation, conceived in liberty and dedicated to the proposition that all men are created equal. [Applause]. Now we are engaged in a great civil war, testing whether that nation, or any nation so conceived and so dedicated, can long endure. We are met on a great battle-field of that war. We are met to dedicate a portion of it as the final resting-place of those who here gave their lives that that nation might live. It is altogether fitting and proper that we should do this. But in a larger sense we cannot dedicate. We cannot consecrate, we cannot hallow this ground. The brave men, living and dead, who struggled here have consecrated it far above our power to add or detract. [Applause]. The world will little know or long remember, what we say here, but it can never forget what they did here. [Applause]. It is for us, the living, rather to be dedicated here to the refinished work that they have thus so far nobly carried on. [Applause]. It is rather for us to be here dedicated to the great task remaining before us, that from these honored dead we take increased devotion to that cause for which they here gave the last full measure of devotion; that we here highly resolve that the dead shall not have died in vain; [applause] that the Nation shall under God have a new birth of freedom, and that Governments of the people, by the people and for the people, shall not perish from the earth, [Long continued applause].

Three cheers were then given for the President and the Governors of the States.

After the delivery of the addresses, the dirge and the benediction closed the exercises, and the immense assemblage separated at about 4 o'clock. . . .

PART FOUR

1864

Union bandsmen—swords by side, horns at the ready—played the war's tunes.

The New-York Times.

VOL. XIII—NO. 3939. NEW-YORK, MONDAY, MAY 9, 1864.

GLORIOUS NEWS

Defeat and Retreat of Lee's Army.

TWO DAYS BATTLE IN VIRGINIA

Lieut.-General Grant Against Gen. Lee.

The Struggle of Thursday and of Friday in the Wilderness.

IMMENSE REBEL LOSSES.

Lee Leaves His Killed and Wounded in Our Hands.

OUR LOSS TWELVE THOUSAND.

GEN. BUTLER'S OPERATIONS.

Capture of City Point and Reported Occupation of Petersburgh.

rebel deserter that HUNTER was dangerously wounded PICKETT also, and JONES and JENKINS were killed. Nothing has been heard from Gen. SHERMAN.

EDWIN M. STANTON, Secretary of War.

SPECIAL DISPATCHES TO THE N. Y. TIMES

FRIDAY'S BATTLE.

FIRST DISPATCH.

WASHINGTON, Sunday, May 5, 1864.

The latest news from the army received here is up to seven o'clock yesterday evening, at which time GRANT fully maintained his position. The fighting on Thursday and Friday was very severe, with skirmishing only on Saturday. LEE's first onset was made upon our left, but failing he then fell upon our centre and finally upon our right, where the hardest contest took place. Here the rebels charged upon our lines twice, but were repulsed each time with severe loss. HANCOCK's corps charged back twice, and at one time entered that portion of the enemy's entrenchments commanded by A. P. HILL, but were at length compelled to fall back. SEDGWICK's division of HANCOCK's corps was badly cut. Gens. WADSWORTH and BARTLETT were badly wounded, the former having been knocked off his horse by a spent minie ball. The rebels were reported retreating yesterday morning. The number of wounded is reported at about ten thousand; the killed at two thousand. The loss of the enemy exceeds this. He left his dead and disabled on the field, in our hands. The Ambulance Corps, with its admirable organization, is working up to its full capacity, carrying the wounded to Rappahannock Station. Sixteen trains of cars, dispatched from Alexandria to-day, will receive them. It is expected that they will return, with their bruised and mangled freight, about daylight. Several car-loads of ice were also sent down for the comfort of the wounded. The Sanitary and Christian Commissions are on the field, with a full force of assistants, and with plentiful supplies of everything necessary for the wounded. The Gov-

the Yankees had crossed in force at Germanna and Ely's Fords. There is absolutely nothing known of the movements of the enemy at headquarters to-night. It is supposed, however, that LEE is concentrating, and that we will meet him in force to-morrow. Efforts will be made, at all events, to ascertain his whereabouts. The army will be pushed southwestwardly to the open country beyond the Wilderness, provided developments in regard to the enemy do not necessitate a change of this purpose. The movements to-day were made in fine order, and with creditable precision. There was hardly any straggling, notwithstanding the hard work during the night and day. The troops are full of spirit; the most auspicious weather favors the advance. Gen. BURNSIDE's command, consisting of four (4) divisions, commanded by Gens. POTTER, FERRERO, WILSON and CRITTENDEN, is expected to come up with the army to-morrow afternoon.

GEN. GRANT'S HEADQUARTERS, May 5—8 P. M.

As expected, last night, the army came up with the enemy to-day. A battle has been fought between parts of it and the whole rebel army, but, as at Gettysburgh, the bloody scenes of this day were only a prelude to the bloody work, and it is to be hoped more auspicious results, to-morrow. Reveille was sounded at 3 A. M., and the whole army was again in motion at daylight. According to the order of the day, Gen. HANCOCK's corps was to march upon Chancellorsville, southwestwardly on the Pamunkey road to Greve Church, Gen. WARREN's from Old Wilderness Tavern to Parker's Store, on the Orange Courthouse plank road. SEDGWICK's corps was to follow behind WARREN's.

Gen. SHERIDAN was to concentrate the whole cavalry corps at Piney Branch Church, a few miles south of Chancellorsville, and start upon a general hunt after STEWART's cavalry, the main body of which was reported to be concentrating for a fight. The different bodies had been in motion but a short time, when, at about 6 o'clock, reports came in from both turnpike and plank-road running almost parallel from this vicinity to Orange Court-house, that the enemy were advancing with infantry and artillery toward us from near Old and New Verdiersville. The evidence accumulating in the course of the next two hours that strong rebel columns were moving upon us from the directions mentioned, Gens. GRANT and MEADE came up from Germanna Ford, and orders were issued to halt the various columns of infantry, concentrate and form them for battle at this point. Commanding

that it was brought about by an advance on our side to clear our front.

WASHINGTON REPORTS.

Speculations, Rumors, &c.—Everything Looking Bright—The Success of Butler and Sherman.

WASHINGTON, Sunday, May 8.

The *National Republican* has the following:

We are glad to be able to state that the result of the fighting on Thursday and Friday is all that the most sanguine friends of the Government can desire. The dawn of day on Saturday exhibited no evidence of the presence of the enemy. Gen. GRANT with great promptness took advantage of the fact and ordered a forward movement. It is proper to say here that in consequence of such movement nothing has been heard directly from Gen. GRANT. He has more important duties to perform. It is believed by those who have the best means of knowing, that LEE is hastening to the works of Richmond, not only to save the remnant of his own army, but to rescue, if possible, the rebel capital from falling into the hands of that dreaded chieftain, Gen. BUTLER. There is little doubt that LEE will have to make good time to prevent such a disaster to DAVIS' rebel dominions. There are many things known to the Government, all of a cheerful tendency, which it is not proper to state at this time. For instance, it would not be proper to state what we know about the operations on the Peninsula, up James River, &c.; but at the same time, in general terms, it is not improper for us to state that everything is progressing successfully. We are in possession of information that the rebel authorities at Richmond, seeing the fate which awaits the city, have taken measures to remove everything of value to them from the city. The ten thousand wounded men upon the field mentioned in our last extra to-day, some of which have at this writing probably reached Rappahannock Station, *includes the wounded on both sides*. The list of killed and wounded have not reached the city yet, and probably will not before

THE PENINSULAR MOVEMENT

Capture of Petersburgh—The City Burned by the Rebels—Gunboat Commodore Jones Blown up by a Torpedo—Handsome Achievements by Colored Cavalry.

FORTRESS MONROE, Friday, May 6—6 P. M.

Our troops, under Major-Gen. BUTLER, are in possession of Petersburgh, Va.

LATER.

NEW-YORK, Sunday, May 8—6 P. M.

By the arrival at this port of the steam transport *Western Metropolis*, Capt. MILTON, from Fortress Monroe, Capt. MILTON reports that, on leaving, he gained the following information:

"On the 6th inst. our forces, who had landed at City Point, moved on Petersburgh, when the enemy immediately set fire to the place and abandoned it.

On the morning of the same date, the United States gunboat *Commodore Jones*, while on picket duty in the James River, near Turkey Bend, was blown up by a torpedo, one of the cigar-shaped infernal machines, and several of her officers and men killed and some forty wounded. The rebel who had charge of the torpedo was shot, and two of his companions made prisoners.

On the 5th inst. the First and Second regiments of Colored Cavalry, under Col. WEST, made a dash across the Chickahominy River, and two companies dismounted and charged into the camp of the Forty-sixth Virginia Cavalry, killing 30 men and capturing 35 horses. The horses were immediately mounted by our troops, who pursued the rebels to within ten miles of Richmond."

Official Dispatch from Gen. Butler to Gen. Grant.

OFF CITY POINT, Va., May 5, 1864.

Lieut.-Gen. Grant, Commanding Armies of the United States, Washington, D. C.:

We have seized Wilson's Wharf Landing. A brigade of WILD's colored troops are there. At Fort Powhatan Landing two regiments of the same brigade have landed. At City Point HINKS' Division, with the remaining troops and battery, have landed. The remainder of both the Eighteenth and Tenth Army Corps are being landed at Bermuda Hundreds, above the Appomattox.

After Grant's Army of the Tennessee captured Vicksburg, Grant went to Chattanooga in October 1863 to take charge of units from three different Union armies that had been combined there after a Confederate victory in the battle of Chickamauga south of Chattanooga on September 19–20. Grant melded these troops together and in an attack on November 24–25 won a lopsided victory that drove the enemy into northern Georgia to set the stage for Sherman's Atlanta campaign the next year. In March 1864 Grant was called to Washington as general in chief of all Union armies. He devised simultaneous advances on all fronts beginning in early May, and made his headquarters with the Army of the Potomac in its campaign against Lee in Virginia. Northerners expected the one-two punch of Grant and Sherman to floor the Confederacy for the count by the summer of 1864. The first clash in Virginia took place in a region of scrub oak and pine woods called the Wilderness, near the site of the battle of Chancellorsville a year earlier. The fighting was equally vicious this time, but on May 7, instead of retreating as previous Union commanders in Virginia had done, Grant headed south. This news caused elation in the North, as reflected in these headlines and dispatches in *The Times*.

by straggling and desertion commences, and the enemy's loss in killed and wounded must weaken him more than we are weakened.

Nothing later than my last night's dispatch has been received from Gen. BUTLER.

A dispatch from Gen. SHERMAN, dated at 5 o'clock P. M. yesterday, states that Gen. THOMAS had occu-

vented it from being a crushing defeat. The loss on both sides has been very heavy, but at this hour of hasty writing, I cannot even give an estimate.

THURSDAY'S BATTLE.

FULL DETAILS.

and the remainder of the army. GETTY's division of SEDGWICK's corps was ordered at once to stay this dangerous demonstration. HANCOCK's advance, MOTT's division, arrived just in time to form with GETTY's, to the left and right of the plank road leading directly from Chancellorsville to Orange Court-house. Gen. GRANT ordered them to attack the advancing enemy, in order to give the remaining divisions of HANCOCK's time to come up and form. They

on Saturday morning, say there had been two days' severe fighting on Thursday and Friday, and that it was believed that the enemy were retreating.

Our wounded were being sent to the rear, showing that we had lost no ground in the fighting.

It is believed that our forces were pressing forward.

Nothing further has been heard from Gen. BUTLER. Reports from Chattanooga, dated at 5 o'clock yes-

that not the slightest symptom of resistance on part of the enemy to our advance in the direction of Richmond has been encountered, either from guerrillas, torpedoes or any other source, I shall go be a few weeks, and briefly trace from its conception the enterprise which, to the present point, in all details, has been a wonderful success.

THE PLAN.

May 9, 1864.

GLORIOUS NEWS.

DEFEAT AND RETREAT OF LEE'S ARMY.

TWO DAYS BATTLE IN VIRGINIA.

Lieut.-General Grant Against Gen. Lee.

The Struggle of Thursday and of Friday in the Wilderness.

IMMENSE REBEL LOSSES.

Lee Leaves His Killed and Wounded in Our Hands.

OUR LOSS TWELVE THOUSAND.

GEN. BUTLER'S OPERATIONS.

Capture of City Point and Reported Occupation of Petersburgh.

Railroad Communication Destroyed.

Gen. Sherman's Movements in Georgia.

ADVANCE TO TUNNELL HILL.

Retreat of Joe Johnston's Army Toward Atlanta.

DISPATCHES FROM THE WAR OFFICE.

First Dispatch.

GEN. GRANT SUCCESSFUL — LEE REPORTED TO BE RETIRING — GEN. SHERMAN ADVANCING — TUNNELL HILL OCCUPIED.

While Lincoln suffered with less than competent commanders in the east, Ulysses S. Grant was piling success upon success in the western theater, including key victories at Vicksburg and Chattanooga. Four months after Chattanooga, Lincoln appointed Grant as the commander of all Union forces.

To Gen. John A. Dix, New York:

WASHINGTON, Sunday May 8—9 A.M.

We have no official reports from the front, but the Medical Director has notified the Surgeon-General that our wounded were being sent to Washington, and will number from six to eight thousand.

The Chief Quartermaster of the Army of the Potomac has made requisition for seven days' grain, and for railroad construction trains, and states the enemy is reported to be retiring.

This indicates Gen. GRANT's advance, and affords an inference of material success on our part.

The enemy's strength has always been most felt in his first blows, and their having failed, and our forces not only having maintained their ground, but preparing to advance, lead to the hope of full and complete success, for when either party fails, disorganization by straggling and desertion commences, and the enemy's loss in killed and wounded must weaken him more than we are weakened.

Nothing later than my last night's dispatch has been received from Gen. BUTLER.

A dispatch from Gen. SHERMAN, dated at 5 o'clock P.M. yesterday, states that Gen. THOMAS had occupied Tunnell Hill, where he expected a battle, and that the enemy had taken position at Buzzard Roost Pass, north of Dalton. Skirmishing had taken place, but no real fighting yet.

Nothing later from Gen. BANKS.

You may give such publicity to the information transmitted as you deem proper.

It is designed to give accurate official statements of what is known to the department of this great crisis, and to withhold nothing from the public.

EDWIN M. STANTON, SECRETARY OF WAR.

SECOND DISPATCH.

NO FIGHTING ON SATURDAY—THE WOUNDED AT RAPPAHANNOCK STATION—SEVERE FIGHTING BY GEN. BUTLER'S ARMY—THE RICHMOND AND PETERSBURGH RAILROAD DESTROYED.

WASHINGTON, SUNDAY MAY 8—5 P.M.

Major-Gen. John A. Dix, New York:

We are yet without any official dispatches from the Army of the Potomac, except those referred to this morning from the Medical Director and Chief Quartermaster, and nothing additional has been received by the department from any other source. It is believed that no fighting took place yesterday.

A part of the wounded arrived in ambulances this morning at Rappahannock Station, and are on the way in by railroad. The department will probably receive dispatches by that train, which will arrive to-night.

A dispatch from Gen. BUTLER, just received, and which left him yesterday, states that a demonstration had been made by his forces on the railroad between Petersburgh and Richmond, and had succeeded in destroying a portion of it, so as to break the connection; that there had been some severe fighting, but that he had succeeded. He heard from a rebel deserter that HUNTER was dangerously wounded PICKETT also, and JONES and JENKINS were killed. Nothing has been heard from Gen. SHERMAN.

EDWIN M. STANTON, SECRETARY OF WAR.

SPECIAL DISPATCHES TO THE N.Y. TIMES.

FRIDAY'S BATTLE.

FIRST DISPATCH.

WASHINGTON, SUNDAY, MAY 8, 1864.

The latest news from the army received here is up to seven o'clock yesterday evening, at which time GRANT fully maintained his position. The fighting on Thursday and Friday was very severe, with skirmishing only on Saturday. LEE's first onset was made upon our left, but failing, he then fell upon our center and finally upon our right, where the hardest contest took place. Here the rebels charged upon our lines twice, but were repulsed each time with severe loss. HANCOCK's corps charged back twice, and at one time entered that portion of the enemy's entrenchments commanded by A.P. HILL, but

Union hospital Number 1, Chattanooga, Tennessee, 1864–1865.
(*Illinois State Historical Library*)

were at length compelled to fall back. SEYMOUR's division of HANCOCK's corps was badly cut. Gens. WADSWORTH and BARTLETT were badly wounded, the former having been knocked off his horse by a spent minie ball. The rebels were reported retreating yesterday morning. The number of wounded is reported at about ten thousand; the killed at two thousand. The loss of the enemy exceeds this. He left his dead and disabled on the field, in our hands. The Ambulance Corps, with its admirable organization, is working up to its full capacity, carrying the wounded to Rappahannock Station. Sixteen trains of cars, dispatched from Alexandria to-day, will receive them. It is expected that they will return, with their bruised and mangled freight, about daylight. Several car-loads of ice were also sent down for the comfort of the wounded. The Sanitary and Christian Commissions are on the field, with a full force of assistants, and with plentiful supplies of everything for the wounded. The Government has hospital accommodations here for thirty thousand, which will probably meet all demands.

SECOND DISPATCH.

WASHINGTON, SUNDAY MAY 8—MIDNIGHT

Your special correspondent, writing from headquarters at Wilderness Tavern, Friday evening, May 6, gives the following intelligence of the great battle on Friday:

The day has closed upon a terribly hard-fought field, and the Army of Potomac has added another to its list of murderous conflicts. LEE's tactics, so energetically employed at Chancellorsville and Gettysburgh, of throwing his whole army first upon one wing and then upon another, have again been brought to bear, but I rejoice to say that the army of the Potomac has repulsed the tremendous onslaught of the enemy, and stands to-night solidly in the position it assumed this morning. The first attempt was made upon HANCOCK, upon the right, somewhat weakened in numbers by the battle of yesterday; but the iron old Second Corps nobly stood its ground; then the enemy hurled his battalions upon SEDGWICK, and once or twice gained a temporary advantage, but our veterans were nobly rallied, and the rebels repulsed with awful slaughter. About half-past four P.M., LEE made a feint attack upon the whole line, and then suddenly fell, with his whole force, upon SEDGWICK, driving him back temporarily, but the advantage was soon regained, and the rebels hurled back with great loss. Night had now come on, and it is believed at headquarters, at this hour, that LEE has withdrawn from our front. Although the nature of the ground has been of a terrible character, most of it being so thickly wooded as to render movements all but impossible, and to conceal entirely the operations of the enemy, yet he has been signally repulsed in all his attacks, and nothing but the nature of the battle-field has prevented it from being a crushing defeat. The loss on both sides has been very heavy, but at this hour of hasty writing, I cannot even give an estimate.

The pattern established in the battle of the Wilderness persisted for the next six weeks in Virginia—hard fighting and heavy casualties in the battles of Spotsylvania, North Anna, and Cold Harbor, followed by flanking movements southward around Lee's right that forced the Confederates to retreat to a new defensive position and entrench. On June 12 the Army of the Potomac silently vacated its trenches at Cold Harbor just east of Richmond and marched south another twenty miles, crossing the James River to attack the formidable defensive works at Petersburg, a vital rail junction whose loss would force the abandonment of Richmond. Repeated Union attacks from June 15 to 18 failed to capture Petersburg, however, despite the initial reports of its fall that were reflected in these headlines and dispatches in *The Times.*

June 18, 1864.

IMPORTANT.

PETERSBURG CAPTURED.

The Fortifications Stormed by General Smith.

BOTH LINES CARRIED.

Four Hundred Prisoners and Sixteen Guns Taken.

Distinguished Gallantry of the Black Legion.

Gen. Smith Tenders His Thanks to Them.

PETERSBURG UNDER OUR GUNS.

The Rebels on the West Side of the Appomattox.

The Army All Across the James.

HANCOCK IN JUNCTION WITH SMITH.

GRANT WELL AHEAD OF LEE.

SECRETARY STANTON TO GENERAL DIX

[OFFICIAL.]

WASHINGTON, SUNDAY JUNE 17, 1864.

To Major-Gen Dix:

The following dispatches have been received by this Department:

CITY POINT, June 15, VIA JAMESTOWN ISLAND,
5:30 A.M., 16—1864.

SMITH, with 15,000 men, attacked Pittsburgh this morning.

Gen. BUTLER reports, from his observatory near Bermuda Hundred, that there had been sharp fighting and that the troops and trains of the enemy were, as he writes, moving from the City across the Appomatox as if retreating.

HANCOCK is not near enough to render Gen. SMITH any aid.

The Richmond papers have nothing to indicate a suspicion of our crossing the James River. They expect to be attacked from the direction of Malvern Hill.

CITY POINT, Va., 5:30 P.M., June 15, 1864.

Our latest report from SMITH was at four P.M. he had carried a line of entrenchments at Beatty's House, the colored troops assaulting and carrying the rifle-pits with great gallantry, but he had not yet carried the main line. He describes the rebel artillery as very heavy.

He expected to assault this line just before dark. HANCOCK is within three miles of SMITH.

CITY POINT, VA., 7 A.M., JUNE 16,
VIA JAMESTOWN ISLAND, 11:45 A.M.

At 7:20 P.M. yesterday, SMITH assaulted and carried the principal line of the enemy before Petersburgh, taking thirteen cannon, several stands of colors, and between three and four hundred prisoners. This line is two miles from Petersburgh. HANCOCK got up and took position on SMITH's left at 3 A.M. to-day. There was heavy firing in that direction from 5 to 6 o'clock. No report has been received yet.

DON'T HARD LANDING, VA., JUNE 16—1 P.M.

After sending my dispatch of this morning from the heights southeast of Petersburgh, I went over the conquered lines with Gen. GRANT and the engineer officers. The works are of the very strongest kind, more difficult to take than was Missionary Ridge, at Chattanooga. The hardest fighting was done by the black troops. The forts they stormed were the worst of all. After the affair was over, Gen. Smith went to thank them, and tell them he was proud of their courage and dash. He says they cannot be exceeded as soldiers, and that hereafter he will send them in a difficult place as readily as the best white troops.

They captured six out of the sixteen cannons which he took.

The prisoners he took were from BEAUREGARD's command. Some of them said they had just crossed the James above Drewry's Bluff.

Confederate soldier of Ewell's Corps killed at Spotsylvania, May, 1864. Photograph by Timothy O'Sullivan.

I do not think any of LEE's army had reached Petersburgh when SMITH stormed it. They seem to be there this morning, however, and to be making arrangements to hold the west side of the Appomatox.

The town they cannot think of holding, for it lies directly under our guns.

The weather continued splendid.

CITY POINT, VA., JUNE 16, 1864—4:15 P.M.

Gen Butler reports from Bermuda Hundred that the enemy have abandoned the works in front of that place. His troops are now engaged in tearing up the railroad between Petersburgh and Richmond.

GRANT'S LAST MOVEMENT.

Its Military Aspects and Objects—Its Probable Effect upon the Campaign.

From Our Special Correspondent.

WASHINGTON, THURSDAY, JUNE 16, 1864.

The clear and succinct dispatches of the Secretary of War have made the country acquainted with the outline facts of the last great move of Gen. GRANT—the transfer of the Army of the Potomac from the Chickahominy to the James River. I can add no details of fact to the official statement, having been absent from the army since the battle of Chickahominy on the 3d inst. There are, however, some suggestions of moment that may not be out of place.

Your readers will recollect that in my letter on the battle of the Chickahominy, in which I endeavored to recognize the true military character and bearings of that battle, I put on record the opinion that Gen. GRANT would make no further effort to pass the Chickahominy, and hinted that his eyes were even then, "turned away to lines and combinations more bold than any yet essayed." Well, what could then only be thus obscurely foreshadowed, is to-day a realized fact. Indeed, I may now go further, and state that *from the very start, the transfer of the army to the south side of Richmond has formed an integral part of Gen. Grant's plan of campaign;* and while the battle of Chickahominy was still in progress, the whole question of the pontooning of the James River was elaborately discussed. And now recognizing the relations which that section holds to the general plan of operations—noting that it now stands defined as the pivotal point of the whole campaign—would it be too much for me to ask those presses that abused me for having so recognized it a fortnight ago, to take back their abuse?

The battle of the Chickahominy was an experiment made for a specific purpose—to test the feasibility of an assault on Richmond from the northern side. It was an experiment perfectly proper to be made; and it was satisfactory. It convinced every reflecting mind that nothing was to be gained in that direction. This was obvious to every one; and every one waited to see what card GRANT would play next. But it was only those who knew something of the boldness of his military conception, that could have ventured to anticipate a repetition of the Vicksburgh strategy—the same strategy, the same audacity, only on a far grander scale!

This splendid stroke, comparable only to MOREAU's passage of the Rhine and flank march on Ulm, stands to-day an accomplished fact; the Army of the Potomac, taken up, as in the arms of a giant, is transported from the Chickahominy and planted south of the James River and south of Richmond. Now begins a new act in the grand war drama. We shall operate on new and unattempted lines, looking to new and hitherto unattainable results. I think there are a few military men who do not now feel that *the present position of the Army of the Potomac gives us reason to indulge in brighter hopes of ultimate success than has been possible any time since the war began.*

The south side is the true line of operation against Richmond looking to great ulterior results. Of the three cardinal maxims of strategy, the most important of all prescribes "to operate on the enemy's communications without endangering your own." Now, the operations of the Virginia campaign have been conducted under circumstances that made it impossible to apply this principle. Gen. GRANT has aimed assiduously to bring on a great decisive field fight with the hope of *crushing* the rebel army. But from the nature of the country, its prodigious facilities for defence, and the skill of the opposing General, this has been impossible. We gained victories; we steadily pushed the enemy back, and in an unparalleled campaign of twenty-nine days, forced LEE from the Rapidan to the front of Richmond. But no *decisive* results were accomplished. LEE's army is an army of veterans; it is an instrument sharpened to a perfect edge. You turn its flanks; well, its flanks are *made* to be turned; that effects little or nothing. All that we can reckon as gained, therefore, is the loss of life inflicted on the enemy, and of having reached a point thus near the objective; but no brilliant military results. In loss of life we were undoubtedly suffering more severely than the rebels; I think we may fairly say in the proportion of *five* to their *three*. Now it is obvious that we could not have long stood thus. Whatever preponderance of numbers we might have would soon disappear—would soon become an equality, and presently an inferiority. The rebel army might have been wore away by attrition; but we should ourselves have been exhausted in the process. The hammer would have been broken on the anvil.

By the present move a new order of operation begins. We not only threaten the communications of the enemy, we plant ourselves across his communications. The communications of the rebel army are the great lines of railroad by Petersburgh and Danville and their connections.

Richmond, as a city, Richmond, as a military center, is strictly dependent on these lines for its supplies. Cut it off from these and you have a tourniquet around its throat. It may have a month's supplies, or three months', or six months'; but these exhausted and it must succumb. If LEE allows himself to be shut up within Richmond, therefore, the problem reduces itself to a repetition of Vicksburgh over again. Will he do so? That is a question.

But this is the pitiless alternative to which LEE is now reduced; to stay in Richmond and suffer the fatal lines of circumvallation to be drawn around him, or to come out of his works and give battle. Now a fair field-fight is precisely what the Army of the Potomac invites and welcomes; it will gladly give the rebel man for man, and engage to defeat them withal. If LEE is unwilling to run this risk, he retires within the defences of Richmond, *and we then hold precisely the relations held by the Allies to Napoleon defending Paris in 1814.* It was in vain then that the consummate master put forth a generalship that recalled the splendors of the first great Italian campaign; in vain he threw his masses on different points of the investing line. If LEE is not a better General than NAPOLEON, he can hardly hope for a much better fate.

With the army of the Potomac planted at the north of Petersburgh, we there tap the great railroad line connecting Richmond with the Atlantic seaboard and Gulf States. When there Grant may be able to throw his left across the Danville Road, and in this case Richmond is isolated. If his plan does not contemplate so great a development of front, he will at least provide for the effectual *destruction* of the latter road; and this, as well as the destruction of the Western (Lynchburgh) Road and the James River Canal, will be an easy prey to our cavalry, which, under the hands of SHERI-

DAN, has almost put the rebel cavalry out of existence. The reduction of Fort Darling is an incidental piece of work, which will be gladly contended for by some of the able engineering heads of the Army of the Potomac. In the meantime, we have a perfectly secure and convenient base—the James River—to which all the transportation lately at White House has been forwarded.

There is another aspect of the move to the south side of the James, which from the point of view of its relation to the whole theatre of war, is not less important than its bearing on the problem immediately before us. *It is a division of the two great rebel armies, and gives us an interior position relative to the army of Lee in Virginia, and the army of Johnston in Georgia.* It has been reported that large detachments of JOHNSTON's army are already en route to reinforce LEE, and, if not actually under way, we may depend upon it that the able military heads that rule the war councils at Richmond, thoroughly imbued with the conception of *concentration*, and willing to risk everything to save Richmond, would willingly have sacrificed Southwestern territory to secure the great point in Virginia. But how does it stand now? JOHNSTON coming to reinforce LEE *would find his progress to Richmond barred by the same opponent who stopped his junction with Pemberton in Vicksburgh!* We secure this, therefore: first, that the enemy shall receive no addition to his strength, while our position effects a concentration of both the forces of BUTLER and HUNTER with the main operating force.

While, however, we have reason to look forward to great and important results as coming from the new position of the army, I am very far from looking on our success as a foregone conclusion. We have opposed to us an enemy of the highest skill, handling an army of sufficient strength still to attempt great things, and animated by a spirit of desperation. I fully expect some bold, audacious initiative on the part of LEE, and the greater the straits in which he finds himself, the more energetically he will attempt to retrieve himself, and the fortunes of the Confederacy bound up with him.

WILLIAM SWINTON

The high hopes of the Northern people at the beginning of the military campaigns in May 1864 had been dashed by August after 100,000 Union casualties on all fronts with no end in sight. Grant was bogged down in a stalemate before Richmond and Petersburg while Sherman, after a rapid advance to the outskirts of Atlanta, also appeared to be stymied. General Jubal Early's corps of the Army of Northern Virginia had raided into Maryland, approaching Washington in July. On July 30, two events occurred that reinforced the impression of futility in the Northern war effort. At the Battle of the Crater at Petersburg the Union forces exploded a mine under Confederate lines, but the followup attack was botched and a Confederate counterattack contained it. One of the four Union divisions in this attack was composed of African Americans, most of them liberated slaves. Contrary to reports that they were principally to blame for the humiliating failure, the black division bore the least responsibility. They had received special training to spearhead the assault, but almost at the last minute General Meade ordered that the three white divisions go in first. By the time the black division went in, the attack had failed. The second humiliation on July 30 was the burning of Chambersburg, Pennsylvania by a Confederate cavalry brigade—in retaliation, they said, for the earlier burning of Virginia Military Institute in Lexington by Union troops.

August 2, 1864.

THE PETERSBURG LINES.

The Assault by Our Troops on Saturday.

Desperate Attempt to Carry the Enemy's Position.

FAILURE OF THE ATTEMPT.

The Colored Troops Charged With the Failure.

The Loss on Both Sides Between Four and Five Thousand.

A Detailed Sketch of the Whole Matter.

FIRST DISPATCH.

HEADQUARTERS OF THE ARMY OF THE POTOMAC,
SATURDAY, JULY 30—9 O'CLOCK P.M.

After the explosion at an early hour this morning, everything betokened a brilliant victory, but soon after matters assumed a different aspect, part of the attacking force having given way, thus exposing the balance to an enfilading fire from both artillery, and infantry.

The programme was as follows:

The mine was to be exploded at 3 o'clock in the morning; the batteries to open at once along the entire line immediately after the explosion, and the Ninth Corps to make the charge, supported by the Eighteenth Corps, AYER's division of the Fifth Corps, and the Third Division of the Second Corps.

The greater part of the arrangement was carried out as ordered, although the commencement was later than the hour designated, on account of the fuse going out twice.

The explosion took place at precisely 4:40 o'clock.

The roar of the artillery that immediately followed was almost deafening.

At 5½ o'clock the charge was made, and the fort, with part of the line each side, was carried in the most brilliant style.

The Second Division, which was in the center, advanced and carried the second line, a short distance beyond the fort, and here rested, holding their ground with the utmost determination.

It was at this time the Colored Division, under the command of Brig. Gen. WHITE, was pushed forward and ordered to charge and carry the crest of the hill, which would have decided the contest.

The troops advanced in good order as far as the first line, where they received a galling fire, which shocked them, and although quite a number kept on advancing, the greater portion seemed to become utterly demoralized, part of them taking refuge in the fort, and the balance running to the rear as fast as possible.

The were rallied, and again pushed forward, but without success, the greater part of their officers being killed or wounded.

During this time they seemed to be without anyone to manage them, and finally they fell back to the rear and out of the range of the volleys of canister and musketry that were plowing through their ranks.

Their losses were very heavy, particularly in officers as will be seen by the following figures:

TWENTY-THIRD UNITED STATES, COLORED.

Fifteen officers killed and wounded; 400 men, including the missing.

TWENTY-EIGHTH UNITED STATES, COLORED.

Eleven officers, and about 150 men killed, wounded and missing.

TWENTY-SEVENTH U.S. COLORED.

Six officers and about 150 men killed, wounded and missing.

TWENTY-NINTH U.S. COLORED.

Eight officers and about two hundred and seventy-five men killed, wounded and missing.

THIRTY-FIRST U.S. COLORED.

Seven officers and about two hundred men killed, wounded and missing.

FORTY-THIRD U.S. COLORED.

Six officers and a large number of men killed, wounded and missing.

THIRTY-NINTH U.S. COLORED.

Several officers and about two hundred and fifty men killed, wounded and missing.

The loss in the Second Division of the Ninth Corps, Gen. LEDLIE commanding, was very severe, and is estimated at from 1,000 to 1,200, while many make the figure larger.

Among those missing I regret to announce the name of Gen. BARTLETT. He succeeded in reaching the fort with his command, but having accidentally broken his cork leg he was unable to get off the field. He however held possession of the ground for several hours, and only surrendered when all hope of escape was gone. Some 200 men, both black and white, were with him at the time, a few of whom managed to get back to our lines amidst a storm of bullets. . . .

We captured five hundred prisoners in the assault.

The loss on both sides was considerable, probably from four to five thousand.

286 THE ASSAULT—ITS CHARACTER AND RESULTS.

From Our Special Correspondent.

HEADQUARTERS, IN FRONT ARMY OF POTOMAC
SATURDAY EVENING, JULY 30, 1863

I am called to the fulfillment of an ungracious task to-night. Instead of success and victory which the morning fairly promised, I have to write of disaster and defeat. To-day's brief history affords another striking proof of the uncertain issues of battle, showing how the shrewdest and most elaborate strategic planning may be completely thwarted by an error or an accident in tactics. To-day's disaster finds solution in the old story that "some one has blundered" in a manner "worse than a crime," but precisely who the blunderer is I do not know, and if I knew it would not devolve upon me at present to tell. A military tribunal must decide that point. Happily, however, the blunder is not irreparable. It fills us with poignant grief and disappointment, necessitates a long interval of delay before future operations, has lost to us the labor of a month's preparation, and, worse than all this, has sacrificed thousands of valuable lives. But the result does not dishearten the Army of Potomac, and it should not depress the people. The soldiers who fought on Saturday have received the baptism of blood on other fields, and know how to bear reverses manfully, as they bear success modestly. They bate not a jot of heart or hope, and they only ask as the lesson to the country from to-day's mishap, that their thinned ranks shall be promptly reinforced. The army is still unfaltering in its faith, and will try and try again until the day of decisive victory.

With so much by way of exordium, I shall attempt to give, as clearly as I may, an account of the battle, in summarizing in the first place, the relative positions of the opposing armies, the object sought to be gained by the attack, and the admirable strategic devices of the past few days.

With the passage of the James was exhausted all possibilities of a movement by the left flank, with Richmond as the objective point. Nothing, therefore, remained to Gen. GRANT but to assault the rebel lines in front of him at Petersburgh. The past six weeks have been devoted to preparation for this assault. From day to day, by the aid of the shovel and the pick, our lines have been insidiously advanced by zig-zags and covered ways, until the outlying pickets of both armies have scarcely averaged 500 yards' distance between them. Along portions of the line, the interval between the rifle-pits was scarcely 150 yards. The ground over which our advances have been made, is itself a series of natural fortifications, adding vastly to the difficulty of taking possession of it. Perhaps your readers will form a more perfect opinion of its features, if I tell them that it very much resembles Greenwood Cemetery in its profile. There are similar hills and eminences, sloping more or less precipitously into ravines which intersect at every conceivable angle, and many of the elevations are thickly wooded. Over ground of this impracticable nature our men have sturdily fought and dug their way, driving the enemy before them, *until only one hill remained for them to take* to place our guns in a position commanding at easy range the town of Petersburgh. It is known as Cemetery Hill. Its crest, frowning with guns, is not more than 800 yards distant from our advanced works, and its gently-sloping sides are welted with long rows of earth-works, pitted with redoubts and redans, and ridged with serried salients and curtains and all the skillful defences known to skillful military engineers.

The vital importance to us at this point will readily be admitted. To gain it by direct assault must necessarily cost many lives, but to gain it in the cheapest manner gave occasion for the display of that high strategy of which Gen. GRANT has long since proved himself the master. Therefore, it was that on Tuesday night last the Second Corps, under Gen. HANCOCK, and two divisions of cavalry under Gen. SHERIDAN, and another division under Gen. KAUTZ, crossed the James River for the purpose of engaging the enemy, who, misled by some preliminary operations of Gen. FOSTER's command at Deep Bottom, and of a portion of the Nineteenth Corps at Strawberry Plains a mile below—had a day or two earlier heavily reinforced the troops in the vicinity of Malvern Hill. The demonstration here had precisely the effect which Gen. GRANT desired. Fearing a serious attack, LEE dispatched a column, estimated at from 12,000 to 15,000 strong, from before Petersburgh, and the railroad between Petersburgh and Richmond was kept busy on Friday and Friday night in transporting the troops. To keep up the rebel General's delusion, an immense train of more than 400 empty covered wagons, mainly the transportation of the Sixth Corps, crossed the Appomattox on Friday in broad daylight, in full view of the rebel signal lookouts at Bermuda Hundred, as if destined for the army at Deep Bottom. But on Friday night, as the rebels were hurriedly taking possession of their new line, the

Second Corps and the cavalry were quietly withdrawn with an additional facility for rapid movement in a third pontoon bridge laid across the James in the afternoon. By daylight this morning, these troops were nearly all in position to cooperate with the remainder of the army in the attack. The strategy was, therefore, perfect, and no share of the reverse can be attributed to failure in this part of the programme.

All these stratagems, too, were conducted with such secrecy, that information of their precise bearing was narrowed down to the circle of the corps Commanders. Until late on Friday night, few persons in the army were disposed to believe differently from what Gen. LEE suspected, viz.: that a movement upon Richmond was intended from the north side of the James, and were only undeceived when, at one o'clock this morning, the troops were got into position for the assault.

The tactics of the movement were under Gen. MEADE's direction. His arrangement of troops and order of battle was as follows: The Eighteenth Corps (Gen. ORD) was withdrawn on Thursday morning from his position on the extreme right, resting on the Appomattox, (being relieved by MOTT's division of the Second Corps,) and massed in rear of the Ninth Corps, (BURNSIDE's,) the centre of our line, in front of which the attack was to be initiated. The extreme left held by the Fifth Corps, (WARREN's,) was to be in readiness to advance as soon as BURNSIDE pierced the works in front of him. Collaterally, but in unison with the advance of the infantry, every piece of siege artillery posted along the line was ordered to open simultaneously upon the enemy at a given signal made by the explosion of a mine containing eight tons of powder, which was placed directly beneath the rebel battery which BURNSIDE was to assault. Not only were the siege places to open a fierce fire, but all the field artillery which could be got into position after the opening of the battle was to advance as opportunity offered, and bring their batteries into play. Upon this awful fire of heavy guns it was natural that great stress should be placed, in the expectation that the shock of its suddenness would have a demoralizing effect, and so make the way of the infantry easier. So far all was well arranged; success was promising, and much confidence was felt in the result.

The time fixed for the assault was 3½ o'clock, when, without any moon, an almost Cimmerian darkness, would effectually shut out from the enemy the unavoidable stir and bustle of the troops as they got into position. But just here the first misfortune of the day occurred. Upon attempting to fire the mine the fuse or slow-match failed, and another was tried, I am told, with a similar result. The third fuse was successful in its mission, but the hour's delay had made it broad daylight, and, in consequence, the enemy's suspicions were aroused, (at least along a portion of his front,) and we were robbed of the advantage of a surprise.

This was a very great misfortune. The army felt it to be such as they stood in suspense and silent impatience in the cold gray of the morning, crouching on their arms. Of the effect of the explosion you have been already apprised. The mine has been talked of in the army for weeks, but only talked of with bated breath, although whisperings concerning it have been wafted over from the rebels. Clearly they did not know its precise locality, and few on our side, I suspect, were any wiser. It has been tacitly acknowledged as an improper subject for conversation, and the most curious have appeared to feel the propriety of checking themselves. The noise of the explosion was a dull, rumbling thud, preceded, I am told, by a few seconds' swaying and quaking of the ground in the immediate vicinity. The earth was rent along the entire course of the excavation, heaving slowly and majestically to the surface, and folding sideways to exhibit a deep and yawning chasm, comparable, as much as anything else, to a river gorged with ice, and breaking up under the influence of a freshet. But there was a grander effect than this observable also. Where the charge in the burrow was heaviest, directly under the rebel work, an immense mass of dull red earth was thrown high in the air, in three broad columns, diverging from a single base, and, to my mind, assuming the shape of a Prince of Wales' feather, of colossal proportions. Those near the spot say that clods of earth weighing at least a ton, and cannon, and human forms, and gun-carriages, and small-arms were all distinctly seen shooting upward in that fountain of horror, and fell again in shapeless and pulverized atoms. The explosion fully accomplished what was intended. It demolished the six-gun battery and its garrison of one regiment of South Carolina troops, and acted as the wedge which opened the way to the assault. Our men were to rush through this breach, and so beyond upon the second line of works which crown the crest of Cemetery Hill, thus compelling the enemy to evacuate the first line, or what was more probable, to surrender under the fire of our artillery.

A black soldier in the Union army. (*Chicago Historical Society*)

The awful instant of the explosion had scarcely passed when the dull morning air was made stagnant by the thunder of our artillery. From ninety-five pieces, niched in every hillside commanding the enemy's position, there belched out sheets of flame and milk-white smoke, while the shot and shell sped forward, screeching, howling, rumbling like the rushing of a hundred railroad trains. But why attempt to give an idea of such indescribable and awful sound! The sudden transition from utter silence to fiercest clamor was terrible. So the rude combat raged without sign of slackening for two long hours. At first the enemy was slow in replying to our fire, but gradually their pieces were brought into action, and in less than half an hour banks of angry smoke partially veiled the scene from both sides.

Union General Robert Potter (fourth from left) posed with his staff while a casual Mathew Brady cut a rakish figure at the far right of the photograph. While Brady took few wartime photographs himself, the photographers he sent out into the field made a major contribution to the visual record of the war.

In accordance with the plan of battle, the First Division of the Ninth Corps (LEDLIE'S) was made the assaulting column. Gen. LEDLIE formed his troops in three lines of battle, having each a front of about six hundred. The Second Brigade of this division (Col. MARSHALL) led the assault, followed by the First Brigade, (Gen. W. F. BARTLETT,) and the third line made up of the Third Brigade (Col. GOULD'S.) The left of LEDLIE'S division was supported by Brig.-Gen. HARTRANFT'S brigade of the Third Division (WILCOX'S) and its right by Gen. GRIFFIN'S brigade of POTTER'S division. The Fourth Division of the Ninth Corps (all negroes) was posted directly in rear of the assaulting column, to press forward whenever practicable. The Fourteenth New-York Heavy Artillery were the first to enter the breach made by the explosion. They bounded forward at the word, in the midst of the shock of the artillery, through the dense clouds of flying dust, and clambering over the debris, found themselves violently pushed down into the yawning crater. The sight which there met them must have been appalling. Bodies of dead rebels crushed and mangled out of all resemblance to humanity, writhing forms partly buried, arms protruding here and legs struggling there—a very hell of horror and torture, confined to a space 50 feet in length and half as many wide. But the time was not favorable to the play of humane promptings. This chaos of mangled humanity mixed with debris of implements and munitions of war must be unheeded. Enough for the storming party to do was found in exhuming two pieces of rebel cannon with their caissons, and, in obedience to the law of self-preservation, turning these guns upon the enemy, who was throwing into the crater a shower of shells and minie balls from the hill beyond, and from points on either side, which they still held on this first line. Getting these pieces into position promptly, and under cover of their fire, the assaulting column was reformed, and at the word of command dashed forward once more to storm the crest of the hill. It was a task too great. They gallantly essayed it, and nearly gained the summit, subjected all the time to a withering fire, which increased in fierceness at every step, until they became the centre of a converging storm of shot and shell. Attacked on the right flank and the left flank, in front and rear, they were compelled to fall back to the partial protection of the crater, leaving their course thickly strewn with the dying and the dead.

The colored troops, upon the heels of this repulse, were ordered to charge, and they moved out gallantly. A hundred yards gained and they wavered. Then the Thirty-ninth Maryland Regiment, which led, became panic-stricken and broke through to the rear, spreading demoralization swiftly. Their officers urged them, entreated them, threatened them, but failed to rally them, and, the mass, broken and shattered, swept back like a torrent into the crater which was already choked with white troops. The confusion, incident to this wholesale crowding and crushing of the negro soldiers into the ranks of the white troops, very nearly caused the panic to spread. Had such been the result, it might have been fortunate, and many a brave fellow who afterwards fell, might have escaped his fate. But at the moment the rebel fire, which had been murderously directed upon the place, materially slackened, and the white soldiers recovered their stamina. Our lines were once more straightened, and just in time to check an impetuous charge, which was afterwards repeated, and with a similar result of heavy loss to the assailants.

So the morning waned. It became apparent, doubtless, that the position gained could not be held without more sacrifice of life than could well be afforded at this time. At any rate, this seems a false inference, or the other corps would have been ordered to advance upon those portions of the first line still held by the enemy, and, as far as I can ascertain, no such order was given. On the contrary, about noon the order was given to retire—a matter not easy of execution, as to gain our works an open space must be traversed, over which one man in every twenty was sure to be brought down by the crossfire which swept the spot.

I omitted to say that when the negro division advanced to the charge, they were supported on the right of the Prince George Court-house Road by TURNER's division of the Tenth Corps, which gallantly advanced a long way beyond the spot where the negroes broke, and strove unavailingly to breast the storm of their retreat. The list of casualties in this division was heavy. I forward the names of those in hospital.

The losses on both sides, considering the numbers engaged, were very severe. The wounded in the hospitals are more than one thousand. Probably 1,800 were taken prisoners, and the killed would swell the list materially.

H. J. W.

War weariness and defeatism in the North grew so serious by August 1864 that the Democratic party adopted a platform for the presidential campaign declaring the war a failure and calling for peace negotiations. If the election had been held on September 1, Lincoln almost surely would have lost. But on September 3 a telegram arrived in Washington from General Sherman: "Atlanta is ours, and fairly won." This news electrified the North and transformed morale by 180 degrees—as indicated by one of the subheads in the *Times's* headline: "A Thunderbolt for Copperheads" (The Copperheads were the peace wing of the Democratic party). The capture of Atlanta broke the stalemate that had prevailed since the spring. Northern arms went on to win battle after battle during the next six months, and Lincoln was triumphantly reelected in November on a platform calling for the unconditional surrender of the Confederacy.

September 3, 1864.

ATLANTA.

FALL OF THE REBEL STRONGHOLD.

A Great Battle on the Macon Railroad.

HOOD'S ARMY CUT IN TWAIN.

The Rebel General Hardee Killed.

SHERMAN ENTERS THE CITY.

Official Bulletin from the War Department.

A THUNDERBOLT FOR COPPERHEADS.

THE APPROACHING DRAFT.

Its Burdens Materially Lightened.

Grant Wants but One Hundred Thousand More Men.

These to Finish the Rebellion and Restore Peace.

[Official Dispatch.]

General William Sherman (below, hand on hip) leaned on the breech of a 20-pounder Parrott gun at a Union fort in Atlanta during the Federal occupation of the city. The devastation inflicted on Atlanta by Sherman's wrecking crews made him perhaps the most hated man in the South. His instructions to his men charged with the demolition of Atlanta's transportation infrastructure included the order that "the destruction be so thorough that not a rail or tie can be used again." *(Library of Congress)*

WAR DEPARTMENT
WASHINGTON, SEPT. 2—8 P.M.

To Maj.-Gen. Dix, New-York:

This Department has received intelligence this evening that Gen. SHERMAN's advance entered Atlanta about noon to-day. The particulars have not yet been received, but telegraphic communication during the night with Atlanta direct is expected.

It is ascertained with reasonable certainty that the naval and other credits required by the act of Congress will amount to about 200,000, including New-York, which has not been reported yet to the Department; so that the President's call of July 10 is practically reduced to 300,000 men to meet and take the place of—

First—The new enlistments in the navy;

Second—The casualties of battle, sickness, prisoners and desertion; and

Third—The hundred day's troops, and all others going out by expiration of service this Fall.

One hundred thousand new troops promptly furnished are all that Gen. GRANT asks for the capture of Richmond and to give a finishing blow to the rebel armies yet in the field. The residue of the call would be adequate for garrisons in forts and to guard all the lines of communication and supply, free the country from guerrillas,

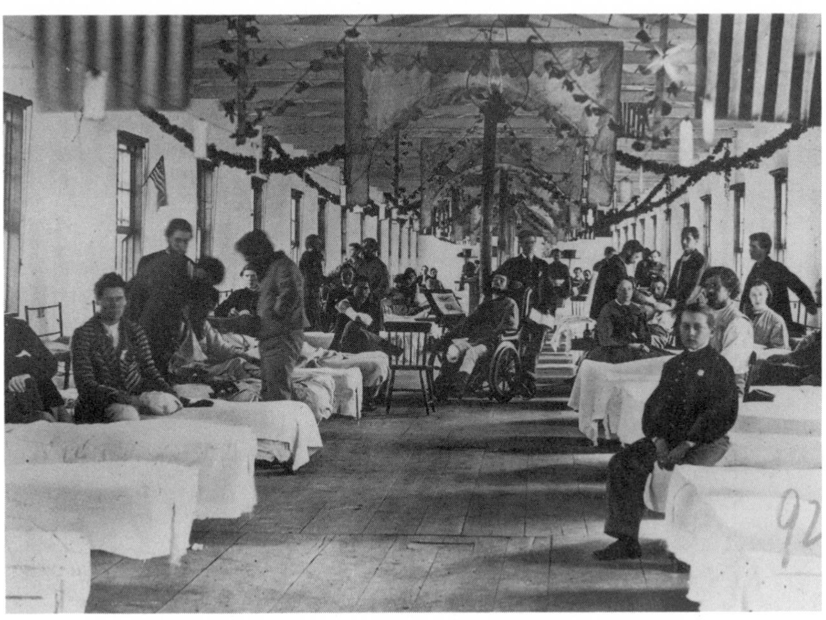

Union wounded in Carver Hospital, Washington, photographed by Mathew Brady, September, 1864.

give security to trade, protect commerce and travel, and establish peace, order and tranquillity in every State

EDWIN M. STATON,
SECRETARY OF WAR.

THE CAPTURE CONFIRMED.

[Official.]

WAR DEPARTMENT, WASHINGTON, SEPT. 2, 1864.

To Maj.-Gen. Dix:

The following telegram from Maj.-Gen. SLOCUM, dated this day in Atlanta, and just received, confirms the capture of that city:

Gen. SHERMAN has taken Atlanta. The Twentieth Corps occupies the city. The main army is on the Macon road, near East Point.

A battle was fought near that point, in which Gen. SHERMAN was successful. Particulars are not known.

(Signed) H. W. SLOCUM, MAJ.-GEN.

PART FIVE

1865

Abraham Lincoln, 1865. Photograph by Alexander Gardner.
(*National Portrait Gallery, Smithsonian Institute, Washington, D.C.*)

The New-York Times

VOL. XIV......NO. 4167. NEW-YORK, WEDNESDAY, FEBRUARY 1, 1865.

THE PEACE QUESTION.

ITS LATEST ASPECT.

Three Commissioners Coming from Richmond.

They Apply for Admission to General Grant's Lines.

A. H. Stephens of Georgia, R. M. T. Hunter of Virginia, and A. J. Campbell of Alabama.

A FLAG OF TRUCE AND A PARLEY.

General Grant in Communication with the Government.

Expected Arrival of the Commissioners at Annapolis.

Special Dispatch to the New-York Times.

WASHINGTON, Tuesday, Jan. 31.

In regard to the rebel Peace Commissioners, the following facts are known:

ALEXANDER H. STEPHENS of Georgia, R. M. T. HUNTER of Virginia, and A. J. CAMPBELL of Alabama, the latter formerly of the United States Supreme Court, arrived at Gen. GRANT's lines last Sunday afternoon and desired permission to come to Gen. GRANT's headquarters.

After considerable delay and parley they were allowed to come to Gen. GRANT's headquarters at City Point. It appears that Gen. GRANT immediately notified the Government of the fact, but up to this time we are not aware of the decision arrived at, though they are expected to reach Washington presently, via Annapolis.

FROM WASHINGTON.

ABOLITION OF SLAVERY.

Passage of the Constitutional Amendment.

One Hundred and Nineteen Yeas against Fifty-six Nays.

Exciting Scene in the House.

ENTHUSIASM OVER THE RESULT.

THE PEACE MISSION IN THE SENATE.

A Resolution Calling for Information.

Passage of Retaliation Resolutions in the Senate.

THIRTY-EIGHTH CONGRESS.

SECOND SESSION.

The Republican platform in 1864 had pledged the complete abolition of slavery by constitutional amendment. The Senate, in which the Republicans had more than a two-thirds majority, had passed such an amendment in April 1864. But the House, in which the Democrats were stronger, could not summon the necessary two-thirds vote to pass the amendment. After Lincoln's reelection, however, enough Democrats saw the handwriting on the wall to vote aye or abstain when the Thirteenth Amendment again came before the House on January 31, 1865. This time it passed. The Amendment became part of the Constitution when three-quarters of the states ratified it by December 1865.

February 1, 1865.

FROM WASHINGTON.

ABOLITION OF SLAVERY.

Passage of the Constitutional Amendment.

One Hundred and Nineteen Yeas against Fifty-six Nays.

Exciting Scene in the House.

ENTHUSIASM OVER THE RESULT.

THE PEACE MISSION IN THE SENATE.

A Resolution Calling for Information.

Passage of Retaliation Resolutions in the Senate.

Special Dispatches to the New-York Times.

WASHINGTON, TUESDAY, JAN. 31

THE PASSAGE OF THE CONSTITUTIONAL AMENDMENT.

The great feature of the existing rebellion was the passage to-day by the House of Representatives of the resolutions submitting to the Legislatures of the several States an amendment to the Constitution abolishing slavery. It was an epoch in the history of the country, and will be remembered by the members of the House and spectators present as an event in their lives. At 3 o'clock, by general consent, all discussion having ceased, the preliminary votes to reconsider and second the demand for the previous question were agreed to by a vote of 113 yeas, to 58 nays; and amid profound silence the Speaker announced that the yeas and nays would be taken directly upon the pending proposition. During the call, when prominent Democrats voted aye, there was suppressed evidence of applause and gratification exhibited in the galleries, but it was evident that the great interest centered entirely upon the final result, and when the presiding officer announced that the resolution was agreed to by yeas 119, nays 56, the enthusiasm of all present, save a few disappointed politicians, knew no bounds, and for several moments the scene was grand and impressive beyond description. No attempt was made to suppress the applause which came from all sides,

Lincoln addressing the crowd from the eastern portico of the Capitol at his second inauguration, March 4, 1865. Photograph by Alexander Gardner.

every one feeling that the occasion justified the fullest expression of approbation and joy. . . .

Dispatches to the Associated Press.

WASHINGTON, TUESDAY, JAN. 31.

THE VOTE ON THE AMENDMENT.

Soon after the passage of the Anti-Slavery Constitutional Amendment this afternoon, a salute was fired in honor of that event. The vote last June, when it was defeated for the want of the requisite two-thirds majority, was yeas, 96; nays, 65; absent, 21. Those who at that time voted against the amendment, but who changed their votes and cast them in the affirmative to-day, are Messrs. BALDWIN of Michigan, COFFROTH, MCALLISTER, GANSON, HERRICK, RADFORD, STEELE, KING, ROLLINS of Missouri, and HUTCHINS. Those who were absent on the former occasion, and who now voted aye, are as follows: Messrs. BROWN of West Virginia, DAVIS of Maryland, DAVIS of New-York, GRINNELL, MCBRIDE, NELSON, POMEROY, RAN-

DALL WORTHINGTON and YEAMAN. The following who were absent or not voting when the June vote was taken, voted nay: Messrs. HALL, HARRIS, of Maryland, HARRIS of Illinois, WINFIELD, BEN. WOOD and TOWNSEND. Those who voted against the resolution last year, and were to-day absent or not voting, are Messrs. LAZEAR, LE BLOND, MCKINNEY, MARCY, MCDOWELL and ROGERS.

MR. WADE ON THE PEACE MISSION.

During the debate on the retaliation resolution, while Mr. WADE was speaking about Mr. BLAIR'S mission to Richmond, Mr. JOHNSON asked how he came to go there. Mr. WADE replied: "I would like to know. I intend to know if there is power in the United States Senate to be informed on that subject. Yes, Sir. I intend to know why it was that any man was permitted to go with impunity through our lines, and confer with the arch traitor of the Confederacy, and come back here and go again." Mr. JOHNSON said he went in a Government vessel the last time. Mr. WADE responded: "Yes, I understand he went on a Government vessel. He had no more right to be on that vessel on a mission to hold communication with this arch traitor and devil, than he had to be on his road to the lower regions in a vehicle furnished by the Government."

After the fall of Atlanta on September 2, 1864, everything was downhill for the Confederacy, which never won another battle. On April 1, 1865, General Philip Sheridan's cavalry and the 5th Corps of the Army of the Potomac crushed the right wing of Lee's defenses at Five Forks southwest of Petersburg and cut the last railroad into the city. Next day Grant attacked all along the line and broke through at several points, forcing the Confederates to evacuate both Petersburg and Richmond. When this news reached the North it set off wild celebrations. But the war was not over yet.

April 4, 1865.

GRANT.

RICHMOND AND VICTORY!

The Union Army in the Rebel Capital.

Rout and Flight of the Great Rebel Army from Richmond.

Jeff. Davis and His Crew Driven Out.

Grant in Close Pursuit of Lee's Routed Forces.

Richmond and Petersburgh in Full Possession of Our Forces.

ENTHUSIASM IN THE REBEL CAPITAL.

The Citizens Welcome Our Army with Demonstrations of Joy.

RICHMOND FIRED BY THE ENEMY.

Our Troops Save the City from Destruction.

THE EVACUATION OF PETERSBURGH

First Dispatch

City Point, Monday, April 3—11 A.M.

To Edin M. Stanton, Secretary of War:

Gen. Weitzel telegraphs as follows:

"We took Richmond at 8:15 this morning. I captured many guns. The enemy left in great haste. The city is on fire in one place. Am making every effort to put it out. The people receive us with enthusiastic expressions of joy."

Gen. Grant started early this morning with the army toward the Danville road, to cut off Lee's retreating army, if possible.

President Lincoln has gone to the front.

T. S. Bowere, A. A. G.
E. M. Stanton.

OUR SPECIAL ACCOUNTS

MOVEMENTS BY GEN. SHERIDAN—HIS CALL FOR REINFORCEMENTS—FOUR THOUSAND PRISONERS CAPTURED—OPERATIONS ON THE PETERSBURGH FRONT—THE GUNBOAT FLEET DOING ITS PART.

From Our Own Correspondent.

Headquarters Army of the Potomac,
Sunday, April 2—5 A.M.

After we quitted the field on Friday evening the left of the Fifth Corps swung about half a mile further round, and drove the enemy before them. But intelligence being received from Gen. Sheridan that the condition of the ground on his front was such that he could not operate with cavalry, and his advance had, therefore, been compelled to fall back. The Fifth Corps was ordered to go to his assistance, in order to relieve it and prevent its withdrawal. Being perceived and taken advantage of by the enemy, Gen. Miles' division of the Second Corps was advanced by the left flank in its front, and it was then withdrawn to the Boydtown road.

Gen. Miles' division of the Second then fell back to a position on the plankroad behind a temporary embankment that had been thrown up on Wednesday, leaving in the line he recently occupied nothing more than skirmishers, who were directed to fall back if attacked. The Second Division of the Fifth Corps, Gen. Ayers, set out early this morning to support Gen. Sheridan, and the division of Gen. Griffin and Gen. Crawford followed it about noon. They all formed a junction with Gen. Sheridan's Corps at a distance of some five miles from the Mrs. Butler house, and a general engagement commenced there about 3 o'clock.

Freight cars and wood-burning locomotive on the City Point Line. The 13-inch mortar shown in the foreground was used by the Federal artillery around Petersburg during the closing months of the war. This gun was so heavy—it weighted 17,000 pounds—that it was necessary to mount it on a railroad car for easy movement. The "Dictator" fired a 200-pound shell with 20 pounds of powder.

I was not able to go out, as the distance is too great for me to accomplish anything in time for the mail. I understand, however, that the combined forces of Gens. SHERIDAN and WARREN succeeded, after a hotly contested fight, in putting the enemy to flight. They captured four thousand prisoners, four batteries of artillery, a large train of loaded wagons and a number of cattle. The rebel loss in killed and wounded, as well as our own was very heavy, but I am unable to give any estimate of the number.

On our lines during the day there was no fighting except on the Twenty-fourth Corps front. The rebels assaulted the pickets of that corps, and attempted to retake the picket line, from which they were driven yesterday. They were speedily repulsed with a loss of about twenty-five killed and wounded and sixty-four prisoners. Our loss was fifteen in the aggregate.

In the afternoon our troops were massed at three places in the Ninth Corps front, at two in the Sixth, and one in the Twenty-fourth, one in the Twenty-fifth, and two in the Second, with a view of making several demonstrations on the enemy's works and going through them, if necessary, for the complete development of the plan of attack. In pursuance with this design our artillery opened a furious cannonading along the entire front at about 11 P.M., which was continued with little intermission until 6 o'clock this morning. At 3 this morning, such of our troops as it was deemed proper to send in were got into position in front of our works and held ready to make the assault.

I have not yet had time to ascertain which troops were led to the assault, nor the results at different points, and am only able to speak of the Second Division, Gen. POTTER's, of the Ninth Corps. This division was posted on that part of the line between forts Sedgwick and Davis, and some time before the hour of attack arrived the Brigade Commanders Gens. GRIFFIN and CURTIN, perceiving the opportunity to do so without endangering their own men made a sortie and captured one hundred and thirty-three men and four officers of the rebel pickets.

His picket-line was completely surprised, and only knew of the attack when called upon to surrender. At this hour, 6 A.M., there is exceedingly heavy firing along the entire line from Deep Bottom to the Boydtown plank-road, and the fleet of gunboats on the James River are participating in it.

The assault on the enemy's works commenced at 4 o'clock in several places, and is still progressing, but with what success is not yet known. In the front of the Second Division of the ninth Corps there seems to be more artillery engaged than elsewhere on the line, except at the point where the gunboats are engaged. But Gen. POTTER and his two able Brigade Generals, GRIFFIN and CURTIN, are holding their men well up the work, and the determination is universal throughout the division to go through if required. Gen. POTTER and his staff are in the hottest part of the field, overseeing the assault in person. The General feels, no doubt, that his front is one of the most important positions on the whole line, and from its proximity to the rebel works, most liable to be broken through, except that opposite Fort Steadman, and he is consequently extremely solicitous respecting it. The front at Fort Steadman is ably defended by Gen. WILCOX.

LATER.

Part of the line on the left is said to have made a successful demonstration and captured a number of prisoners. If possible to get it through in time, I will send you particulars, dispatching it to City Point by express before the boat leaves.

The fighting was so severe that the loss on both sides must necessarily be very heavy. The rebels fought our men hand to hand when we were about climbing the parapet of the fort, although lying down at the time to avoid the fire of our advancing line. Gen. GRIFFIN, of the Second Brigade of the Division, led the way into their works, and when Gen. POTTER sent to ask if he could hold the works, and if not to fall back, his reply was, "Tell Gen. POTTER I can hold the works. Send me more men if you can; but I will hold the works." He took command of the division on Gen. POTTER being wounded. Gen. CURTIN, of the First Brigade, also behaved with great gallantry, holding his men up to the works till an entrance was effected, and then dashing forward at their head driving the enemy before him. This fight, even if not ultimately successful, proves the old Ninth corps to be equal to any emergency. The task set for it is the worst this army ever had to do, and so far it has accomplished the

Picket line in front of Fort Malone, Petersburg, Virginia, 1865.

object unaided. Everybody here thinks those who are left of us will quarter in Petersburgh to-night, and that the old Stars and Stripes will wave over the cockade city ere the setting of the sun. In taking Petersburgh we draw the cord that will soon strangle the rebellion in Richmond.

Gen. WILCOX is also in the field with his staff. The lines here are also very close together, and if our forces should be repulsed and disordered, the enemy would have an excellent opportunity to inflict serious damage, and make us pay dearly for the temerity we have evinced in attempting to assault such almost impregnable works as those he occupies along this line.

Gen. HARTRANFT's Division is engaged in the assault, but I am not able to say at what particular point or with what success. It is composed wholly of new troops who have never been in any engagement but that of the 25th ult., but they behaved so nobly on that occasion that great things were expected of them. And they have such regard for their brave and noble Division Commander that they will no doubt strive hard for the sake of his reputation and their own. Gen. PARKS, the Corps Commander, is also near the scene of action with his staff and within range of the enemy's guns directing the operations. From the present aspect of affairs he will have cause to be proud of his corps ere the day closes as we are no doubt already partially within the enemy's lines, strong as they are, whether we can hold them will soon be known. It is thought here that we can both take and hold them.

1 o'clock. A.M.—The demonstration in front of the Second division of the Ninth

Corps promises to be a success. We have captured two of their forts, guns and all, and the line of works between and on either flank, and have taken two hundred more prisoners. The fight is still raging furiously. Our loss must be heavy, but at this hour it is impossible to give any estimate. We have succeeded in compelling them to bring their forces from the left and thus opened the way there for SHERIDAN and WARREN to operate successfully. Their force in this front, and which we are now fighting, is Gen. GORDON's corps, principally Southern troops from Alabama, Ga., and South Carolina. They have fought hard since the attack commenced, and still continue to dispute the ground inch by inch. . . .

H. H. YOUNG

THE GLORIOUS NEWS.

Rejoicings in City and Country.

Enthusiasm, Solemnity and Thanksgiving.

Business Suspended and Flags Displayed.

The Praise of the Army on Every Tongue.

Great Mass Meetings in Wall Street and at Union Square.

Patriotic Speeches and Patriotic Songs.

The Whole City Aglow with Excitement.

ILLUMINATIONS AND FIREWORKS.

At no time since the Fall of Sumter has the City of New-York been so thoroughly excited as it was yesterday upon the announcement of the occupation of Richmond. The news in the morning journals was sufficient to arouse the most latent patriotism, and cause the hardest heart to beat with gratitude. Scarcely, however, had the people settled themselves at their various avocations when a strange whisper filled the air, penetrating to the counting-room, the workshop and the school, as if by magic, and long before the newspaper extras stamped the joyful news upon the public mind, it was everywhere known that great news had come to hand, and that victory was ours. An interested crowd gathered about the TIMES Bulletin, and as the cheering words were read again and again, great hearty cheers went up from the multitude, and joy beamed from every eye. Soon the nimble feet of the newsboys had sped with the official dispatch throughout the town, and what had been but an intuitive surmise became a patent truth. The manifestations of exhilaration were boundless; flags were flung to the breeze from innumerable stores and dwellings, making Broadway to shine with the Stars and Stripes, and casting a stream of glory upon the harbor. At the ferries, as soon as the announcement was formally made, an order was issued to deck the boats with bunting, and at once the several fleets of double-enders steamed across the river gay with the flutter of our flag. The down-town shipping houses, most of which are provided with staffs, ran up their colors, so that South-street and West-street, Broad-street and Beaver-street, with the neighboring marts of traffic, vied in patriotic display with the hotels of Broadway and the mansions of the upper end. The magnetism of delight was upon every man. Not a dismal face, not an averted eye, not a pursed-up mouth was seen, nor a croaking tongue heard. No one suggested an "if" or a "but," but every one accepted the glad tidings as truth from the pen of an "honest man." Hand grasped hand in places where "how much" and "how low" are the ordinary salutation; "glorious news" and "thank God" sprang from lips more accustomed to "buyer sixty" and "seller ten;" hard pebbled spectacles that have weathered the beatings of the world and the buffetings of care for sixty years without a moisture, were wet with tears of gratitude, and men estranged for months grasped each others willing palm, while their hearts beat in harmonious thanksgiving. In the public and private schools as much as genuine enthusiasm was displayed as in the harsher schools of Wall and William streets. Appropriate addresses were made in several of them by the Principals, and the national hymns were sung with a gusto which only school boys and girls can give. One theme was upon every lip—the boats, the cars, the restaurants, the stages, the streets were full of cheerful, happy, exulting, forgiving people, who waived all ceremony, all points of etiquette, and chattered busily each with his neighbor upon the one great occurrence of the day.

It would be idle to disguise the fact that our people rejoiced particularly over the fact that Richmond, the rebel capital, the home of the Confederate President, the seat of their government, the hub and centre of the contest, was at length occupied by our troops. Atlanta, Savannah, Wilmington and Charleston especially were each in turn the object of public attention and anxiety, but after all Richmond was the point after which the popular heart had yearned. There it was that JEFF. and his satellites had reared their temple, there the skill of rebel engineers and the energies of their Gen. LEE had been spent in lines of defense and fortifications of strength. It has been the boast of any Southern man that come what might Richmond was forever theirs; that no power this side of Heaven could take it. For years this kind of talk has been made by the Southern people, and for years the sympathizing newspapers of this city and elsewhere have indorsed it, so that our people have felt within them an irrepressible longing for its possession. They wanted its lines of defense broken and its fortifications captured—they wanted JEFF. DAVIS driven out or hanged at his door post, and Gen. LEE swept from his entrenchments by besom of the Union. At length it came, and came, too, so suddenly, that the people were quite unprepared for it. It took the city several hours to accept the startling fact, to recognize its magnitude; and it is very doubtful if even yet the vast extent of the victory is duly appreciated. As each successive dispatch was placed upon the bulletins of the newspapers, the crowds increased in numbers, but the cup of enthusiasm was too full for further addition. Hardly would the paper be placed upon its board, before its contents would be thundered out to the people by some quick-sighted person, and after cheers were given for the news, he would be called upon for a repetition, and no let up was vouchsafed him until, hoarse with shouting and perspiring with exertion, he gave way to a successor, who, in turn, read and reread the stirring dispatches.

Many were the jokes made at the expense of JEFF. and his gray coats; many were the queer suggestions and odd ideas thrown out as to Mr. LINCOLN's probable course. One man, who kept the crowd near our bulletin in a constant uproar, suggested that it would be a good idea if Old ABE would take rooms at the Spottswood House, and issue from thence a proclamation of amnesty to every mother's son in rebeldom, always excepting old JEFF. . . .

After evacuating Petersburg and Richmond, Lee's ragged, tired troops slogged westward hoping to turn south and link up in North Carolina with the remnants of the Confederate Army of Tennessee under General Joseph Johnston. Sheridan's cavalry raced west on a parallel road and prevented them from turning south, while the Union infantry caught up with them at Appomattox, Virginia. Virtually surrounded, Lee had no choice but to meet with General Grant in Wilmer McLean's parlor to accept Grant's generous surrender terms. In subsequent weeks the other Confederate armies accepted similar surrender terms. The war was over.

April 10, 1865.

UNION VICTORY!

PEACE!

SURRENDER OF GENERAL LEE AND HIS WHOLE ARMY.

THE WORK OF PALM SUNDAY.

Final Triumph of the Army of the Potomac.

The Strategy and Diplomacy of Lieut.-Gen. Grant.

Terms and Conditions of the Surrender.

The Rebel Arms, Artillery, and Public Property Surrendered.

Rebel Officers Retain Their Side Arms, and Private Property.

Officers and Men Paroled and Allowed to Return to Their Homes.

The Correspondence Between Grant and Lee.

OFFICIAL.

War Department, Washington,
April 9, 1865—9 o'clock P.M.

To Maj.-Gen. Dix:

This department has received the official report of the SURRENDER, THIS DAY, OF GEN. LEE AND HIS ARMY TO LIEUT.-GEN. GRANT, on the terms proposed by Gen. Grant.

Details will be given as speedily as possible.

Edwin M. Stanton,
Secretary of War.

Headquarters Armies of the United States,
4:30 P.M., April 9.

Hon. Edwin M. Stanton, Secretary of War:

GEN. LEE SURRENDERED THE ARMY OF NORTHERN VIRGINIA THIS AFTERNOON, upon the terms proposed by myself. The accompanying additional correspondence will show the conditions fully.

(Signed) U. S. Grant, Lieut.-Gen'l.

Sunday, April 9, 1865.

General—I received your note of this morning, on the picket line, whither I had come to meet you and ascertain definitely what terms were embraced in your proposition of yesterday with reference to the surrender of this army.

I now request an interview in accordance with the offer contained in your letter of yesterday for that purpose.

Very respectfully, your obedient servant,

R. E. Lee, General.
To Lieut.-Gen. Grant, Commanding United States Armies.

Sunday, April 9, 1865.

Gen. R. E. Lee, Commanding Confederate States Armies:

Your note of this date is but this moment, 11:50 A.M., received.

In consequence of my having passed from the Richmond and Lynchburgh road to the Farmville and Lynchburgh road, I am at this writing about four miles West of Walter's church, and will push forward to the front for the purpose of meeting you.

Notice sent to me, on this road, where you wish the interview to take place, will meet me.

VERY RESPECTFULLY, YOUR OB'D'T SERVANT,
U. S. GRANT,
LIEUTENANT-GENERAL.

APPOMATTOX COURT-HOUSE, April 9, 1865.

General R. E. Lee, Commanding C. S. A.:

In accordance with the substance of my letters to you of the 8th inst., I propose to receive the surrender of the Army of Northern Virginia on the following terms, to wit:

Rolls of all the officers and men to be made in duplicate, one copy to be given to an officer designated by me, the other to be retained by such officers as you may designate.

The officers to give their individual paroles not to take arms against the Government of the United States until properly exchanged, and each company or regimental commander sign a like parole for the men of their commands.

The arms, artillery and public property to be packed and stacked and turned over to the officers appointed by me to receive them.

This will not embrace the side-arms of the officers, nor their private horses or baggage.

This done, EACH OFFICER AND MAN WILL BE ALLOWED TO RETURN TO THEIR HOMES, not to be disturbed by United States authority so long as they observe their parole and the laws in force where they reside.

VERY RESPECTFULLY,
U. S. GRANT, LIEUTENANT-GENERAL.

HEADQUARTERS ARMY OF NORTHERN VIRGINIA,
April 9, 1865.

Lieut.-Gen. U. S. Grant, Commanding U. S. A.:

GENERAL: I have received your letter of this date, CONTAINING THE TERMS OF SURRENDER OF THE ARMY OF NORTHERN VIRGINIA, as proposed by you: As they are substantially the same as those expressed in your letter of the 8th last, THEY ARE ACCEPTED. I will proceed to designate the proper officers to carry the stipulations into effect.

VERY RESPECTFULLY,
YOUR OBEDIENT SERVANT,
R. E. LEE, GENERAL.

THE PRELIMINARY CORRESPONDENCE.

The following is the previous correspondence between Lieut.-Gen. GRANT and Gen. LEE, referred to in the foregoing telegram to the Secretary of War:

CLIFTON HOUSE, VA., April 9, 1865.

Hon. Edwin M. Stanton, Secretary of War:

The following correspondence has taken place between Gen. LEE and myself. *There has been no relaxation in the pursuit during its pendency.*

U. S. GRANT, LIEUTENANT-GENERAL.

APRIL 7, 1865.

Gen. R. E. Lee, Commanding C. S. A.:

GENERAL: The result of the last week must convince you of the hopelessness of further resistance on the part of the Army of Northern Virginia in this struggle. I feel that it is so and regard it as my duty to shift from myself the responsibility of any further effusion of blood, by asking of you the surrender of that portion of the Confederate States Army, known as the Army of Northern Virginia.

VERY RESPECTFULLY,
YOUR OBEDIENT SERVANT,
U. S. GRANT,
LIEUTENANT-GENERAL,
COMMANDING ARMIES OF THE UNITED STATES.

APRIL 7, 1865.

General: I have received your note of this date.

Though not entirely of the opinion you express of the hopelessness of further resistance on the part of the army of Northern Virginia, I reciprocate your desire to avoid useless effusion of blood, and therefore, before considering your proposition, *ask the terms you will offer, on condition of its surrender.*

R. E. LEE, GENERAL.
TO LIEUT.-GEN. U. S. GRANT,
COMMANDING ARMIES OF THE UNITED STATES.

APRIL 8, 1865.

To Gen. R. E. Lee, Commanding C. S. A.:

GENERAL: Your note of last evening in reply to mine of same date, asking the conditions on which I will accept the surrender of the Army of Northern Virginia, is just received.

In reply, I would say that *peace being my first desire, there is but one condition that I insist upon, viz.:*

That the men surrendered shall be disqualified for taking up arms again against the Government of the United States until properly exchanged.

I will meet you, or designate officers to meet any officers you may name, for the same purpose, at any point agreeable to you, for the purpose of arranging definitely the terms upon which the surrender of the Army of Northern Virginia will be received.

U. S. GRANT, LIEUT.-GENERAL,
COMMANDING ARMIES OF THE UNITED STATES.

APRIL 8, 1865.

GENERAL: I received, at a late hour, your note of to-day, in answer to mine of yesterday.

I did not intend to propose the surrender of the Army of Northern Virginia, but *to ask the terms* of your proposition. To be frank, I do not think the emergency has arisen to call for the surrender.

But as *the restoration of peace should be the sole object of it all.* I desire to know whether your proposals would tend to that end.

I cannot, therefore, meet you with a view to surrender the Army of Northern Virginia, but *as far as your proposition may affect the Confederate States forces under my command, and tend to the restoration of peace,* I should be pleased to meet you at 10 A.M., to-morrow, on the old stage road to Richmond, between the picket lines of the two armies.

Very respectfully, your obedient servant,

R. E. LEE,
GENERAL, C. S. A.
TO LIEUT.-GEN. GRANT, COMMANDING ARMIES OF THE UNITED STATES.

APRIL 9, 1865.

To Gen. R. E. Lee, commanding C. S. A.:

GENERAL: Your note of yesterday is received. As I have no authority to treat on the subject of peace, the meeting proposed for 10 A.M. to-day could lead to no good. I

General Robert E. Lee posed with his son, General George Washington Curtis Lee (left), and his aide, Colonel Walter Taylor (right), on the rear veranda of his home in Richmond, Virginia, several days after returning from his surrender at Appomattox. On April 10, Lee wrote his final words to his men: With "admiration of your constancy and devotion to your country and a grateful remembrance of your kind and generous consideration of myself, I bid you all an affectionate farewell."

will state, however, General, that *I am equally anxious for peace with yourself;* and the whole North entertain the same feeling. *The terms upon which peace can be had are well understood. By the South laying down their arms, they will hasten that most desirable event, save thousands of human lives, and hundreds of millions of property not yet destroyed.*

Sincerely hoping that all our difficulties may be settled *without the loss of another life,* I subscribe myself,

Very respectfully,
Your obedient servant,.
U. S. Grant,
Lieutenant-General United States Army.

THE VICTORY

Thanks to God, the Giver, of Victory.

Honors to Gen. Grant and His Gallant Army.

A NATIONAL SALUTE ORDERED.

Two Hundred Guns to be Fired at the Headquarters of Every Army, Department, Post and Arsenal.

FIRST IMPRESSIONS OF RICHMOND—THE GREAT CONFLAGRATION IN THE CITY—WHO WAS RESPONSIBLE FOR IT?—THE LIBBY AND CASTLE THUNDER—SUFFERING FOR FOOD—DISTRIBUTION OF SUPPLIES—LEE'S FAMILY.

From Our Own Correspondent.

RICHMOND, THURSDAY, APRIL 6, 1865.

So many thousand facts are presented to the mind of the visitor here in such a very short space of time, that to record them systematically is almost impossible. The great features of the evacuation, the entrance of our troops, the conflagration, the President's visit and reception, have already been forwarded to you in detail by your correspondents who came in with troops, and I will, therefore, allude to them only in a general way.

Let me say, though, at the outset, that the best part of the city is a ruin. That the awful fire kindled by the enemy, and which at first promised to consume but a few buildings, was so fanned by the rising wind, that before it could be got under subjection, *thirty squares, comprising not less than eight hundred buildings in the very best and most valuable business part of Richmond were in ashes*. What the pecuniary loss is no one can estimate. Nearly all the principal mills, factories, warehouses, stores, banks and insurance offices were destroyed, and the losses being so heavy, the insurance companies, perhaps insolvent already from their countenance of the rebel currency, are now more than bankrupted, and thousands of property owners, computed wealthy in their actual possessions three days ago, are now reduced to beggary. It is among the things easily discernable, that this ruin, wrought by their own friends, to whom they have given all, and to whose tyranny they have submitted, with even cheerfulness, is the cause of far deeper gloom among many than that produced by the loss of the city or the defeat of their army. It is apparent indeed that the transfer of the city to the Union flag was not only *not distasteful to a very large portion of the people, many of them among the best classes, but even highly gratifying.* No captured city, not even Savannah nor Columbia, can present the ruin apparent here in Richmond. It will carry the painful evidences for half a score of years, and the only thing which will speedily alleviate the dire distress that must prevail, and give the city a chance for a speedy recovery from its present stagnation, is immediate peace. It is Richmond's only salvation. The origin of the fire and the incendiaries are so well and positively known that no extended investigation on these points is required. It seems that *Gen. Lee was not responsible for it, but that Jeff. Davis and his Secretary of War, Breckenridge, were.* The destruction of the supplies and the arsenal involved the destruction of the city, and it was so decided by the leading citizens. Gen. EWELL and Maj. CARRINGTON both protested against it in the most earnest manner, as did also a committee of citizens, but BRECKINRIDGE, in reply, exclaimed *that he didn't care a d-m if every house in Richmond was consumed, the warehouse must be burned.* Thus this wretched rebel, foisted into a powerful position with no constituents, is responsible for the dreadful ruin, and his master DAVIS is likewise responsible, because he silently countenanced it.

The fire was started in two places, among the supply warehouses near the wharves, and at the Danville Depot, where there were 1,500 hogsheads of tobacco belonging to the Confederate Government. This consumed the Danville Depot, also the Petersburgh Depot, and the bridge over the James to Manchester. The famous Libby Prison, and Castle Thunder, as I have already informed you, were not burned. They were reserved for a far more appropriate fate. I visited them yesterday, and found Castle Thunder used as a guard-house for factious and thieving negroes, caught in acts of plunder, while the Libby contained 700 rebel prisoners, officers and privates, temporarily shut up together. They looked through the iron gratings with gloomy countenances, while the Union guard outside seemed to richly enjoy the transition that the famous building had undergone, evidently having been there himself. The whirligig of time makes all things even, and the thousands of loyal officers and soldiers who have suffered the tortures and horrors of these dungeons may now contemplate their present users with serene satisfaction, and yet without resentment.

A close inspection of Castle Thunder reveals one of the most hideous dungeons that can be conceived. We failed to see it, however, in all its filth and nastyness, for a strong force of men had been engaged two days in carrying out the accumulation of the past three years. The corporal of the guard who conducted us through, pointed out a spot on the floor on one of the main halls, not yet cleaned, where the dirt was three inches thick, and alive with vermin, *and yet on this floor, in this condition, prisoners were obliged to sleep either upon the dirt itself or upon pallets of decaying straw.*

But I will not descant further upon this vile relic of the rebellion. Its career is too well known. The prisoners confined here, it will be recollected, were those against whom special vengeance was directed, prisoners of State, persons charged with harboring Union prisoners, Union officers charged with being special blockade-runners,

&c. Well has it been said that a confinement in Castle Thunder is a foretaste of the tortures of the damned.

This building, together with the Libby belongs to the estate of \JOHN ENDERS, and was leased by the rebel Government. They were originally built for stores, but subsequently turned into tobacco manufactories. But their base uses are now at an end.

This is the fourth day of the Union occupation, and the confusion in the city necessarily attendant upon such an evacuation, and such an occupation, is gradually subsiding. Could the ruins of the fire be removed from sight, Richmond would present an attractive appearance, for it is really a handsome city; but, after all, the saddest scenes are at the headquarters of the Provost-Martial, the Commissioners of Subsistence, and the office of Sanitary Commission, the latter being already established here. Gen. WEITZEL had no sooner established his headquarters here than thousands of citizens besieged him for rations. And as the city is now shut out from all supplies from the country, the crowd of applicants for subsistence is rapidly increasing. This morning there was nothing in the markets but a few small fish caught by negroes. The Capitol, the City Hall and the Capitol-square are filled with a great throng of all classes, condition, sexes and ages, with basket in hand and an appealing expression of face. What the regulations yet are in regard to the issue of rations to the citizens, I do not know, but a limited quantity is being supplied them at present.

In order to study this peculiar social feature of the rebellion, I mingled with these crowds this morning for a short time, to observe their temper, desires and condition. They were, of course, largely made up of what appeared to be the poorer classes, and many negroes were among them, some for subsistence for themselves and some as servants of families. I found many whose intelligent expression of countenance, fair features and attempted gentility of dress, indicated that they were of the higher classes, on whom the demands of want and hunger were as insatiable as upon those of less position. I noticed several ladies approach the officer in charge at the City Hall, genteelly attired, and with their faces so closely veiled as to defy the gaze of the keenest eye. They spoke in such tremulous tones when giving their names as to cause us to suspect their names were as foreign to them as the hunger they now sought to appease had been in days gone by. Many of the wealthiest families, however, who had the means, have far larger supplies of provisions on hand than was consistent with the repeated appeals of Confederate officials for such to spare from their bounty to feed the army.

The exodus of prominent citizens was confined mainly to those connected with the rebel government, and a few who had made themselves very conspicuous in rebel politics—all the rebel Cabinet and their chief assistants, though not much of their clerical force, got away. The preparations for the evacuation began very quietly among the officials. At noon of Sunday the important records of the departments were boxed up and carted to the depot; but very little suspicion was excited among the citizens as to the real state of the case. A strong guard was stationed at the

Danville depot, and four trains were got ready, the first of which left, with DAVIS on board, at seven o'clock in the evening, and the last at midnight. DAVIS' family had gone into the country on the Friday preceeding, but not because of any apprehension that the city was to be given up. Very few families left the city, and there are very few vacant houses, the mansions of JEFF. DAVIS and GOV. BILLY SMITH being among those now in want of tenants. The family of Gen. LEE, consisting of a wife, who is an invalid, and three daughters, are among those who remain. They occupy a stylish house on Franklin-street, and for their protection a well disciplined guard is placed at the dwelling, and the family are scrupulously protected from annoyance of any character, the staring gaze of the passer-by hardly being allowed. This is the second time that Mrs. Gen. LEE has been in our hands. She was once captured by our cavalry near White House, in 1862, and sent through our lines to Richmond under flag of truce, by order of Gen. MCCLELLAN.

L. L. CROUNSE.

UNION SENTIMENT IN RICHMOND—PROJECTS OF RECONSTRUCTION—DISTINGUISHED VISITORS—RECRUITING NEGRO TROOPS—THE TRUTH ABOUT REBEL ENLISTMENT OF NEGROES.

From Our Own Correspondent.

RICHMOND, FRIDAY, APRIL 7, 1865.

I can give you news, to-day, which will gratify the heart of every loyal American. Virginia will return to the Union, and that right speedily. Desiring to ascertain the exact truth with reference to the alleged existence of a strong Union sentiment in the city, I availed myself of an opportunity to call upon certain gentlemen here whom I had heard alluded to by Secessionists as Union men, and I must say, that I spent two of the happiest hours of my life in full and free conversation with some of the most thorough and radical Union men in the country; men of wealth and position, whose faith has never wavered for an instant, and who, slaveholders, as they are, *demand that Virginia shall be taken back into the Union "under the Emancipation Proclamation;" that no vestige of the rebellion shall be tolerated; that the usurpation State, and Confederate, which has wrecked Virginia, shall not be recognized in a single respect;* that the State Government must be organized anew, by a convention of the people, as soon as that can be properly effected, and the State and its inhabitants thoroughly purged of treason in every shape.

Union sentiments, in this strong form exist here to a far greater extent than has yet been conceived; not alone among the poorer classes—mechanics and laborers—*but in wealthy and influential circles, where may be found men who have never lost faith in the Union;* who have confidently anticipated its triumph, and who greeted the old flag with tears of joy. They are men of the John Minor Botts school, and they are the leaven which shall leaven the whole lump here in this venerable old commonwealth of Virginia. They will delight to see the mass of the people treated with magnanimity, but they have felt too deeply the iron heel of despotism to permit the amnesty of the prominent leaders of the rebellion. I am not at liberty to-day to mention the names of the most prominent of these men; but were I to do so, many of your readers would recognize them as of the most sterling character.

In the final days of the war, with Union victory all but assured, Lincoln turned his attention to the task of reuniting the fractured nation. As he declared in his second inaugural address: "With malice towards none; with charity for all; with firmness in the right, as God gives us to see the right, let us strive on to finish the work we are in; to bind up the nation's wounds. . . ." Forty-two days later he was dead. (*Maryland Historical Society*)

In addition to this, there is another element, not so thoroughly Union, but ready to stop and talk about the best terms of reconstruction. When the President was here on Tuesday a committee waited on him, headed by Judge CAMPBELL, of Alabama, and late Assistant Secretary of War, also late Peace Commissioner, and asked him what were the best terms he could offer to Virginia—what plan of action must the people adopt to secure reconstruction on the most favorable terms? The President wrote on a slip of paper, without address or signature: *That the Emancipation Proclamation must stand;* that in all other matters the people *would be treated with liberality;* that passports might possibly be granted to the Governor, members of the Legislature, or any other public men to come to Richmond and decide the destiny of Virginia.

This little document was the basis of a private conference held this afternoon at the office of the Whig, at which were assembled Judge CAMPBELL, Gen. J.R. ANDERSON of the Tredegær Iron Works, and the following members of the State and city governments: Senators MARSHALL of Fauquier, GARRISON of Accomac, and Messrs. ENGLISH, HALL, BURR and SCOT, of the House of delegates; Joseph MAYO, Mayor of the City, WILLIAM THOMAS, city auditor, and Messrs. WALKER, BURR, SAUNDERS and SCOTT, of the city council. There were also several prominent Union citizens present. Mr. ANDERSON was called to the chair, and Judge CAMPBELL stated what he had obtained from the President. The meeting was intended to be private, and I have not been able to learn fully what transpired, but I believe it is proposed to send four Commissioners to Gen. LEE with the terms proposed by Mr. LINCOLN, and see if he can be induced to cease hostilities while the Legislature is convened to deliberate and decide the fate of the State, and that the village of Charlottesville be made neutral ground, there to convene the Legislature and deliberate.

This project contains several impracticable features, and does not express the views of the thoroughly loyal people here, who declare that "BILLY" SMITH, the present Governor, is a far worse rebel than JEFF. DAVIS himself, and *that he must be repudiated, and the Legislature with him*, for both were elected, not by the people, but by a terrible despotism under which no freedom of choice could be exercised. But even such signs are vastly encouraging, though the completeness of our great victory should never be marred by any compromise, when there is *an absolute majority of Union men here in the city of Richmond to-day.*

There will be further developments of deep interest in a few days, which I trust I may have the pleasure of chronicling.

The city is thronged with distinguished visitors. Yesterday two steamers arrived with Mr. LINCOLN, Mrs. GRANT, Senator SUMNER, Senator HARLAN, and other well-known people. To-day there arrived Vice-President JOHNSON, PRESTON KING and others. The city is really crowded. All the sutlers and traders at City Point have rushed up here, and trade will soon be lively.

The recruiting of negro troops goes on with great rapidity, two or three hundred per day being enlisted. A branch of Gen. CASEY'S Examining Board is already established, by Col. FREDERICKS and Maj. TAGGART, of the War Department. The truth about the rebel enlistment of negroes here appears to be that about two hundred only were ever sworn into service. *No inducements could tempt the black man to enter the rebel army.*

The great news to-day that SHERIDAN has captured 12,600 more prisoners, including Gens. EWELL, KERSHAW, and FITZHUGH LEE, thrills every heart with enthusiasm, and there is the greatest good feeling everywhere tonight.

As I close my letter, bands are playing in the Capitol Square, the moon shines brilliantly overhead, and the scene seems not at all one of war.

L. L. CROUNSE.

The North was still celebrating Lee's surrender when chilling news sent the nation into mourning. On April 14 the careworn Lincoln relaxed by attending a comedy at Ford's Theater. In the middle of the play, John Wilkes Booth gained entrance to Lincoln's box and shot him in the head. Lincoln died the next morning. A prominent actor, the Maryland-born Booth was a frustrated, unstable egotist who supported the Confederacy and hated Lincoln. He had plotted for months to kidnap Lincoln and, with the help of the Confederate secret service, to take him to Richmond and hold him hostage for concessions to the Confederacy. This scheme collapsed when Richmond fell, so Booth decided, apparently on his own, to kill Lincoln. He assigned accomplices to assassinate Vice-President Andrew Johnson and Secretary of State Seward. The man assigned to kill Johnson lost his nerve, and Seward survived the attempt on his life. Lincoln lay in state at the White House on April 19 and then his funeral train began the long trip back to Springfield over the same route he had taken to Washington four years earlier, stopping in nine cities where tens of thousands paid tribute to the martyred president. Seven million people viewed Lincoln's funeral train as it steamed slowly westward.

April 15, 1865.

AWFUL EVENT.

PRESIDENT LINCOLN SHOT BY AN ASSASSIN.

The Deed Done at Ford's Theatre Last Night.

THE ACT OF A DESPERATE REBEL.

The President Still Alive at Last Accounts.

No Hopes Entertained of His Recovery.

Attempted Assassination of Secretary Seward.

DETAILS OF THE DREADFUL TRAGEDY.

[OFFICIAL.]

War Department,
Washington, April 15—1:30 A.M.

Maj.-Gen. Dix:

This evening at about 9:30 P.M., at Ford's Theatre, the President, while sitting in his private box with Mrs. Lincoln, Mrs. Harris, and Major Rathburn, was shot by an assassin, who suddenly entered the box and approached behind the President.

The assassin then leaped upon the stage, brandishing a large dagger or knife, and made his escape in the rear of the theatre.

The pistol ball entered the back of the President's head and penetrated nearly through the head. The wound is mortal. The President has been insensible ever since it was inflicted, and is now dying.

About the same hour an assassin, whether the same or not, entered Mr. Seward's apartments, and under the pretence of having a prescription, was shown to the Secretary's sick chamber. The assassin immediately rushed to the bed, and inflicted two or three stabs on the throat and two on the face. It is hoped the wounds may not be mortal. My apprehension is that they will prove fatal.

The nurses alarmed Mr. Frederick Seward, who was in an adjoining room, and hastened to the door of his father's room, when he met the assassin, who inflicted upon him one or more dangerous wounds. The recovery of Frederick Seward is doubtful.

It is not probable that the President will live throughout the night.

Gen. Grant and wife were advertised to be at the theatre this evening, but he started to Burlington at 6 o'clock this evening.

At a Cabinet meeting at which Gen. Grant was present, the subject of the state of the country and the prospect of a speedy peace was discussed. The President was very cheerful and hopeful, and spoke very kindly of Gen. Lee and others of the Confederacy, and of the establishment of government in Virginia.

All the members of the Cabinet except Mr. Seward, are now in attendance upon the President.

I have seen Mr. Seward, but he and Frederick were both unconscious.

EDWIN M. STANTON,
Secretary of War.

DETAIL OF THE OCCURENCE.

WASHINGTON, FRIDAY, APRIL 14—12:30 A.M.

The President was shot in a theatre to-night, and is, perhaps, mortally wounded. Secretary SEWARD was also assassinated.

SECOND DISPATCH.

WASHINGTON, FRIDAY, APRIL 14.

President LINCOLN and wife, with other friends, this evening visited Ford's Theatre for the purpose of witnessing the performance of the *American Cousin.*

It was announced in the papers that Gen. GRANT would also be present, but he took the late train of cars for New-Jersey.

The theatre was densely crowded, and everybody seemed delighted with the scene before them. During the third act, and while there was a temporary pause for one of the actors to enter, a sharp report of a pistol was heard, which merely attracted attention, but suggesting nothing serious, until a man rushed to the front of the President's box, waving a long dagger in his right hand, and exclaiming *"Sic semper tyrannis,"* and immediately leaped from the box, which was in the second tier, to the stage beneath, and ran across to the opposite side, making his escape amid the bewilderment of the audience from the rear of the theatre, and, mounting a horse, fled.

The screams of Mrs. LINCOLN first disclosed the fact to the audience that the President had been shot, when all present rose to their feet, rushing toward the stage, many exclaiming "Hang him! Hang him!"

The excitement was of the wildest possible description, and of course there was an abrupt termination of the theatrical performance.

There was a rush toward the President's box, when cries were heard: "Stand back and give him air." "Has any one stimulants." On a hasty examination, it was found that the President had been shot through the head, above and back of the temporal bone, and that some of the brain was oozing out. He was removed to a private house opposite to the theatre, and the Surgeon-General of the army, and other surgeons sent for to attend to his condition.

On an examination of the private box blood was discovered on the back of the cushioned rocking chair on which the President had been sitting, also on the partition and the floor. A common single-barreled pocket pistol was found on the carpet.

A military guard was placed in front of the private residence to which the President had been conveyed. An immense crowd was in front of it, all deeply anxious to learn the condition of the President. It had been previously announced that the wound was mortal; but all hoped otherwise. The shock to the community was terrible.

The President was in a state of syncope, totally insensible, and breathing slowly. The blood oozed from the wound at the back of his head. The surgeons exhausted every effort of medical skill, but all hope was gone. The parting of his family with the dying President is too sad for description.

At midnight, the Cabinet, with Messrs. SUMMER, COFLAX and FARNSWORTH, Judge CURTIS, Gov. OGLESBY, Gen. MEIGS, Col. HAY, and a few personal friends, with Surgeon-General BARNES and his immediate assistants, were around his bedside.

The President and Mrs. LINCOLN did not start for the theatre until fifteen minutes after eight o'clock. Speaker COLFAX was at the White House at the time, and the President stated to him that he was going, although Mrs. LINCOLN had not been well, because the papers had announced that Gen. GRANT and they were to be present, and, as Gen. GRANT had gone North, he did not wish the audience to be disappointed.

He went with apparent reluctance and urged Mr. COLFAX to go with him; but that gentleman had made other engagements, and with Mr. ASHMAN, of Massachusetts, bid him good-bye.

When the excitement at the theatre was at its wildest height, reports were circulated that Secretary SEWARD had also been assassinated.

On reaching this gentleman's residence a crowd and a military guard were found at the door, and on entering it was ascertained that the reports were based on truth.

Everybody there was so excited that scarcely an intelligible word could be gathered, but the facts are substantially as follows:

About 10 o'clock a man rang the bell, and the call having been answered by a colored servant, he said he had come from Dr. VERDI, Secretary SEWARD's family physician, with a prescription, at the same time holding in his hand a small piece of folded paper, and saying in answer to a refusal that he must see the Secretary, as he was entrusted with particular directions concerning the medicine.

He still insisted on going up, although repeatedly informed that no one could enter the chamber. The man pushed the servant aside, and walked heavily toward the Secretary's room, and was then met by Mr. FREDERICK SEWARD, of whom he demanded to see the Secretary, making the same representation which he did to the servant. What further passed in the way of colloquy is not known, but the man struck him on the head with a "billy," severely injuring the skull and felling him almost senseless. The assassin then rushed into the chamber and attacked Major SEWARD, Paymaster of the United States army and Mr. HANSELL, a messenger of the State Department and two male nurses, disabling them all, he then rushed upon the Secretary, who was lying in bed in the same room, and inflicted three stabs in the neck, but severing, it is thought and hoped, no arteries, though he bled profusely.

The assassin then rushed downstairs, mounted his horse at the door, and rode off before an alarm could be sounded, and in the same manner as the assassin of the President.

It is believed that the injuries of the Secretary are not fatal, nor those of either of the others, although both the Secretary and the Assistant Secretary are very seriously injured.

Secretaries STANTON and WELLES, and other prominent officers of the government, called at Secretary SEWARD's house to inquire into his condition, and there heard of the assassination of the President.

They then proceeded to the house where he was lying, exhibiting of course intense anxiety and solicitude. An immense crowd was gathered in front of the President's house, and a strong guard was also stationed there, many persons evidently supposing he would be brought to his home.

The entire city to-night presents a scene of wild excitement, accompanied by violent expressions of indignation, and the profoundest sorrow—many shed tears. The military authorities have dispatched mounted patrols in every direction, in order, if possible, to arrest the assassins. The whole metropolitan police are likewise vigilant for the same purpose.

The attacks both at the theatre and at Secretary SEWARD's house, took place at about the same hour—10 o'clock—thus showing a preconcerted plan to assassinate those gentlemen. Some evidence of the guilt of the party who attacked the President are in the possession of the police.

Vice-President JOHNSON is in the city, and his headquarters are guarded by troops.

ANOTHER ACCOUNT.

Special Dispatch to the New-York Times.

WASHINGTON, FRIDAY, APRIL 14.
11:15 P.M.

A stroke from Heaven laying the whole of the city in instant ruins could not have startled us as did the word that broke from Ford's Theatre a half hour ago that the President had been shot. It flew everywhere in five minutes, and set five thousand people in swift and excited motion on the instant.

It is impossible to get at the full facts of the case, but it appears that a young man entered the President's box from the theatre, during the last act of the play of *Our American Cousin,* with pistol in hand. He shot the President in the head and instantly jumped from the box upon the stage, and immediately disappeared through the side scenes and rear of the theatre, brandishing a dirk knife and dropping a kid glove on the stage.

The audience heard the shot, but supposing it fired in the regular course of the play, did not heed it till Mrs. LINCOLN's screams drew their attention. The whole affair occupied scarcely half a minute, and then the assassin was gone. As yet he has not been found.

The President's wound is reported mortal. He was at once taken into the house opposite the theatre.

As if this horror was not enough, almost the same moment the story ran through the city that Mr. SEWARD had been murdered in his bed.

Inquiry showed this to be so far true also. It appears a man wearing a light coat, dark pants, slouch hat, called and asked to see Mr. SEWARD, and was shown to his room. He delivered to Major SEWARD, who sat near his father, what purported to be a physician's prescription, turned, and with one stroke cut Mr. SEWARD's throat as he lay on his bed, inflicting a horrible wound, but not severing the jugular vein, and not producing a mortal wound.

In the struggle that followed, Major SEWARD was also badly, but not seriously, wounded in several places. The assassin rushed down stairs, mounted the fleet horse on which he came, drove his spurs into him, and dashed away before anyone could stop him.

Reports have prevailed that an attempt was also made on the life of Mr. STANTON.

MIDNIGHT.

The President is reported dead. Cavalry and infantry are scouring the city in every direction for the murderous assassins, and the city is overwhelmed with excitement. Who the assassins were no one knows, though every body supposes them to have been rebels.

SATURDAY MORNING—1 O'CLOCK.

The person who shot the President is represented as about 30 years of age, five feet nine inches in height, sparely built, of light complexion, dressed in dark clothing, and having a genteel appearance. He entered the box, which is known as the State box, being the upper box on the right hand side from the dress-circle in the regular manner, and shot the President from behind, the ball entering the skull about in the middle, behind, and going in the direction of the left eye; it did not pass through, but apparently broken the frontal bone and forced out the brain to some extent. The President is not yet dead, but is wholly insensible, and the Surgeon-General says he cannot live till day-break. The assassin was followed across the stage by a gentleman, who sprang out from an orchestra chair. He rushed through the side door into an alley, thence to the avenue and mounted a dark bay horse, which he apparently received from the hand of an accomplice, dashed up F, toward the back part of the city. The escape was so sudden that he effectually eluded pursuit. The assassin cried *"sic sempre"* in a sharp, clear voice, as he jumped to the stage, and dropped his hat and a glove.

Two or three officers were in the box with the President and Mrs. LINCOLN, who made efforts to stop the assassin, but were unsuccessful, and received some bruises. The whole affair, from his entrance into the box to his escape from the theatre, occupied scarcely a minute, and the strongest of the action found everybody wholy unprepared. The assault upon Mr. SEWARD appears to have been made almost at the same moment as that upon the President. Mr. SEWARD'S wound is not dangerous in itself, but may prove so in connection with his recent injuries. The two assassins have both endeavored to leave the city to the northwest, apparently not expecting to strike the river. Even so low down as Chain Bridge, cavalry have been sent in every direction to intercept them.

SATURDAY, 1:30 O'CLOCK A.M.

The President still lies insensible. Messrs. STANTON, WELLS, MCCULLOCH, SPEED and USHER are with him, as also the Vice-President, the Surgeon-General, and other Surgeons.

There is a great throng about the house, even at this hour.

2 O'CLOCK A.M.

The President still lives, but lies insensible, as he has since the first moment, and no hopes are entertained that he can survive.

The most extravagant stories prevail, among which one is to effect, that Gen. GRANT was shot while on his was to Philadelphia, of course this is not true.

Another is, that every member of Mr. SEWARD'S family was wounded in the struggle with the assassin there. This also is untrue. Mr. FRED. SEWARD, the Assistant Secretary, and Major CLARENCE SEWARD, of the army, were wounded, neither of them dangerously.

THE CONDITION OF THE PRESIDENT.

WASHINGTON, APRIL 15—2:12 A.M.

The President is still alive; but he is growing weaker. The ball is lodged in his brain, three inches from where it entered the skull. He remains insensible, and his condition is utterly hopeless.

The Vice-President has been to see him; but all company, except the members of the Cabinet and of the family, is rigidly excluded.

Large crowds still continue in the street, as near to the house as the line of guards allows.

April 16, 1865.

OUR GREAT LOSS.

DEATH OF PRESIDENT LINCOLN.

The Songs of Victory Drowned in Sorrow.

CLOSING SCENES OF A NOBLE LIFE.

The Great Sorrow of an Afflicted Nation.

Party Differences Forgotten in Public Grief.

Vice-President Johnson Inaugurated as Chief Executive.

MR. SEWARD WILL RECOVER.

John Wilkes Booth Believed to be the Assassin.

Manifestations of the People Throughout the Country.

OFFICIAL DISPATCHES.

WAR DEPARTMENT, WASHINGTON,
APRIL 15–4:10 A.M.

To Maj.-Gen. Dix:

The President continues insensible and is sinking.

Secretary SEWARD remains without change.

Frederick SEWARD's skull is fractured in two places, besides a severe cut upon his head.

The attendant is still alive, but hopeless. Maj. SEWARD's wound is not dangerous.

It is now ascertained with reasonable certainty that two assassins were engaged in the horrible crime, WILKES BOOTH being the one that shot the President, and the other companion of his whose name is not known, but whose description is so clear that he can hardly escape. It appears from a letter found in BOOTH's trunk that the murder was planned before the 4th of March, but fell through then because the accomplice backed out until "Richmond could be heard from." BOOTH and his accomplice were at the livery stable at six o'clock last evening, and left there with their horses about ten o'clock, or shortly before that hour.

It would seem that they had for several days been seeking their chance, but for some unknown reason it was not carried into effect until last night.

One of them has evidently made his way to Baltimore—the other has not yet been traced.

EDWIN M. STANTON,
SECRETARY OF WAR.

WAR DEPARTMENT, WASHINGTON, April 15.

Major-Gen. Dix:

ABRAHAM LINCOLN died this morning at twenty-two minutes after seven o'clock.

EDWIN M. STANTON,
SECRETARY OF WAR.

WAR DEPARTMENT, WASHINGTON,
April 15—3 P.M.

328 *Maj.-Gen. Dix, New-York:*

Official notice of the death of the late President, ABRAHAM LINCOLN, was given by the heads of departments this morning to ANDREW JOHNSON, Vice-President, upon whom the constitution devolved the office of President. Mr. JOHNSON, upon receiving this notice, appeared before the Hon. SALMON P. CHASE, Chief Justice of the United States, and took the oath of office, as President of the United States, assumed its duties and functions. At 12 o'clock the President met the heads of departments in cabinet meeting, at the Treasury Building, and among other business the following was transacted:

First—The arrangements for the funeral of the late President were referred to the several Secretaries, as far as relates to their respective departments.

Second—WILLIAM HUNTER, Esq., was appointed Acting Secretary of State during the disability of Mr. SEWARD, and his son, FREDERICK SEWARD, the Assistant Secretary.

Third—The President formally announced that he desired to retain the present Secretaries of departments of his Cabinet, and they would go on and discharge their respective duties in the same manner as before the deplorable event that had changed the head of the government.

All business in the departments was suspended during the day.

The surgeons report that the condition of Mr. SEWARD remains unchanged. He is doing well.

No improvement in Mr. FREDERICK SEWARD.

The murderers have not yet been apprehended.

EDWIN M. STANTON,
SECRETARY OF WAR.

THE ASSASSINATION.

Additional Details of the Lamentable Event.

WASHINGTON, SATURDAY, APRIL 15.

The assassin of President LINCOLN left behind him his hat and a spur.

The hat was picked up in the President's box and has been identified by parties to whom it has been shown as the one belonging to the suspected man, and accurately described as the one belonging to the suspected man by other parties, not allowed to see it before describing it.

The spur was dropped upon the stage, and that also has been identified by parties to whom it has been shown as the one procured at a stable where the same man hired a horse in the evening.

Two gentlemen who went to the Secretary of War to apprize him of the attack on Mr. LINCOLN met at the residence of the former a man muffled in a cloak, who, when accosted by them, hastened away.

It had been Mr. STANTON'S intention to accompany Mr. LINCOLN to the theatre, and occupy the same box, but the press of business prevented.

It therefore seems evident that the aim of the plotters was to paralyze the country by at once striking down the head, the heart and the arm of the country.

As soon as the dreadful events were announced in the streets, Superintendent RICHARDS, and his assistants, were at work to discover the assassin.

In a few moments the telegraph had aroused the whole police force of the city.

Maj. WALLACE and several members of the City Government were soon on the spot and every precaution was taken to preserve order and quiet in the city.

Every street in Washington was patrolled at the request of Mr. RICHARDS.

Gen. AUGUR sent horses to mount the police.

Every road leading out of Washington was strongly picketed, and every possible avenue of escape was thoroughly guarded.

Steamboats about to depart down the Potomac were stopped.

The Daily *Chronicle* says:

"As it is suspected that this conspiracy originated in Maryland, the telegraph flashed the mournful news to Baltimore and all the cavalry was immediately put on active duty. Every road was picketed and every precaution taken to prevent the escape of the assassin. A preliminary examination was made by Messrs. RICHARDS and his assistants. Several persons were called to testify and the evidence as elicited before an informal tribunal, and not under oath, was conclusive to this point. The murderer of

President LINCOLN was JOHN WILKES BOOTH. His hat was found in the private box, and identified by several persons who had seen him within the last two days, and the spur which he dropped by accident, after he jumped to the stage, was identified as one of those which he had obtained from the stable where he hired his horse.

This man BOOTH has played more than once at Ford's Theatre, and is, of course, acquainted with its exits and entrances, and the facility with which he escaped behind the scenes is well understood.

The person who assassinated Secretary Seward left behind him a slouched hat and an old rusty navy revolver. The chambers were broken loose from the barrel, as if done by striking. The loads were drawn from the chambers, one being but a rough piece of lead, and the other balls smaller than the chambers, wrapped in paper, as if to keep them from falling out."

CLOSING SCENES.

Particulars of His Last Moments—Record of His Condition Before Death—His Death.

WASHINGTON, SATURDAY, APRIL 15—11 O'CLOCK A.M.

The *Star* extra says:

"At 7:20 o'clock the President breathed his last, closing his eyes as if falling to sleep, and his countenance assuming an expression of perfect serenity. There were no indications of pain, and it was not known that he was dead until the gradually decreasing respiration ceased altogether.

Rev. Dr. GURLEY, of the New-York-avenue Presbyterian Church, immediately on its being ascertained that life was extinct, knelt at the bedside and offered an impressive prayer, which was responded to by all present.

Dr. GURLEY then proceeded to the front parlor, where Mrs. LINCOLN, Capt. ROBERT LINCOLN, Mrs. JOHN HAY, the Private Secretary, and others, were waiting, where he again offered a prayer for the consolation of the family.

The following minutes, taken by Dr. ABBOTT, show the condition of the late President throughout the night:

11 o'clock—Pulse 44.
11:05 o'clock—Pulse 45, and growing weaker.
11:10 o'clock—Pulse 45.
11:15 o'clock—Pulse 42.
11:20 o'clock—Pulse 44; respiration 27 to 29.

11:25 o'clock—Pulse 42.
11:32 o'clock—Pulse 48, and full.
11:40 o'clock—Pulse 45.
11:45 o'clock—Pulse 45; respiration 22.
12 o'clock—Pulse 48; respiration 22.
12:15 o'clock—Pulse 48; respiration 21—ecchymosis both eyes
12:30 o'clock—Pulse 45.
12:32 o'clock—Pulse 60.
12:35 o'clock—Pulse 66.
12:40 o'clock—Pulse 69; right eye much swollen, and ecchymosis.
12:45 o'clock—Pulse 70.
12:55 o'clock—Pulse 80; struggling motion of arms.
1 o'clock—Pulse 86; respiration 30.
1:30 o'clock—Pulse 95; appearing easier.
1:45 o'clock—Pulse 86—very quiet, respiration regular.
Mrs. LINCOLN present.
2:10 o'clock—Mrs. LINCOLN retired with ROBERT LINCOLN to an adjoining room.
2:30 o'clock—President very quiet—pulse 54—respiration 28.
2:52 o'clock—Pulse 48—respiration 30.
3 o'clock—Visited again by Mrs. LINCOLN.
3:25 o'clock—Respiration 24 and regular.
3:35 o'clock—Prayer by Rev. Dr. GURLEY.
4 o'clock—Respiration 26 and regular.
4:15 o'clock—Pulse 60—respiration 25.
5:50 o'clock—Respiration 28—regular—sleeping.
6 o'clock—Pulse falling—respiration 28.
6:30 o'clock—Still falling and labored breathing.
7 o'clock—Symptoms of immediate dissolution.
7:22 o'clock—Death.

Surrounding the death-bed of the President were Secretaries STANTON, WELLES, USHER, Attorney-General SPEED, Postmaster-General DENNISON, M. B. FIELD, Assistant Secretary of the Treasury; Judge OTTO, Assistant Secretary of the Interior; Gen. HALLECK, Gen. MEIGS, Senator SUMMER, R. F. ANDREWS, of New-York; Gen. TODD, of Dacotah; JOHN HAY, Private Secretary; Gov. OGLESBY, of Illinois; Gen. FARNSWORTH, Mrs. and Miss KENNEY, Miss HARRIS, Capt. ROBERT LINCOLN, son of the President, and Doctors E. W. ABBOTT, B. K. STONE, C. D. GATCH, NEAL HALL, and Mr. LIEBERMAN. Secretary MCCULLOCH remained with the President until about 5 o'clock, and Chief-Justice CHASE, after several hours' attendance during the night, returned early this morning.

Immediately after the President's death a Cabinet meeting was called by Secretary STANTON, and held in the room in which the corpse lay. Secretaries STANTON, WELLES and USHER, Postmaster-General DENNISON, and Attorney-General SPEED, were present. The results of the conference are as yet unknown."

REMOVAL OF THE REMAINS TO THE EXECUTIVE MANSION—FEELING IN THE CITY.

WASHINGTON, SATURDAY, APRIL 15.

The President's body was removed from the private residence opposite Ford's Theatre to the executive mansion this morning at 9:30 o'clock, in a hearse, and wrapped in the American flag. It was escorted by a small guard of cavalry, Gen. AUGUR and other military officers following on foot.

A dense crowd accompanied the remains to the White House, where a military guard excluded the crowd, allowing none but persons of the household and personal friends of the deceased to enter the premises, Senator YATES and Representative FARNSWORTH being among the number admitted.

The body is being embalmed, with a view to its removal to Illinois.

Flags over the department and throughout the city are at half-mast. Scarcely any business is being transacted anywhere either on private or public account.

Our citizens, without any preconcert whatever, are draping their premises with festoons of mourning.

The bells are tolling mournfully. All is the deepest gloom and sadness. Strong men weep in the streets. The grief is wide-spread and deep and in strange contrast to the joy so lately manifested over our recent military victories.

This is indeed a day of gloom.

Reports prevail that Mr. FREDERICK W. SEWARD, who was kindly assisting the nursing of Secretary SEWARD, received a stab in the back. His shoulder blade prevented the knife or dagger from penetrating into his body. The prospects are that he will recover.

A report is circulated, repeated by almost everybody, that BOOTH was captured fifteen miles this side of Baltimore. If it be true, as asserted, that the War Department has received such information, it will doubtless be officially promulgated.

The government departments are closed by order, and will be draped with the usual emblems of mourning.

The roads leading to and from the city are guarded by the military, and the utmost circumspection is observed as to all attempting to enter or leave the city.

AUTOPSY UPON THE BODY OF ABRAHAM LINCOLN.

WASHINGTON, SATURDAY, APRIL 15.

An autopsy was held this afternoon over the body of President LINCOLN by Surgeon-General BARNES and Dr. STONE, assisted by other eminent medical men.

The coffin is of mahogany, is covered with black cloth, and lined with lead, the latter also being covered in white satin.

A silver plate upon the coffin over the breast bears the following inscription:

ABRAHAM LINCOLN
SIXTEENTH PRESIDENT OF THE UNITED STATES.
Born July 12, 1809.
Died April 15, 1865.

The remains have been embalmed.

A few locks of hair were removed from the President's head for the family previous to the remains being placed in the coffin.

THE ASSASSINS.

Circumstances Tending to Inculpate J. W. Booth— Description of his Confederate in the Crime.

WASHINGTON, SATURDAY, APRIL 15.

There is no confirmation of the report that the murderer of the President has been arrested.

Among the circumstances tending to fix a participation in the crime on BOOTH, were letters found in his trunk, one of which, apparently from a lady, supplicated him to desist from the perilous undertaking in which he was about to embark, as the time was inauspicious, the mine not yet being ready to be sprung.

The *Extra Intelligencer* says: "From the evidence obtained it is rendered highly probable that the man who stabbed Mr. SEWARD and his sons, is JOHN SURRATT, of Prince George County, Maryland. The horse he rode was hired at NAYLOR'S stable, on Fourteenth-street. SURRATT is a young man, with light hair and goatee. His father is said to have been postmaster of Prince George County."

About 11 o'clock last night two men crossed the Anacostia Bridge, one of whom gave his name as BOOTH, and the other as SMITH. The latter is believed to be JOHN SURRATT.

Last night a riderless horse was found, which has been identified by the proprietor of one of the stables previously mentioned as having been hired from his establishment.

Accounts are conflicting as to whether Booth crossed the bridge on horseback or on foot; but as it is believed that he rode across it, it is presumed that he had exchanged his horse.

From information in the possession of the authorities it is evident that the scope of the plot was intended to be much more comprehensive.

The Vice-President and other prominent members of the Administration were particularly inquired for by suspected parties, and their precise localities accurately obtained; but providentially, in their cases, the scheme miscarried.

A boat was at once sent down the Potomac to notify the gunboats on the river of the awful crime, in order that all possible means should be taken for the arrest of the perpetrators.

The most ample precautions have been taken, and it is not believed the culprits will long succeed in evading the overtaking arm of justice.

The second extra of the *Evening Star* says:

> "Col. Ingraham, Provost-Marshal of the defenses north of the Potomac, is engaged, in taking testimony to-day, all of which fixes the assassination upon J.. Wilkes Booth.
>
> Judge Olin, of the Supreme Court of the District of Columbia, and Justice Miller, are also engaged to-day, at the Police Headquarters, on Tenth-street, in taking the testimony of a large number of witnesses.
>
> Lieut. Tyrell, of Col. Ingraham's staff, last night proceeded to the National Hotel, where Booth had been stopping, and took possession of his trunk, in which was found a Colonel's military dress-coat, two pairs of handcuffs, two boxes of cartridges and a package of letters, all of which are now in the possession of the military authorities."

One of these letters, bearing the date of Hookstown, Md., seems to implicate Booth. The writer speaks of "the mysterious affair in which you are engaged," and urges Booth to proceed to Richmond, and ascertain the views of the authorities there upon the subject. The writer of the letter endeavors to persuade Booth from carrying his designs into execution at that time, for the reason, as the writer alleges, that the government had its suspicions aroused. The writer of the letter seems to have been implicated with Booth in "the mysterious affair" referred to, as he informs Booth in the letter that he would prefer to express his views verbally; and then goes on to say that he was out of money, had no clothes, and would be compelled to leave home, as his family were desirous that he should dissolve his connection with Booth. This letter is written on note paper, in a small neat hand, and simply bears the signature of "Sam."

At the Cabinet meeting yesterday, which lasted over two hours, the future policy of the government toward Virginia was discussed, the best feeling prevailed. It is stated that it was determined to adopt a very liberal policy, as was recommended by the President. It is said that this meeting was the most harmonious held for over two years, the President exhibiting throughout that magnanimity and kindness of heart which has ever characterized his treatment of the rebellious States, and which has been so [word?] requited on their part.

One of the members of the Cabinet remarked to a friend he met at the door, that "The government was to-day stronger than it had been for three years past."

WASHINGTON, SATURDAY, APRIL 15—3:30 P.M.

To-day no one is allowed to leave the city by rail conveyance, or on foot, and the issuing of passes from the Headquarters of the Department of Washington has been suspended by Gen. AUGUR.

PROBABLE ATTEMPT OF THE ASSASSINS TO ESCAPE INTO CANADA— ORDER FROM THE WAR DEPARTMENT.

[CIRCULAR.]

WAR DEPARTMENT,
PROVOST-MARSHAL GENERAL'S BUREAU,
WASHINGTON, D. C.—9:40 A.M., APRIL 15.

It is believed that the assassins of the President and Secretary SEWARD are attempting to escape to Canada. You will make a careful and thorough examination of all persons attempting to cross from the United States into Canada, and will arrest all suspicious persons. The most vigilant scrutiny on your part, and the force at your disposal, is demanded. A description of the parties supposed to be implicated in the murder will be telegraphed you to-day. But in the meantime be active in preventing the crossing of any suspicious persons.

By order of the Secretary of War,

N. L. JEFFERS, BREVET BRIG.-GEN.,
ACTING PROVOST-MARSHAL GENERAL.

THE SUCCESSION.

Mr. Johnson Inaugurated as President.

The Oath Administered by Secretary Chase.

He Will Perform His Duties Trusting in God.

WASHINGTON, SATURDAY, APRIL 15–12 A.M.

ANDREW JOHNSTON was sworn into office as President of the United States by Chief-Justice Chase, to-day, at eleven o'clock.

Secretary McCULLOUGH and Attorney-General SPEED, and others were present.

He remarked:

"The duties are mine. I will perform them, trusting in God.

SECOND DISPATCH.

WASHINGTON, SATURDAY, APRIL 15.

At an early hour this morning, Hon. EDWIN M. STANTON, Secretary of War, sent an official communication to Hon. ANDREW JOHNSON, Vice-President of the United States, that in consequence of the sudden and unexpected death of the Chief Magistrate, his inauguration should take place as soon as possible, and requesting him to state the place and hour at which the ceremony should be performed.

Mr. JOHNSON immediately replied that it would be agreeable to him to have the proceedings take place at his rooms in the Kirkwood House as soon as the arrangements could be perfected.

Chief Justice CHASE was informed of the fact and repaired to the appointed place in company of Secretary McCULLOUGH, of the Treasury Department, Attorney-General SPEED, J. P. BLAIR, Sr., Hon. MONTGOMERY BLAIR, Senators FOOT, of Vermont, RAMSAY, of Minnesota, YATES, of Illinois, STEWART, of Nevada, HALE, of New Hampshire, and Gen. FARNSWORTH, of Illinois.

At eleven o'clock the oath of office was administered by the Chief Justice of the United States, in his usual solemn and impressive manner.

Mr. JOHNSON received the kind expressions of the gentlemen by whom he was surrounded in a manner which showed his earnest sense of the great responsibilities so suddenly devolved upon him, and made a brief speech, in which he said:

"The duties of the office are mine. I will perform them. The consequences are with God. Gentlemen, I shall lean upon you. I feel that I shall need your support. I am deeply impressed with the solemnity of the occasion and the responsibility of the duties of the office I am assuming.

Mr. JOHNSON appeared to be in remarkably good health, and has a high and realizing sense of the hopes that are centred upon him. His manner was solemn and dignified, and his whole bearing produced a most gratifying impression upon those who participated in the ceremonies.

It is probably that during the day President JOHNSON will issue his first proclamation to the American people.

It is expected, though nothing has been definitely determined upon, that the funeral of the late President LINCOLN will take place on or about Thursday next. It is supposed that his remains will be temporarily deposited in the Congressional Cemetery.

April 17, 1865.

OUR GREAT LOSS.

The Assassination of President Lincoln.

DETAILS OF THE FEARFUL CRIME.

Closing Moments and Death of the President.

Probable Recovery of Secretary Seward.

Rumors of the Arrest of the Assassins.

The Funeral of President Lincoln to Take Place Next Wednesday.

Expressions of Deep Sorrow Throughout the Land.

LAST MOMENTS OF THE PRESIDENT.

Interesting Letter from Maunsell B. Field, Esq.

On Friday evening, April 14, 1865, I was reading the evening paper in the reading-room of Willard's Hotel, at about 10½ o'clock, when I was startled by the report that an attempt had been made a few minutes before to assassinate the President at Ford's Theatre. At first I could scarcely credit it, but in a few minutes the statement was confirmed by a number of people who came in separately, all telling the same story. About fifteen minutes previously I had parted with Mr. MILLER, of the Treasury Department, and he had retired to his room. Immediately on receiving this intelligence I notified him of it, and we together proceeded to the scene of the alleged assassination. We found not only considerable crowds on the streets leading to the theatre, but a very large one in front of the theatre, and of the house directly opposite, where the President had been carried after the attempt upon his life. With some difficulty I obtained ingress to the house. I was at once informed by Miss HARRIS, daughter of Senator HARRIS, that the President was dying, which statement was confirmed by three or four other persons whom I met in the hall; but I was desired not to communicate his condition to Mrs. LINCOLN, who was in the front parlor. I went into this parlor, where I found Mrs. LINCOLN, no other lady being present, except Miss HARRIS, as already mentioned. She at once recognized me, and begged me to run for Dr. STONE, or some other medical man. She was not weeping, but appeared hysterical, and exclaimed in rapid succession, over and over again: "Oh! Why didn't he kill me? why didn't he kill me?" I was starting from the house to go for Dr. STONE, when I met at the door, Major ECKERT, of the War Department, who informed me he was going directly to STONE's house, STONE having already been sent for, but not having yet arrived. I then determined to go for Dr. HALL, whose precise residence I did not know. Upon inquiring of the crowd, I was told it was over FRANK TAYLOR's bookstore, on the avenue. This proved to be a mistake, and I was compelled to return to his actual residence on the avenue, above Ninth-street. I found the doctor at home and dressed, and he at once consented to accompany me. Arrived in the neighborhood of the house, I had great difficulty in passing the guard, and only succeeded at last in having the doctor introduced, admission being refused to myself. I returned to Willard's, it now being about 2 o'clock in the morning, and remained there until between 3 and 4 o'clock, when I again went to the house where the President was lying, in company with Mr. ANDREWS, late Surveyor of the port of New-York. I obtained ingress this time without any difficulty, and was enabled to take Mr. ANDREWS in with me. I proceeded at once to the room in which the President was lying, which was a bedroom in an extension, on the first or parlor floor of the house. The room is small, and is ornamented with prints—a very familiar one of LANDSEER's, a white horse, being prominent directly over the bed. The bed was a double one, and I found the President lying diagonally across it, with his head at the outside. The pillows were saturated with blood, and there was considerable blood upon the floor immediately under him. There was a patchwork coverlet thrown over the President, which was only so far removed, from time to time, as to enable the physicians in attendance to feel the arteries of the neck or the heart, and he appeared to have been divested of all clothing. His eyes were closed and injected with blood, both the lids and the portion surrounding the eyes being as black as if they had been bruised by violence. He was breathing regularly, but with effort, and did not seem to be struggling or suffering.

The persons present in the room were the Secretary of War, the Secretary of the Navy, the Postmaster General, the Attorney-General, the Secretary of the Treasury, (who, however, remained only till about 5 o'clock,) the Secretary of the Interior, the Assistant-Secretary of the Interior, myself, Gen. AUGUR. Gen. HALLECK, Gen. MEIGS, and, during the last moments, Capt. ROBERT LINCOLN and Maj. JOHN HAY. On the foot of the bed sat Dr. STONE; above him, and directly opposite the President's face, an army surgeon, to me a stranger; another army surgeon was standing, frequently holding the pulse, and another gentleman, not in uniform, but whom I understood to be also an army surgeon, stood a good deal of the time leaning over the head-board of the bed.

For several hours the breathing above described continued regularly, and apparently without pain or consciousness. But about 7 o'clock a change occurred, and the breathing, which had been continuous, was interrupted at intervals. These intervals became more frequent and of longer duration, and the breathing more feeble. Several times the interval was so long that we thought him dead, and the surgeon applied his finger to the pulse, evidently to ascertain if such was the fact. But it was not till 22 minutes past 7 o'clock in the morning that the flame flickered out. There was no apparent suffering, no convulsive action, no rattling of the throat, none of the ordinary premonitory symptoms of death. Death in this case was a mere cessation of breathing.

The fact had not been ascertained one minute when Dr. GURLEY offered up a prayer. The few persons in the room were all profoundly affected. The President's eyes after death were not, particularly the right one, entirely closed. I closed them myself with my fingers, and one of the surgeons brought pennies and placed them on the eyes, and subsequently substituted for them silver half-dollars. In a very short time the jaw commenced slightly falling, although the body was still warm. I called attention to this, and had it immediately tied up with a pocket handkerchief. The expression immediately after death was purely negative, but in fifteen minutes there came over the mouth, the nostrils, and the chin, a smile that seemed almost an effort of life. I had never seen upon the President's face an expression more genial and pleasing. The body grew cold very gradually, and I left the room before it had entirely stiffened. Curtains had been previously drawn down by the Secretary of War.

Immediately after the decease, a meeting was held of the members of the Cabinet present, in the back parlor, adjacent to the room in which the President died, to which meeting I, of course, was not admitted. About fifteen minutes before the decease, Mrs. LINCOLN came into the room, and threw herself upon her dying husband's body. She was allowed to remain there only a few minutes, when she was removed in a sobbing condition, in which, indeed, she had been during all the time she was present.

After completing his prayer in the chamber of death, Dr. GURLEY went into the front parlor, where Mrs. LINCOLN was, with Mrs. and Miss KINNEY and her son ROBERT, Gen. TODD, of Dacotah, (a cousin of hers,) and Gen. FARNSWORTH, of Illinois. Here another prayer was offered up, during which I remained in the hall. The prayer was continually interrupted by Mrs. LINCOLN's sobs. Soon after its conclusion, I went into the parlor, and found her in a chair, supported by her son ROBERT. Presently her carriage came up, and she was removed to it. She was in a state of tolerable composure at that time, until she reached the door, when, glancing at the theatre opposite, she repeated three or four times: "That dreadful house!—that dreadful house!"

Before I myself left, a guard had been stationed at the door of the room in which the remains of the late President were lying. Mrs. LINCOLN had been communicated with, to ascertain whether she desired the body to be embalmed or not, and the Secretary of War had issued various orders, necessary in consequence of what had occurred.

I left the house about 8:30 o'clock in the morning, and shortly after met Mr. Chief-Justice CHASE, on his way there. He was extremely agitated, as, indeed, I myself had been all through the night. I afterward learned that, at the Cabinet meeting referred to, the Secretary of the Treasury and the Attorney-General were appointed a committee to wait on the Vice-President, which they did, and he was sworn into office early in the morning by the Chief-Justice.

MAUNSELL B. FIELD.

THE GREAT CALAMITY.

WASHINGTON, APRIL 16.

THE CORPSE.

The corpse of the late President has been laid out in the room known as the "guests' room," northwest wing of the White House. It is dressed in the suit of black clothes worn by him at his late Inauguration. A placid smile rests upon his features, and the deceased seems to be in a calm sleep. White flowers have been placed upon the pillow and over the breast.

The corpse of the President will be laid out in state in the east room on Tuesday, in order to give the public an opportunity to see once more the features of him they loved so well. The preparations are being made, to that end, under the supervision of the upholsterer. The catafalque upon which the body will rest is to be placed in the south part of the east room, and is somewhat similar in style to that used on the occasion of the death of President HARRISON. Steps will be placed at the side to enable the public to mount to a position to get a perfect view of the face. The catafalque will be lined with fluted white satin, and on the outside it will be covered with black cloth and black velvet.

THE FUNERAL.

The funeral of President LINCOLN will take place on Wednesday next. Rev. Dr. GURLEY, of the New-York-avenue Presbyterian Church, where the President and his family have been accustomed to worship, will doubtless be the officiating clergyman.

The remains will be temporarily deposited in the vault of the Congressional Cemetery, and hereafter taken to Mr. LINCOLN's home at Springfield, Illinois.

THE FUNERAL CAR.

The funeral car, which is being prepared for the occasion, is to be a magnificent affair. It is to be built on a hearse body. Its extreme length will be fourteen feet. The body of the car will be covered, with black cloth, from which will hang large festoons of cloth on the sides and ends, gathered and fastened by large rosettes of white and black satin over bows of white and black velvet. The bed of the car, on which the coffin will rest, will be eight feet from the ground, in order to give a full view of the coffin; and over this will rise a canopy, the support of which will be draped with black cloth and velvet. The top of the car will be decorated with plumes. The car will be drawn by six or eight horses, each led by a groom.

BOOTH NOT ARRESTED.

Up to this time it has not been ascertained that the assassin of the President has been captured.

THE PRESIDENT'S PLACE OF WORSHIP.

This morning, at the New-York-avenue Presbyterian Church, which Mr. LINCOLN formerly attended, a large crowd of persons assembled in anticipation that the pastor, Rev. P. D. GURLEY, D. D., would make some allusion to the nation's great calamity. The pulpit and the choir, and the President's pew were draped in mourning.

THE ASSASSINATION A CONSPIRACY.

The Extra *Star* has the following:

"Developments have been made within the past twenty-four hours, showing conclusively the existence of a deep laid plot of a gang of conspirators, including members of the order of the Knights of the Golden Circle, to murder President LINCOLN and his Cabinet. We have reason to believe that Secretary SEWARD received, several months since, an intimation from Europe that something of a very desperate character was to transpire at Washington; and it is more than probable that the intimation had reference to the plot of the assassination."

THE CONSPIRACY.

The pickets encircling this city on Friday night, to prevent the escape of the parties who murdered President LINCOLN and attempted the assassination of Secretary SEWARD and his sons, were fired upon at several points by concealed foes. Arrests of the parties charged with the offence will be promptly made.

It was ascertained some weeks ago, from personal friends of the late President, that he had received several private letters warning him that an attempt would probably be made upon his life. But to this he did not seem to attach much, if any, importance. It has always been thought that he was not sufficiently careful of his individual safety on his last visit to Virginia.

It is known that on frequent occasions he would start from the Executive mansion for his Summer country residence at the Soldier's Home without the cavalry escort, which often hurried and overtook him before he had proceeded far. It has always been understood that this escort was accepted by him only on the importunity of his friends as a matter of precaution.

The President before retiring to bed, would, when important military events were progressing, visit the War Department, generally alone, passing over the dark intervening ground, even at late hours, on repeated occasions; and after the warning letters had been received, several close and intimate friends armed for any emergency were careful that he should not continue his visits without their company. For himself, the President seemed to have no fears.

The above facts have heretofore been known to the writer of this telegram, but for prudential reasons, he has not stated them until now.

THE LAST HOURS OF THE PRESIDENT.

As everything pertaining to the last hours of the late President must be interesting to the public, the following incidents of the last day of his life have been obtained
342 from several sources.

His son, Capt. LINCOLN, breakfasted with him on Friday morning, having just returned from the capitulation of LEE, and the President passed a happy hour listening to all the details. While at breakfast he heard that Speaker COLFAX was in the house, and sent word that he wished to see him immediately in the reception room. He conversed with him nearly an hour about his future policy as to the rebellion, which he was about to submit to the Cabinet. Afterwards he had an interview with Mr. HALE, Minister to Spain, and several Senators and Representatives.

At 11 o'clock the Cabinet and Gen. GRANT met with him, and in one of those most satisfactory and important Cabinet meetings held since his first inauguration, the future policy of the Administration was harmoniously and unanimously agreed on. When he adjourned Secretary STANTON said he felt that the government was stronger than at any previous period since the rebellion commenced.

In the afternoon the President had a long and pleasant interview with Gen. OGLESBY, Senator YATES, and other leading citizens of his State.

In the evening Mr. COLFAX called again, at his request, and Mr. ASHMUN, of Massachusetts, who presided over the Chicago Convention of 1860, was present. To them he spoke of his visit to Richmond; and when they stated that there was much uneasiness at the North while he was at the rebel capital, for fear that some traitor might shoot him, he replied jocularly that he would have been alarmed himself if any other person had been President and gone there, but that he did not feel any danger whatever. Conversing on a matter of business with Mr. ASHMUN, he made a remark that he saw Mr. ASHMUN was surprised at; and immediately with his well-known kindness of heart said, "You did not understand me, ASHMUN, I did not mean what you inferred, and I will take it all back and apologize for it." He afterward gave Mr. ASHMUN a card to admit himself and friend early the next morning, to converse further about it.

Turning to Mr. COLFAX he said: "You are going with Mrs. LINCOLN and me to the theatre, I hope." But Mr. COLFAX had other engagements, expecting to leave the city the next morning.

He then said to Mr. COLFAX, "Mr. SUMNER has the gavel of the Confederate Congress, which he got at Richmond, to hand to the Secretary of War. But I insisted then that he must give it to you; and you tell him for me to hand it over." Mr. ASHMUN alluded to the gavel which he still had, and which he had used at the Chicago Convention, and the President and Mrs. LINCOLN, who was also in the parlor, rose to go to the theatre. It was a half an hour after the time they had intended to start, and they spoke about waiting half an hour longer, for the President went with reluctance, as Gen. GRANT had gone North, and he did not wish the people to be disappointed, as they had both been advertised to be there. At the door he stopped, and said: "COLFAX, do not forget to tell the people in the mining region as you pass through them, what I told you this morning about the development, when peace comes, and I will telegraph you at San Francisco." He shook hands with both gentlemen with a pleasant good-bye, and left the Executive Mansion, never to return to it alive.

The President and Cabinet, at the meeting, today, entrusted to Assistant Secretary of the Treasury, HARRINGTON, the general arrangement of the programme for the funeral of the late President. Maj. FRENCH, the Commissioner of Public Buildings, will attend to the carrying out of so much of it as directly appertains to the corpse, and Maj.-Gen. AUGUR, in charge of the defences of Washington, will be in charge of the military part of the procession. Assistant Secretary HARRINGTON has been in consultation to-night, relative to the arrangements, with Gov. OGLESBY, Senator YATES and Ex-Representative ARNOLD, of Illinois, and Gens. GRANT, HALLECT and AUGUR and Admirals FARRAGUT and SHUBBRICK.

The funeral ceremonies of the late President will take place on Wednesday. The time for the remains to leave the city, as well as the route by which they will be taken to Springfield, is as yet undetermined. The procession will form at 11 o'clock, and the religious services will commence at noon, at which hour throughout the whole land, the various religious societies have been requested to assemble in their respective places of worship for prayer. The procession will move at 2 P.M. Details will be made known as soon as perfected.

The acting Secretary of State has issued the following address:

To the People of the United States:

The undersigned is directed to announce that the funeral ceremonies of the lamented Chief Magistrate will take place at the Executive Mansion, in this city, at 12 o'clock noon on Wednesday, the 19th instant.

The various religious denominations through the country are invited to meet in their respective places of worship at that hour for the purpose of solemnizing the occasion with appropriate ceremonies.

(Signed) W. HUNTER,

Acting Secretary of State.

Department of State, Washington, April 17, 1865.

Washington, Saturday, April 15.

To-day, Surgeon General Barnes, Dr. Stone, the late President's family physician; Drs. Crane, Curtis, Woodward, Toft and other eminent medical men, performed an autopsy on the body of the President.

The external appearance of the face was that of a deep black stain about both eyes. Otherwise the face was very natural.

The wound was on the left side of the head behind, on a line with and three inches from the left ear.

The course of the ball was obliquely forward, toward the right eye, crossing the brain obliquely a few inches behind the eye, where the ball lodged.

In the track of the wound were found fragments of bone which had been driven forward by the ball.

The ball was found imbedded in the anterior lobe of the west hemisphere of the brain.

The orbit plates of both eyes were the seat of comminuted fracture, and the orbits of the eyes were filled with extravasated blood.

The serious injury to the orbit plates was due to the centre coup, the result of the intense shock of so large a projectile fired so closely to the head.

The ball was evidently a derringer, hand cast, and from which the neck had been clipped.

A shaving of lead had been removed from the ball in its passage of the bones of the skull, and was found in the orifice of the wound. The first fragment of bone was found two and a half inches within the brain. The second and a larger fragment about four inches from the orifice. The ball lay still further in advance. The wound was half an inch in diameter.

THE NEW PRESIDENT.

INAUGURATION OF ANDREW JOHNSON.

BRIEF AND IMPRESIVE CEREMONIES.

The Oath of Office Administered on Saturday by by Chief-Justice Chase.

PRESIDENT JOHNSON'S INAUGURAL ADDRESS.

WASHINGTON, SUNDAY, APRIL 16.

Yesterday morning Attorney-General SPEED waited upon Hon. ANDREW JOHNSON, Vice-President of the United States, and officially informed him of the sudden and unexpected decease of President LINCOLN, and stated that an early hour might be appointed for the inauguration of his successor. The following is a copy of the communication referred to:

WASHINGTON CITY, April 15, 1865

SIR: ABRAHAM LINCOLN, President of the United States, was shot by assassin last evening at Ford's Theatre, in this city, and died at the hour of twenty-two minutes after seven o'clock. About the same time at which the President was shot, an assassin entered the sick chamber of Hon. W. H. SEWARD, Secretary of State, and stabbed him in several places in the throat, neck and face, severely, if not mortally, wounding him. Other members of the Secretary's family were dangerously wounded by the assassin while making his escape.

By the death of President LINCOLN, the office of President has devolved, under the Constitution, upon you. The emergency of the government demands that you should immediately qualify, according to the requirements of the Constitution, and enter upon the duties of the President of the United States. If you will please make known you pleasure, such arrangements as you deem proper will be made.

Your obedient servants,

HUGH McCULLOCH,
Secretary of the Treasury.
EDWIN M. STANTON,
Secretary of War.
GIDEON WELLES,
Secretary of the Navy.
WILIAM DENNISON,
Postmaster-General.
J. P. USHER,
Secretary of the Interior.
JAMES SPEED,
Attorney-General.

To ANDREW JOHNSON, Vice-President of the United States.

Mr. JOHNSON requested that the ceremony take place at his rooms at the Kirkwood House, in this city, at 10 o'clock in the morning.

Hon. SALMAN P. CHASE, Chief-Justice of the Supreme Court of the United States, was notified of the fact, and desired to be in attendance to administer the oath of office.

At the above-named hour the following gentlemen assembled in the Vice-President's room to participate in the ceremony:

Hon. SALMAN P. CHASE.
Hon. HUGH McCULLOCH, Secretary of the Treasury,
Mr. Attorney-General SPEED,
F. P. BLAIR, Senior,
Hon. MONTGOMERY BLAIR,
Senator FOOT, of Vermont,
Senator YATES, of Illinois,
Senator RAMSAY, of Minnesota,

Senator STEWART, of Nevada,
Senator HALE, of New-Hampshire,
Gen. FARNSWORTH, of Illinois.

After the presentation of the above letter, the Chief Justice administered the following oath to Mr. JOHNSON:

"I do solemnly swear that I will faithfully execute the office of President of the United States, and will, to the best of my ability, preserve, protect and defend the Constitution of the United States."

After receiving the oath, and, being declared President of the United States, Mr. JOHNSON remarked:

ADDRESS OF PRESIDENT JOHNSON.

"Gentlemen, I must be permitted to say that I have been almost overwhelmed by the announcement of the sad event which has so recently occurred. I feel incompetent to perform duties so important and responsible as those which have been so unexpectedly thrown upon me. As to an indication of any policy which may be presented by me in the administration of the government, I have to say that that must be left for the development as the Administration progresses. The message or declaration must be made by the acts as they transpire. The only assurance that I can now give of the future is by reference to the past. The course which I have taken in the past in connection with this rebellion, must be regarded as a guarantee of the future. My past public life, which has been long and laborious, has been founded as I, in good conscience believe, upon a great principle of right, which lies at the basis of all things. The best energies of my life have been spent in endeavoring to establish and perpetuate the principles of free government, and I believe that the government, in passing through its present trials, will settle down upon principles consonant with popular rights, more permanent and enduring than heretofore. I must be permitted to say, if I understand the feelings of my own heart, I have long labored to ameliorate and alleviate the condition of the great mass of the American people. Toil and an honest advocacy of the great principles of free government have been my lot. The duties have been mine—the consequences are God's. This has been the foundation of my political creed, I feel that in the end the government will triumph, and that these great principles will be permanently established. In conclusion, gentlemen, let me say that I want your encouragement and countenance. I shall ask and rely upon you and others in carrying the government through its present perils. I feel in making this request that it will be heartily responded to by you and all other patriots and lovers of the rights and interests of a free people."

At the conclusion of the above remarks, the President received the kind wishes of the friends by whom he was surrounded.

A few moments were devoted to conversation. All were deeply impressed with the solemnity of the occasion, and the recent sad occurrence that caused the necessity for the speedy inauguration of the President was gravely discussed.

Mr. JOHNSON is in fine health and has an earnest sense of the important trust that has been confided in him.

WM. HUNTER, Esq., the Chief Clerk of the State Department, has been appointed Acting Secretary of State.

A special meeting of the Cabinet was held at the Treasury Department, at 10 o'clock this morning.

NEWS FROM WASHINGTON.

Special Dispatches to the New-York Times.

WASHINGTON, SUNDAY, APRIL 16.

APPROPRIATE RELIGIOUS SERVICES.

Easter Sunday has been, for the most part, a cool, and fair, and sunny, and breezy day; yet the tones of all voices have been low, and the great bereavement has been the subject of all conversation. Dr. GURLEY's Church, where Mr. LINCOLN attended, was overflowingly full at an early hour. The pulpit, the front of the choir, gallery and the vacant pew were heavily draped in mourning.

The day had been set apart for sacramental purposes, but the Rev. Doctor prefaced the services with some feeling remarks upon the death of Mr. LINCOLN. He urged the audience to look beyond the hand of the assassin to the hand of the wise God, who overrules all things, and makes even the wrath of man to praise him. He admitted the soreness of this affliction, but doubted not that time would show God's purpose in bringing it upon us.

Most of the churches of the city are draped in mourning, and in each of them was to-day appropriate and touching remembrance of the national sorrow.

A meeting of all clergymen in the city is called at nine o'clock, to-morrow morning, to take such action as becomes a Christian community at this time. Meetings are also called for to-morrow, of a large number of State, social, literary, benevolent and religious organizations, to take action appropriate to the occasion.

THE INVESTIGATION OF THE MURDER.

The city and military authorities have been quietly pursuing investigations since yesterday morning, and persons conversant to some extent with the results thereof, are very confident that the murder of Mr. LINCOLN and the attempted murder of Mr. SEWARD, are only part of the fruits of a carefully planned conspiracy that intended the murder also of other members of the Cabinet, and the destruction of some of the public buildings, and perhaps certain sections of the city. Nothing has yet been brought to light calculated to fix the identity of the assassin of Mr. SEWARD, though various parties have been arrested and examined, and two or three are held for further examination.

RUMORS OF BOOTH'S ARREST.

Rumor has arrested Booth a dozen times already, and many persons will retire to-night in the confident belief that he is confined on a gunboat at the Navy-yard, but so far as can be learned from the authorities he not only has not been arrested, but very little is known as to the route he took in escaping. The aggregate reward now offered here for the arrest of these men is thirty thousand dollars.

MRS. LINCOLN.

Mrs. LINCOLN is yet much depressed, though less so than yesterday. She remains at the White House. Hon. MONTGOMERY BLAIR has tendered to her the use of his house till such time as she leaves the city, and President JOHNSON has communicated to her that he expects her to occupy the White House while she remains in Washington.

THE BODY OF MR. LINCOLN.

The body of Mr. LINCOLN, dressed in the plain black suit he wore on inauguration day, is lying in the northwest corner room of the second floor of the White House. The head lies amidst white flowers, and the features wear the calm peaceful expression of deep sleep. The corpse will be laid in state in the east room on Tuesday, and the funeral will be held on Wednesday.

Hundreds of instances of Mr. LINCOLN'S personal kindness and graceful courtesy have come to light within the last two days. The *Intelligencer* says his last official act was to sign a permit allowing JACOB THOMPSON, late Secretary of the Interior, to leave the country for Europe.

LIEUT.-GEN. GRANT.

Gen. GRANT is still here and at Willard's. He has been in consultation to-day some time with the President and Cabinet. It is said that as soon as he arrived yesterday he ordered the arrest at Richmond of various prominent late rebels.

ARRIVALS IN THE CITY.

There are numerous arrivals of distinguished persons from the North, consequent upon the national bereavement. Among others are Hon. L. F. S. FOSTER, Senator and Vice-President pro tem., and Gov. BUCKINGHAM and Staff, of Connecticut.

INTENSE FEELING OF SORROW.

There is intense feeling in all parts of the city, and any man showing the least disrespect to the memory of the universally lamented dead, is sure to find rough treatment. One of the long-haired wandering preachers, named TOMLINSON, and hailing from Buffalo, while speaking at a soldier's camp, this afternoon, indulged in the remark that if the new President pursued Mr. LINCOLN'S policy he would meet Mr. LINCOLN'S fate in two weeks. He was immediately set upon by the soldiers, and only escaped severe bodily harm because he was at once arrested. In another case, a crowd of curious persons in front of the Provost-Marshal's office, on Ninety-fourth-street, where were a number of rebel soldiers and parties brought in under arrest, became incensed at the remark of one of them about Mr. LINCOLN, and set upon him in such a manner that his life was only saved by hustling him out of the back door and off to the Old Capitol, while JOHN B. HOLE and Gen. F. E. SPINNER made speeches to the crowd, and urged coolness and obedience to law.

April 18, 1865.

THE ASSASSINATION.

Condition of Secretary Seward Improving.

NEW FACTS ABOUT THE MURDERERS.

Preparations for the President's Funeral.

Official Directions from Heads of Departments.

DESCRIPTION OF ASSASSINS.

Reward of Thirty Thousand Dollars Offered for Their Apprehension.

Additional Details of the Conspiracy.

APPEARANCE OF THE CITY.

WASHINGTON, D.C.,
TUESDAY, APRIL 17—9:20 P.M.

The city has to some extent resumed its wonted appearance, though the great grief is still uppermost in all hearts, and its signs are apparent on every hand. Every yard of black fabric in the city on Saturday, was brought up at an early hour on that day, and hundreds of persons who wished to testify their grief by draping the residences were unable to do so. This morning, however, further supplies arrived here, and this afternoon many more houses have been draped in mourning.

Business has been partially resumed, though large numbers of stores have simply contented themselves with opening their doors and not taking down their shutters. In the Public Departments some work has been done during the day, but business generally will not be resumed therein until after the funeral. . . .

CONDITION OF SECRETARY SEWARD AND SON.

The condition of Secretary SEWARD and son Frederick, at the hour of nine o'clock this evening, is so far improved as to encourage the hope of the speedy recovery of both. Secretary SEWARD has slept well to-day, and his condition generally is much easier. The Assistant Secretary is so far improved that the hope of his recovery strengthens with every hour. The others of the injured are doing well.

ARRESTS OF SUSPECTED PERSONS.

Several arrests of parties suspected of being connected with murder of Mr. LINCOLN and the attempted assassination of Secretary SEWARD and sons have been made. Yesterday four men dressed in female attire were arrested in Georgetown and committed to the Old Capitol. Investigations by the civil and military authorities are still in progress, and the testimony of a large number of witnesses has already been taken. These investigations are proceeding quietly, however, as it is deemed best for the ends of justice that no publicity should be given at present to the facts elicited.

EFFECT ON THE FINANCES OF THE COUNTRY.

The effect of the late tragedy upon the finances of the country is most strikingly illustrated by the subscriptions to the popular Seven-thirty loan, which for Friday and Saturday last amounted to the enormous aggregate of *nine million one hundred and thirty-four thousand seven hundred dollars.* This sum was composed entirely of small subscriptions and does not include those made by heavy holders of government vouchers, who by the Loan Act of the last Congress can receive these bonds in payment of their claims. If any evidence was wanted of the determination of the people to sustain the government finances against all attempts of traitors of every dye. This is conclusive.

Dispatches to the Associated Press.

WASHINGTON, MONDAY, APRIL 17.

The deep interest felt in Secretary SEWARD has thronged his residence with visitors, among them the members of the Cabinet, foreign ministers, and a large number of others.

He was informed yesterday, for the first time, of the assassination of President LINCOLN, and of the attempted assassination of himself and of the Assistant Secretary, and to some extent of the condition in which the latter lay.

Mr. SEWARD, though moved with the most intense sorrow and horror at the recital of the awful facts, nevertheless bore it with considerable firmness and composure, his strength having so far returned as to enable him to undergo the trying ordeal.

Every effort that ingenuity, excited by fervor, can make, is being put forth by all the proper authorities to capture or trace the assassin of Mr. LINCOLN and the would-be assassin of Mr. SEWARD.

The Common Council have offered a reward of $20,000 for the arrest and conviction of the assassins, and to this sum another of $10,000 is added by Col L. C. BARKER, Agent of the War Department, making a total of $30,000.

Description of J. WILKES BOOTH, who assassinated the President on the evening of April 14, 1865:

Height, five feet eight inches; weight, 160 pounds; compact built; hair jet black, inclined to curl, of medium length, and parted behind; eyes black, and heavy, dark eyebrows; wears a large seal ring on his little finger; when talking inclines his head forward and looks down.

Description of the person who attempted to assassinate Hon. WM. H. SEWARD, Sectary of State:

Height six feet, one inch; hair black, thick, full and straight; no beard nor appearance of beard; cheeks red on the jaws; face moderately full; twenty-two or twenty-three years of age; eyes large, not prominent, color unknown; brows not heavy but dark; face not large but rather round; complexion healthy; nose straight and well formed, and of medium size; mouth small; lips thin; the upper lip protrudes when he talks; chin pointed and prominent; head medium size; neck short; hands soft and small, fingers tapering, showing no signs of hard labor; broad shoulders; taper waist; straight figure; strong looking man; manner not gentlemanly but vulgar; wears an overcoat with pockets in the side and one on the breast, with lapels or flaps; pants black, and of common stuff; new, heavy boots; voice small and thin, and inclined to tremor . . .

The *National Intelligencer* says:

"We can state on the highest authority that it has been ascertained that there was a regular conspiracy to assassinate every member of the Cabinet, together with the Vice-President. BOOTH, it is said, sent his card up to the Vice-President at the hotel, but Mr. JOHNSON would not conveniently see him.

We understand from authority, which we deem unquestionable, that a few days ago, after an interview between the late Chief Magistrate and the present one, Mr. LINCOLN expressed himself gratified with their concurrent views, and that he placed implicit confidence in the then Vice-President.

The names of the severally appointed assassins, are, we understand, known, and after the present investigation is concluded and published, the public will be astonished at the developments. From motives of public interest we refrain from mentioning many of them that reach us.

A member of the Cabinet remarked on the day after the murder of Mr. LINCOLN, that the rebels had lost their best friend: that Mr. LINCOLN invariably, at every Cabinet meeting, counseled forbearance, kindness and mercy to these misguided men."

REPORTS ABOUT BOOTH'S ARREST.

Report still prevails that BOOTH has been arrested and is on board of a gunboat in the Potomac. The origin of the story was in this wise: A prominent military officer came into the Navy Department on Saturday and said he had just learned that BOOTH was overtaken some miles out on the road leading from Seventh-street, and asked whether the department would consent that he be placed on board of a gunboat. The reply was in the affirmative. Unfortunately the same officer received later information that the report was not true. The military authorities have received no intelligence as to his arrest.

THE FLAG TORN BY THE ASSASSIN.

The National flag draped round the box at the theatre, occupied by the President, belonged to the Treasury Department Regiment. It was torn by the spur of the assassin as he leaped to the stage.

CONDITION OF SECRETARY SEWARD AND SON.

At 10:30 o'clock to-day, Secretary SEWARD was represented to be in an improving condition, though he rested rather uncomfortably last night from mental excitement, caused by conversation with friends in relation to recent events.

His son FREDERICK has partially recovered consciousness, and his symptoms are otherwise somewhat favorable.

MR. HANSELL IS BETTER.

Mr. HANSELL, the Messenger of the State Department, who was stabbed in the back at the same time, is a great sufferer, but believed to be out of danger.

A GRAY COAT STAINED WITH BLOOD FOUND.

WASHINGTON, MONDAY, APRIL 17.

Yesterday a gray coat stained with blood, and which evidently had been worn as an overcoat, was found near Fort Bunker Hill, just back of Glenwood Cemetery. In the pocket was a false moustache, a pair of riding gloves, and a slip of paper, upon which was "MARY E. GARDNER, 410." The coat is supposed to have been worn by the man who attacked Secretary SEWARD, although the weight of the evidence indicates that all the conspirators took the same route—that of the navy-yard bridge.

BOOTH'S MISTRESS.

This morning, Detective KELLEY and a detail of patrolmen of the Second Ward, by order of Judge OLIN, proceeded to the house of MOLLIE TURNER, on the corner of Thirteenth and Ohio-avenue, and arrested all the inmates, from the mistress to the cook, eight in all, and carried them to the police headquarter, to be held as witnesses. This is the house where BOOTH spent much of his time, ELLA TURNER, the woman who attempted suicide, being his kept mistress.

BOOTH'S RECENT BEHAVIOR.

The *Evening Star* says on Friday last, BOOTH was about the National Hotel, as usual, and strolled up and down the avenue several times. During one of these strolls he stopped at the Kirkwood House, and sent to Vice-President JOHNSON a card, upon which was written:

"I do not wish to disturb you. Are you in?

J. WILKES BOOTH."

A gentleman of BOOTH's acquaintance at this time met him in front of the Kirkwood House, and in the conversation which followed, made some allusion to BOOTH's business, and, in a jesting way, asked: "What makes you so gloomy? Have you lost another thousand in oil?" BOOTH replied he had been hard at work that day, and was about to leave Washington never to return. Just then a boy came out and said

to BOOTH: "Yes, he is in his room." Upon which the gentleman walked on, supposing BOOTH would enter the hotel. About 7 o'clock Friday evening he came down from his room at the National and was spoken to by several concerning his paleness, which, he said, proceeded from indisposition. Just before leaving, he asked the clerk if he was not going to Ford's Theatre, and added: "There will be some very fine acting there to-night." The doorkeeper at the theatre noticed BOOTH as he passed in, and shortly after the latter entered the restaurant and in a hurried manner, called for "Brandy, brandy, brandy," rapping at the same time on the bar.

The *Star* also contained the following article, headed, "A Clue to the Assailant of Mr. SEWARD:"

About three weeks ago, a man named ATZERODT, represented as being a merchant at Brigantown, Charles Co., Md., went to the stables of THOMPSON NAYLOR, corner of Thirteen and a half and E streets, for the purpose of selling a stallion, and a brown horse blind in one eye. ATZERODT made several attempts to sell the horses to the government, but without success, and finally disposed of the stallion to Mr. THOMPSON NAYLOR, stage contractor to Port Tobacco. He continued to visit Mr. NAYLOR's stables, however, and in a short time reported that he had also sold his brown horse.

On Friday afternoon a man named HEROLD, who appeared to be intimate with ATZERODT, came to the stable and hired a roan pacing horse, and shortly afterward ATZERODT appeared with a bay horse, which he left, telling the hostler to have it ready for him at 10 o'clock. Upon calling for the horse at the appointed time, the hostler asked what had become of his friend HEROLD and the roan, to which ATZERODT replied: "Has he not returned yet? He'll be here directly." Some time after the hostler heard the pace of the roan coming down from the direction of the Treasury, and went out to meet him, but the rider, apparently to avoid the hostler, turned up Fourteenth and then down F-street. The latter went back to the stable, and fearing HEROLD intended to make off with the horse, saddled another, and followed him to the Navy Yard Bridge, where, in answer to his inquiries, the guard stated that a man riding such a horse had passed over, and was probably about a quarter of a mile in advance. He was told that he might go over, but could not return before morning. He then came back to the stable, and, hearing that a horse had been picked up in the street by the detectives, made inquiries, and, after giving his statement to the Provost-Marshal, was shown a saddle, which he identified beyond doubt as the one used on the brown horse when at NAYLOR's stable, which ATZERODT said he had sold.

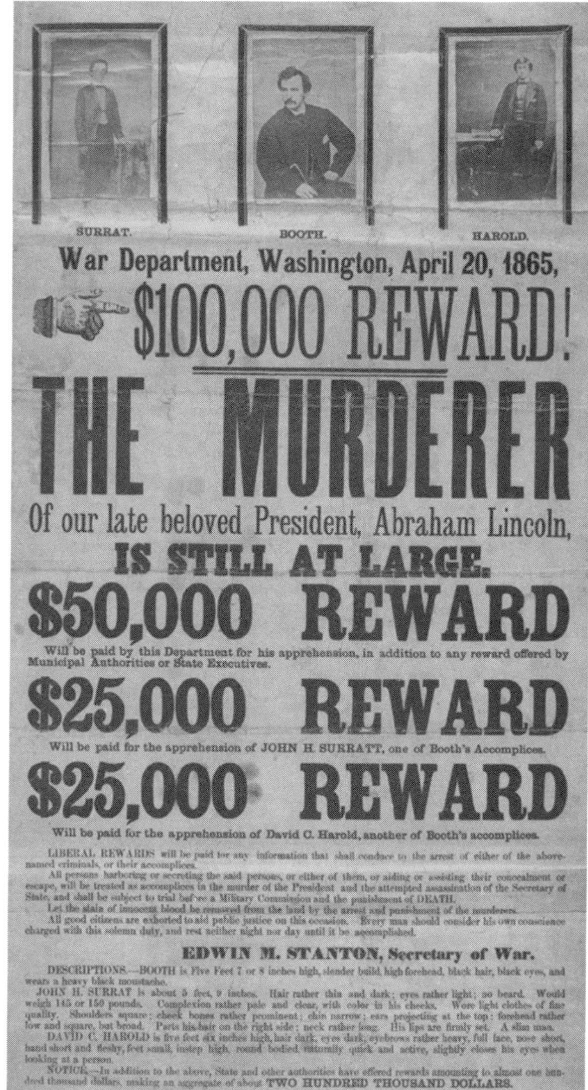

A week after the assassination, the War Department issued a wanted poster offering large rewards for the capture of assassin John Wilkes Booth and conspirators John Surratt and David Herold. (The names of Surratt and Herold were misspelled on the poster.) Six days later, on April 27, 1865, Booth was killed and Herold surrendered, but Surratt was able to escape and flee the country. *(Library of Congress)*

This forenoon several prisoners from Prince George's County were brought to Washington. As they were being taken to the Old Capitol from Provost-Marshal INGRAHAM'S office a large crowd followed, increasing in numbers at every corner, although, as a precautionary measure, the route taken was down the back streets. The crowd was a motly one, of all ages and colors. It being represented, and the report that the parties were BOOTH and SURRATT gaining credit, as they reached the Baltimore depot, the cry was raised, "Hang them," "Kill them," and at the same time the prisoners were attacked with stones, who were struck several times, as were also the guard. Some orderly persons attempted to quiet the crowd by remonstrating with them and assuring them that they were mistaken, but they failed to stop the riotous proceedings, which, however, were soon quieted. After the guard were struck a number of times, they faced about and made ready to defend themselves with their muskets. The prisoners were delivered to the superintendents of the prison, each of them having been somewhat bruised by the flying missiles.

Among other arrests to-day were, it is said, several men in female apparel.

April 21, 1865.

THE MURDERER OF MR. LINCOLN.

Extraordinary Letter of John Wilkes Booth—Proof that He Meditated His Crime Months Ago—His Excuses for the Contemplated Act—His Participation in the Execution of John Brown.

From the Philadelphia Inquirer.

The following verbatim copy of a letter, in writing which is the hand-writing of JOHN WILKES BOOTH, the murderer of President LINCOLN, has been furnished us by the Hon. WM. MILLWARD, United States Marshal of the Eastern District of Pennsylvania. It was handed over to that officer by JOHN S. CLARKES, who is a brother-in-law of Mr. BOOTH . . .

"TO WHOM IT MAY CONCERN":

Right or wrong, God judge me, not man. For be my motive good or bad, of one thing I am sure, the lasting condemnation of the North.

I love peace more than life. Have loved the Union beyond expression. For four years have I waited, hoped and prayed for the dark clouds to break, and for a restoration of our former sunshine. To wait longer would be a crime. All hope for peace is dead. My prayers have proved as idle as my hopes. God's will be done. I go to see and share the bitter end.

I have ever held the South were right. The very nomination of ABRAHAM LINCOLN, four years ago, spoke plainly, war—war upon Southern rights and institutions. His election proved it. "Await an overt act." Yes, till you are bound and plundered. What folly! The South was wise. Who thinks of argument or patience when the finger of his enemy presses on the trigger? In a *foreign war* I, too, could say, "country, right or wrong." But in a struggle *such as ours,* (where the brother tries to pierce his brother's heart,) for God's sake, choose the right. When a country like this spurns justice from her side she forfeits the allegiance of every honest freeman, and should leave him, untrammeled by any fealty soever, to act as his conscience may approve.

People of the North, to hate tyranny, to love liberty and justice, to strike at wrong and oppression, was the teaching of our fathers. The study of our early history will not let *me* forget it, and may it never.

This country was formed for the *white,* not for the black man. And looking upon *African Slavery* from the same stand-point held by the noble framers of our constitution, I for one, have ever considered it one of the greatest blessings (both for themselves and us,) that God has ever bestowed upon a favored nation. Witness heretofore our wealth and power; witness their elevation and enlightenment above their race elsewhere. I have lived among it most of my life, and have seen *less* harsh treatment from master to man than I have beheld in the North from father to son. Yet, Heaven knows, *no one* would be willing to do *more* for the negro race than I, could I but see a way to *still better* their condition.

But LINCOLN's policy is only preparing the way for their total annihilation. The South are *not, nor have they been fighting* for the continuance of slavery. The first battle of Bull Run did away with that idea. Their causes *since* for *war* have been as *noble and greater far than those that urged our fathers on. Even* should we allow they were wrong at the beginning of this contest, *cruelty and injustice* have made the wrong become the *right,* and they stand *now* (before the wonder and admiration of the world) as a noble band of patriotic heroes. Hereafter, reading of *their deeds,* Thermopylæ will be forgotten.

When I aided in the capture and execution of JOHN BROWN (who was a murderer on our Western border, and who was fairly *tried and convicted,* before an impartial judge and jury, of treason, and who, by the way, has since been made a god), I was proud of my little share in the transaction, for I deemed it my duty, and that I was helping our common country to perform an act of justice. But what was a crime in poor JOHN BROWN is now considered (by themselves) as the greatest and only virtue of the whole Republican party. Strange transmigration! *Vice* to become a *virtue,* simply because *more* indulge in it.

I thought then, as *now,* that the Abolitionists *were the only traitors* in the land, and that the entire party deserved the same fate of poor old Brown, not because they wish to abolish slavery but on account of the means they have ever endeavored to use to effect that abolition. If Brown were living I doubt whether he *himself* would set slavery against the Union. Most or many in the North do, and openly curse the Union, if the South are to return and retain a *single right* guaranteed to them by every tie which we once *revered as sacred.* The South can make no choice. It is either extermination or slavery for *themselves* (worse than death) to draw from. I know my choice.

I have also studied hard to discover upon what grounds the right of a State to secede has been denied, when our very name, United States, and the Declaration of Independence, *both* provide for secession. But there is no time for words. I write in haste. I know how foolish I shall be deemed for undertaking such a step as this, where, on the one side, I have many friends, and everything to make me happy, where my profession *alone* has gained me an income of *more than* twenty thousand dollars a year, and where my great personal ambition in my profession has such a great field for labor. On the other hand, the South have never bestowed upon me one kind word; a place now where I have no friends, except beneath the sod; a place where I must either become a private soldier or a beggar. To give up all of the *former* for the *latter,* besides my mother and sisters whom I love so dearly, (although they so widely differ with me in opinion,) seems insane; but God is my judge. I love *justice* more than I do a country that disowns it; more than fame and wealth; more (Heaven pardon me if wrong,) more than a happy home. I have never been upon a battle-field;

but O, my countrymen, could you all but see the *reality* or effects of this horrid war, as I have seen them, (in *every State* save Virginia,) I know you would think like me, and would pray the Almighty to create in the Northern mind a sense of *right* and *justice,* (even should it possess no seasoning of mercy,) and that he would dry up this sea of blood between us, which is daily growing wider. Alas! poor country, is she to meet her threatened doom? Four years ago I would have given a thousand lives to see her remain (as I had always known her) powerful and unbroken. And even now, I would hold my life as naught to see her what she was. O, my friends, if the fearful scenes of the past four years had never been enacted, or if what has been had been but a frightful dream, from which we could now awake, with what overflowing hearts could we bless our God and pray for his continued favor. How I have loved the *old flag,* can never now be known. A few years since and the entire world could boast of *none* so pure and spotless. But I have of late been seeing and hearing of the *bloody deeds* of which she has *been made the emblem,* and would shudder to think how changed she had grown. O, how I have longed to see her break from the mist of blood and death that circles round her folds, spoiling her beauty and tarnishing her honor. But no, day by day has she been dragged deeper and deeper into cruelty and oppression, till now (in my eyes) her once bright red stripes look like bloody gashes on the face of Heaven. I look now upon my early admiration of her glories as a dream. My love (as things stand to-day) is for the South alone. Nor do I deem it a dishonor in attempting to make for her a prisoner of this man, to whom she owes so much of misery. If success attends me, I go penniless to her side. They say she has found that "last ditch" which the North have so long derided, and been endeavoring to force her in, forgetting they are our brothers, and that it's impolite to goad an enemy to madness. Should I reach her in safety and find it true, I will proudly beg permission to triumph or die in that same "ditch" by her side.

A Confederate doing duty upon his own responsibility.

J. Wilkes Booth.

April 26, 1865.

THE OBSEQUIES.

Sombre Grandeur of the Funeral Pageant.

Imposing Demonstrations of the People's Respect.

Tremendous Crush and Pressure in the Streets.

Suburban, Metropolitan and Miscellaneous Crowds.

Sixty Thousand Citizens in the Funeral Procession.

The Closing Scenes About the Coffin and in the Streets.

Mr. Bancroft's Oration at the Union Square.

DEPARTURE OF THE FUNERAL TRAIN.

The coffin in which was deposited the dead body of our deceased President was kept open from 12 o'clock Monday noon, until 12 o'clock Tuesday noon. From the earliest moment to the latest, every facility compatible with the narrow arrangements of the committees, was afforded the public for viewing the remains. The Guard of Honor, divided into twelve watches, did duty until the lid was fastened on the casket, relieving each other every two hours.

THE EIGHTH WATCH

took charge at 2 o'clock Tuesday morning, down to which time the TIMES account of yesterday was complete. . . .

These gentlemen stood patiently and quietly until 4 o'clock in the morning. Doubtless they had anticipated a season of reflection rather than action; they knew that at such hours honest men were asleep and that rogues were watched by the police. For once they were mistaken. The crowds that filed through the Hall exceeded those which but two hours before preceded them. A glance from the balcony toward Chatham-street revealed not only a broad line of pilgrims wending slowly their way to the bier of the martyr, but far beyond stood the dense masses of immovable people, with but one apparent thought, one determination; turning to the west end of the Park a still greater force of men and women, and not a few children, who, provided

The funeral train that would carry the slain president's body from Washington to Springfield, Illinois, waited to begin its sad journey. Heavily draped in black crepe, the engine and its nine cars departed Washington on April 21, 1865, and stopped in nine cities—the president lying in state in each one—before reaching the final destination of Springfield.

by the courtesy of the members of the committee, had passed the sentinels and now stood silent and glum in vain expectancy of success. But these vast hosts were only the exponents of the civic multitudes which were massed solid in the streets. One could go neither up nor down the street; crossing was perilous, as it involved an encounter with scores of hundreds of irate citizens, some of whom would like no better sport by which to relieve the tedium of the hour than a tossing and whipping of any such offender, and a passage from point to point by persons who had no desire even to visit the Hall was a simple impossibility. Of course these people did not get into the Hall; many of them stood there for hours in the hot sun, exposed to the wind and dust; some came early in the evening and braved the long weariness of time between 8 and 2, and then from excess of faintness gave up their places and trudged, provoked and out of temper, homeward. Others however, held on, and many of them were so fortunate as to get foothold upon the City Hall basement steps, but their difficulties were but then commenced. From the bottom step to the top, thence along the corridor to the second flight, and thence again to the Governor's room, stood in every place a man, or what was worse, a woman. Little by little, the fagged-out man, and the toil-worn women, and the pallid, sleepy children, moved toward the desired point; a step at a time, and a very little step at that, was all they could even think of, and this was taken with fear and trembling, for on each side, in front and behind, stepped likewise a neighbor—an unpleasant eager neighbor, one of the anxious, imperative sort, who push and haul, elbow and knuckle violently at every opportunity, but with no good result to himself. If graciously permitted to enter the Governor's Room, how short was the stay, how unsatisfactory the look on the dead man's face, how instantly the police moved them on—on and out of the door at the other end of the room, around the rotunda and back again in the dense crowd, with long flights of stairs before them, up which came the eager ones, as the disappointed and weary went down. To the public, the exhibition of the discolored face of the President was not desirable. Sympathy and love for the deceased led many doubtless to the side of the coffin, but if we may judge from the effect produced upon them by the sight, by their subsequent action, curiosity had a still greater power over them, and took them through troubles and over difficulties, which, under ordinary circumstances, would have been deemed insurmountable. The features were so very unnatural, the color so thoroughly turned, and the general appearance so unpleasant, that none could regard the remains with even a melancholy pleasure. . . .

After shooting Lincoln, Booth jumped to the stage and shouted "sic semper tyrannis" ("Thus always to tyrants"), the state motto of Virginia. Either then or in a fall of his horse as he escaped from Washington he broke his leg, which was set by Dr. Samuel Mudd in southern Maryland as Booth headed for Virginia along the same route he had planned to take the kidnapped Lincoln. Union cavalry finally caught up with Booth at a farm in Virginia and shot him dead when he refused to surrender. The rest of his accomplices (with the exception of John Surratt, who may have been assigned to assassinate Grant, and who escaped to Europe) were rounded up and tried by a military tribunal. Three received a life sentence (President Johnson pardoned them in 1869) and four were hanged on July 7, including Mary Surratt, John's mother, at whose boarding house the conspirators had held their meetings.

April 28, 1865.

BOOTH KILLED.

Full Account of the Pursuit and its Result.

He is Traced into St. Mary's County, Maryland.

Herold and Booth Discovered in a Barn.

Booth Declares He Will not be Taken Alive.

The Barn Set on Fire to Force Them Out.

SERGT. BOSTON CORBETT FIRES AT BOOTH

He is Shot Through the Neck and Dies in Three Hours.

His Body and Herold Brought to Washington.

[OFFICIAL]

War Department,
Washington, April 27, 1865—9:20 A.M.

Maj.-Gen. John A. Dix, New-York:

J. Wilkes Booth and Herold were chased from the swamp in St. Mary's County, Maryland, to Garrett's farm, near Port Royal, on the Rappahannock, by Col. Baker's force.

The barn in which they took refuge was fired.

Booth, in making his escape, was shot through the head and killed, lingering about three hours, and Herold was captured. Booth's body and Herold are now here.

EDWIN M. STANTON,
Secretary of War.

DETAILS OF THE CAPTURE OF BOOTH.

Special Dispatch to the New-York Times.

Washington, Thursday, April 27.

About 8 o'clock last evening we received the intelligence of the capture of J. Wilkes Booth, the assassin of Abraham Lincoln, and one of his accomplices in the murder, David E. Herold. The following are such of the particulars as we were enabled to gather, which, with the exception of the precise locality where the occurrence took place, we give as being reliable and correct. It having been pretty clearly ascertained that Booth and his accomplice had crossed the Potomac River at or near Aquia Creek, our cavalry scouts in that vicinity have been in consequence unusually active in their endeavors to get on their trail. Early yesterday morning a squad of about twelve men, belonging to the Sixteenth New-York Cavalry, under command of a Lieutenant, whose name we did not learn, succeeded in discovering the fugitives in a barn on the road leading from Port Royal to Bowling Green in Caroline County, Va. As soon as they were discovered, the place was surrounded and the assassins ordered to surrender. This they both refused to do, Booth declaring that he would not be taken alive, and offering to fight the whole squad if he would be permitted to place himself twenty yards distant from them. His proposition was not, however, acceded to, and as they persisted in their refusal to surrender, the Lieutenant determined to burn them out, and accordingly set fire to the barn, shortly after which Herold came out and gave himself up. Booth remained in the burning building for some time, and until driven out by the fire, when he rushed out and was immediately shot through the neck by the sergeant of the squad.

Since the above we have had an interview with two of the cavalrymen engaged in the capture of the assassins. From them we learn that the whole party consisted of twenty-eight, including two detectives. The first information respecting BOOTH's crossing the river, and his probable whereabouts, was obtained from disbanded rebel soldiers who were met with in all directions in that part of the country. From one and another of these the clue to BOOTH's movements was gathered and held until just at daybreak they came upon the barn, where he and HEROLD were secreted. A parley was held, and BOOTH manifested the most desperate determination not to be taken alive, and to take as many of the lives of the party as possible. Lieut. EDWARD P. DOHERTY, who commanded the scouting party, determined to make short work of him. When HEROLD saw the preparations for firing the barn, he declared his willingness to surrender, and said he would not fight if they would let him out. BOOTH, on the contrary, was impudently defiant, offering at first to fight the whole squad at one hundred yards, and subsequently at fifty yards. He was hobbling on crutches, apparently very lame. He swore he would die like a man, etc. HEROLD having been secured, as soon as the burning hay lighted the interior of the barn sufficiently to rend the scowling face of BOOTH, the assassin, visible, Sergeant BOSTON CORBETT fired upon him and he fell. The ball passed through his neck. He was pulled out of the barn, and one of his crutches, and carbine and revolvers secured; the wretch lived about two hours, whispering blasphemes against the government, and messages to his mother, desiring her to be informed that he died for his country. At the time BOOTH was shot he was leaning upon one crutch and preparing to shoot his captors. Only one shot was fired in the entire affair—that which killed the assassin.

Lieut. DOHERTY is one of the bravest fellows in the cavalry service, having distinguished himself in a sharp affair at Culpepper Court-house and on other occasions. The Sixteenth New-York Cavalry is commanded by Col. NELSON SWEITZER, and has been doing duty in Fairfax County. This regiment formed part of the cavalry escort on the day of the President's obsequies in Washington. The body of BOOTH and the assassin's accomplice, HEROLD, were placed on board the *John S. Ide* and sent to Washington, arriving here about 1 o'clock this morning.

ACCURATE ACCOUNT OF THE PURSUIT AND CAPTURE OF BOOTH.

Special Dispatch to the New-York Times.

WASHINGTON, THURSDAY, APRIL 27.

Without recurring to the circumstances that brought together and put to work a large body of detectives in pursuit of the assassin BOOTH AND HIS ACCESSORIES IN CRIME, I PROPOSE TO STATE BRIEFLY AND CONSECUTIVELY THE INCIDENTS IN THE PURSUIT

FROM THE TIME THE DETACHMENT STARTED FROM THIS CITY UNTIL THEIR ARRIVAL HERE THIS MORNING WITH THE CORPSE OF Booth and the body of HEROLD. The following facts I obtained from Col. BAKER and the other persons engaged with him.

From the time the Secretary of War telegraphed Col. L. C. BAKER at New-York, twelve days ago, to come here immediately and take charge of the matter of ferreting out the facts, and arresting the criminals in the assassination, up to last Sunday, but little progress was made in the right direction. All the lower counties of Maryland were scoured by a large force consisting of 1,600 cavalry and 500 detectives and citizens. On Sunday last Col. BAKER learned of a little boy in Maryland some facts which satisfied him that BOOTH and HEROLD had crossed the river about 11 o'clock A.M. and had gone into Virginia. A telegraph operator with a small body of soldiers was sent down the river to tap the wires at a given place and make certain inquiries. This party returned on Monday morning last, bringing with them a negro man whom they picked up at Swan Point, who, on being closely interrogated, disclosed that he had seen parties cross in a boat, and the description of these parties assured Col. BAKER that BOOTH and HEROLD were the men. No examination or search had yet been made by official authority in Virginia. Demand was made upon Gen. HANCOCK for a detachment of cavalry, and twenty-eight of the Sixteenth New-York were immediately sent to Col. BAKER, under command of Lieut. DOHERTY, one of this detachment being BOSTON CORBETT. The whole party were put in charge of Lieut. L. B. BAKER and Lieut.-Col. E. J. CONGOR. They were instructed to go immediately to Port Royal; that BOOTH had crossed the river, and had had time to reach that point; that he could not ride on horseback, and must therefore have traveled slowly.

At twenty-five minutes past four o'clock on Monday afternoon, this force left the Sixth-street wharf in the steamer *John S. Ide*. They were directed that when they arrived at the land place—Belle Plain—they should shove or swim their horses to shore, if they could not make a landing, for they must have the horses on land. That night the party went down the river four miles, but heard nothing satisfactory. They finally, at daylight, brought up below Port Royal some miles. They returned, finding no trace of the criminals till they got to Port Royal Ferry. Lieut. BAKER rode up, found the ferryman, and made inquiries. The ferryman stoutly denied having seen any such persons as those described. Lieut. BAKER throttled him and threatened him, yet he denied any knowledge of the persons sought. By the side of the ferryman a negro was sitting. Lieut. BAKER presented a likeness of BOOTH and HEROLD. The negro upon looking at these exclaimed, "Why, Massa, them's the gentlemen we brought cross the river yesterday." The ferryman then admitted that he had brought BOOTH and HEROLD over the river in his boat. The cavalry was started off and went fourteen miles beyond GARRETT's place. There they met a negro who said he saw two men sitting on GARRETT's porch that afternoon. The description of one accorded with that of BOOTH. Lieut. BAKER and his party returned to GARRETT's house. GARRETT denied that the two men had been there. BAKER threatened to shoot him if he did not tell the truth. Garrett's son thereupon came out of the house and said the two men were in the barn. The barn was at once surrounded. This was about 2 A.M. Baker went up and rapped at the door. Booth asked "Who are you, friends or foes? Are you Confederates? I have got five men in here, and we can protect ourselves." Col. Baker replied, "I have fifty men out here; you are surrounded, and you may as well come out and surrender." Booth answered, "I shall never give up; I'll not be taken alive." The instructions were that every means possible must be taken to arrest Booth alive, and Baker, Conger and Doherty held a consultation a few feet from the barn. In the meantime Booth was cursing Herold for his cowardice, charging him with a desire to meanly surrender, etc.

Col. Baker and his party returned and held a parley with Booth, thus consuming about an hour and a quarter. Another consultation of officers was held, and it was determined that, in view of the probability of an attack from a tolerably large force of rebel cavalry, which they had learned were in the neighborhood, the barn should be fired, and Booth thus forced to come out.

Conger gathered a lot of brush, and placed it against and under the barn, and pulled some hay out of the cracks, in the mean time holding a lighted candle in his hand. Booth could now see through the openings of the barn all their movements. The lighted candle was applied to the hay and brush, and directly the flames caught the hay inside the barn. Booth rushed forward towards the burning hay and tried to put out the fire. Failing in this, he ran back to the middle of the floor, gathered up his arms and stood still pondering for a moment. While Booth was standing in this position Sergt. Boston Corbett ran up to the barn door and fired. Col. Baker, not perceiving where the shot came from, exclaimed "he has shot himself," and rushed into the barn and found Booth yet standing with a carbine in hand. Baker clasped Booth around the arms and breast; the balance of the party had also, in the mean time, got inside. Corbett then exclaimed "I shot him." Booth fell upon the floor apparently paralyzed. Water was sent for and the wound bathed. It was now just 3:15 o'clock. The ball had apparently passed through the neck and the spine. In a few moments Booth revived. He made an effort to lift his hands up before his eyes. In this he was assisted, and upon seeing them he exclaimed somewhat incoherently. "Useless!—useless!—useless!—blood!—blood!! and swooned away. He revived from time to time, and expressed himself entirely satisfied with what he had done. He expired at 7:10 yesterday morning.

The body was placed in a cart and conveyed to the steamer *John S. Ide*, and brought upon that vessel to the navy-yard, where the boat arrived at 5:20 o'clock this morning.

While the barn was burning, Herold rushed out and was grappled by Lieut. Baker, thrown to the ground and secured.

Corbett says he fired with the intention of wounding Booth in the shoulder, and did not intend to kill him.

BOOTH had in his possession a diary, in which he had noted events of each day since the assassination of Mr. LINCOLN. This diary is in possession of the War Department. He had also a Spencer carbine, a seven-shooter, a revolver, a pocket pistol and a knife. The latter is supposed to be the one with which he stabbed Major RATHBURN. His clothing was of dark blue, not Confederate gray, as has been stated.

CORBETT, who shot BOOTH, was born in England, and is about 33 years old. He came to this country some years since, and resided for several years in Troy, N. Y. He resided for a time in Boston, where he became a member of a Methodist Church, and took in baptism the name of "Boston." He is a man of small stature, slight form, mild countenance and quiet deportment.

Surgeon-Gen. BARNES says the ball did not enter the brain. The body, when he examined it this afternoon, was not in a rapid state of decomposition, but was considerably bruised by jolting about in the cart. It is placed in charge of Col. BAKER, in the attire in which he died, with instructions not to allow any one to approach it, nor to take from it any part of apparel, or thing for exhibition hereafter; in brief, it is necessary for the satisfaction of the people that two points shall be positively ascertained: first, that the person killed in GARRETT'S barn, and whose body was brought to this city, was J. WILKES BOOTH; secondly, that the said J. WILKES BOOTH was positively killed. The first point was to-day confirmed by overwhelming testimony, such as no jury would hesitate to accept. The substantial one of the second point is shown in the report of Surgeon-General BARNES, which will be officially announced.

BOOTH'S leg was not broken by falling from his horse, but the bone was injured by the fall upon the stage at the theatre.

Besides the articles heretofore mentioned, BOOTH had on his person a draft for sixty pounds drawn by the Ontario Bank of Canada on a London banker. The draft was dated in October last.

May 30, 1865.

THE TRIAL OF THE ASSASSINS.

Full Report of the Proceedings on Monday.

Progress of Testimony for the Defense.

Examination of Hyams, the Yellow-Fever Distributor.

The Story of His Employment by Dr. Blackburn.

Full Knowledge of the Infernal Plot by the Rebel Leaders in Canada.

Special Dispatch to the New-York Times.

WASHINGTON, MONDAY, MAY 29.

Most of to-day's session of the commission for the trial of the assassins was taken up by testimony for the defendant, Dr. MUDD. An effort was made to break down the evidence of THOMAS, a government witness, who testified, some days ago, that Dr. MUDD had told him the President and members of the Cabinet were to be killed. The defence also offered evidence to prove that Dr. MUDD was not with BOOTH at the several places in Washington, on given days of March and April last, as testified by WEICHMAN and others.

Probably the most fiendish acts in the whole catalogue of diabolical crimes proved against the rebels were disclosed this afternoon, in the testimony of the witness HYAMS, who gave an account of his employment by Dr. BLACKBURN, in Toronto, to convey to this city several packages of clothing, infected with yellow fever and smallpox, to be sold here indiscriminately. The work was faithfully performed by the witness HYAMS, so far as he engaged to execute the devilish job. No credit could be attached to the evidence of this wretch, were there not some other circumstances and credible witnesses to corroborate enough of his testimony to make it probable that the whole of it is true. He rattled off his story without hesitancy, and there was that in his manner which impressed the hearer that he was telling the truth, notwithstanding in it be discovered himself to be one of the most heartless, cold-blooded, wholesale would-be assassins of them all. HYAMS is a genteelly dressed man, of small stature, of dark complexion, and Israelitish features, and is said to be of the Jewish persuasion. During his recital of the transaction the audience gave, in suppressed murmurs and exclamations, unmistakable demonstrations of what their verdict would be were the witness himself on trial before them. That verdict seemed to be unanimous, "Hang the wretch."

The audience was principally composed of ladies, and the room again packed to its utmost capacity. There were about a dozen Congressmen present, among them, Hon. BENJAMIN EGGLESTON, member elect from First District of Ohio, the successor of Mr. PENDLETON.

SYNOPSIS OF TESTIMONY TAKEN ON MONDAY.

WASHINGTON, MONDAY, MAY 29.

Today, the counsel for Mrs. SURRATT asked to have HENRY VON STEINECKER recalled; they wished to show that VON STEINECKER had been attached to BLESKER's staff, but, subsequently, while under sentence of death, for desertion, he escaped to the rebel service, and was employed as a draughtsman to Gen. J. E. B. STUART. They wanted to show there was no such secret meeting as VON STEINECKER had described in the camp of the Second Virginia Regiment, at which BOOTH was alleged to be present, and the assassination of President LINCOLN discussed.

Gen. WALLACE, a member of the court, said the application just made, which was
370 in writing, contained a bitter aspersion on the witness in his absence and was inflammatory in its character. It was discreditable to the parties concerned and too offensive to the court to be placed on record.

Mr. CAMPBELL disclaimed any intention on the part of counsel to reflect upon the court. The only object was to impeach the testimony of a witness.

The court voted not to put the paper on record, but was perfectly willing, as was expressed the other day, that the counsel for the accused should call witnesses to impeach VON STEINECKER's testimony.

Mr. AIKEN said they had Gen. EDWARD JOHNSON, late of the rebel service, and members of his staff, to prove that no such secret meeting as VON STEINECKER represented took place in the Second Virginia Regiment, at which BOOTH was said to be present, having for its object the assassination of President LINCOLN.

Witnesses were examined by the defence to impeach those who had testified against Dr. MUDD.

The prosecution called Mr. HYAMS, who testified meeting Dr. BLACKBURN at Toronto in December, 1862, and knew that he was in the service of the rebellion. That BLACKBURN took witness to a private room, and asked him if he was willing to go on an expedition. He told him he would make a $100,000 and receive more glory than LEE. Witness consented and received a letter from BLACKBURN, dated May 10, at Havana, stating that he would arrive at Halifax, and witness made his way there and perfected arrangements for the distribution of infected clothing, and bringing the trunks to New York, Philadelphia, etc. BLACKBURN stated that his object was to destroy the Federal army; that the clothing had been infected with yellow fever, and that other parties were engaged with him in infecting goods amounting to $1,000,000 worth, with that disease and the small-pox.

Witness understood that the clothing in a valise, which was sent to President LINCOLN, was infected with both diseases.

When witness returned to Hamilton he met CLAY and HOLCOMBE, who congratulated him on his success, and he telegraphed to Dr. BLACKBURN, who came down the next night; and when witness had told him what he had done, he said it was all right, as "Big No. 2" had gone to Washington, and he was sure it would kill at sixty yards.

BLACKBURN said THOMPSON would pay him, and he went to THOMPSON, who stated that he would be paid when they heard the goods had been delivered according to instructions.

Witness showed them a letter from Wall & Co., when THOMPSON gave witness fifty dollars on account.

July 7, 1865.

THE CONSPIRATORS.

FINDING OF THE COURT.

Herold, Payne, Atzerodt and Mrs. Surratt to be Hung.

The Execution to Take Place This Morning.

Dr. Mudd, Arnold and O'Laughlin to be Imprisoned for Life.

Spangler to be Confined in the Penitentiary at Albany for Six Years.

Delivery of the Death Warrants to the Condemned.

A Resume of the Testimony in Each Case.

Washington, Thursday, July 6.

In accordance with the finding and sentences of the Military Commission, which President Johnson approved yesterday, David E. Herold Lewis Payne, Mrs. Mary E. Surratt and George A. Atzerodt, are to be hung to-morrow, by the proper military authorities.

Dr. Mudd Samuel Arnold and O'Laughlin, are to be imprisoned for life.

Spangler is sentenced to six years' imprisonment at hard labor in the penitentiary at Albany.

THE EXECUTIVE ORDER.

Washington, Thursday, July 6.

The following important order has just been issued:

War Department, Adjutant-General's Office,
Washington, July 5, 1865.

To Maj.-Gen. W. S Hancock, United States Volunteers, Commanding Middle Military Division, Washington, D. C.:

Whereas, by the Military Commission appointed in paragraph four, Special Orders No. 211, dated, War Department, Adjutant-General's Office, May 6, 1865, and of which Maj.-Gen. DAVID HUNTER, United States Volunteers, is President, the following persons were tried and sentenced as hereinafter stated, as follows:

First—DAVID E. HEROLD.

Finding—Of the specification "Guilty," except combining, confederating and conspiring with EDWARD SPANGLER, as to which part thereof, "Not guilty." Of the charge "Guilty," except the words of the charge that "he combined, confederated and conspired with EDWARD SPANGLER," as to which part of the charge, "Not guilty."

Sentence—And the commission therefore sentence him, the said DAVID E. HEROLD, to be hanged by the neck until he be dead, at such time and place as the President of the United States shall direct, two-thirds of the members of the commission concurring therein.

Second—GEORGE A. ATZERODT.

Finding—Of the specification "guilty," except combining, confederating and conspiring with EDWARD SPANGLER. Of this "not guilty."

Sentence—And the commission does therefore sentence him, the said GEORGE A. ATZERODT, to be hung by the neck until he be dead, at such time and place as the President of the United States shall direct, two-thirds of the members of the commission concurring therein.

Third—LEWIS PAYNE.

Finding—Of the specification "guilty," except combining, confederating and conspiring with EDWARD SPANGLER—of this not guilty. Of the charge "guilty," except combining, confederating and conspiring with EDWARD SPANGLER—of this not guilty.

Sentence—And the Commission does therefore sentence him, the said LEWIS PAYNE, to be hung until he be dead, at such time and place as the President of the United States shall direct, two-thirds of the members of the commission concurring therein.

Fourth—MARY E. SURRATT.

Finding—Of the specification "guilty," except as to the receiving, entertaining, harboring and counseling SAMUEL ARNOLD and MICHAEL O'LAUGHLIN, and except as to combining, confederating and conspiring with EDWARD SPANGLER. Of this not guilty. Of the charge "guilty," except as to combining, confederating and conspiring with EDWARD SPANGLER. Of this not guilty.

Sentence—And the commission does, therefore, sentence her, the said MARY E. SURRATT, to be hung by the neck until she be dead, at such time and place as the President of the United States shall direct, two-thirds of the members of the commission concurring therein.

And whereas the President of the United States has approved the foregoing sentences in the following order, to wit:

Executive Mansion, July 5, 1865.

The foregoing sentences in the cases of David E. Herold, George A. Atzerodt, Lewis Payne and Mary E. Surratt are hereby approved, and it is ordered that the sentences in the cases of David E. Herold, Geo. A. Atzerodt, Lewis Payne and Mary E. Surratt, be carried into execution by the proper military authority, under the direction of the Secretary of War, on the 7th day of July, 1865, between the hours of 10 o'clock A.M., and two o'clock, P.M., of that day.

Andrew Johnson, President.

Therefore, you are hereby commanded to cause the foregoing sentences in the cases of David E. Herold, G. A. Atzerodt, Lewis Payne and Mary E. Surratt to be duly executed in accordance with the President's order.

By command of the President of the United States.

E. D. TOWNSEND,
Assistant Adjutant-General.

374 In the remaining cases of O'Laughlin, Spangler, Arnold and Mudd, the finding sentences are as follows:

Fifth—Michael O'Laughlin.

Finding—Of the specification "guilty," except the words thereof as follows: "And in the further prosecution of the conspiracy aforesaid, and its murderous and treasonable purposes aforesaid, on the nights of the 13th and 14th of April, A. D., 1865, at Washington City, and within the military department and military lines aforesaid, the said Michael O'Laughlin did then and there lie in wait for Ulysses S. Grant, then Lieutenant-General and Commander of the Armies of the United States, with the intent then and there to kill and murder the said Ulysses S. Grant." Of said words "not guilty; and except "combining, confederating and conspiring with Edward Spangler." Of this "not guilty." Of the charge "guilty," except combining, confederating and conspiring with Edward Spangler. Of this "not guilty."

Sentence—The commission does, therefore, sentence Michael O'Laughlin to be imprisoned at hard labor for life.

Sixth—Edward Spangler.

Finding—Of the specification "not guilty," except as to the words "The said Edward Spangler, on said 14th day of April, A. D., 1865, at about the same hour of that day as aforesaid, within said military department and military lines aforesaid, did aid and abet him," meaning John Wilkes Booth, "in making his escape," after the said Abraham Lincoln had been murdered in the manner aforesaid, and of these words, "guilty." Of the charge, not guilty, but guilty of having feloniously and traitorously aided and abetted John Wilkes Booth in making his escape; after having killed and murdered ABRAHAM LINCOLN, President of the United States, he, the said EDWARD SPANGLER, at the time of aiding and abetting as aforesaid, well knowing that the said ABRAHAM LINCOLN, President as aforesaid, had been murdered by the said JOHN WILKES BOOTH, as aforesaid.

The commission sentenced SPANGLER to be confined at hard labor for six years.

Seventh—SAMUEL ARNOLD.

Finding—Of the specification "guilty," except combining, confederating and conspiring with EDWARD SPANGLER; of this "not guilty." Of the charge "guilty," except combining, confederating and conspiring with EDWARD SPANGLER; of this "not guilty."

Sentence—The commission sentenced him to imprisonment at hard labor for life.

Eighth—SAML. A. MUDD.

Finding—Of the specification "guilty," except combining, confederating and conspiring with EDWARD SPANGLER; of this "Not guilty;" and accepting, receiving, and entertaining and harboring, and concealing said LEWIS PAYNE, JOHN W. SURRATT, MICHAEL O'LAUGHLIN, GEORGE A. AZTERODT, MARY E. SURRATT, and SML. ARNOLD; of this "not guilty." Of the charge "guilty," except combining, confederating and conspiring with EDWARD SPANGLER; of this "not guilty."

Sentence—The commission sentence Dr. MUDD to be imprisoned at hard labor for life.

The President's order in these cases, is as follows:

> It is further ordered that the prisoners SAMUEL ARNOLD, SAMUEL A. MUDD, EDWARD SPANGLER and MICHAEL O'LAUGHLIN, be confined at hard labor in the penitentiary at Albany, New-York, during the period designated in their respective sentences.

ANDREW JOHNSON, PRESIDENT.

VISIT TO THE PRISONERS—PREPARATIONS FOR THE EXECUTION.

Special Dispatch to the New-York Times.

WASHINGTON, THURSDAY, JULY 6.

At 11 o'clock to-night we visited the Arsenal, in which the condemned prisoners are confined. The grounds and buildings are more strictly guarded than heretofore.

A double guard is on duty, the first of the sentinels being out at the gate, about a quarter of a mile north of the prison. About half-way between the gate and the building another body of armed soldiers halted us, and after making the required showing, we passed on to the prison. Here the greatest care is observed as to who pass in or out of the building.

Gen. HANCOCK arrived just as we alighted, and held a short consultation with Gen. HARTRANFT, who has charge of the prisoners, and Rev. Mr. BUTLER, of the Lutheran

Church of this city, passed in at the same moment to the cell of ATZERODT, who was sitting in close conversation with his brother, the latter preparing to take a final leave of the unhappy culprit.

The regular physician of the arsenal had just made his report of the condition of the prisoners. Mrs. SURRATT was, and had been since the sentence was read to her, dangerously prostrated, and the physician had prescribed wine of valerian. ATZERODT was also equally prostrated, and for him brandy was ordered. The other prisoners were about as usual.

The spiritual advisors of Mrs. SURRATT were with her. The other prisoners were alone. PAYNE expresses no hope of life beyond the hour of execution to-morrow. Nor does he talk much to-night. He says JOHN SURRATT is acting cowardly, most villainously, in failing to appear and be with his mother. Being asked if he had any direction to give as to the disposition of his body, he answered that he had no friends within reach or immediate communication, and therefore his body must be subject to such disposal as the officers shall direct. He maintains that his relatives are all in Florida, and that his real name is POWELL. He expresses the deepest regret that Mrs. SURRATT is to be a sufferer by reason of any act of his, and evinces a solicitude for her not unlike that of a tender child for its parent, seemingly thinking only of her fate and the suffering she is about to undergo.

HEROLD is as he has been all through the trial, apparently inappreciative of his fearful position, and is scarcely more serious to-night than he has been at any time since the trial commenced. He has been visited several times to-day by his sisters, who are bowed in the most painful grief. He, too, expects no mercy, and makes no request other than that his body may be delivered to his family.

ATZERODT is, characteristically, weighed down, and in fear and trembling. He is bewildered, stunned, and only appears to consider the bodily pain he is condemned to suffer. For his soul he has manifested no care. He was a coward when the time arrived for him to fulfill his part in the horrible drama on the night of the 14th of April. He is a greater coward now that he is to face death. He is devoid of sensibility other than to bodily harm.

The findings and sentences were read to the condemned separately, to-day, about 12 o'clock, by Gen. HARTRANFT, in the presence of Gen. HANCOCK, to whom the warrant for execution is directed, and of several officers of Gen. HARTRANFT'S staff. At the moment of reading the warrant no outward signs of emotion were visible on the part of the prisoners, save Mrs. SURRATT and AZTERODT, each of whom trembled and grew deathly pale. Mrs. SURRATT faintly uttered a few words, saying: "I had no hand in the murder of the President."

In a few moments after the reading, however, all except PAYNE and HEROLD were deeply moved, though none had much to say, and their emotions being generally discoverable from their demeanor.

Soon after the promulgation of the sentences the friends and relatives of the prisoners began to arrive at the arsenal. Miss SURRATT, the daughter of the wretched woman of that name, was among the first to visit the prison.

The meeting of the criminal mother and sorrow-stricken daughter was most heart-rending. Soon, however, the former rallied, and straightway visited the President, to plead for a commutation of the sentence to an imprisonment for life.

She was joined by two Catholic priests and her mothers attorneys, who urged that the sentence and findings be set aside upon the ground that new and important evidence has been discovered which will exculpate their client.

The President was too ill to give them an audience, and referred them to Judge HOLT. The latter after hearing Miss SURRATT promised to present the subject to the President, but as yet nothing further is known to have transpired in the matter.

The sisters of HEROLD, five in number, called also in a body at the Executive Mansion to ask for a commutation, and they, too, were referred to Judge HOLT. There is no reason to believe that the President will pardon or commute the sentence of any, unless it may be in the case of Mrs. SURRATT.

As to whom it is understood that all the members of the Commission added to the sentence of a recommendation to the President, that in the exercise of his clemency it might be advisable to commute her sentence to imprisonment for life.

A scaffold is prepared and will be erected early in the morning, in the enclosed lot south of the arsenal, upon which the four prisoners condemned to death will be executed.

They will all be hung at the same moment. One o'clock is the hour at which the execution will take place. The lot in which the scaffold is to be erected is about one hundred and fifty by two hundred feet.

Surprise is expressed, almost unanimously, that the execution should be fixed for a day so immediate after the promulgation of the sentence. A week or ten days, it is thought, should have intervened between the announcement of the judgment and the day of execution.

It is believed that Mrs. SURRATT's sentence will be commuted to imprisonment for life. Such appears to be the general desire so far as can be determined this evening.

Dispatch to the Associated Press.

WASHINGTON, WEDNESDAY, JULY 6.

Major-Gen. HANCOCK repaired to the arsenal at noon to-day, and delivered the death-warrants of PAYNE, HEROLD, Mrs. SURRATT and ATZERODT, to Major-Gen. HARTRANFT, who is in charge of the prisoners, when they together visited the condemned to inform them of the sentences pronounced, and the time fixed for their execution. PAYNE was the first to whom the intelligence was communicated. It did not seem to take him by surprise, as doubtless he anticipated no other sentence, and had nerved himself accordingly. The other prisoners were naturally more or less affected. Mrs. SURRATT, particularly, sank under the dread announcement, and pleaded for four days' additional time to prepare herself for death.

All the prisoners will be attended by clergymen of their own designation. The scaffold has been erected in the South yard of the old Penitentiary building which is enclosed by a high brick wall. The coffins and burial clothes have already been prepared. Only a limited number of persons will be admitted to the scene. The sentences of the conspirators who are to be imprisoned will be carried into immediate effect.

RESUME OF THE EVIDENCE, AND PERSONAL DESCRIPTION OF THE PRISONERS.

DAVID E. HEROLD.

The evidence against HEROLD of having assisted BOOTH in the assassination, and aided him to escape, was clear. As early as February last he was found to have been in confidential relations with the assassin, and was proved to have been present on several occasions at secret meetings with BOOTH, ATZERODT and others of the conspirators. Once he was at Mrs. SURRATT's in company with them. He called with SURRATT and ATZERODT at the tavern in Shurattsville, and left the two carbines and ammunition which were taken away from the tavern by him and BOOTH on the night of the assassination. During their flight he acknowledged to WILLIE JETT and other rebel soldiers that he and BOOTH were the assassins of Mr. LINCOLN, and he was captured in the barn with BOOTH. There can be no doubt whatever of his guilt. His personal appearance during the trial was described as that of a boy of nineteen, dressed in a faded blue suit, in height about five feet four inches, dusky black, neglected hair, lively, dark hazel eyes, slight tufts of beard along the chin and jaws and faintly surrounding the mouth, rather round face, full but not prominent nose, full lips, foolish, weak, confiding countenance indicating but little intelligence, and not the faintest trace of ferocity. HEROLD seemed to live but in the smile of BOOTH, following him devotedly in his flight, and sharing his privations, perils and capture.

GEORGE A. ATZERODT

It was shown beyond doubt that ATZERODT was a co-conspirator in the assassination plot. He like HEROLD made his first appearance at Mrs. SURRATT's house in the early part of February, inquiring for JOHN H. SURRATT or Mrs. SURRATT and was thereafter found in secret communication with BOOTH and his confederates. To him was assigned the murder of President JOHNSON at the Kirkwood House but notwithstanding it appears that there was no obstacle in the way of its performance, he does not seem to have made any effort to get access to his intended victim on the evening of the 14th of April. On the afternoon of the 14th he was seeking to obtain a horse, thereafter to secure his own safety by flight, after he should have performed the task which he had voluntarily under taken. He was traced to the Kirkwood House on horseback, about 9 o'clock in the evening, but did not remain there long, and was not seen near the house after that hour. He proved false to his confederates no [unintelligible] for want of pluck to do the murder, but is proud to have been in active cooperation with them throughout the night and to have absconded at day light the next morning, first throwing away the knife with which he was to have assassinated Mr. JOHNSON, and disposing of a pistol, which belonged to HEROLD. During the trial ATZERODT looked rather unconcernedly on, and at no time evinced a high sensibility of his almost inevitable doom. He is a man of small stature, Dutch Face, sallow complexion, dull dark blue eyes, rather light-colored hair, bushy and unkempt.

LEWIS PAYNE

This prisoner is shown to have been the confederate of BOOTH, and to have been intimate with JOHN H. SURRATT. There has never been the slightest intimation on the part of himself or his counsel to deny his guilt. He went to Secretary SEWARD's house with the intent to kill him, representing to the servant, as he hurriedly passed him by, that he had brought medicine from Dr. VERDI, the family physician. Before he left the house, he not only stabbed Secretary SEWARD, but also nearly succeeded in killing Mr. FREDERICK W. SEWARD, and inflicted serious wounds upon Mr. AUGUSTUS H. SEWARD, Mr. FREDERICK W. HANSELL and Mr. GEO. F. ROBINSON, Secretary Seward's nurse. PAYNE is a native of Florida, and served some time in the rebel army, from which he deserted. He made his appearance at Mrs. SURRATT's in the early part of March, when he stated that his name was WOOD, and afterward was a frequent visitor at the house, staying there on one occasion two or three days, and participating with JOHN H. SURRATT, ATZERODT and BOOTH in the secret consultations. He and SURRATT were discovered in the bed-room of the latter, playing with bowie-knives. In this room were also found two revolvers and four sets of spurs, of the same kind as the spurs and revolvers found in ATZERODT's room in the Kirkwood House. After doing his bloody work, PAYNE made his escape from Washington, whither he returned on the evening of the 17th, when he presented himself at Mrs. SURRATT's house, dressed as a laboring man, and carrying a pick-ax on his shoulder, saying that he had been engaged to dig a gutter. He was then arrested. In appearance, PAYNE is described as a wild and savage-looking man, showing no marks of culture or refinement—the most perfect type of the ingrain, hardened criminal. He is fully six feet high; of slender, bony, angular form, square and narrow across the shoulders, hollow breasted, hair black, straight, irregularly cut, and hanging indifferently about his forehead, which is rather low and narrow; blue eyes, large, staring, and at times wild; square face, angular nose, thin at the top, but expanding abruptly at the nostrils, thin lips and a slightly twisted mouth, curved unsymmetrically a little to the left of the middle line of the face.

MARY E. SURRATT.

This woman appears to have been cognizant of the intended crime almost from its inception, even if she were not its instigator. Her house had been a refuge for blockade runners, and she was an active participant in overt acts. Her character appears to have been that of general manager. She received and entertained all the prisoners except Dr. MUDD O'LAUGHLIN and ARNOLD. With Dr. MUDD she planned the means and assistance for the escape of the assassins. She visited Surrattville at 5 o'clock on the day of the assassination to see that the carbines, &c., should be in readiness, and informed LLOYD, the tavern-keeper, that they would be called for that night. BOOTH frequently called at her house and held long and confidential talks with her. He was in her company a few minutes on the afternoon of the 14th. When confronted with PAYNE on the night of his arrest, when he went to her house in disguise, she protested that she had never seen him, and added, "I did not hire him; I don't know him." It was proved that she knew PAYNE well, and that he had lodged at her house. She is described as a large woman of the Amazonian style, aged about fifty years. Her form is square built, her hands masculine, her face full, her eyes dark gray and lifeless, her hair not decidedly dark, and her complexion swarthy. During the trial she bore up strongly against the weight of crushing testimony against her, only once seeming to be at all disturbed.

MICHAEL O'LAUGHLIN.

To this prisoner appears to have been assigned the murder of Gen. GRANT; but whether he failed to make the attempt from lack of courage, from disinclination or from missing the opportunity, does not appear. Gen. GRANT was announced to visit the theatre, but suddenly and unexpectedly took the cars to Philadelphia. ATZERODT made the remark the next day when it was reported that Gen. GRANT had been shot, that "probably it is the fact, if he was followed by the man that was to do it." O'LAUGHLIN was clearly shown to have been in conspiracy with BOOTH. He was found lurking in the hall of Secretary STANTON's house on the night of the 13th of April, evidently watching the movements of Gen. GRANT, who was Secretary STANTON's guest, that he might be able with certainty to identify him. During the day and night before, he had been visiting BOOTH, and on the night and at the very hour of the assassination was in position at a convenient distance to aid and protect BOOTH in his flight, as well as to execute his own part of the conspiracy by inflicting death upon Gen. GRANT, who, happily, was not at the theatre nor in the city, having left the city that day. O'Laughlin is an ordinary looking individual, about five feet five inches in height, bushy black hair, of luxuriant growth, pale face, black eyes, slight black whiskers, delicate silky moustache and thin goatee; weight about 130 pounds.

EDWARD SPANGLER.

The prisoner does not appear to have been in the conspiracy at an earlier period than a few hours before the commission of the crime. He was recognized as being one of three men in company with Booth in front of the theatre, and was heard that day to promise Booth assistance. His participation appears to have been in preparing the means of escape by keeping the passage-way clear on the stage, and by closing the door after Booth had passed through, so as to retard the movements of pursuers. Standing at the door after Booth had passed out, he exclaimed, "Hush, don't say anything about it!" He appears to have been Booth's drudge, sometimes taking care of and feeding his horse. During the progress of the trial his bearing was somewhat stolid. He is of short, thick stature, full face, showing indications of excessive drink, dull, gray eyes, unsymmetrical head, and light hair, closely cut.

SAMUEL ARNOLD.

Arnold was proven to have been at one time in full communion with the conspirators. His counsel claimed that at this time the plot was simply to abduct the President, and that Arnold and Booth quarreled, and the former withdrew from the conspiracy. The prisoner afterward went to Fortress Monroe, and took a situation as clerk in a sutler's store, where he remained till his arrest, two days after the assassination. Arnold was at one time in the rebel service. He is about thirty years of age, five feet eight inches in height, dark hair and eyes, clear light complexion, and an intelligent and prepossessing countenance.

SAMUEL A. MUDD.

Dr. Mudd was shown to have been in the full confidence of Booth as long ago as last November. He had a suspicious meeting with Surratt and Booth at the National Hotel in January. He introduced Booth to Surratt. Booth visited him at his room in the Pennsylvania House. Booth and Herold fled to his house directly after committing the murder. He dressed Booth's broken leg and assisted the escape, into Lower Maryland, of the latter and Herold. Three days afterward, when called upon by the officers, he doubted that he knew either of the criminals. When arrested on the Friday following, he prevaricated, lied outright, and finally admitted that he knew Booth. He said he first heard of the assassination on Sunday at Church, and it was shown by abundant proof that he was at Bryantown on the day preceeding (Saturday,) at an hour when the populace was all excitement, the town guarded by and full of soldiers and every man, woman and child in the place had not only heard of the murder, but knew the name of the assassin of Dr. MUDD's being an accomplice in the assassination there can be no shadow of doubt. In appearance MUDD is described as being five feet ten inches in height, slender in form, hair red or sandy, and of thin growth, pale oval intelligent face, blue eyes, high forehead, rather prominent nose, thin lips, and a red tuft of hair upon his chin.

July 8, 1865.

END OF THE ASSASSINS.

Execution of Mrs. Surratt, Payne, Herold and Atzerodt.

Their Demeanor on Thursday Night and Friday Morning.

Attempt to Release Mrs. Surratt on a Writ of Habeas Corpus.

Argument of Counsel—Order of the President.

SCENES AT THE SCAFFOLD.

The Four Hang Together and Die Simultaneously.

INTERESTING INCIDENTS—EXCITEMENT IN WASHINGTON—ORDER AND QUIET IN THE CITY.

Special Dispatch to the New-York Times.

WASHINGTON, FRIDAY, JULY 7, 1865.

The conspirators have gone to their long home, the swift hand of justice has smitten them, and they stand before the judgment seat. Electrified—saddened as the country was by the terrible calamity brought upon it by the damnable deeds of these deep-dyed villains, astounded as it has been by the daily revelations of the trial of the criminals, it was doubtless unprepared, as were all here, for the quick flash of the sword of power, whose blade to-day fell upon the guilty heads of the assassins of our lamented President.

Tried, convicted and sentenced, they stood this morning upon the threshold of the house of death, all covered with the great sin whose pall fell darkly upon the land. Young and old, equal in crime, they spent the night as is told hereafter, and when the first grey pencilings of the early morning traced the dawning day upon the sky, the city was all agog for the coming scene of retribution and of justice.

THE HABEAS CORPUS.

Mrs. SURRATT's friends have been constant and faithful. They have manipulated presses and created public sentiment. The papers received here to-day were singularly unanimous in the supposition that the President would commute the sentence of Mrs. SURRATT to imprisonment for life. Such a sentiment found no echo here. It was well known that the counsel, family and friends of the culprit were determined to make every exertion, to strain every nerve in a strong pull and tug at the tender heart of the President in her behalf. She was a woman, and a sick woman at that. Her daughter was with her, and her cowardly son, with secrets in his possession that might mitigate her guilt—these and like arguments, it was said, would be brought to bear upon the President, backed with certain political strength which could not fail to succeed. But such talk has seemed idle from the first. Woman as she was, she knew her business well; sick as she was, she had strength sufficient for her fearful purpose, and stern as the sentence was, its justice was absolute, its execution certain. We have heard many express the desire that the woman's life might be spared and its weary hours passed in the quiet of the prison, but no one who knew the President and his unmoveable nature supposed for an instant that the sentence would be changed in jot or tittle.

The hotels were thronged on Thursday. The streets were filled with restless, impatient people. The headquarters were surrounded by crowds of anxious men, who desired above all things to witness the execution, and who were willing to spend hundreds of dollars for that poor privilege. All day long the trains came in loaded with people from the North; all night long the country roads were lined with pedestrians, with parties hurrying on to the city, where they might at least participate in the excitements of the occasion.

Officials of every grade and name, with or without influence, were pestered by applications for tickets; the subordinate officers of the department were approached in every conceivable way, and by every possible avenue, by those whose idle or morbid curiosity impelled them to come to this hot and sweltering city in search of food for gossip and remembrance. Of course all endeavor was futile. Major-Gen. HANCOCK, who had charge of everything, had carefully prepared the list of people entitled to admission, and beyond those therein named, no one was permitted to be present. The

SCENES AT THE OLD CAPITOL

Prison on Thursday night were by no means so harrowing in intensity as the public doubtless can imagine. So far as the authorities were concerned, there was possibly an increased vigilance, and extra precautions were taken with Mrs. SURRATT; but beyond that, matters went along quite in accordance with the general custom.

MRS. SURRATT,

about whose fearful participation in the murder of the President has been thrown so much mystery, was a very remarkable woman, and, like most remarkable women, had an undertone of superstition which served her in place of true religion, and enabled her to sleep peacefully even while cognizant of such a crime as that for which she has now suffered. She was fifty years of age, but, although since her illness of the past two weeks she has grown old and looked pale and thin, she would be called rather forty-two or three. Firmness and decision were part and parcel of her nature. A cold eye, that would quail at no scene of torture; a close, shut mouth, whence no word of sympathy with suffering would pass; a firm chin, indicative of fixedness of resolve; a square, solid figure, whose proportions were never disfigured by remorse or marred by loss of sleep—these have ever marked the *personnel* of MARY SURRATT—these, her neighbors say, were correct indices of her every-day and every-year life.

Those who have watched her through the whole of this protracted trial have noticed her utter indifference to anything and everything said or suggested about her. The most terrible flagellation produced no effect upon her rocky countenance, stolid, quiet, entirely self-possessed, calm as a May morning, she sat, uninterested from the opening to the close.

Her guardians say she anticipated an acquittal, she alone knew why. When, therefore, she was informed of the finding of the court, the sentence, and its near execution, she might well be roused from the state of utter listlessness she had thitherto maintained. Weakened by continued illness, with head stunned by the sudden blow, she for a moment forgot the SURRATT in the woman, and felt the keenness of her position. Fainting, she cried aloud in the bitterness of her woe, wailing forth great waves of sorrow, she fell upon the floor and gave vent to a paroxysm of grief, partially hysterical, and wholly nervous. This was so unlike her, so entirely different from any conduct previously noticed, that the officer and her attendants were alarmed for her life. They sent at once for the regular physician of the arsenal, who pronounced her system deranged and dangerously prostrated. Wine of valerian and other quieting drink was given to her, and she revived, but no longer was she the Mrs. SURRATT of the court-room. She desired to see her spiritual advisers, and they were sent for. The sacred vail of ghostly comfort should not be rudely rent nor lightly lifted, but we may state with entire propriety that the miserable woman expressed the most emphatic desire for prayer and holy consolation. Desirous of clearing her mind first of all worldly affairs, she indicated the disposition she wished made of her property, and talked long and earnestly of her children and their future prospects. Toward her cowardly son JOHN she quite naturally entertained feelings of deep-seated bitterness. This she in a measure overcame after having relieved her mind about him and his conduct, and finally appeared reconciled to his desertion. What the feelings of the scoundrel must be to-day we cannot well imagine. If, as Mrs. SURRATT's friends more than intimated, his testimony would save her, if, as his own offer proved, his revelations would keep her from a death of infamy, we cannot believe he will dare survive her. Suicide and the unknown possibilities of the future, would seem preferable to life and the certain remorse and disgrace attending it here.

As the night wore on Mrs. SURRATT, who had been removed from the larger room where she has been confined since her illness, began to toss uneasily on her narrow bed. She was really ill and the kind offices of the physician were frequently needed. Conscious of the approach of day, she betook herself again to the preparation of her soul for its infinite journey. She rallied mentally and physically and determined evidently to bear and brave the scaffold. Her daughter, whose faithful service has been most touching in its constancy, had done all she could. The President had been seen, Judge HOLT had been visited. To both of them the most fervent appeals, inspired by a filial love as devoted as it was disinterested, had been presented, but in vain. Five of the members of the court had joined in a recommendation for commutation to imprisonment for life, and it was understood that the entire court concurred in the same, but this too was in vain. These facts the heartbroken daughter had communicated to her sentenced mother, and as she bent her head upon her neck she bathed her shoulders with tears of unfeigned grief and sympathy.

Seemingly convinced of the utter hopelessness of her situation, and apparently desirous of quieting the exceedingly demonstrative outbursts of her daughter, Mrs. SURRATT rose from her bed and again betook herself to her devotional exercises. It may seem strange that this woman, who was proven to know all about the projected

assassination, who kept open house for the scoundrels who planned and the villains who did the deed, who insisted that she had never seen and never knew PAYNE, and who said, when informed of her sentence, "I had no hand in the murder of the President," should seem so calm and consistent in her preparation for death. Nevertheless the fact is that after turning her back upon hope, she gave herself with apparent sincerity and with heartiness to prayer and communion, the effect of which it is not for us to judge. . . .

Concerning PAYNE or POWELL, as he called himself, there has been a great deal of unnecessary mystery and foolish surmisings. His name, as far as the public is concerned, is

LEWIS PAYNE,

and if behind that he hid the honest name of a respectable family, the fact is one to his credit; but of that no one cares. He is dead; gone before the bar of a higher tribunal than that which last judged him, and with his future we have naught to do. The cool villainy, the absolute savagery of the fellow, has been consistent with the atrocity of his crime, until, with singular emotion, he became the apologist for his fellow-criminal, and the assailer of her son. By no means handsome, or of the romantic scoundrel stamp, PAYNE seems to have been a very common kind of person, with an exceedingly hard head and apparently no heart. No mere man would or could have deliberately cut and slashed the face of a sick and dying sufferer; it required the instinct of a demon and the temper of a brute to suggest and execute such a project. He was a species of idiot, an intelligent beast, with wit enough to understand his duty, sense enough to do it thoroughly, but unable to talk or maneuver himself out of such a scrape as he fell into at the door of Mrs. SURRATT's house.

Throughout the trial he has been unmoved. Never sullen nor morose, he kept his eyes about him, seeing everybody and everything, but never for an instant admitting by sign or gesture that he recognized anything. The confinement didn't annoy him at all. Quite likely he would have enjoyed a night in the town, and been as ready for a spree or a murder as ever; but he rarely opened his mouth, and as rarely closed his eyes, which wandered around and around, as if in continual search for an object of rest.

In his cell, PAYNE manifested no different appearance. His conduct was the same everywhere and at all times. He was a fit tool for the hand that used him—a reliable blade for a bloody purpose. At night he slept; in the morning he awoke early; his appetite was always good, and when the time for the meeting of the court was announced, he went along quietly as a lamb, as docile as an ox in yoke. When, therefore, his sentence was read to him, it was to be expected that his don't-careativeness, or stupidity, or *sang froid,* or whatever it may be termed, would still characterize him. He neither appeared surprised nor disappointed. Had he been pronounced "not guilty," it would have been the same—until he was freed; then he might have developed differently, though that is more conjecture, baseable upon no reliable data.

Doubly ironed, doubly guarded, PAYNE spent the day and night before his death. No future presented aught of hope or fear for him; no God or devil stared him in the face with searching scrutiny or tantalizing punishment. He simply felt nothing, and yet in the midst of apathy and indifference, we find him explaining that Mrs. SURRATT had nothing to do with the murder, inveighing against John SURRATT as a coward and scoundrel who had deserted his mother, leaving her to die when he should fill her place, and expressing tenderest regret that any act of his should have brought her into trouble and put her life in jeopardy. It is difficult to reconcile these two phases of character, so entirely different. Common sense forbids the belief that he feigned stupidity and was in reality a man of birth and breeding, and it likewise scouts the theory that he was entitled to sympathy on account of idiocy. Declining to participate in any religious mummery, and wholly averse to any religious reality, he passed his last hours in quiet stupidity, exerting himself to please no one, caring apparently nothing, either for the people here or the probabilities of the hereafter. His body was a source of no earthly considerations. Until he died it was not his—his keepers had it; after his death it was not his, and he did not care who had it. His friends, he said, lived in Florida. Before they could come, if they would, he would be gone, and the senseless clod which tenemented his scared soul would be en route to corruption. Why should he care? He didn't care.

One redeeming feature stood prominent. Noticing the kind consideration of Miss SURRATT toward her mother, PAYNE expressed regret that they should be compelled to part. He said he would do anything, say anything which could help Mrs. SURRATT, who was an innocent woman. He emerged from his brutism and became humane; he left his carelessness behind him and asserted the case of the mother against her recreant son; he forgot the idiot and resumed for the moment the attitude and intelligence of a man. With the clergymen he had but little to say. He seemed entirely careless as to his future, and down to the very last maintained his stolid, indifferent, hang-dog manner.

Perhaps there was more sympathy expressed for

DAVID E. HEROLD

than for any of the prisoners. He was young, thoughtless, light and trivial. He probably had never known a serious moment nor a sober thought. His following of BOOTH was very much such a companionship as a dog affords, and it seemed as if he might have been so thoroughly under the influence of that fascinating fiend as to be entirely *non compos.* The legal evidence against him was, however, clear and conclusive. As early as February last he was found to have been in confidential relations with the assassin, and was proved to have been present on several occasions at secret meetings with BOOTH, ATZERODT and others of the conspirators. Once he was at Mrs. SURRATT'S in company with them. He called with SURRATT and ATZERODT at the tavern in Surattville, and left the two carbines and ammunition which were taken away from the tavern by him and BOOTH on the night of the assassination. During their flight he acknowledged to WILLIE JETT and other rebel soldiers that he and BOOTH were the assassins of Mr. LINCOLN, and he was captured in the barn with BOOTH. His personal appearance was that of a boy of nineteen, dressed in a faded blue suit, in height about five feet four inches, dusky black, neglected hair, lively, dark hazel eyes, slight tufts of beard along the chin and jaws, and faintly surrounding the mouth, rather round face, full but not prominent nose, full lips, foolish, weak, confiding countenance, indicating but little intelligence, and not the faintest trace of ferocity. His sisters, who are apparently very estimable young women, labored with him, hoping to make some serious impression upon him, but in vain. He was full of levity almost to the very hour of his death. At the announcement of the finding of the court, HEROLD was unmoved. Indeed, none of the prisoners at first manifested any great concern—HEROLD and PAYNE least of any. PAYNE was sullen and indifferent, HEROLD careless and free. After a little, when the later hours of the night were passing silently by, he became more tractable and for the time left his habit of joking and gossiping, and when asked if he had any requests to make, desired that his body might be given to his family. With the clergyman he was ever respectful, but beyond a routine representation of words and phrases seemed to know and care little more about the coming than the present world. Impressible to a remarkable degree, but equally elastic, he talked and wept with the ministers, but was as ready for a quib or joke immediately after as ever. It is difficult to say that he was not a responsible person, and yet he seemed more like a butterfly than a man. He was at no time manly in deportment, and his exit from this world, was in accordance with his variable temperament while in it.

GEORGE A. ATZERODT

was a coward, mentally, morally and physically. He failed to grasp the magnitude of the conspiracy as unfolded to him by the leaders; he failed to accomplish his part of the assassination scheme, and he failed to make any one care a rap whether he lived or died. During the trial he was unconcerned; since his imprisonment, was peevish and full of complaints, and on the night before his death he was restless and uneasy. He couldn't sleep at all, and, unlike PAYNE, had no appetite. He was a poor, miserable fellow, and his death amounted to no more than did his life.

THE MORNING OF THE DAY

appeared, and with it came thousands of people from afar to witness the execution. They might as well have come to see GEORGE WASHINGTON, the one was easy as the other. As above stated, every person in any way connected with the government, was tortured and annoyed by applications for passes to the prison. This morning the crowd of besiegers again appeared before 7 o'clock, and most of them failing to receive the desired pass, the curious wended their way to the arsenal grounds, two miles distant, in the hot sun, there to renew their importunities. When we arrived at the latter place, about 10 o'clock, the streets and avenues were blocked up by hundreds of vehicles, and probably 2,000 lookers-on, whose only reward for their exposure and labor was a peep at the prison walls in the distance. Four and One-half-street, the thoroughfare leading directly to the arsenal, was strongly and thickly guarded from Pennsylvania-avenue to the arsenal lot, and at the entrance to the latter, and completely surrounding it, were numerous soldiers on guard. Entering the enclosure, we found several regiments on duty—in all, two brigades of HANCOCK'S corps—scattered here and there between the gates and the prison.

Pedestrians were flocking rapidly toward the building, and when we entered the latter, we found already several hundred persons—a mixed assembly of civilians and military men. We learned that none of the prisoners had slept during the past night save PAYNE and HEROLD, both of whom had a sound, quiet rest of about two hours. None of them had eaten anything scarcely except PAYNE, who partook heartily of breakfast. During the night opiates had been given Mrs. SURRATT to produce rest, but without avail. The spiritual advisers and friends of the condemned left the prison shortly after 11 o'clock last night, and none returned until this morning, except Miss SURRATT, who remained with her mother from about midnight until 5 o'clock A.M. No confessions had been made. None, indeed, could have been expected from either

PAYNE, HEROLD or ATZERODT, who had already from time to time, given in the main, probably, the truthful account of their relations to the bloody tragedy in which they were participants. Mrs. SURRATT was the only one remaining who had not acknowledged the full measure of her guilt. She, it was rumored, had made a full confession to her confessor, but on inquiry we found her confession in preparation for receiving the sacrament, was confounded with an acknowledgement of guilt for publicity. She had hope up to almost the hour of her execution that her sentence would be respited, if not commuted, and she had apparently lost sight of her own interest in deep solitude for her daughter, of whom she constantly talked, and repeatedly, frantically and with wringing of hands asked: "What will become of her—what will be ANNA's fate?"

STATEMENTS OF PAYNE.

PAYNE, last evening, informed Col. DODD, who has special charge of the prisoners, that so far as he knew, Mrs. SURRATT had nothing to do with the plot for assassination. Certainly she had never said a word to him on the subject, nor had any of his co-conspirators mentioned her in connection with the matter. She may have known what was going on, but to him she never disclosed her knowledge by word or act. That immediately after he had made the murderous attack upon Mr. SEWARD, he felt he had done wrong, and he had wandered around and slept in the woods that night, frequently feeling inclined to come to the city and give himself up. That when, finally, he was by hunger and loss of rest driven to Mrs. SURRATT's house he had doubts about his reception there and whether she would not deliver him to the officers of the law for punishment. Col. DODD, who has been constantly in conversation with PAYNE, recently says the latter has never varied from one straightforward, consistent story, claiming at all times that he was informed and believed that he was acting under an order from the rebel authorities, and did not, therefore, originally view his act as a murderous one. HEROLD says in the original plot to him was assigned the duty of shutting off the gas in the theatre, and he had once rehearsed the work with BOOTH; that, however, on the night of the assassination, he was only required to be in waiting near the Navy-yard Bridge to assist BOOTH in his escape.

These statements embrace substantially all the prisoners have given in the nature of confessions, other than what is found in the proofs and admissions on the trial.

DEMEANOR OF THE CONDEMNED.

We were permitted to look in upon the cells on several occasions during the forenoon, and up to a few minutes before the execution. The four prisoners condemned to death were removed yesterday from the upper floor of the prison to a tier of cells on the first floor South. ATZERODT occupied the eastern apartment, No. 151,

Mrs. SURRATT the next West, No. 153, HEROLD, No. 155, and PAYNE, No. 157, thus leaving a vacant cell between each of the prisoners.

Our first observation of ATZERODT, found him in company with the Rev. Mr. BUTLER, a Lutheran minister of the gospel. The prisoner was lying upon his bed an intent and quiet listener to the whisperings of the minister. At another time ATZERODT seemed utterly unnerved and tossed about, frequently clasping his hands together and wringing them as in hopelessness and despair. At noon and thereafter he became calmer and scarcely spoke or moved.

Mrs. SURRATT throughout the day continued in physical prostration, but grew calmer as the hour approached for execution. The parting between herself and daughter was borne with more fortitude than was expected of her, and whilst the latter swooned away, and was carried to an adjoining apartment senseless, Mrs. SURRATT appeared to rally in strength for the moment. Soon again, however, she lost strength, and when taken from her cell to the scaffold, she had to be almost literally lifted and borne along by the officers.

HEROLD's demeanor was somewhat after the manner he has shown from the commencement of the trial—listlessness and lack of appreciation of his fearful position, with alternatives of serious reflection.

PAYNE was, throughout the day, quiet and firm, occasionally joining the Rev. Dr. GILLETTE in earnest prayer.

THE SCAFFOLD.

in the lot south of the prison, and surrounded by a wall thirty feet high, the scaffold was erected. The structure is about seventy feet from the prison nearby, say thirty feet distant, were four freshly dug graves, and beside them four large pine coffins coarsely constructed.

The scaffold was so arranged that the four condemned could be hung at the same time.

The enclosure was much larger than was stated in my dispatch of last night, and there must have been present within the lot and upon the top of the wall, which was literally packed with soldiers, quite 3,000 spectators, three-fourths of whom were soldiers.

About 12:30 o'clock, gen. HANCOCK arrived, and remained personally inspecting all the official acts.

THE PROCESSION OF DEATH.

At 1:15 the procession proceeded from the prison to the scaffold in the following order, preceded by Gen. HARTRANFT:

Mrs. SURRATT, supported by an officer and a noncommissioned officer, and attended by Rev. Fathers WALTER and WIGETT.

AZTERODT, attended by an officer, with whom walked his spiritual advisers, Rev. J. G. BUTLER, of the Lutheran Church, and Chaplain WINCHESTER.

HEROLD came next, attended by Rev. Dr. OLDS, of Christ Church; Episcopal.

PAYNE, attended by Rev. Dr. GILLETTE, of the First Baptist Church, of this city, and Rev. Dr. STRIKER, of Baltimore.

Mrs. SURRATT, attended by two soldiers. Her waist and ankles were ironed; she was attired in a plain black alpacca dress, with black bonnet and thin veil. Her face could be easily seen. She gazed up at the horrid instrument of death, and her lips were moving rapidly as in prayer. She was assisted upon the scaffold and seated in a chair near the drop. She gazed upon the noose, which dangled in the wind before her face, and again her lips moved as if in prayer.

ATZERODT, followed, with a glaring, haggard look. He seemed to have changed in appearance greatly since his incarceration. He, also, was assisted by two soldiers, and seemed very feeble, but appeared to rally when on the scaffold, and took an evident interest in the proceedings.

HEROLD came next, supported on each side. He seemed very feeble, but revived a little subsequently. He realized his position now, if he never did before. He was very pale and careworn. He examined the scaffold closely, upon approaching it, and especially the drop.

PAYNE came next, with his usual bold, straight attitude, looking with seeming indifference upon the instrument of death. He wore a blue shirt and straw hat. There was not firmness in his step as he marched to the scaffold.

REMARKS AND PRAYERS OF THE ATTENDING CLERGY.

The Catholic priest in attendance upon Mrs. SURRATT declined making any public remark. Dr. GILLETTE stepped forward and said:

The prisoner, LEWIS THORNTON POWELL, known as PAYNE, requests me on this occasion, to say for him, that he thanks, publicly and sincerely thanks, Gen. HARTRANFT, all the officers and soldiers who had charge of him, and all persons who have ministered to his wants, for their unwavering kindness to him in this trying hour. Not an unkind word nor an illfeeling act has been made toward him.

Almighty God, our Heavenly Father, as we pray thee to permit us to commit this soul into thy hands, not for any claim we have to make for it in ourselves, but depending as we do upon the merits of our Lord Jesus Christ, grant, O Heavenly Father, we beseech thee, that his spirit may be accorded an easy passage out of this world, and, if consistent with thy purposes of mercy, and thou delightest in mercy, receive him. This we humbly ask, through Jesus Christ, our Lord and our Redeemer. Amen.

Dr. OLDS, in behalf of HEROLD, followed, saying:

"DAVID E. HEROLD, who is here about to undergo the extreme penalty of offended law, desires me to say that he hopes your prayers may be offered up to the Most High

God for him; that he forgives all who may at any time have wronged him, and asks of all forgiveness for all the wrong or supposed wrong he has done unto them, that he thanks the officers who have had charge of him during his confinement in prison for their deeds of kindness toward him, he hopes that he dies in charity with all the world and is convinced that his soul is in the hands of God. Amen.

Rev. Mr. BUTLER, the spiritual adviser of ATZERODT, then rose and said:

"George A. ATZERODT requests me thus publicly to return his unfeigned thanks to Gen. HARTRANFT, and all associated with him in this prison, for their uniform courtesy and kindness during his imprisonment. And now, GEORGE A. ATZERODT, may God have mercy upon you. The ways of the transgressor is hard. The wages of sin is death; but if we freely confess our sins, God will in mercy pardon them. Christ came into the world to save sinners—even the chief of sinners. Believe in the Lord Jesus Christ, and thou shalt be saved. The blood of the blessed redeemer, Jesus Christ, cleanseth from all sin. You profess to have thus believed to have peace in your heart; and may God be with you in this hour of trial and suffering; and may you be enabled so to commend your soul to the Creator of it that you may have peace in this last moment of life. The Lord God Almighty, Father of Mercy, have mercy upon you, and receive you into His heavenly keeping. Lord God, Redeemed of the world, have mercy upon this man. Lord God, Holy Spirit of the Father and the Son, have mercy upon him and grant him thy peace. Amen."

THE LAST PAINFUL SCENE.

Gen. HARTRANFT read the order of the War Department, embracing the President's Executive Order, for the execution.

The limbs of each of the prisoners were now pinioned. The caps were drawn over their heads, Mrs. SURRATT exclaiming in a faint voice, "Don't let me fall; hold on!"

ATZERODT exclaimed in a loud tone: "Gentlemen, take warning;" then, after an interval of about two minutes he said: "Good-by, gentlemen who are before me; may we all meet in the other world."

It was now twenty-five minutes past 1 o'clock. The officer in charge of the scaffold here made some preconcerted motions to the attendant soldiers to step back from the drop, and then, with a motion of his hand, the drop fell and the bodies of the criminals were suspended in the air.

The bodies fell simultaneously, and swayed backward and forward for a few minutes. Mrs. SURRATT, appeared to suffer very little. PAYNE and HEROLD, on the contrary, writhed in apparent agony, the first for about two minutes, and the later for about five minutes. The muscles of their feet and hands were visibly contracted. Payne's hands, which were more exposed than the others, became purpled, as did his neck near where the rope was fastened. ATZERODT's agony seemed, like Mrs. SURRATT's, to be of but very short duration.

On July 7, 1865, four condemned conspirators—Mary Surratt, Lewis Powell, David Herold, and George Atzerodt—were hanged in the courtyard of Washington's Old Arsenal Prison for their involvement in the plot to assassinate the president. *(Library of Congress)*

After the lapse of ten minutes, the medical officers, Surgeon WOODWARD, U. S. A., Dr. OTIS, U. S. V., and Dr. PORTER, U. S. A., and Surgeon of the post examined severally the bodies, and pronounced life extinct. The ropes were cut, the bodies lowered, stretched upon the tops of the coffins, and a further and more minute examination was made by the Surgeons, who state that the necks of each were instantly broken.

At about 4 o'clock the bodies were placed in the coffins and buried.

The soldiers who were required to let fall the trap of the scaffold, are of Company F, Fourteenth Veteran Reserves. They were chosen by the Commander of that regiment who, without making known what was his purpose, required four able bodied men of the regiment to be selected from the left of the line, to perform a special and important duty. The selection was accordingly made before the service to be performed became known to the members of the regiment.

MUDD, ARNOLD, O'LAUGHLIN and SPANGLER will probably be sent to the Penitentiary to-morrow.

PART SIX

Obituaries

The New-York Times.

VOL. XXXIV......NO. 10,574. NEW-YORK, FRIDAY, JULY 24, 1885.—TRIPLE SHEET.

A HERO FINDS REST

GEN. GRANT'S PEACEFUL, PAINLESS DEATH.

THE END COMING IN THE EARLY MORNING.

THE LAST BREATH AT SIX MINUTES AFTER EIGHT O'CLOCK.

THE SORROWING GROUP AROUND THE DEATHBED.

HIS LAST WORDS FULL OF REGARD FOR OTHERS.

THE LONG STRUGGLE AGAINST DISEASE ONLY ENDED WHEN VITALITY WAS THOROUGHLY EXHAUSTED—CONSCIOUSNESS PRESERVED NEARLY TO THE LAST WHEN ALL OTHER FACULTIES WERE DEAD.

HIS BURIAL PLACE.

NEW-YORK.—*Because the people of that city befriended me in my need.*

U. S. GRANT.

Robert E. Lee became president of Washington College in Lexington, Virginia, after the war. In 1870 he died of a heart attack at the age of sixty-three.

By coincidence, Grant died at the same age thirteen years later of throat cancer probably caused by heavy cigar smoking. From the time of Lincoln's death until his own twenty years later, Grant was the most popular man in the country as savior of the Union. His reputation survived the uneven record of his two presidential terms. Grant's obituary and other stories associated with his life and death were probably the longest such copy ever published in *The New York Times*. Selections of the reporting are reprinted below.

By comparison the two columns on Jefferson Davis, who died of pneumonia in 1889 at the age of eighty-one, testify to the difference of reputation between Grant and Davis in the postwar North.

The last of these old protagonists to go was William T. Sherman, who also succumbed to pneumonia at the age of seventy-one in 1891. The tributes paid to him were second only to those showered on Grant.

October 13, 1870.

OBITUARY

Gen. Robert E. Lee.

Intelligence was received last evening of the death at Lexington, Va., of Gen. Robert E. Lee, the most famous of the officers whose celebrity was gained in the service of the Southern Confederacy during the late terrible rebellion. A report was received some days ago that he had been smitten with paralysis, but this was denied, and though it was admitted that he was seriously ill, hopes of his speedy recovery seem to have been entertained by his friends. Within the last two or three days his symptoms had taken an unfavorable turn, and he expired at 9½ o'clock yesterday morning of congestion of the brain, at the age of sixty-three years, eight months and twenty-three days.

ROBERT EDMUND LEE was the son of Gen. HENRY LEE, the friend of WASHINGTON, and a representative of one of the wealthiest and most respected families of Virginia. Born in January, 1807, he grew up among all the advantages which wealth and family position could give in a republican land, and received the best education afforded by the institutions of his native State. Having inherited a taste for military studies, and an ambition for military achievements, he entered the National Academy at West Point in 1825, and graduated in 1829, the second in scholarship in his class. He was at once commissioned Second Lieutenant of engineers, and in 1835 acted as assistant astronomer in drawing the boundary line between the States of Michigan and Ohio. In the following year he was promoted to the grade of First Lieutenant, and in 1838 received a Captain's commission. On the breaking out of the war with Mexico he was made Chief-Engineer of the army under the command of Gen. WOOL. After the battle of Cerro Gordo, in April, 1847, in which he distinguished himself by his gallant conduct, he was immediately promoted to the rank of Major. He displayed equal skill and bravery at Contreras, Cherubusco and Chapultepec, and in the battle at the last-mentioned place received a severe wound. His admirable conduct throughout this struggle was rewarded before its close with the commission of a Lieutenant-Colonel and the brevet title of Colonel. In 1852 he was appointed to the responsible position of Superintendent of the Military Academy at West Point, which he retained until 1855. On retiring from the charge of this institution he was made Lieutenant-Colonel of the Second Cavalry, and on the 16th of March, 1861, received the commission of Colonel of the First Cavalry.

Thus far the career of Col. LEE had been one of honor and the highest promise. In every service which had been entrusted to his hands he had proved efficient, prompt and faithful, and his merits had always been readily acknowledged and rewarded by promotion. He was regarded by his superior officers as one of the most brilliant and promising men in the army of the United States. His personal integrity was well known, and his loyalty and patriotism was not doubted. Indeed, it was in view of the menaces of treason and the dangers which threatened the Union that he had received his last promotion, but he seems to have been thoroughly imbued with that pernicious doctrine that his first and highest allegiance was due to the State of his birth. When Virginia joined the ill-fated movement of secession from the Union, he immediately threw up his commission in the Federal Army and offered his sword to the newly-formed Confederacy. He took this step, protesting his own attachment to the Union, but declaring that his sense of duty would never permit him to "raise his hand against his relatives, his children, and his home." In his farewell letter to Gen. SCOTT, he spoke of the struggle which this step had cost him, and his wife declared that he "wept tears of blood over the terrible war." There are probably few who doubt the sincerity of his protestation, but thousands have regretted, and his best friends will ever have to regret, the error of judgment, the false conception of the allegiance due to his Government and his country, which led one so rarely gifted to cast his lot with traitors, and devote his splendid talents to the execution of a wicked plot to tear asunder and ruin the Republic in whose service his life had hitherto been spent.

He resigned his commission on the 25th of April, 1861, and immediately betook himself to Richmond, where he was received with open arms and put in command of all the forces of Virginia by Gov. LETCHER. On the 10th of May he received the commission of a Major-General in the army of the Confederate States, retaining the command in Virginia, and was soon after promoted to the rank of General in the regular army. He first took the field in the mountainous region of Western Virginia, where he met with many difficulties, and was defeated at Greenbrier by Gen. J. J. REYNOLDS on the 3rd of October, 1861. He was subsequently sent to take command of the Department of the South Atlantic Coast, but after the disabling of Gen. JOSEPH E. JOHNSTON at the battle of Fair Oaks, in the Spring of 1962, he was recalled to Virginia, and placed at the head of the forces defending the capital, which he led through the remainder of the campaign of the Chickahominy. He engaged with the Army of the Potomac under his old companion-in-arms, Gen. MCCLELLAN, and drove it back to the Rappahannock. He afterward, in August 1862, attacked the Army of Virginia, under Gen. POPE, and, after driving it back to Washington, crossed the Potomac into Maryland, where he issued a proclamation calling upon the inhabitants to enlist under his triumphant banners. Meantime MCCLELLAN gathered a new army from the broken remnants of his former forces, and met LEE at Hagerstown, and, after a battle of two days, compelled him to retreat. Reinforced by "STONEWALL" JACKSON, on the 16th of September, he turned to renew the battle, but after two days of terrible fighting at Sharpsburgh and Antietam, was driven from the soil of Maryland. Retiring beyond the Rappahannock, he took up his position at Fredericksburgh, where he was attacked, on the 13th of December, by Gen. BURNSIDE, whom he drove back with terrible slaughter. He met with the same success in May, 1863, when attacked by HOOKER, at Chancellorsville. Encouraged by these victories, in the ensuing Summer he determined to make a bold invasion into the territory of the North. He met Gen. MEADE at Gettysburgh, Penn., on the 1st of July, 1863, and after one of the most terrible and destructive battles of modern times, was driven from Northern soil. Soon after this, a new character appeared on the battle-fields of Virginia, and Gen. LEE found it expedient to gather his forces for the defense of the Confederate capital against the determined onslaughts of Gen. GRANT. In the Spring and Summer of 1864, that indomitable soldier gradually enclosed the City of Richmond as with a girdle of iron, which he drew closer and closer with irresistible energy and inexorable determination, repulsing the rebel forces whenever they ventured to make an attack, which they did several times with considerable vigor. In this difficult position, holding the citadel of the Confederacy, and charged with its hopes and destinies, LEE was made Commander-in-Chief of the armies of the South. He held out until the Spring of 1865, vainly endeavoring to gather the broken forces of the Confederacy, and break asunder the terrible line which was closing around them. After a desperate and final effort at Burkesville, on the 9th of April, 1865, he was compelled to acknowledge his defeat, and surrendered his sword to Gen. GRANT on the generous terms which were dictated by that great soldier. LEE retired under his parole to Weldon, and soon after made a formal submission to the Federal Government. Subsequently, by an official clemency, which is probably without a parallel in the history of the world, he was formally pardoned for the active and effective part he had taken in the mad effort of the Southern States to break up the Union and destroy the Government. Not long after his surrender he was invited to become President of Washington University, at Lexington, Va., and was installed in that position on the 2nd of October, 1865. Since that time he has devoted himself to the interests of that institution, keeping so far as possible aloof from public notice, and by his unobtrusive modesty and purity of life, has won the respect even of those who most bitterly deplore and reprobate his course in the rebellion.

July 24, 1885.

A HERO FINDS REST.

GEN. GRANT'S PEACEFUL, PAINLESS DEATH.

THE END COMING IN THE EARLY MORNING.

THE LAST BREATH AT SIX MINUTES AFTER EIGHT O'CLOCK.

THE SORROWING GROUP AROUND THE DEATHBED.

HIS LAST WORDS FULL OF REGARD FOR OTHERS.

THE LONG STRUGGLE AGAINST DISEASE ONLY ENDED WHEN VITALITY WAS THOROUGHLY EXHAUSTED—CONSCIOUSNESS PRESERVED NEARLY TO THE LAST WHEN ALL OTHER FACULTIES WERE DEAD.

HIS BURIAL PLACE.

NEW-YORK—*Because the people of that city befriended me in my need.*

U. S. GRANT

MOUNT MCGREGOR, JULY 23—SURROUNDED BY ALL OF HIS FAMILY AND WITH NO SIGN OF PAIN, GEN. GRANT PASSED FROM LIFE AT SIX MINUTES AFTER EIGHT O'CLOCK THIS MORNING. THE END CAME WITH SO LITTLE IMMEDIATE NOTICE AS TO BE IN THE NATURE OF A SURPRISE. ALL NIGHT HAD THE FAMILY BEEN ON WATCH, PART OF THE TIME IN THE PARLOR, WHERE HE LAY, RARELY VENTURING FURTHER AWAY FROM HIM THAN THE PORCH ON WHICH THE PARLOR OPENS. THERE SEEMED NO HOPE THAT DEATH COULD BE HELD OFF THROUGH THE NIGHT. IT WAS EXPECTED AT 9 O'CLOCK, AGAIN AT ABOUT MIDNIGHT, AND AGAIN NEAR 4 O'CLOCK. THERE WAS SERIOUS FAILURE AT 4 O'CLOCK AND AT MIDNIGHT, BUT NOT AT 4 O'CLOCK, AND AS THE DAY CAME, BRINGING BUT SLIGHT CHANGE, THE HOPE WAS THAT HE MIGHT LAST UNTIL MIDDAY . . .

The General, knowing his disease, foreseeing the result, and apprehending death sooner than did the doctors, had only one wish in regard to it. He wanted to die painlessly. The brandy, the hot appliances, and anodynes made the end what he wanted it to be. Otherwise the feverish coursing of the pulse, the panting, shallow breath, and the sense of dissolution which he might have felt extending upward to the brain might have made the end anything but a peaceful sinking into sleep. These symptoms and the treatment for them make a basis for doubt if the General could have been at any time during the night in clear mind. His posture in bed was most of the time on the right side. The head was bolstered. Toward the end he was turned on his back, dying in that position.

The end was characteristic, the doctors say, of the disease as diagnosed by them. It was a case of clear exhaustion, the emaciation having left him, it is said, weighing less than 100 pounds. This morning, when the first shock was over, the doctors recalled to the family the question raised in regard to the diagnosis, and asked the privilege of an autopsy. The family would not hear of it. They were satisfied, they said, with the diagnosis. The matter was dropped at once.

Dr. DOUGLAS said there was nothing peculiar about the death except the resisting force of remarkable vitality. It was nine months yesterday since Dr. DOUGLAS took charge of the General. The General had not been dead two minutes when the wires were sending it over the country. It was known in New-York before some of the guests heard of it at the hotel, where it spread very quickly. Undertaker HOLMES was on his way from Saratoga almost as soon as the family had withdrawn to their rooms from the bedside. A special train which had waited for him all night was at once dispatched for him. A message was sent to STEPHEN MERRITT, at New-York, to come on at once to take charge of the funeral services. . . .

LOCAL TRIBUTES OF GRIEF.

WIDE EXTENT OF THE POPULAR REGARD FOR THE DEAD HERO.

The bells of old Trinity began tolling at 8:15 o'clock yesterday morning. Tidings of Gen. GRANT's death had been conveyed to Sexton Brown by a special messenger. The mournful music of the bells floated up upon the brisk breezes, and caused hundreds of hurrying pedestrians in the streets below to pause and listen. Business men, who had just reached their stores and offices, ran eagerly to doors and windows to catch the sound more clearly. There was no mistaking the meaning of that ominous pealing of the bells. "Gen. Grant is dead!" was spoken in hushed voices, and the listeners turned to their work with mingled feelings of relief and of sadness.

Soon from the belfry of the venerable St. Paul's rang out startling and significant peals. Then the bells of St. John's, St. Augustine's, St. Chrysostom's, Trinity Chapel, and other churches successively took up the sad refrain and spread it throughout the city. Noisy news vendors began to appear, and by 8:30 o'clock their shrill cries of "Extra!" "Extra!" were heard in all of the principal down-town thoroughfares. The boys had no need to solicit patronage. They were unable to distribute their hastily printed papers fast enough to satisfy the impatient buyers. Some of these news vendors disposed of their stocks before they could get two blocks away from Printing House Square. Others, with heavy piles of papers slung across their shoulders, sped recklessly by would-be purchasers and betook themselves to the ferry landings and the railroad stations.

While the bells in the church towers were yet tolling, and while the exciting cries of the news vendors were resounding through the streets, the custodians of public and private buildings down town climbed to the roofs and placed the flags at half mast. The city had not fairly awakened before it was known in every public space and hotel that Gen. GRANT was dead, and a thousand flags were fluttering from the middle of their staffs. The sight of those tell-tale flags was the first intimation given to a good many residents of this city and of the suburbs that the sufferer at McGregor was a sufferer no longer. Persons who came into the city by the early trains and boats were met at the stations and landings by the black-bordered "extras," the sight of which abruptly conveyed to them the sad news.

The dissemination of the news of Gen. GRANT's death was followed by a development of keen and expressive sorrow. In every part of the city, among all nationalities, and in every grade of society this manifestation of human sympathy was noticeable. Nothing could be more touching than some of the brief dialogues so frequently heard in the street cars or near the newspaper bulletin boards.

"The great General has gone at last," one person would say.

"Yes; God bless him! He was a great man," somebody would reply.

"The greatest soldier of his time."

"Yes, and a hero up to the very last."

"That's true! That's true!"

Such verbal expressions of regard and affection for the dead soldier were heard wherever men congregated to discuss the all absorbing topic. And besides these verbal expressions there were innumerable mute ones, which caught the eye on almost every hand. It was no uncommon thing yesterday to see a brawny laborer step before a shop window, gaze steadfastly upon a portrait of Gen. GRANT, and turn hastily away to conceal a suspicious moistening about the eyes. Teamsters of jaunty and reckless bearing were observed fitting little crape bordered flags in the harnesses of their horses. Conductors of many of the street cars arranged, with apparent pride, tiny portraits of GRANT in their cars. Nearly all of the Third-avenue surface cars carried flags, the edges of which were bordered with black. Shop keepers who seldom display any sentimental weakness were seen to scan the fronts of their buildings with critical eyes and subsequently to dispatch messengers with orders for mourning cambric for decorative purposes.

The forenoon was not more than half spent before a general disposition to display emblems of mourning began to manifest itself. This disposition embraced private residences as well as places of business. Portraits of Grant, bordered with black crepe, and in some instances adorned with white flowers, were placed in the windows of private residences in many parts of the city. Sometimes the portraits would be framed in the folds of an American flag, and frequently, where there were no portraits, flags would be looped up with black and white cambric over doorways and beneath broad windows. In the store windows on Broadway, Sixth-avenue, Third-avenue, Grand-street, and in fact in almost every thoroughfare from the Battery to Harlem, portraits of the dead General could be counted by the hundred. Some of them were elaborately draped and others were unadorned. Beneath some of them were the words, "The Nation's Hero," or "We Mourn Our Loss," or "Unconquerable to The Last," or "The Foremost Solider of his Time." Wherever such portraits were displayed there also were to be found knots of sorrowing admirers of the dead General. . . .

EDITORIAL

GEN. GRANT.

The name of Gen. GRANT will be remembered by Americans as that of the savior of their country in a crisis more appalling than any it has passed through since the United States became a nation. His fame as a soldier, entering the Union Army at the first call of the President, and rising steadily by the sheer force of his faithful and precious service until, in the command of all Union forces, he crushed the stubborn rebellion on the ground where it had first shown a formidable front, will survive as long as the history of our country is read. It is near a quarter of a century now since he modestly offered himself as a recruiting officer to the Governor of Illinois; it is twenty years since he received the sword of LEE at Appomattox. The country is in profound peace, and the Union is not only restored but established on a basis infinitely firmer and more enduring than before it was assailed in the shock of civil war. There is a deeper national sentiment, a closer unity of aims and interest and hopes than ever before. The passions of that dreadful conflict are dying out under the steady advance of common freedom and common justice. The wounds war made are healing or have healed. But the new generation that did not feel the heat or the apprehension of the war, in the South and in the North, will join with those who watched or shared in the long and momentous struggle in a tribute of sorrow, of gratitude, of honor toward the great leader who has passed away.

There is a singular unity in the career of Gen. GRANT as a military commander, springing from the constancy and firmness of his mental and moral qualities. He was from the first and to the last marked by prompt and sustained energy. He saw with great quickness and clearness the work immediately before him, and pursued it without hesitation, without vacillation, patiently watching his opportunity, seizing it with instant and tremendous vigor, absolutely unshaken by doubt, never discouraged, never turning back, as calmly resolute after a check as after an advance, giving his enemy no rest and his armies no chance for the suspicion of failure. The people who watched his career from Belmont, Fort Henry, and Fort Donelson to Richmond were not the best judges of whether he was a master of the art of war, but they saw that he was the winner of battles, and they placed their utmost resources in men and money at his command because they relied instinctively upon his indomitable courage, his invincible faith in the cause, in his armies, and in himself. It may be easy to attribute to him faults of strategy and to deny his relative merits, but no one can deny that he was at every instant ready to do all that could be hoped from him and more than any other dared to undertake, that in every situation he took upon himself the heaviest responsibility, bore it calmly and steadily, and made the utmost use of his resources. When before Fort Donelson, the Confederates having made a gallant sortie, and his own troops being thrown into confusion, he remarked, "Whichever party now attacks first will whip," he showed the temper which, seizing instinctively the decisive moment of action, sprang to the decision it suggested, and risked all to win all. And this was the secret of his wonderful successes, of Vicksburg as of Donelson, of Chattanooga as of his more extended series of battles in the East. He has been criticized as wasting life in Virginia and seeking to simply wear out his weaker foe. But the unflinching resolution that fought and flanked the army of LEE from the Wilderness to Five Forks, while directing the campaigns in the West with the same steadiness, which dared to use the immense resources at his command with such singleness of purpose, despite the awful cost in life, and treasure, was in itself the proof of the rarest quality of leadership. It fully justified the confidence the people conceived in him, and was at the time the supreme condition of success.

The fame of Gen. GRANT will be the fame of a soldier, and there are features of his career in the Presidency that somewhat dimmed its luster. But while these will not be remembered, there are other features that are fully in harmony with the character that has won him his lasting distinction, and which add to his title to the grateful respect of the American Nation. The chief of these is the clearness of view and the firmness with which, while President, he supported the good faith of the Government in its finances. It was a period when the public mind was obscured, when the distinction between money and promises to pay was not everywhere recognized, when patriotism joined with speculative greed to sustain and extend the use of the deceptive legal tender currency. Men far more experienced than he in matters of finance, in public and in business life, were confused or cowardly in the struggle between difficult honesty and easy and popular dishonesty. President GRANT put aside the sophistries and the temptations of the hour with the same simple directness he showed in the pursuit of his military aims, and when he vetoed the Inflation bill and called upon the Government to pay in coin the promises it had compelled its creditors to take he rendered a service not less heroic and hardly less valuable than when he took his army by the batteries of Vicksburg and, staking its very existence, won the freedom of the Mississippi. That simple integrity, that unconquerable fidelity to his conception of duty, that quiet support of a great responsibility were characteristic of the man. Nor ought there to be withheld a sincere expression of respect for the manner in which he entered the reform of the civil service, which he surrendered because on the one hand his experience had not taught him its real value, and on the other because there was but a feeble public opinion supporting it anywhere, and in the Congress of the country there was only indifference and contempt. It is but justice to say that, viewing his whole remarkable life, the tributes of gratitude, of admiration, and of affection that will be paid to him by the whole American people have been richly deserved. The last of the two greatest Americans of their generations is gone.

December 6, 1889.

JEFFERSON DAVIS'S LIFE.

CAREER OF THE LEADER OF THE CONFEDERACY

HIS SERVICES IN UNITED STATES POLITICAL AFFAIRS AND HIS MANAGEMENT OF AFFAIRS OF THE CONFEDERATE STATES—AFTER THE WAR.

The death of Jefferson Davis removes the most conspicuous figure in that civil war which more than any series of events since the independence of the United States decided the destinies of the American people. Not only as the President of the Confederate States during their brief and stormy period of existence, but as an expounder and advocate of the doctrine of secession, and as a leader in the complex political movements that led to the attempt to carry out that doctrine, Jefferson Davis will hold a considerable place in the history of the United States.

406 After Gettysburg and Vicksburg the fate of the Confederacy was sealed, and in the desperate period that followed Davis presented a sorry figure. He maintained to the last his narrow and obstinate energy, but it was manifested largely in persistent meddling with his commanders in the field and in spiteful personal wrangles with the prominent men of the Confederacy, among whom he had managed to make many bitter enemies. As the crisis approached steadily and surely, it cannot be said that he rose to the occasion either in force of intellect or in dignity of character. The game was too desperate not to be played to the end, but the more trust-worthy of the accessible accounts of the events of that time within the Confederacy, necessarily confused and incomplete as they are, reveal a scene of waspian quarreling, of acrid personal jealousies and resentments, and of mutual recrimination between Davis and his chief associates that forbids us to regard him as a "great man struggling with adversity." He was rather a man of very moderate gifts, either mental or moral, who, in the tremendous transaction in which he had sought the post of leadership, was incapable of leading, and with whom intense personal vanity and obstinacy, unfailing but narrow, deprived his cause of much of the service which he might have rendered. The exact history of the close of the rebellion from the Confederate side has not yet been written, and probably will not be, but enough is known to make it evident that at the last Davis fell below rather than rose above his previous level in his influence upon affairs. After Grant had closed in upon the army of Lee, and Sherman, thanks largely to Davis's change of commanders at Atlanta, had swept unopposed through Georgia, and was steadily pushing upward through the Carolinas, and Davis had fled from Richmond, he still proclaimed to his people that the army, relieved of the necessity of defending the Government,

would be able to turn back the conquering armies of the Union. But the people were no longer to be deceived, and DAVIS's capture, as he was making his way southward and westward with a wild scheme of joining the remnant of the Confederate forces beyond the Mississippi, was, in its mortifying details, no unfitting close to his career. His subsequent confinement and final release tended to restore to him the regard of the people of the South, which had been much weakened during the last year of the war. He then retired to his beloved Mississippi, where, in comparative retirement, he prepared and published an extensive history of *The Rise and Fall of the Confederate Government*, and from time to time, in letters and speeches, avowed his undying attachment to the principles that had led him to secession. The restoration of the Union, in the feelings and habits of the people, received no aid from him, and his latest public utterances revealed still strong in him the inveterate vanity of personal consistency in narrow ideas which made him so mischievous as a promoter and so feeble as a leader of the wretched rebellion with which his name will be forever connected.

Jefferson Davis brought a wealth of experience to his duties as president of the Confederacy, having been a soldier, congressman, senator, and U.S. secretary of war. At the time of his inauguration he described the reasons for secession: "Through many years of controversy with our late associates, we have vainly endeavored to secure tranquility and to obtain respect for the rights to which we are entitled. As a necessity, not a choice, we have resorted to the remedy of separation." (*Chicago Historical Society*)

It would be a serious mistake, however, to attribute to JEFFERSON DAVIS and to the error of his views or the defects of his character a controlling influence upon the course of the events with which he was so conspicuously linked. He was, as has been said, a fairly complete representative of the people in which he played his part, and was rather a product than a decisive factor in the forces that led to the rebellion and to its failure. The theory of the sovereignty of the State, which his mind embraced with such clinging ardor, and which he advocated and applied with such untiring energy, was the off-spring of slavery, since it was the only one by which slavery could be maintained or the unceasing expansion of slave territory, so vital to its maintenance, be defended. It was readily waived on repeated occasions, when the needs of slavery dictated that course, but in the main it was the natural and logical view of the Union for those to whom slavery was not merely the accepted but the inevitable basis of the society in which they lived. The unyielding and arrogant claims put forth in the name of State rights were in close harmony with the ideas of their personal and class pretensions which slavery bred in the minds of the leading slaveholders. It was in the nature of things that this institution, resting on the absolute denial of the common rights of men, should give rise to a class of able, sincere, energetic, imperious, and ambitious leaders, and that these leaders, when brought in conflict with the representatives of the free and progressive society of the North, should conceive a theory of their political relations that would, if long enough pursued, lead to an open rupture. And it was equally inevitable that when the rupture came the slaveholding class should go down under the influence of the tendencies they represented and the ideas they had conceived and applied. The Confederacy was from the first hampered and enfeebled by the very theory for which it was fighting. It never really commanded its own resources, for it was impossible to organize an orderly, concentrated and well-directed Government to collect or use them. JEFFERSON DAVIS was peculiarly unfitted for this task, because he was the embodiment of the ideas that made it an impossible one. Those of his critics who maintained that, given the relative strength of the Union and the Confederacy, their material forces, their territorial relations, the war ought not to have ended in four years, were sound in their premises as far as they went, but they were mistaken in thinking that Mr. DAVIS could have in any serious degree changed or even delayed the result. The fact that the slaves never rose in insurrection and made no considerable contribution to the Union forces was more than counterbalanced by the fact that, performing all the needed labor, they left the whites free for military service. But it was none the less slavery that doomed the Confederacy, because it had through successive generations paralyzed the material and moral forces of the ruling class, and because it had compelled the adoption of a political system utterly inconsistent with sustained and united action. Nor was its effect confined to the leaders. Midway in the struggle the "public spirit" of the South gave out. As early as the close of 1862 Mr. DAVIS complained with curious blindness to the significance of the fact, that if one-third of those who ought to be in the ranks would join his armies they would be invincible, and in spite of the general and bitter feeling of animosity to the Union, there cannot be said after this date to have been an efficient public sentiment for the war in the South. The common people had by that time come to feel, if not to know, that it was in no sufficient sense their war. It is not to be reasonably denied that JEFFERSON DAVIS did substantially as much and as well for his evil cause as any Southern man would or could have done, and he was in many ways possessed of the most admirable traits of the ruling class of the South. He failed, and was bound to fail, because these traits were overborne by others equally characteristic and fatal to success, and because the system which he sought to maintain was opposed to the merciless laws of human progress. In this view of his career, it is easy to see that there was injustice in the detestation with which he was regarded in the North, and exaggeration in the admiration he won and to the time of his death retained in the South. History will regard him as the singularly exact representative of a society that in free America, in the third quarter of the nineteenth century, was dominated by the ideas of human rights that belonged, at the latest, to France a century before, and that was defeated in the inevitable and "irrepressible conflict" with a society animated by the real forces of time.

February 15, 1891.

GENERAL SHERMAN IS DEAD.

DISEASE FINALLY CONQUERED THE NOBLE OLD SOLDIER

HE PASSED QUIETLY AWAY A LITTLE BEFORE TWO O'CLOCK YESTERDAY AFTERNOON SURROUNDED BY HIS FAMILY AND HIS FRIENDS.

Gen. Sherman died yesterday afternoon at 1:50 o'clock. So gently and peacefully did the spirit of the great soldier depart that the sorrowing relatives at his bedside could scarcely realize at the time that death had completed its work. The dying man was surrounded by all of the members of his family except his eldest son, the Rev. T. E. SHERMAN, who is now on the Atlantic homeward bound.

All hope of Gen. SHERMAN's recovery was practically abandoned early yesterday morning. The wonderful vitality displayed by the distinguished invalid had kept hope alive up to that time in the hearts of the affectionate watchers. But soon after 5 o'clock yesterday morning there were alarming symptoms. It was evident to Dr. ALEXANDER that the General was sinking rapidly. His strength seemed to have been spent.

In the belief that death was near, the members of the household who had retired about 2 o'clock A.M. were summoned to the sick chamber. Lieut. FITCH and Ms. THACKARA had left the house for the night, and they were sent for. It was a sad group that gathered about the couch of the dying soldier just before the dawn of day. The General was very weak indeed. His lungs were almost dormant, and but the faintest bit of breath came from them. The doctors observed symptoms of pneumonia.

No word had passed Gen. SHERMAN's lips since very early Friday, when he addressed some brief remark to his nurse. Members of his family listened eagerly for some utterance from him yesterday morning, but none came. Once or twice it seemed to the watchers as though the dying man was trying to speak. His eyes bespoke affectionate recognition of those about him, but his swollen tongue was incapable of articulation. His jaws, too, became too stiff to work, and the great hero of the famous march to the sea, although living, was as silent and helpless as a sleeping babe. The hours dragged wearily along and the members of the family waited mournfully and patiently the coming of the destroyer. The faithful doctors could give them no hope.

Soon after daylight telegrams were sent to Gen. O. O. HOWARD at Governors Island and to Gen. HENRY W. SLOCUM in Brooklyn, asking them to come to the house as soon as possible. Both of these well-known soldiers were old comrades in arms of Gen. SHERMAN. They responded to the summons as speedily as they were able.

Senator John Sherman, who had spent the night at his brother's house and had scarcely slept, sent the following dispatch to his wife at 8:25 o'clock A.M.:

"Gen. Sherman still lives, faintly conscious and without pain. His asthmatic breathing is shorter and his strength weaker."

A little before 9 o'clock the following bulletin, dated at 8:30 o'clock A.M. was posted:

The physicians, after consultation, declare that Gen. Sherman's condition is now hopeless. He is dying and the end is near.

C. T. ALEXANDER.

INDEX